INTRODUCTION
TO
ADMINISTRATIVE
LAW

Neil Hawke, LLB (Hons), PhD
Professor of Environmental Law
Head of the Department of Law
De Montfort University

Neil Parpworth, LLB, MA
Lecturer in Law
De Montfort University

Cavendish
Publishing
Limited

First published in Great Britain 1996 by Cavendish Publishing Limited, The Glass House, Wharton Street, London WC1X 9PX.

Telephone: 0171-278 8000 Facsimile: 0171-278 8080

British Library Cataloguing in Publication Data.

Hawke, Neil
Introduction to Administrative Law
I Title II Parpworth, Neil
344.2026

ISBN 1-85941-191-6

Printed and bound in Great Britain by
Biddles Ltd, Guildford and King's Lynn

Preface

'Government, even in its best state, is but a necessary evil; in its worst state, an intolerable one.'

(Thomas Paine, 1737–1809)

Administrative law provides many of the safeguards which prevent government becoming an intolerable evil. It is the purpose of this book to provide an introduction to administrative law and its control of government power indicating, wherever possible, the nature of those powers, the purpose of governmental functions as well as the scope and effectiveness of legal control. The book is divided into four parts covering the administrative agencies of government, the nature, characteristics and sources of its powers, the judicial review of administrative action and the remedies for unlawful and irregular administrative action. To help the reader through the subject, a glossary of terms used in the book is provided, together with a selected bibliography of further reading and a range of self-assessment questions. The book is designed for use by those pursuing degree level courses in Law or Public and Social Administration. Equally, the book will be of use to those undertaking sub-degree or professional courses in similar areas.

The last decade has seen some very significant changes in administrative law, driven mainly by government policy. This is vividly illustrated by changes in the status and functions of local government and the stringency of central government control of local administration. Elsewhere privatisation has produced many more pages in the statute book. The government's reliance on prerogative powers has also been reappraised by the courts, particularly through the landmark decision in the GCHQ case. It is clear that the courts are prepared to be far more proactive in adjudicating prerogative acts, even if only to delay the government's actions on the ground of unfairness. More generally, the courts' willingness to develop an increasingly comprehensive view of the requirements in law of 'fairness' has coloured a good deal of judicial review. In the same way there has been a continuing expansion of those bodies amenable to judicial review: the self-regulatory bodies in the financial markets, for example. Finally, reference is made in the book to the rapidly expanding influence of the law of the European Union which affects the framework of municipal administrative law as much as it affects any other area of relevant 'national' law.

We are indebted to Liz Steward of the Department of Law for her unfailing energy and helpfulness in word-processing the text. Without her efforts we would have found it very difficult to meet any of our deadlines!

Professor Neil Hawke

Neil Parpworth

Department of Law

1 September 1995

Contents

Part 2   Administrative Powers

Table of Cases

Table of Statutes

UK Law

EU Law

Glossary of Terms

administrative action – the acts of administrative agencies, covering any of their administrative, judicial or (limited) legislative functions.

affidavit – a written statement made on oath.

alter ego – in the administrative law context, the other person (a civil servant) through whom the minister acts.

appellant – one who undertakes an appeal.

Attorney General – the principal law officer of the Crown.

audi alteram partem – no man shall be condemned unheard.

common law – the unwritten law of England, developed by the courts, and in many instances, reported in the law reports as cases decided by the courts.

Conseil d'Etat – the superior French administrative court.

courts of record – superior and inferior courts possessing the power to punish for contempt.

ex gratia **payment/compensation** – money paid as a matter of favour.

hearsay evidence – evidence relating to a matter of fact which was not witnessed by the person giving the evidence.

inferior courts – courts such as the county courts and magistrates' courts whose jurisdiction is limited, geographically and financially.

intra vires – within (statutory) powers.

Judicial Committee of the Privy Council – a court comprising mainly members of the House of Lords sitting as a judicial body, acting principally as a final appeal court for some Commonwealth countries.

justiciable – some matter which is subject to adjudication by a person or body, usually possessing legal authority for the purpose.

locus standi – standing or status in law, giving a right to be heard.

Lord Advocate – the principal law officer of the Crown in Scotland.

Lord Chancellor – the head of the judiciary, Speaker of the House of Lords and a member of the government.

nemo judex in causa sua – no man shall be judge in his own cause.

null and void – of no effect in law, as with an *ultra vires* decision.

plaintiff – a person who seeks some remedy or relief against another in legal proceedings.

prerogative – powers peculiar to the monarch which exist independently of the law and which are frequently subject to conventional exercise by ministers of the Crown.

prima facie – at first sight: consequently, *prima facie* evidence will appear to be in favour of the person who presents it.

probative – something that is capable of providing proof.

respondent – a person or body required to answer an appeal.

Solicitor General – the second law officer of the Crown.

statute law – written law, legislated by or with the authority of Parliament.

superior courts – courts whose jurisdiction is not limited: the House of Lords (in its judicial capacity); the Court of Appeal; the High Court (comprising the Queen's Bench, Chancery and Family Divisions); the Crown Court; the Judicial Committee of the Privy Council; the Restrictive Practices Court; and the Employment Appeal Tribunal.

Supreme Court of Judicature – the High Court and the Court of Appeal whose procedures are governed by the Rules of the Supreme Court.

tort – a civil wrong comprising something other than a breach of contract.

ultra vires – beyond or outside (statutory) powers.

vicarious liability – liability for the act of another arising from the (legal) status of their relationship.

voidable – legally binding until quashed.

Table of Abbreviations

AC } App Cases }	Appeal Cases
Admin LR	Administrative Law Reports
All ER	All England Reports
Ch	Chancery (Law Reports)
CLR	Commonwealth Law Reports (Australia)
CMLR	Common Market Law Reports
Crim LR	Criminal Law Review
ECR	European Court Reports
EG	Estates Gazette
ER	English Reports
ICR	Industrial Court Reports
IRLR	Industrial Relations Law Reports
JPL	Journal of Planning and Environment Law
KB	King's Bench (Law Reports)
LGR	Local Government Reports
Ll LR	Lloyds Law Reports
LR HL	House of Lords Law Reports
LR QB	Queen's Bench Law Reports
NZLR	New Zealand Law Reports
P & CR	Property and Compensation Reports
PD	Law Reports Probate Divorce and Admiralty Division
QB	Queen's Bench (Law Reports)
QBD	Queen's Bench Division (Law Reports)
TLR	Times Law Reports
WLR	Weekly Law Reports

1   The Scope and Purpose of Administrative Law

1.1   Definition of Administrative Law

Administrative law deals with the legal control of government and related administrative powers. This means that a significant emphasis of the subject is the control exercised by the High Court over the use of statutory powers by a wide range of administrative agencies.

In supervising the fulfilment of governmental and related administrative functions by these agencies, the sole concern of the High Court is to ensure that they exercise their functions within the limits of the statutory powers, that is, *intra vires*. This is achieved by applying the rules developed by the common law, described in Chapters 9–11 and collectively referred to as the doctrine of *ultra vires*. Where it is found that an administrative agency has acted outside or beyond its statutory powers, any resulting decision or other act may be recognised as *ultra vires*, that is, null and void so that in law it has never existed. Accordingly, the High Court will probably grant one of the remedies described in Chapter 13, eg an order of *certiorari* to quash the *ultra vires* decision or action. This supervision and control of the exercise of statutory powers by the High Court is referred to as judicial review and is a vital part of the Rule of Law.

The legal control of government and other administrative powers also occurs in other ways, eg through the vast array of general appeals to the courts and, in particular, the inferior courts below the High Court. At the grass roots one finds that many 'informal' rules are made and applied for the purpose of applying government powers, often without any challenge before the courts.

Accordingly, the reference above to 'legal control' represents the lowest common denominator of administrative law. The network of governmental and other administrative powers is necessarily complex, stretching now to include the European Community (also referred to as the European Union). As a result the dynamics of the controls available point to an important role for the courts. However, internal checks and balances within the system of administration do suggest that 'control' is manifested both through the law, be it statute or common law, and through extra-legal devices such as budgetary control. However, the word 'control' may itself be too restrictive. Above all, administrative law should be capable of operating positively in order to facilitate action both on the part of administrative agencies such as local authorities and on the part of the courts in granting remedies to those subject to irregular, unlawful administrative action.

1.2 The Rule of Law

There have been a number of attempts to define the Rule of Law, from the considered academic definition to the popular newspaper headline telling us that some powerful group of workers is threatening the Rule of Law with strike action. One of the best-known definitions is that of Professor A V Dicey contained in his famous book *The Law of the Constitution*, published in 1885. He considered that the Rule of Law requires the recognition of the predominance of the regular law (as opposed to arbitrary or wide discretionary powers), equality before the law and that the British constitution is the product of the ordinary law. In essence, therefore, the Rule of Law requires that there should be government according to law and an avoidance of arbitrary action. This prescription may be seen to be rather negative, emphasising the need for a definition of the Rule of Law that is more pro-active for the purpose of allowing more positive political and other pressure in aid of the ever expanding dimensions of 'government according to law'.

Dicey's Rule of Law depends on the capacity of the court to control abuses of administrative power. That the courts are incapable of undertaking this control function is seen in the fact that not all administrative action is contained in statute amenable to judicial interpretation. Increasingly, administrative functions are dissipated, particularly with the development of privatisation. In this and many other governmental contexts some functions are carried out by means of contracts governed, not by public, administrative law, but by the *private* law of contract. Even if Dicey's Rule of Law depended on the supremacy and sovereignty of Parliament, there would be an important question about Parliament's capacity to control the executive. For so many different purposes the reality is that the executive government of the day influences and controls Parliament.

The first part of Dicey's definition emphasises the central feature of administrative law as a means of limiting the scope of statutory powers through the doctrine of *ultra vires*. Although we have a supreme, sovereign Parliament which is capable of legislating very extensive laws which may appear to confer arbitrary or very wide discretionary powers on an administrative agency, the High Court, ever mindful of the Rule of Law, will be reluctant to see some powers as being without limit. A vivid example occurs in *Customs and Excise Commissioners v Cure and Deeley Ltd* (1961) where the Commissioners were empowered by the Finance (No 2) Act 1940 to 'make regulations providing for any matter for which provision appears to them to be necessary for the purpose of giving effect to the provisions of this Part of this Act'. As will be seen in

Chapter 11 where this case is dealt with in more detail, Sachs J rejected the view that these words 'necessarily make [the] authority the sole judge of what are its powers as well as the sole judge of the way in which it can exercise such powers as it may have'. Although this case represents an important step in the development of the doctrine of *ultra vires* as a means of controlling the statutory powers of administrative agencies, Parliament continues to legislate a number of very wide discretionary powers which pose a real threat to Dicey's view of the Rule of Law. Such is the width of some of these powers that their control may be increasingly difficult for the court. This was certainly the case in *Norwich City Council v Secretary of State for the Environment* (1982) where the Court of Appeal was concerned with the powers conferred on the Secretary of State by s 164 of the Housing Act 1985. This section empowers the Secretary of State to intervene and take over the functions of a local authority in relation to the sale of council houses where it appears to [him] that tenants ... have or may have difficulty in exercising the right to buy effectively and expeditiously'. It was decided by the Court that the determining factor in deciding whether to exercise these powers was the view of the Secretary of State himself whether council tenants had or might have difficulty in exercising the right to buy effectively and expeditiously, for whatever reason. The Court contrasted the words of s 68 of the Education Act 1944 whereby the Secretary of State for Education is empowered to serve a direction against a local education authority if he is satisfied that the authority 'have acted or are proposing to act *unreasonably* with respect to the exercise of any power conferred or the performance of any duty imposed by or under this Act'. The contrast is based on the fact that the powers in s 164 of the Housing Act are wider than those in s 68 of the Education Act because they do not involve any objective standard of 'reasonableness' to be determined by the court. As Kerr LJ observes: ' ... the determinative factor is the view of the Secretary of State'. He also observes that the powers in s 164 are 'Draconian' and that, 'short of seeking to exclude altogether any power of review by the courts, the wording of section 164 has clearly been framed by Parliament in such a way as to maximise the power of the Secretary of State and to minimise any power of review by the court', a position which can be explained by the likelihood of political controversy between central government and some local authorities showing reluctance to implement the council tenant's right to buy under the Housing Act.

(2) The second part of Dicey's definition of the Rule of Law concerns the necessity for equality before the law. Compared with the first part of the definition, there would appear to be fewer anxieties in this context. There are certain groups in society, such as trade unionists, who require limited immunity from legal liability in order to undertake strike and other industrial action. It will be seen in Chapters 2 and 14 that the Crown as an entity in administration also has a limited immunity in law, but, theoretically, the limits in law of much administrative action is supervised by the ordinary courts. The UK courts are indepen-

dent of the executive government and it is vitally important that administrative agencies should not be judges in their own cause. In some countries, notably France, there is a special system of administrative courts whose sole concern is with administrative law. Dicey criticised this system which, in France, comprises local administrative courts headed by a central *Conseil d'Etat*, on the ground that it imported special rules of law and legal immunities for the administrative agencies of government. In reality and although the judges involved in this system are government employees, it is a truly impartial and objective aspect of the French judiciary. Although a significant focus of English administrative law is the power of the High Court to review the legality of action taken by administrative agencies, it will be seen in Chapter 5 that various administrative tribunals and inferior courts (ie courts such as the county courts which are beneath the 'superior' courts) the Supreme Court of Judicature (comprising the High Court and Court of Appeal) and the House of Lords, have a part to play in the adjudication of administrative disputes. In particular, it will be seen that the tribunals are, to an extent, independent of the government departments which create them and that more generally, both tribunals and inferior courts are subject to the supervision of the High Court along with other administrative agencies.

The third part of Dicey's formulation of the Rule of Law is that the Constitution is but part of the ordinary law. Whereas most countries have a written constitution which expressly guarantees fundamental rights such as freedom from arbitrary arrest, any constitutional rights in the UK are products of the ordinary law. As a consequence, and despite the Police and Criminal Evidence Act of 1984, it may appear more difficult to define the scope of police powers of arrest, for example, although our unwritten constitution does mean that the law may be changed rather more easily than a written constitution, which may require, say, a two-thirds majority. It will be noted, however, that membership of the European Union requires adherence to the Treaty of Rome and other European Union legislation. Increasingly therefore analogies with a written constitution are relevant to the enforcement of certain Community-wide freedoms. Overall, this third part of Dicey's formulation emphasises the importance of the courts' role in protecting individual liberty through their ability to interpret and apply the ordinary law. In other words, where the law is not being changed by Parliament, the courts are the final arbiters of individual rights. In this context such rights are usually referred to as civil rights and are very much the concern of constitutional law whereas administrative law is concerned with the matters referred to at the beginning of this chapter. There are overlaps between these two areas of law, eg in the area of the Crown's status in law, bearing in mind the Crown's position and importance in the constitutional structure of the country and the fact that various statutory powers are exercised by individuals and organisations acting as servants or agents of the Crown.

1.3 The Constitutional Background to Administrative Law

Although the British constitution is unwritten and not therefore embodied in any one document, it is usually possible to define some aspect of the British constitutional framework from the existing law, difficult though that may be. In the previous section on the Rule of Law reference was made to police powers of arrest. Where it is necessary to ascertain the scope of police powers to enter and question a person on his own property such an issue has probably arisen from that person's refusal to be questioned in such circumstances. If as a result he is arrested for the obstruction of a police officer in the execution of his duty, contrary to s 51 of the Police Act 1964, his conviction will depend on whether there was an obstruction and whether the officer was acting in the execution of his duty. Because these terms are not defined by the Act, their definition has been left to the courts; that is, they are terms of art developed through the common law. Consequently, this area of the constitution regulating powers of the police can be defined only by reference to statute and common law, that is, a combination of Act of Parliament and case law. Accordingly, it is likely that a court would conclude that there could be no conviction for obstruction under s 51 where the police officer is told to leave the person's property because, as a trespasser, he would not have been acting in the execution of his duty.

There can be no doubt that the Rule of Law requiring government according to law is fundamental to the constitutional background of administrative law. There are, however, other facets of the constitutional structure which must be examined in order to appreciate the true significance of the law's ability to control government powers. These other facets include the sovereignty and supremacy of Parliament, the separation of powers, conventions and prerogative powers.

1.3.1 The sovereignty and supremacy of Parliament

In many countries it is the written constitution which is supreme. Consequently, where certain fundamental rights are guaranteed by such a constitution, Parliament cannot legislate in order to remove or modify those rights. This, therefore, indicates that Parliament is not the sovereign, supreme law-maker. The Fifth Amendment of the United States constitution, for example, prohibits the taking of property without just compensation. Accordingly, any legislation attempting to authorise the compulsory acquisition of a person's land with little or no compensation entitlement would be struck down by a court in the United States as being *ultra vires* the constitution, indicating that the court is the guardian of such fundamental constitutional provisions. In the UK, with its unwritten constitution, it is Parliament which is sovereign and supreme. In other words, Parliament is the ultimate and, in theory, unlimited law-maker.

The 'primacy' of enacted legislation (subject to the status of the law of the European Union) is well illustrated in three cases where it was argued that the European Convention on Human Rights should be accepted as part of our municipal law. In the first of these cases – *R v General Medical Council ex p Colman* (1990), dealing with a restriction on the advertising of holistic medicine – it was held by the Court of Appeal that the General Medical Council's power was not subject to the Convention because there was no ambiguity in the statute concerned, the Medical Act 1983. Furthermore the relevant section of the statute did not deal with the international obligations of the UK under the Convention. The leading case for present purposes is undoubtedly *R v Secretary of State for the Home Department, ex p Brind and Others* (1991) where it was held by the House of Lords that the Convention does not form part of English law. On the facts of this case, concerning certain statutory discretionary powers of the Home Secretary in relation to broadcasting restrictions in Northern Ireland, it was concluded that there is no presumption that that discretion should be exercised in accordance with the Convention. Nevertheless if there is some uncertainty or ambiguity in an English enactment, resort may be made to the Convention. This, presumably, would extend to any similar international Convention. In *R v Secretary of State for the Environment and Secretary of State for Wales, ex p NALGO* (1992) the High Court affirmed the principle that there is no presumption that formal, substantive legislation should conform to the Convention here in the context of a dispute about restrictions on the political activities of local government officers. More recently, in *R v Secretary of State for the Home Department, ex p McQuillan* (1995), Sedley J in the High Court stressed that the jurisprudence of the European Court of Justice showed that the principles of the Convention now inform the law of the European Union. Accordingly, our own national law can now take notice of the Convention in setting its own standards. Ignorance of the Convention by the common law would therefore be unreal and potentially unjust. Although the learned judge did not depart from *Brind*, he concluded that the legal standards by which the decisions of public bodies are supervised could, and should, differentiate between 'fundamental' rights and those not enjoying such pre-eminence. At this point Sedley J considered that the standard of justification of infringements of rights and freedoms by executive decision must vary in proportion to the significance of the right in issue.

Because Parliament, ie the Queen, House of Commons and House of Lords, has a theoretically unlimited power to make law by statute, it could legislate on any matter, but in practice there are all sorts of constraints on its power, such as political opinion. As a result it is usually accepted that Parliament will not enact retrospective legislation in order, eg to penalise action which has taken place previously in the absence of any legal sanctions. Nevertheless, there are occasional exceptions, as in the case of the War Damage Act 1965. This Act was passed as a result of the decision in *Burmah Oil Co v Lord Advocate* (1964) where it was decided that compensation was payable by the government to the company where it had, during wartime, destroyed one of its oil refineries to prevent it falling into the hands of the advancing Japanese army. In order to prevent similar claims for compensation for such events which had occurred previously, the Act of 1965 was framed to act retrospectively.

Such retrospective legislation might be necessary where (for example) money is spent or action is taken in advance of legislation appearing on the statute book if there are no statutory powers to justify such expenditure or other action. This was the issue before the High Court in *R v Secretary of State for Health and Others, ex p Keen* (1990) where it was held that pre-existing statutory powers in the National Health Service Act 1977 were wide enough to justify various acts such as the preparation of applications for National Health Service 'trust' status prior to new legislation reaching the statute book. Had this not been the case so-called 'paving' legislation would have been necessary in order to justify these preparatory acts. However, 'paving' powers are to be found in the Health Authorities Act 1995 in anticipation of the replacement of existing health authorities. Section 3 of the Act stipulates that the functions of 'existing' authorities 'shall include the power to do anything which appears appropriate for facilitating the implementation of any provision made by or by virtue of the Act'.

One area of law-making by Parliament which has had profound constitutional implications relates to the UK's accession to membership of what was known originally as the European Economic Community (EEC), and now known as the European Union (EU). As a result of the European Communities Act 1972 the UK became part of an economic union of Member States of the EU through acceptance of the Treaty of Rome, which contains the fundamental laws and constitution of the EU. Accordingly, where EU law governs a situation then Parliament has disabled itself through the Act of 1972 from legislating in that area. By way of an example, Article 48 of the Treaty stipulates that there shall be no discrimination against the workers of Member States from moving freely between those states. Any attempt by Parliament to legislate, eg to protect the jobs of UK workers, would be contrary to Article 48 where the legislation appeared to permit discrimination against workers from other Member States. More generally, it appears that Parliament gave away some of its sovereignty and supremacy in legislating the European Communities Act. In theory, Parliament could repeal the Act to regain its sovereignty and supremacy in full, although it is argued that the financial and economic implications for the country would make this very difficult.

In the meantime the European Court of Justice continues to limit the scope of sovereignty. In *Factortame Ltd and Others v Secretary of State for Transport* (No 2) (1990) it was held that where a national court has made a reference to the European Court of Justice, an English court may grant an injunction against the Crown or even suspend the operation of an Act of Parliament although there is no power to do so under English law. It was held by the House of Lords in *R v Secretary of State for Employment, ex p Equal Opportunities Commission* (1993) that a

7

Divisional Court of the High Court had power to make declarations that certain aspects of employment law in the UK were incompatible with Article 119 of the Treaty of Rome and accompanying Directives. The issue referred to the European Court of Justice in *Factortame* concerned the need to set aside a rule of national law considered to be the sole obstacle preventing the grant of interim relief in a case before the court concerning the law of the European Union if, otherwise the full effectiveness of a decision on the substantive issues of Union law would be impaired. However, in *R v Secretary of State for the Environment, ex p RSPB* (1995) the House of Lords has held that while a reference to the European Court of Justice on questions relating to the conservation of wild birds and protection of their habitats is extant, it is inappropriate for the national court to make an interim declaration that it would be unlawful for the Secretary of State to fail to act so as to avoid deterioration of habitats and the disturbance of species in an area whose status as a special protection area is under consideration. The reason for this limit is the uncertainty of the scope and nature of any such obligation to act, an uncertainty that may be resolved only following the response of the European Court of Justice.

Where Parliament has enacted statute law its legality cannot be challenged in the High Court, as is the case in a country like the United States of America, where laws cannot be made which contravene fundamental provisions of the written constitution. In the leading case of *Pickin v British Railways Board* (1974) Lord Reid said that 'the function of the court is to construe and apply the enactments of Parliament. The court has no concern with the manner in which Parliament or its officers ... perform these functions'. There are two qualifications to this fundamental rule. First, and as seen previously in the reference to the EU, any attempt by Parliament to legislate contrary to the terms of EU law might be challenged directly or indirectly in the High Court or the European Court of Justice. In the case of any clash then clearly EU law would have to prevail. However, where such a challenge is made in the High Court it could be argued that, because the judges have to interpret and apply the latest law, any statute which is inconsistent with the requirements of the European Communities Act should prevail. In other words, and particularly where Parliament has legislated in full knowledge of the European Communities Act and its full effect, any later Act which is inconsistent with EU law would have to be applied by the High Court. The second qualification depends on the important distinction between primary and delegated or secondary legislation which is dealt with in Chapter 8. Where a statute confers a power to make rules, regulations, bylaws and so on, the minister, local authority or other agency exercising such a power to make delegated legislation must remain within the terms of the primary legislation. Failure to do so means that the delegated legislation is *ultra vires* the primary, enabling legislation. In practice these problems tend to arise where a person has been prosecuted for failure to comply with the delegated legislation, in which case his argument will be that he cannot be convicted for breach of, eg statutory regulations which themselves are *ultra vires*.

It has been seen that the High Court cannot question the validity in law of primary legislation so that the Act of Parliament must be interpreted and applied as it appears in the statute book. Although it is not the task of this book to cover the refinements of statutory interpretation, it should be emphasised that such interpretation can sometimes lead to a frustration of Parliament's original intention. There is no better example of this than in the House of Lords decision in *Anisminic v Foreign Compensation Commission* (1969). The Foreign Compensation Act 1950 stated that decisions of the Commission (an administrative tribunal) should 'not be called in question in any court of law'. Despite this apparently clear statement of Parliament's legislative intentions, it was decided that the court could question the legality of a Commission decision if in law it was no decision at all, that is, if it was an *ultra vires* decision. (where administrative agency's have acted without statutory powers.)

1.3.2 The separation of powers

In very general terms it is possible to say that any constitutional structure involves the deployment of legislative, executive and judicial powers. Consequently there are facilities for law-making, the implementation and enforcement of the laws so made, and for the adjudication of disputes arising from one or both of these processes, according to the constitutional context. In some constitutions there is a clear recognition of the need for a separation of these three powers. In the United States, for example, the Federal constitution gives Congress the legislative powers, the President executive powers and the Supreme Court the judicial powers. In the UK the separation of powers is recognised through the guaranteed independence of the judiciary, bearing in mind that the executive government effectively controls the legislative functions of Parliament, as long as it can maintain an effective parliamentary majority. In *R v HM Treasury, ex p Smedley* (1985) the Court of Appeal refused to adjudicate the validity of the government's decision to seek authority for payment of a supplementary EU budget by an Order in Council (an item of subordinate legislation) rather than an Act of Parliament.

This decision is an example of the court's reluctance to interfere with the government's legislative choice. This judicial reluctance to interfere will be seen in greater detail later in the book, in Part 3. It will be seen there that the court is concerned with the legality of administrative action through the process of judicial review. In other words, administrative action may be challenged on the basis that there is no authority under the law. This limitation means that there can be no judicial interference with the *merits* of administrative action, suggesting that Dicey's reliance on judicial control as a cornerstone of the Rule of Law is an over-emphasis on what the courts can achieve in examining administrative action. Nevertheless the courts may be amenable to some creativity as self-styled 'guardians of the public interest'. For example, the Court of Appeal has held that the prescription of a statutory duty may be subject to qualification in the public interest. In *R v Registrar General, ex p Smith* (1991) the Court of Appeal upheld the Registrar General's refusal to produce a birth certificate on the ground that it might be used to commit serious crime.

Where all three powers become vested in the executive government there is clearly cause for anxiety, and many distinguished writers have pointed to the loss of democratic freedom which is likely to flow from such an arrangement. A particularly graphic example comes from a case in Ceylon (as it then was), *Liyanage v R* (1967), where a potentially dangerous situation was saved by a judicial insistence that the separation of powers was a feature of the constitution of that country. In that case the court heard that, following a *coup d'état*, the government introduced retrospective legislation defining a new offence and prescribing a sentence covering the conduct of the captured ring-leaders.

In practice, the separation of powers is a useful doctrine in order to measure any undue shift of power toward the executive. Although it is very difficult to define what is meant by the three powers, it is importance to recognise the scope and extent of a government's executive or administrative powers, and its judicial powers. A Committee on Ministers' Powers, which reported in 1932 and which was also concerned with the growth in the use of delegated legislation, considered that an administrative decision is a matter for the minister's discretion, possibly under the influence of policy, while a true judicial decision involves a dispute between two or more parties where there is an objective application of the law to the facts as found. It was recognised that within government certain decisions arise from the adjudication of disputes, but in a policy atmosphere. In this case the function would be labelled a 'quasi-judicial' function; eg where a landowner's rights are in issue following his objection to a compulsory purchase order made in respect of his land. It is in these circumstances that the law has to be vigilant in order to ensure adequate safeguards for those whose rights are affected by such quasi-judicial decisions of the executive government, particularly in areas where decisions are preceded by statutory inquiries, the subject of Chapter 3. A great deal of administrative adjudication is undertaken by administrative tribunals where, again, it is a matter of importance that their judicial decisions should be seen to be safeguarded from government interference and influence. Consequently the law demands that tribunals and their functions should be effectively separate from the government departments under which they are constituted and with whose decisions they often deal on appeal. Administrative tribunals are the subject of Chapter 5.

Where statute confers a decision-making function on a minister of the Crown within a particular government department it is through an independent judiciary that this function may be supervised to ensure that the decision is made within the relevant statutory powers. Accordingly, through the High Court there may be recognition of the fundamental constitutional requirement of adherence to the Rule of Law and recognition of a limited separation of powers in the existence of an independent judiciary.

The minister, therefore is subject to the law in the exercise of his statutory powers. However, the minister is responsible to Parliament for the way in which he exercises these functions, eg in matters of departmental policy. Because the minister is the political head of his department he is ultimately responsible for the actions of civil servants within that department. This means that while the civil servant remains anonymous, the minister is publicly accountable for his actions although this has not often led to his resignation. In essence, therefore, ministerial responsibility may provide some opportunity for parliamentary criticism of a government department's operation even though a very small proportion of the work carried out is actually referred to the minister. Just as the minister is politically accountable for the actions of his civil servants, so, too, he is legally responsible. In both cases the law considers that the civil servant is the minister's *alter ego*. This matter is explored further in Chapter 9 which deals with the issue of delegation of functions and decisions in government departments and local authorities.

1.3.3 Conventions

Conventions are essentially rules of political practice which arise, and may disappear, as a matter of expediency. Bearing in mind the previous reference to the supremacy of EU law over the municipal law of the individual Member States, it is probably the case that in the UK Parliament there is now a convention that there will be no legislation which is contrary to EU law. There are many other conventions, eg that the Queen invites the leader of the majority party in the House of Commons to form a government. Generally, however, conventions are of marginal interest only to administrative lawyers, primarily because they are not likely to say very much about the scope of statutory powers and their control by the law. In *Smedley* the Court of Appeal recognised the 'fundamental' convention that the legislature and judiciary are independent of each other. Insofar as constitutional conventions are of interest to lawyers they represent ill-defined 'markers' of constitutionality. Where a government acts arbitrarily or oppressively it may be subject to political criticism. Whether it would be subject to challenge as to the legality of its actions here would necessarily depend on the nature and context of the action. However, departure from a convention is not *per se* an unlawful action.

1.3.4 Prerogative powers

Historically, the monarch was able to exercise a great many absolute powers but with the development of democratic, constitutional government it is often the case that these powers are conventionally exercised by ministers of the Crown. There are very few prerogative powers which impinge on and affect individuals and it is for this reason that prerogative powers are employed by the government, through the Crown, principally in order to conclude treaties with foreign governments, to declare war and to make contracts. It has been said that the prerogative is part of the common law because prerogative powers are recognised, but not enforced, by the courts, and that it is the sum total of powers which are peculiar to the Crown because they are powers not possessed by any individual.

The picture of prerogative powers being largely immune from judicial challenge has changed since the decision of the House of Lords in *Council of Civil Service Unions v Minister for the Civil Service* (1985) (the 'GCHQ' case). A decision to exclude union membership from GCHQ in Cheltenham was upheld on grounds of national security. Nevertheless, but for such a justification and in the absence of the usual consultation for changes proposed in working arrangements these prerogative procedures may have been enforced in favour of the unions.

Statutory powers which govern the functions and activities of most administrative agencies are both recognised and may be enforced by the courts. Therefore, the courts will be able to decide where prerogative powers stop and statutory powers begin. Where the Crown acted unlawfully in its dealings with an individual, eg in relation to the grant or withdrawal of a passport, the court had no power to intervene to protect him as long as the action was recognised as an exercise of prerogative powers. Although the granting and withdrawal of passports is generally regarded as being subject to the prerogative, there was until recently some doubt as to whether these powers could be challenged successfully before the courts. In *R v Secretary of State for Foreign and Commonwealth Affairs, ex p Everett* (1988) the Court of Appeal decided that a refusal to renew or reissue a passport was a prerogative discretion reviewable by the court. Because the applicant had suffered no prejudice, even though he was given no reasons for failure to renew, the court declined to quash the decision. Accordingly such powers are recognised by the courts which have considerable influence here in marking the boundary with statutory powers which, in many cases, have superseded prerogative powers. In *Attorney General v De Keyser's Royal Hotel Ltd* (1920), eg, it was argued unsuccessfully by the Crown that compensation for the requisition of an hotel was entirely a matter for its discretion since it was acting under prerogative powers in wartime. It was decided by the court that the requisition and compensation were now governed by statutory provisions which had superseded the prerogative regulation of such matters. No such overlap was found in *R v Secretary of State for the Home Department, ex p Northumbria Police Authority* (1988). The court found that the Home Secretary has an exclusive prerogative power to issue plastic baton rounds or CS gas to a chief constable without the consent of the police authority in order to respond to actual or apprehended breaches of the peace. From the foregoing it is clear that the court has jurisdiction to review the exercise of the royal prerogative of mercy by the Home Secretary. In *R v Secretary of State for the Home Department, ex p Bentley* (1993) the court recognised that the royal prerogative is an important element in the system of criminal justice. Any such prerogative decision ought not to be immune from challenge before the court merely because action is prerogative action. Accordingly, the High Court held that a decision not to recommend a posthumous pardon to Derek Bentley was flawed and, therefore, the Home Secretary was invited to reconsider his decision.

The second point referred to above is that the prerogative is the sum total of powers which are peculiar to the Crown. If it is accepted that the Crown's power to make contracts is part of its prerogative powers, this picture of the prerogative is inaccurate, bearing in mind that most individuals have the capacity to make contracts. Nevertheless, in the case of those prerogative powers which remain unaffected by statutory provisions, most of the prerogative is concerned with matters which do not necessarily interfere with individuals' rights and interests, that is, matters where the executive should (arguably) have relative freedom of action. In practice, that freedom of action may be severely circumscribed by the need for political and financial support for various schemes to be pursued through the use of prerogative powers. In theory, there is no necessity for parliamentary sanction for an exercise of prerogative powers: in practice, however, political and financial support will often be crucial.

While the prerogative can be described as the sum total of powers which are peculiar to the Crown, there may be occasions when the courts find that these powers are closely linked with and sometimes depend on statutory powers and provisions.

In this situation it is also clear that prerogative powers are being subjected to legal enforcement by the courts. A graphic example occurs in the case of *Laker Airways Ltd v Department of Trade* (1977) where the company was granted a licence by the Civil Aviation Authority to operate the Skytrain Service from London to New York. Before the new air service could begin it was necessary for the company to be 'designated' by the government for the purpose of a treaty with the United States called the Bermuda Agreement. This treaty designation was subsequently withdrawn by the government and the Civil Aviation Authority was required to withdraw the licence. It was decided by the Court of Appeal that the Department of Trade was acting *ultra vires* in requiring the withdrawal of a licence by the Authority: at that time the Civil Aviation Act 1971 permitted withdrawal of a licence only in a limited number of situations, such as a wartime emergency. It was also decided that the government could not withdraw its designation of Laker Airways since the company had already obtained its statutory licence. In other words, the statutory powers relating to air route licensing act as a legal restriction on the exercise of the government's prerogative powers. The general issue arose also in *R v Secretary of State for the Home Department, ex p Fire Brigades Union* (1995) where the Secretary of State attempted to perpetuate a prerogative-based, *ex gratia* scheme of compensation for criminal injuries. At the time there was statutory provision for such a scheme, albeit not in force. In these circumstances the Court of Appeal held that while these statutory provisions remained unrepealed it was not possible for the Secretary of State to initiate by prerogative a materially different scheme.

1.4 Administrative Law in Perspective

It has been seen that the essential task of administrative law is to provide a legal control in relation to the exercise of administrative powers conferred on various administrative agencies for all sorts of different purposes. Perhaps the most visible manifestation of this control is an independent judiciary in the shape of the High Court exercising a supervisory role by which it reviews administrative action to ensure that it is not *ultra vires* particular statutory powers or even in excess of prerogative powers. This is the essential character of the subject, but it does not convey the complete picture since administrative law and its rules involve not only a rather negative form of control over the exercise of powers but also a rather more positive aspect. Through its task of interpreting the scope of statutory and other powers the High Court should be concerned to identify, not only the express limits of the powers, but any realistic implied powers which may not be spelt out quite so clearly. In this way it is possible to avoid a situation where a statutory scheme in an Act of Parliament becomes unworkable. In addition, there will be occasions where the interpretation of the statutory powers will expedite administration or where a mere technical non-compliance with the statutory requirements will not lead to the action being condemned as *ultra vires*.

As the rules of administrative law have been developed by the judiciary, so they have influenced the course of administration. In Chapter 11 reference is made to the decision of the Court of Appeal in *Coleen Properties Ltd v Minister of Housing and Local Government* (1971) where the minister's confirmation of a compulsory purchase order was quashed as being *ultra vires* because he had no evidence from the local authority making the Order that it was reasonably necessary to acquire some of the land covered by the Order. In this instance the local authority had not, for some reason, produced evidence for this purpose at the public local inquiry into the Order. There can be little doubt that the lessons to be learned from this case were not lost on local authorities. Of course, it is not every administrative proposal or decision which gets as far as the High Court: such litigation is very much the exception although the principles and rules which emerge from it are often extended or modified to fit the requirements of administration at the grass roots. On many occasions the body or person entrusted with administrative decision-making will have no clear guidance on the law to be applied in a particular case. On other occasions, eg where a minister of the Crown is part of the decision-making hierarchy, he will perhaps develop a body of rules and principles from his own appeal decisions. These rules and principles gain the status of 'quasi-law' unless they are overturned in subsequent litigation. In time it is likely that these rules and principles will shape attitudes to policy or provide a framework for decisions by other bodies in the same decision-making hierarchy, in which case the minister may publish these items, eg in circulars issued to local authorities.

The rules of administrative law governing judicial review and the remedies for unlawful administrative action which are dealt with in Parts 3 and 4 relate to the exercise of statutory powers governing all types of administrative function. It is clearly impossible to know all there is to know about these functions, not only because of the mass of primary and secondary legislation underpinning these functions but also because of the often formidable amounts of non-statutory details, such as policies, which provide their life-blood. Consequently, any study of administrative law will be restricted to an examination of the broad rules arising from the doctrine of *ultra vires* and other principles governing the merits of administrative action, with a general appreciation of the consequences in law of their application to the different statutory powers which govern these many functions.

A study of administrative law cannot be restricted to an examination of judicial review and the doctrine of *ultra vires*, crucially important though they are, for the reasons outlined previously. At various points in this introduction to the subject it will be seen that there are facilities beyond the courts by which administrative action may be challenged, not because it is *ultra vires* any statutory powers, but because it is in some way 'irregular' action. For this reason, some space is devoted to the work of the various 'ombudsmen' whose concern is with maladministration, and some other institutions whose task it is to monitor and deal with the complaints of the individual arising from his dealings with bureaucracy. In this way a complete picture can be conveyed of the way in which administration is accountable either (and perhaps most importantly) to the law directly or to other institutions whose task may be seen in terms of strengthening the traditional methods of dealing with grievances arising from government and administration, through Parliament.

Accountability to the law is not necessarily a comprehensive protection for the individual in his dealings with government and administration. Judicial review in the High Court is concerned only with whether administrative action is within the administrative agency's powers. If it is outside the agency's powers, the court may well quash the resulting decision or other action as *ultra vires*. Beyond this and any general statutory appeals on the merits of some administrative action, the law does not provide many other constructive remedies for the individual affected by unlawful or irregular administrative action. Although the private law of negligence may provide damages for the person suffering loss, eg as a result of negligent advice from a government official, there is no public law remedy providing damages for the person adversely affected by *ultra vires* action. This is clearly a serious gap in the law and one which is only

partially filled by the provision of 'non-legal' remedies like the ombudsmen whose powers do not extend to the making of legally enforceable awards of compensation against the agencies that they are required to investigate.

2 The Crown and Central Government

2.1 The Conduct of Government

On those occasions when the government of the country is being discussed it is not unusual to hear references to 'the Crown'. The impression, therefore, is that it is the Crown which undertakes a great deal of the government of the country, but it may not always be clear what is meant by this expression and what are its legal and practical consequences.

In theory the Crown, epitomised by the monarch, exercises her various statutory and prerogative powers personally. In practice, the constitutional convention is that she exercises virtually all such powers on the advice of and through her ministers. Thus the expression 'the Crown' may have a number of distinct meanings. For example, used in one context it may seek to denote the monarch, that is the constitutional Head of State; whilst used in another context, it refers to the sum total of powers exercised by that body of persons who are collectively termed the executive. Those ministers who form part of the executive and who advise the monarch in relation to her statutory powers are responsible to Parliament for their exercise. However, the normal practice is for Parliament to confer statutory powers on the individual minister who is specifically identified in the legislation. In s 68 of the Education Act 1944, for example, it is provided that:

> If the Secretary of State [for Education] is satisfied ... that any local education authority ... have acted or are proposing to act unreasonably with respect to the exercise of any power conferred or the performance of any duty imposed by or under this Act, he may...give such directions as to the exercise of the power or performance of the duty as appear to him to be expedient.

The consequence of this normal practice is that the minister is again responsible to Parliament in law to ensure that he acts within his statutory powers and not *ultra vires*. Although the minister is acting as 'a minister of the Crown' here, the statutory powers are conferred on him in his capacity as a named minister whereas he acts as a 'servant or agent of the Crown' in his conventional exercise of any powers actually conferred on the Crown. Although in this latter respect the Crown is equally obliged to ensure that its exercise of statutory powers is not *ultra vires*, it is the case that the Crown, including any servant or agent of the Crown, has not been subject to some of the remedies normally granted in the High Court to deal with *ultra vires* administrative action. It will be seen in Chapter 14 that it is the Crown Proceedings Act 1947 which excludes such remedies against the Crown. Consequently, the statutory powers of a minister when he is not acting as a servant or agent of the Crown would appear to be more amenable to judicial review by the High Court.

The normal practice whereby statutory powers are conferred on an individual minister is a clear reflection of the administrative convenience of having responsibility for a particular function placed with the political head of the relevant government department. Such an arrangement may be explained also as a matter of political policy, or as a combination of administrative convenience and political policy. The Education Act 1993 states, in s 1, that the Secretary of State for Education '... shall promote the education of the people of England and Wales'. This duty is matched by the duty of each local education authority under s 8 (as amended) to secure that there should be available for their area sufficient schools for providing full-time education suitable for the requirements of pupils of compulsory school age. This pattern of statutory provision is clearly explained by the original political choice of strategy for education whereby central government policies are implemented locally and subject to some central control through the powers in s 68, referred to previously. By way of contrast, some functions may involve more than one government department. In this case there might well be practical difficulties in conferring a function on one named minister, in which case Parliament would undoubtedly confer the powers on the Crown. One common example occurs in relation to the making of delegated legislation by virtue of various statutory powers. Such a power may be exercised by 'Her Majesty by Order in Council' where formal assent to an Order, an item of delegated legislation referred to in Chapter 8, is given at a meeting of the Privy Council. Again, any minister or ministers exercising such powers in the name of Her Majesty would be acting as servants or agents of the Crown, thereby attracting some legal immunity from certain of the remedies normally available in respect of *ultra vires* administrative action.

A minister of the Crown may be at the head of a government department which may or may not be an 'incorporated' department. If the statutory provisions establishing a government department indicate that it is incorporated, it can undertake its numerous transactions in its own name. Incorporation is therefore of some practical importance, eg to the Department of the Environment in view of its need to hold and dispose of a great deal of property. While this department is incorporated, the Civil Service Department is not, and this may be a reflection of the fact that such a status is not so crucial to such a department. Where the department is incorporated the various functions and powers of that department will be exercised, usually in the name of the designated minister at the political head of that department.

The conferment of statutory powers upon a minister is thus a well established feature of the UK's system of government. Countless Acts of Parliament conform to this practice, whatever the precise formulation of words which they chose to adopt, but, as a matter of convention, it is very rare to discover a statutory provision which expressly confers powers on the Prime Minister. In some respects this may be viewed as an oddity, especially since it is the Prime Minister who is, without doubt, the head of the government in that he effectively has the power to appoint, promote and even dismiss ministerial colleagues. Nevertheless, the pre-eminent position of the Prime Minister in the British system of cabinet government has not ensured that the post is commonly referred to in statute. Indeed, it is widely acknowledged that the first occasion on which the Prime Minister was mentioned in legislation was in the Chequers Estate Act 1917. Thus when this wider statutory anonymity is borne in mind, it is perhaps rather less surprising that statutory powers are rarely conferred upon the *primus inter pares*.

2.2 Legal Immunities of the Crown

It has been seen earlier in this chapter that certain coercive remedies are not available against the Crown, or a servant or agent of the Crown, by virtue of the Crown Proceedings Act 1947. Another immunity under the same Act stipulates that any rights or interests of the Crown shall not be prejudiced by statute unless the statute refers to the Crown expressly or by necessary implication. It is the case that this immunity usually means that the Crown is not liable to pay rates and various types of taxes. Beyond these categories it is difficult to generalise about the scope of the Crown's statutory immunities. One important area of such immunity relates to air pollution control legislation such as the Clean Air Act. This was the issue in *Nottingham No 1 Area Hospital Management Committee v Owen* (1957) where it was the Committee's statutory obligation to carry out its duties on behalf of the Minister of Health. He in turn was required to hold all National Health Service hospitals on trust for 'the Crown'. In these circumstances the court decided that a hospital was Crown property and so exempt from the penal provisions of a statute – the Public Health Act 1936 – which sought to control smoke nuisances. It was in this and similar contexts that the Fifth Report of the Royal Commission on Environmental Pollution (1976) commented that: 'Hospitals seem to take most advantage of Crown privilege ... Nevertheless it is most important that hospitals should do their best to control smoke, particularly when they are in residential areas where smoke control is proposed or operative.'

Whether the Crown is to be covered by and subject to any liabilities under a statute may be a matter of some considerable importance. Unless there is some vigilance on the part of those involved in the legislative process, there is always a danger that an important new statute with perhaps far reaching implications will contain no reference to the Crown. The only certainty in this area is where the Crown is expressly mentioned somewhere in the statutory provisions. The only other possibility whereby the Crown would be bound occurs where it is possible to conclude that the Crown is bound by the statutory provisions 'by necessary implication'. In a case from India decided by the Judicial Committee of the Privy Council, *Province of Bombay v Municipal Corporation of Bombay* (1947), it was concluded that in the absence of any express words the Crown is bound only where its exclusion would completely frustrate the working of the legislation. The case involved certain statutory powers allowing the laying of pipes and mains in land within the city, a statutory scheme which did not require the Crown to be bound by necessary implication in order to achieve such objects. This decision was considered in the Scottish courts in *Lord Advocate v Strathclyde Regional Council* (1988) where it was decided that enforcement notices served under the Town and Country Planning Act on the Ministry of Defence were binding on the Crown. In what appears to be a significant reconsideration of the law here it was concluded that the special rules of statutory construction seen above will apply only where the result will be to encroach on the Crown's rights, interests and privileges. In the instant case no such rights, interests or privileges were in issue as the Ministry sought to encroach on the highway in the process of repairing a perimeter fence.

2.3   Crown Servants and Agents

Bearing in mind that some statutory functions are performed not by a minister in his own name (albeit as a minister of the Crown) but by or in the name of the Crown, it is a matter of some importance to decide which individuals or organisations come under its umbrella as 'servants or agents of the Crown'. This status is of considerable significance for the reasons already given.

Whether any individual or body can be regarded in law as being a Crown servant or agent may be a matter of statutory interpretation. One of the leading cases is *Tamlin v Hannaford* (1949). The issue for the court was whether the British Transport Commission could be regarded as a servant or agent of the Crown. The Commission was landlord of a house whose tenant was Tamlin. In turn, Hannaford was Tamlin's sub-tenant. Tamlin wanted possession of the house from Hannaford. It was claimed by Hannaford that he was protected in proceedings for possession in a county court by the Rent Restriction Acts which were not expressly binding on the Crown. This claim was rejected by the county court which decided that the house was held by the Commission as an agent of the Crown. On appeal in the Court of Appeal it was decided that Hannaford was protected by the Rent Restriction Acts which did apply to the Commission since it was not a body connected with the Crown and its legal immunities in this context. Giving the Court of Appeal's judgment, Denning LJ also observed that:

> ... the Commission's servants are not civil servants, and its property is not Crown property. It is as much bound by Acts of Parliament as any other subject ... It is, of course, a public authority and its purposes, no doubt, are public purposes, but it is not a Government department nor do its powers fall within the province of Government.

On those rare occasions when there is no clear indication in the statute whether a body is a Crown servant or agent, the above words from the judgment in *Tamlin* will provide some indication that where the function is within the general category of industrial and commercial functions it is unlikely that the body will enjoy any Crown status. Accordingly, in *Mersey Docks and Harbour Board v Gibbs* (1866) the trustees of the Liverpool Docks were held to be liable to a shipowner in respect of their negligence which caused damage to a ship through stranding on mud. Although the trustees attempted to hide behind the legal immunities then available to the Crown, the House of Lords considered that this would not be possible, broadly because the trustees were concerned with commercial functions, not governmental functions referable to the Crown. By contrast, in *Pfizer v Ministry of Health* (1965) the House of Lords decided that the treatment of National Health Service patients was a governmental function so that the use of drugs was 'for the services of the Crown', bearing in mind that the Hospital Board in question was found to be acting on behalf of the Minister of Health. Broadcasting, on the other hand, was not considered a governmental function in *British Broadcasting Corporation v Johns* (1965) so that the Corporation could not claim Crown immunity from taxation. However, where premises are let as business premises for use by various central governmental agencies, the likelihood is that they are let to the Crown as tenant, whose business is government. It was in these circumstances that the House of Lords decided in *Town Investments Ltd v Secretary of State for the Environment* (1977) that it was not the Secretary of State for the Environment who was the tenant, but the Crown. Consequently, when the company contracted with the Secretary of State to let the premises they were, in fact, contracting with the Crown, which is synonymous with the government.

It was seen previously that it is rare for there to be any doubt about Crown status. Normally, a body will be a Crown servant or agent, or not. Nevertheless, there may be some hybrid bodies. One of the better-known examples of the exclusion of the Crown status affects the Post Office. The Post Office Act 1969 states that the Post Office 'is not to be regarded as the servant or agent of the Crown, or as enjoying any status, immunity or privilege of the Crown'. By contrast, the Health and Safety at Work Act 1974, referring to the Health and Safety Commission and its Executive, states that: 'The functions of the Commission and of the Executive and of their officers and servants shall be performed on behalf of the Crown'. Finally, an example of a hybrid body, the Atomic Energy Authority, which shares the Crown's immunity from the payment of rates but is not otherwise associated with the Crown. For these purposes the Atomic Energy Authority Act 1954 states that: 'Any land occupied by the Authority shall be deemed for the purposes of any rate on property to be property occupied by or on behalf of the Crown for public purposes'. The same section of the Act goes on to declare that: ' ... save as otherwise expressly provided in this Act, the Authority is not to be treated for the purposes of the enactments and rules of law relating to the privileges of the Crown as a body exercising functions on behalf of the Crown'.

2.4   Central Government Functions

In general terms it is possible to distinguish between those administrative agencies responsible for the initiation of governmental or other administrative action and those which are adjudicative agencies in that they are responsible for the adjudication or resolution of disputes arising from administrative action. Central government departments, local authorities and some public corporations are prime examples of those agencies which initiate governmental or other administrative action. Administrative tribunals and inferior courts are those bodies most obviously responsible for the adjudication of administrative disputes. However, there is no rigid division between these categories since some central government departments in particular act as adjudicative agencies. Where this is the case and a central government department is given the responsibility for an adjudication, this is almost always an indication that there is a significant policy element in the decision-making process. An important example occurs in the Town and County Planning Act 1990 which empowers local authorities and the Secretary of State for the Environment to control most uses of land by the statutory requirement that if a person wishes to carry out 'development' on land, he is normally required to apply to the local planning authority for planning permission to enable (say) the building of houses or some material change in the use of the land such as the storage of motor vehicles on land hitherto used for agricultural purposes. Each local planning authority is obliged to make a policy which provides an element of guidance for some of the important decisions that have to be made on applications for planning permission. Some of these policies must be approved by the Secretary of State who is able to impose his own policy preferences for which he is in turn responsible to Parliament. While the Secretary of State can take the initiative in requiring a planning policy to be made, he remains responsible for the adjudication of planning disputes where, in particular, the local planning authority refuses to grant planning permission from which decision he has to decide any appeal undertaken by the disappointed applicant.

From the foregoing it has been seen that it is the policy element which usually characterises the various administrative functions which are conferred on central government departments. It is this policy element which often explains the nature of the powers conferred by statute on government departments. Whether a government department is required to initiate administrative action, to control other administrative agencies in their performance of various statutory functions or to act as an adjudicative agency from a decision of another administrative agency, such functions are usually defined in terms of a discretion, as illustrated in the earlier reference to s 68 of the Education Act 1944. The essence of any such discretion is that the administrative agency has the opportunity to make a choice of action to take as long as that choice is made within the limits of the statutory powers concerned. Therefore, the Secretary of State for Education could not use his s 68 powers for a purpose unconnected with education. The opportunity to choose a course of administrative action is clearly important where the administrative agency is charged with the function of initiating such action. Equally, it is a matter of importance that there should be some guidance in the exercise of the discretion. Consequently, if the performance of some statutory function depends on the availability of finance, a policy would enable the definition of priorities where such finance is scarce.

Although it is the policy element which usually determines whether a function goes to a central government department or is subject to some control from the same direction, there are other variables which go to make up the picture. For example, there may be a measure of political sensitivity associated with some administrative decisions, for example, in which case such decisions will probably remain with a government department rather than being conferred on an administrative tribunal or some other adjudicative body. A good illustration arises from the context of immigration control under the Immigration Act 1971 where one crucial area of control remains exclusively with the Home Secretary, namely, the question of whether a person's presence in the UK is 'conducive to the public good'. In some cases a function clearly has some local dimensions in which case the option may be between the function being conferred on the relevant local authorities or a local regional division of a particular central government department. Clearly, in these circumstances the option will be between two democratically accountable bodies, that is, the council of a local authority and the relevant minister of the Crown. Whichever option is chosen may depend on factors such as the need to retain a strong central government policy influence, eg in the case of the various localised statutory functions of the Department of Health and Social Security, or the need to recognise local sensitivity and expertise, eg in the case of town and country planning. Even with this latter case and in similar areas such as education it is clear that central government control is not lacking.

Where a statutory function has been conferred on a central government department, it has been seen that there will almost certainly be a policy element involved in that function. This will be true whether the function relates to a decision on whether secondary education should be reorganised or a decision on the question of whether a compulsory purchase order should be confirmed. In both cases and in many others the decision of the responsible minister may be dominated by the need to reconcile any matter of policy with the individual rights and interests of those affected by any proposed action involving (say) the confirmation of proposals for the introduction of comprehensive education or the confirmation of a compulsory purchase order. Is the need for more housing land locally and nationally outweighed by the fact that land contained in the local authority's compulsory purchase order is good quality agricultural land, efficiently farmed by the principal objector to the order? It is this crucial question which can receive close scrutiny, before the minister takes the final decision, through the medium of a public, statutory inquiry. Such an inquiry is provided for by many statutes prescribing administrative action by a minister of the Crown, whether based on local authority proposals or not. As such it is a fundamentally important part of the bureaucratic process. Indeed, in the area of town and country planning it is the case that many planning appeals are now decided by the minister's inspector who conducts the inquiry, so expediting decision-making. These and other aspects of the system of statutory inquiries are examined in the next chapter.

3 Statutory Inquiries

3.1 Categories

It has been seen already that statutory inquiries are provided for as a prerequisite for many decisions by central government departments. Such decisions may arise principally from proposals initiated by local authorities, as seen in the examples already given, or by the central government department itself as where the Department of Transport seeks to provide a trunk road under the Highways Act 1980. In addition to these inquiries there are various other categories of statutory inquiry which, although resorted to much less frequently, need to be noted. These other inquiries fall into three categories: accident inquiries, company inquiries and tribunals of inquiry.

3.1.1 Accident inquiries

Accident inquiries relate mainly to railway, aircraft, factory and shipping accidents. Each category is governed by its own statutory provisions and there are considerable variations although there is usually some measure of formality for the majority of these inquiries. In the case of an inquiry into a railway accident under the Regulation of Railways Act 1871 there are very few formalities and the inquiry culminates with a report from the Department of Transport's railway inspectorate. Nevertheless, the Secretary of State can direct a formal investigation under the chairmanship of, eg a county court judge. In considering the form of a statutory accident inquiry, much may depend on the powers which are conferred. In the case of inquiries into shipping accidents convened by the Department of Trade under the Merchant Shipping Acts 1894–1995 there is a power to withdraw certificates of competence. This power probably explains why such inquiries are very formal, with a number of judicial trappings and right of appeal to the High Court in respect of any suspension or withdrawal of certificates of competence. However, an enduring problem occurs where, as seen in the inquiry into the sinking of *The Herald of Free Enterprise* in March 1987, criticism is forthcoming in relation to the Department of Trade itself. Such criticism might relate to departmental approval of ship design that is eventually found to be defective as a result of an accident at sea.

3.1.2 Company inquiries

Although there are various facilities for inquiries in the general commercial context, one of the best-known areas relates to the power of the Department of

Trade and Industry to appoint an inspector where it appears that fraud is being or has been committed or that the members of a company have not been given all the information they might reasonably expect. This power is found in the Companies Act 1985 and where such an inquiry is convened it is usually the case that any allegations are preceded by an investigation of the company and its financial and other affairs. This two-stage procedure can attract problems. It will be seen in Chapter 10 that natural justice requirements of fair procedure do not apply at the first stage although any inspector from the Department is legally obliged to act fairly so that there may be some occasions where an individual should have some notification of the types of information being investigated. Otherwise the inspectors' powers are very widely drawn and this led Lord Denning to observe in *Re Pergamon Press Ltd* (1971) that:

> Their proceedings are not judicial proceedings. They are not even quasi-judicial, for they decide nothing; they determine nothing. They investigate and report. They sit in private and are not entitled to admit the public to their meetings. They do not even decide whether there is a *prima facie* case.

3.1.3   Tribunals of inquiry

Beyond Parliament tribunals of inquiry have the widest powers of inquiry in English law. They are set up by virtue of the Tribunals of Inquiry (Evidence) Act 1921 following resolutions of both Houses of Parliament and deal with matters of urgent public importance. The chairman is normally a High Court judge and other members may be appointed to the tribunal in addition. Normally, the government requires no special powers to set up an inquiry. However, the powers in the Act of 1921 are necessary because they enable a tribunal of inquiry to use powers of compulsion to require the attendance of witnesses and the production of documents, among other things. The Act also gives all the powers of the High Court for the purpose of dealing with contempts on those occasions when there is a refusal to comply with any requirements of a tribunal of inquiry. One of the most notable tribunals of inquiry investigated the Aberfan disaster in 1966 and since then there has been some anxiety about the operation of these tribunals. It is possible that various allegations may be made against those who may or may not be participating in the inquiry's deliberations and which cannot be made the subject of civil or criminal proceedings in some cases. Consequently, the absence of various safeguards, such as any right to legal representation, rules of evidence or right of appeal, may mean that there is very little protection for those who may be adversely affected by the operation of those tribunals. Bearing in mind the areas which have been subject to this form of inquiry over the years, such as the 'Bloody Sunday' shootings in Londonderry in 1972, the collapse of the Vehicle and General Insurance Co in 1971 and the aforementioned Aberfan disaster in 1966, these are safeguards of fundamental importance.

3.2 Inquiries and the Public Control of Land

Although the statutory inquiry is provided for as a part of many decisions taken by various ministers in central government departments, there is no doubt that the more important and frequent inquiries occur in relation to decisions affecting land. More particularly the Town and Country Planning Act 1990 governing the need for planning permission for the development of land together with a wide variety of other statutes authorising the compulsory purchase of land under the procedures set out in the Acquisition of Land Act 1981 provide for decisions to be made by the Secretary of State for the Environment. Such decisions will in some cases be policy-based. In a previous example it was seen that a proposal to acquire land compulsorily for the building of houses may be supported strongly by the 'confirming authority', the Secretary of State for the Environment. Such support may be grounded in a policy to encourage more house building in areas of pressing need and such a policy may even be used to override strong objections based on the fact that the land in question is of good agricultural quality.

3.2.1 The individual and policy-based decisions

Where statute provides for a policy-based decision there are clear dangers for those affected by any proposal to purchase land for a public function such as the provision of housing or a proposal submitted to a local planning authority to develop land. In the first instance a compulsory purchase order will go to the Secretary of State who will decide whether it should be confirmed while any refusal or conditional grant of planning permission could lead to an appeal to, and a decision by, the same Secretary of State. The dangers inherent in this system of decision-making arise from the fact that in law, the Secretary of State can, in effect, be biased in favour of any particular policy preference so that an individual's rights and interests may not receive adequate recognition. It was against this background that the government appointed the Franks Committee on Tribunals and Inquiries in 1955. Its terms of reference were:

... to consider and make recommendations on:

(a) the constitution and working of tribunals other than the ordinary courts of law, constituted under any Act of Parliament by a minister of the Crown or for the purposes of a minister's functions;
(b) the working of such administrative procedures as include the holding of an inquiry or hearing by or on behalf of a minister on an appeal or as a result of objections or representations, and in particular the procedure for the compulsory purchase of land.

3.3   The Franks Report on Tribunals and Inquiries

The Franks Committee reported in 1957 and its recommendations covered not only inquiries but also administrative tribunals, the subject of Chapter 5. Bearing in mind the Committee's terms of reference set out above, the following recommendations were made in relation to inquiries that:

(a) individuals affected by a decision preceded by an inquiry should have adequate notice of any case to be met;

(b) details of relevant policy should be notified at the inquiry;

(c) inspectors conducting inquiries in this context should be under the control of the Lord Chancellor and not the minister responsible for the decision;

(d) the inspector's report should be published, together with the minister's decision letter;

(e) the decision letter should contain a statement of reasons for the minister's conclusion; and

(f) the minister's decision following the inquiry should be subject to review in the High Court on matters of procedure and substance.

These recommendations were accepted by the government with the exception of the recommendation that inspectors should be under the control of the Lord Chancellor. Implementation has been through statute and administrative action. The principal statute was the Tribunals and Inquiries Act 1958 which was modified and consolidated in the Tribunals and Inquiries Act 1971. In turn this legislation was consolidated in the Tribunals and Inquiries Act 1992. One of the major features of the first Act of 1958 was the establishment of the Council on Tribunals which, despite its name, has equally important supervision of public inquiries. According to the Act of 1971 its principal function in relation to inquiries is:

> ... to consider and report on such matters as may be referred [to it under the Act], or as the Council may determine to be of special importance, with respect to administrative procedures involving, or which may involve, the holding by or on behalf of a minister of a statutory inquiry, or any such procedure.
>
> The term 'statutory inquiry' here means an inquiry or hearing held in pursuance of a statutory duty, or a discretionary inquiry or hearing designated as being under the Council's superintendence and held by virtue of a statutory power. Hearings are private and although various Acts provide for such hearings, most functions in this context are discharged through the public local inquiry.

3.3.1   Implementation of the Franks Report: the Council on Tribunals

There is little doubt that the most important development arising from the Franks Report was the Council on Tribunals although the Report makes only oblique references to such an idea. The Council comprises no more than 15 nor less than 10 members appointed by the Lord Chancellor and the Lord Advocate. There is also a Scottish committee. The Council reports to the Lord Chancellor and the Lord Advocate. In its Annual Report for 1975–76 the Council reviewed its functions in the following terms:

> [O]ur role is entirely an advisory one ... Constituted as we are of part-time members, with a small supporting staff, we cannot do more than exercise a broad oversight over the working of tribunals ... We are not an inspectorial body ... We perform a similar advisory role in overseeing the many and varied procedures applicable to the large number of different kinds of ministerial hearings or inquiries held each year. We are not an appellate body with powers to overturn or alter a tribunal's decision or a decision of a minister reached after an inquiry or hearing; and we cannot concern ourselves with the merits of these decisions ... Our success in achieving changes and improvements in the tribunal and inquiry systems – whether in structure and organisation or in procedure – depends on our ability to persuade the Government of the day to follow our advice ... ministers are under a statutory duty to consult us before making rules of procedure for tribunals under our general supervision. The Lord Chancellor is under a similar duty when he makes procedural rules or regulations for statutory hearings or inquiries ... The Council's powers to deal with complaints are not clearly defined ... [W]e attached great importance to complaints since they help us in discharging our function of supervision, by enabling us to monitor the performance of the tribunal and inquiry systems, to identify weaknesses and shortcomings which might lead to unfairness, and to advise Departments on remedial action ... Inquiry procedures, which in [the] early years gave rise to the most complaints (and the major ones), formed a high proportion of our work. By 1962, new rules for planning appeal and compulsory purchase order inquiries were in operation, and we had fewer complaints about inquiry procedures.

3.3.2   Rules of procedure for statutory inquiries

Apart from the establishment of the Council and its supervision of inquiries, the other major facet of the Report to be implemented is the power of the Lord Chancellor, contained in the Tribunals and Inquiries Act, to make rules of procedure for statutory inquiries. Reference has been made to the Council's comment about the first procedural rules made by the Lord Chancellor in this context and it is important to note that he is required by the Act to ensure that they are in compliance with the terms of the Act under which they are to be used. It has been suggested, eg that when the Town and Country Planning (Inquiries Procedure) Rules were made they unlawfully extended the categories of person having the right to appear at a planning appeal inquiry beyond the categories referred to in the Town and Country Planning Act itself. These and other rules of procedure governing other areas contain the essence of most of the Franks Report recommendations which are in turn characterised by the need for 'openness, fairness and impartiality' in the system of tribunals and inquiries. While this latter standard is perhaps easier to attain in the case of administrative tribunals for reasons which will be seen in Chapter 5, there are certain difficulties with its recognition in the case of inquiries. Of particular significance here is the point emphasised earlier in the present chapter, that the minister's decision may be policy-based. Accordingly, the standard of 'openness, fairness and impartiality' in inquiry procedure has to be seen as a relative standard which provides an important safeguard for the individual's rights and interests as they are reconciled with the minister's statutory responsibility for a policy-based decision.

3.4 Inquiries Procedure and Organisation

In its Annual Report for 1980–81 the Council on Tribunals considered the desirability of statutory rules for public inquiries:

> ... so that the public may have specified legal rights and not merely privileges which can be taken away at the whim of an organising authority. Rules let people know exactly what their rights are and give them a proper foundation for an application to the court if those rights are infringed. Equally, promoting authorities should have no doubt what their obligations are: what notices and statements should be served, on whom and when. Because rules say very little about the conduct of the inquiry itself, and leave the Inspector with an overriding discretion to determine procedure during the inquiry, we do not accept the popular belief that rules must lead to formality and inflexibility of procedure.

These statutory rules are found in statutory instruments and, as such, are items of delegated legislation, a subject which is covered in Chapter 8. It has been seen previously that the rules are made by the Lord Chancellor under the authority of the Tribunals and Inquiries Act for the purpose of inquiries under various Acts. The two most important Acts are the Town and Country Planning Act 1990 (in the case of planning appeals and some other planning decisions by the Secretary of State for the Environment) and the Acquisition of Land Act 1981 (in the case of decisions relating to compulsory purchase orders submitted usually by local authorities and made under a number of different statutory powers). Since it is the case that there are thousands of planning appeals decided each year, the detailed description of statutory inquiries will concentrate on planning inquiries. However, the format and structure of other statutory inquiries is very similar.

3.4.1 Planning appeals and statutory inquiries

The Town and Country Planning Act 1990 s 79 specifies that the Secretary of State shall, before deciding an appeal against a local planning authority's decision to refuse or grant a conditional planning permission, afford 'an opportunity of appearing before, and being heard by, a person appointed by the Secretary of State for the purpose'. Although this provision suggests an alternative of a private hearing or a public inquiry, in practice it is the public local inquiry which is usually convened in order to explore the circumstances of the planning appeal. The 'person appointed' is, in fact, the inspector appointed by the Secretary of State and the power he uses to convene the inquiry is in s 320. Section 320 of the Act states that 'the Secretary of State may cause a local inquiry to be held for the purposes of the exercise of any of his functions under any of the provisions of this Act.' Because this is a discretionary inquiry provision it does not have the status of the mandatory inquiry and is subject to the Tribunals and Inquiries Act only because it was included in a statutory order (an item of delegated legislation) to that effect, along with certain other discretionary inquiries. Clearly, therefore, that status is of crucial importance given the Lord Chancellor's power to make procedural rules for these important inquiries and the fact that such inquiries are superintended by the Council on Tribunals. A further statutory provision which is of significance here is s 250 of the Local Government Act 1972. The material part of this provision states that '[W]here the Secretary of State is authorised to hold an inquiry, either under this Act or under any other enactment relating to the functions of a local authority, he may cause a local inquiry to be held'. Although this provision could be seen as an alternative to the inquiry powers in s 320, that provision may, in fact, borrow some of the inquiry powers specified by s 250 so that they may be used for the purposes of planning inquiries. More particularly, the inspector is empowered to summon persons to give evidence and to take evidence on oath. Failure to adhere to a summons here is a criminal offence. In addition, the Secretary of State is empowered to make orders as to costs in relation to such inquiries. Guidance on the award of costs are usually set down in circulars from the appropriate government department. The Department of the Environment states, eg that successful statutory objectors to compulsory purchase orders can expect an automatic award of costs after making and pursuing a formal objection at the inquiry. The law relating to evidence at planning inquiries has been extended in the Planning Inquiries (Attendance of Public) Act 1982 which contains a general requirement that oral evidence shall be heard in public and that documentary evidence shall be available for public scrutiny. The exceptions occur where the Secretary of State directs that such disclosure relates to national security or the security of premises or property and that it would be contrary to the national interest.

3.4.2 Planning appeal decisions by inspectors

Although it was the case that the Secretary of State decided each planning appeal, there are now facilities by which many such appeals are, in fact, decided by an inspector. As a result, the decision-making process is greatly expedited. Regulations made under the Town and Country Planning Act indicate the prescribed classes of decision transferred to the inspectors although it is always open to the Secretary of State to regain his power to decide a particular appeal, eg where it involves points of peculiar difficulty or controversy. Where an inspector is to decide an appeal the parties may request that they are heard before the inspector in which case a public local inquiry will be convened in most cases and, again the provisions of s 250 of the Local Government Act may be stated to apply. Rules of procedure – the Town and Country Planning (Determination by Inspectors) (Inquiries Procedure) Rules 1992 – apply to the inquiry and differ very little from the rules relating to the Secretary of State's inquiry-based decision. Areas of difference will be examined below. Where, following the inquiry, the parties so desire, they can have advance notice of the inspector's decision, although any formal decision cannot exist in law until the decision letter is received. This is a non-statutory facility which is available only with the consent of the parties. In a puzzling comment about the transfer of appeal decisions to inspectors, the Council on Tribunals remarked in its Annual Report for 1979–80 that:

> ... an inquiry into a planning application which has been transferred to an Inspector for decision becomes in effect a tribunal hearing, which makes it particularly important to emphasise the independent status of the Inspector and the 'openness' of the proceedings.

It has been observed already that the Franks Report standards of 'openness, fairness and impartiality' are more difficult to recognise in the case of inquiries, bearing in mind the policy base for so many decisions in this and similar areas. Because the Inspector has to take note of the policy element affecting decisions here it is really rather difficult to say that he has the judicial characteristics of independence and impartiality although it cannot be denied that the inquiry process is essentially open and public.

3.5 Inquiries Procedure Rules

The Rules divide the inquiry process into three parts: the pre-inquiry process, the procedure at the inquiry and the post-inquiry process. It has been seen that there are some small differences in the Rules, according to whether the decision is that of the Secretary of State or one of his inspectors operating under transferred powers. These differences will be outlined at the end of the following summary of the Town and Country Planning (Inquiries Procedure) Rules 1992.

3.5.1 Inquiry preliminaries

Having accepted the appeal, this fact will be notified by the Secretary of State to the local authority whose adverse planning decision has given rise to the appeal. The authority is then obliged to notify the Secretary of State and appellant of those who have made representations to the local authority in respect of the original application. If he considers it desirable, the Secretary of State may convene a pre-inquiry meeting chaired by the inspector. Thereafter the Secretary of State fixes the time and venue for the inquiry and is obliged to give notice of the inquiry to the various parties. The local authority is then obliged to give a written statement of its submissions to be put at the inquiry. This statement goes to the appellant and those who have made representations about the application. The Rules provide now for a full exchange of information before the opening of the inquiry, a more detailed timetable for the inquiry and regulation of any pre-inquiry meetings between any of the parties involved.

3.5.2   Procedure at the inquiry

The appellant and the local authority are the main actors at the typical inquiry. Together with those who have made representations about certain applications for planning permission, these parties have a legal right to appear at the inquiry: any other party will appear at the discretion of the inspector although that discretion is usually exercised quite freely in favour of any person with a genuine interest in the application for planning permission and the succeeding appeal. At the beginning of the inquiry the inspector will explain the background to the proceedings before allowing the parties – usually through their representatives – to enter their appearances by explaining their identity and interest in the inquiry. Beyond the terms of the Rules and subject to natural justice, the procedure is at the discretion of the inspector. At the outset the appellant opens his case. He produces his evidence, usually by means of witnesses who may be examined either after or instead of reading a proof of evidence. Such witnesses may be cross-examined by the local authority and other parties before a similar process occurs in relation to evidence produced by the local authority and the other parties. The local authority normally sums up its case before the other parties are heard and it is the appellant who normally closes with the final speech, summarising his case. During the inquiry the inspector may ask questions of the parties and it is a matter for his discretion whether evidence is admitted although the rules of evidence are more flexible than those found in a court of law. Consequently, evidence can be admitted where it may be capable of proving some matter of fact. Where any evidence at the inquiry is considered by the inspector to be contrary to the public interest, he is empowered to exclude it. In the same way he can exclude any evidence or questions which appear to relate to the merits of government policy. Much depends on what is defined as 'government policy', as will be seen in Chapter 10 on natural justice which deals with the important decision in *Bushell v Secretary of State for the Environment* (1981). Under normal circumstances an inspector's exclusion of questions or evidence at an inquiry would be in breach of natural justice, but in the foregoing areas of evidence, contrary to the public interest or questions relating to the merits of government policy, the exclusion is made lawful by the Rules' statutory authorisation.

It is normally the case that the inspector undertakes a site inspection once the inquiry is over. It is now possible for the Secretary of State for the Environment to appoint expert assessors to sit with inspectors. This facility will no doubt apply where complicated, technical evidence is in issue at the inquiry.

3.5.3 Procedure following the inquiry

It is in the procedure following the close of the inquiry that there are a number of important safeguards which have been incorporated very largely as a result of the recommendations of the Franks Report. One of the causes for concern before the advent of the Rules was the apparent freedom with which the minister could take into account new evidence or some new issue of fact following the close of the inquiry without giving the parties an opportunity of making representations. Before this area is covered, it should be noted that there is a fundamental requirement whereby the inspector is obliged to make a written report to the Secretary of State following the close of the inquiry. The report must contain the inspector's findings of fact and recommendations or his reasons for refraining from making recommendations. Returning to the provision of safeguards following the close of an inquiry, the Rules proceed on the basis of two possible occurrences: either that (a) there is a difference on a material fact as between the inspector and the Secretary of State, or (b) some new evidence or new matter of fact is taken into consideration by the Secretary of State, as a result of which in either case the Secretary of State is disposed to depart from the inspector's recommendation. In the case of occurrence (a) the Secretary of State is obliged by the Rules to offer the parties an opportunity of making written representations before coming to a decision. In the case of occurrence (b) there is an obligation to offer a re-opening of the inquiry. These are clearly important procedural obligations and whether they apply depends on the legal definition of the key terms such as 'fact' and 'evidence'. In *Luke v Minister of Housing and Local Government* (1967) the difference between the inspector and the minister concerned the question whether a proposed development of land was 'sporadic development' *vis-à-vis* a neighbouring community. The minister did not offer the parties an opportunity of making representations on this difference before coming to his decision. It was decided by the court that the Rules did not oblige the minister to seek representations because the difference related only to a matter of planning policy or opinion, and not a matter of 'fact'. In the case of *Pyrford v Secretary of State for the Environment* (1977) it was decided that whether a firm was a 'local firm' for planning purposes was a question of fact so that there could be no lawful decision until representations had been sought from the parties in respect of this difference which formed the basis of the Secretary of State's decision. In *French Kier Developments Ltd v Secretary of State for the Environment* (1977) it was decided that a policy document on land availability for housing could not be relied on by the Secretary of State without an offer to reopen the inquiry where that document constituted new evidence which had not been in issue at the inquiry. Finally, in *Portsmouth Water plc v*

Secretary of State for the Environment (1993) a disagreement on the question whether development would be detrimental to the locality was characterised as a matter of opinion, not fact.

3.5.4   Notification of a decision and reasons

When the Secretary of State arrives at his decision, the Rules oblige him to notify that decision to the parties and to include a statement of reasons. A copy of the inspector's report will normally accompany the notified decision. Finally, where the provisions of s 250 of the Local Government Act 1972 apply to the inquiry, the Secretary of State may make orders as to costs although this power is usually exercised sparingly.

3.5.5   Procedural differences for decisions by inspectors

Reference has been made to some small differences in the Rules according to whether the decision lies with the Secretary of State or is transferred to one of his inspectors. In the case of a decision by an inspector after an inquiry the discretion as to costs remains with the Secretary of State who is also obliged to notify the parties of the name of the inspector. Following the close of the inquiry, the inspector is not obliged to report to the Secretary of State, in which case he is obliged only to notify his decision and the reasons to the parties.

3.6   Legal Enforcement of the Inquiries Procedure Rules

Reference has been made to the supervisory functions of the Council on Tribunals in relation to statutory inquiries. In addition to this supervision, the High Court undertakes the legal enforcement of the Rules governing the inquiries. Again, the scope of legal enforcement is very similar in relation to most of the decision-making functions of central government where a statutory inquiry is involved. Accordingly, the Town and Country Planning Act 1990 is fairly typical in its provisions which specify that any person aggrieved by the decision of the Secretary of State in a planning appeal can apply to the High Court to have that decision quashed on either or both of two grounds, within six weeks of the decision. The first ground is that the decision is *ultra vires* the Secretary of State's planning powers under the Act, eg where the Secretary of State allows an appeal and grants planning permission on the ground that the applicant, that is, the appellant, proposes to finance his building programme on the site from British, not foreign finance. This topic is pursued in more detail in Chapter 11. The second ground is that the Secretary of State's decision is in breach of the procedural requirements of the Rules and that this breach has caused 'substantial prejudice' to the applicant, ie that there is something more than a mere technical breach of the Rules. Accordingly, in two of the cases previously mentioned, *Pyrford* and *French Kier Developments*, the High Court quashed the Secretary of State's appeal decision for a breach of the relevant post-inquiry Rules. Another area where the High Court has had cause to look critically at appeal decisions of the Secretary of State relates to the requirement for reasons to accompany the decision. In the leading case, *Save Britain's Heritage v Secretary of State for the Environment* (1991), Lord Bridge in the House of Lords stressed that adequacy of reasons cannot be assessed *in vacuo*: the question is whether an applicant has been substantially prejudiced by any inadequacy. Lord Bridge refers to three possible causes of inadequacy:

(a) where reasons are so inadequately or obscurely expressed as to raise a substantial doubt whether a decision has been taken within the powers of the Act;

(b) where the planning considerations on which a decision is based are not explained sufficiently clearly to enable a reasonable assessment of prospects of success in relation to some alternative form of development; and

(c) where there is a failure to explain the planning considerations influencing the decision sufficiently clearly so that there is no clear view of their impact on future applications for planning permission.

The broader scope of the legal obligation to give reasons for administrative decisions is explored further in Chapter 9. Finally, it should be noted that where an inspector makes a decision under transferred powers this decision is, in law, the decision of the Secretary of State so that the foregoing legal enforcement of the Rules and other substantive powers will occur in the normal way.

3.7 Scope of the Statutory Inquiry System

Whether for reasons of efficiency, policy or political expediency, there are occasions when it is necessary, usually from the government's point of view, to exclude, restrict or modify the system of statutory inquiries. Looking again at the context of planning inquiries, there are important examples of exclusion, restriction and modification and each is now examined in turn.

3.7.1 Exclusion of statutory inquiries

There are two situations where the system of statutory inquiries is excluded, in relation to the determination of planning appeals by written representations and by means of hearings. When an applicant for planning permission notifies an appeal against an adverse decision of the local planning authority, he may be invited to choose between a hearing or inquiry on the one hand, and written representations on the other. This latter procedure is statutory, governed by the Town and Country Planning (Appeals) (Written Representations Procedure) Regulations 1987. This is achieved through an exchange of the parties' written statements where, eg the local authority will defend its decision refusing planning permission, while the appellant will, of course, argue that the planning permission should be granted. Thereafter a decision is made in the normal way on the basis of the parties' arguments in the appeal, usually within six to eight weeks. It is not a procedure which is often used where third parties are involved in a planning appeal, usually as objectors to the applicant's proposed development: their participation in the process would tend to defeat the object of more expeditious decision-making. If necessary, and even though the parties have opted for written representations, it is possible for the Secretary of State to insist that the appeal is conducted without written representations but with an inquiry. The second area of exclusion relates to the provision of a hearing rather than the public local inquiry. The hearing is essentially a private process which is not often used in practice.

3.7.2   Restriction of statutory inquiries

In some cases there is a restriction on the coverage of the statutory inquiry. Before examining two significant examples in the context of planning, it should be noted that any objection to a compulsory purchase order which relates to the measure of compensation payable cannot be accepted and, more particularly, cannot be dealt with by a statutory inquiry into such an order. Any such objection is a matter for the Lands Tribunal and so it seems clear that the reason for this restriction reflects on the complexity of compensation questions, an area which is better dealt with by the expert Lands Tribunal. Returning to the planning context, the first example of a restriction on the facilities normally available through the statutory inquiry occurs in the area of immunity given to the treatment of government policy. It has been seen already that under one set of Inquiries Procedure Rules there is an exclusion of questioning which in the inspector's opinion is directed to the merits of government policy. This precedent is also carried into other, similar Rules. The second area of restriction relates to development plans known as structure plans. These are broad, strategic plans for large areas such as counties. They are made by the county planning authorities and submitted to the Secretary of State for the Environment for approval. Before a decision is made, an inquiry must be convened. However, the more conventional statutory public local inquiry is not used, apparently because there was thought to be a danger that a large number of objectors would be attracted and would be concerned only with detailed land use issues, whereas the structure plan is concerned only with broad, strategic questions which are not usually site-specific. For this reason the Town and Country Planning Act 1990 permits the Secretary of State (or the local planning authority) to convene an 'examination in public' of the structure plan. This contrasts with the adversarial statutory inquiry which is, in many respects, a court-like process. The examination in public is, in essence, a round-table discussion of the issues raised by the proposed structure plan. Accordingly, the Act gives an important discretion to do two things: first, to draw up an agenda for the examination in public, and secondly, to identify those persons or groups of persons

who should be allowed to appear.

3.7.3 Statutory inquiries and proposals for controversial development

There may be a fine distinction between the foregoing section on the restriction of the statutory inquiry and the present section dealing with its modification. This section is concerned mainly with the extent to which the conventional statutory inquiry process is adequate to deal with wider issues of national policy, eg in relation to the country's energy requirements. The main focus of this question was the Windscale Inquiry into a proposal by British Nuclear Fuels Ltd to extend its nuclear reprocessing plant at Windscale. The Secretary of State used his power in the Town and Country Planning Act to call in the company's application for planning permission made to the local planning authority for the area. To examine the background to and implications of the application, a public local inquiry was convened with a High Court judge, Parker J, as chairman, together with two assessors. Parker J recognised the wide-ranging implications of the inquiry: 'the issues to be investigated may affect not only those already alive and residing in the immediate neighbourhood but also those who live far away and who will not be born for many years ahead'. The inquiry in common with other similar inquiries such as that into the proposal to build a pressurised water reactor at Sizewell, covered many wide-ranging issues, far beyond the question of whether the site itself was inherently suitable for the proposed expansion of the nuclear processing facility. Major questions covered included the issue of whether there should be reliance on nuclear fuel as opposed to naturally generated energy in the UK and the issue of safety in transporting fuel to and from the site for reprocessing. All the evidence was taken on oath and there was an exclusion of evidence that might prejudice national security or the national interest, together with evidence questioning the merits of government policy, although it appears that this latter exclusion was interpreted quite flexibly during the inquiry. It was finally recommended that planning permission should be granted, a conclusion which was upheld on a vote following a debate in Parliament. For technical reasons the Secretary of State decided to refuse planning permission and then made a Special Development Order (an item of delegated legislation, a subject covered in Chapter 8) granting planning permission but incorporating all the safeguards which had emerged from the report of the statutory inquiry. Despite the controversies surrounding these inquiries, one emerging trend seen at the Sizewell Inquiry is a differing attitude of some government departments to debates about the merits of government energy policy. Many campaigners would argue that these inquiries are the only forum where such debate can occur in a real, detailed context.

3.7.4 The Windscale Inquiry

The major criticism emerging from the Windscale Inquiry was that it and the planning system as a whole are not able to deal adequately with the wider and more controversial questions which are likely to arise from proposals for large-scale energy developments. Somewhat surprisingly, there are facilities in the Town and Country Planning Act for what is known as a Planning Inquiry Commission, which appears to have some, if not all, of the advantages which may be lacking in the ordinary public local planning inquiry for the purpose of dealing with large-scale energy development proposals. The Planning Inquiry Commission, although it has not been used, is intended to operate in two stages. Initially it considers the broad background to a proposal on the basis of evidence provided by the promoters of the scheme, the local authority, objectors, and so on. The second stage involves a local inquiry in conventional form and permits an investigation into the scheme and objections to it. Such a Commission, if it were ever employed in this context, would be comprised of experts in the appropriate fields of activity whose conclusions and recommendations would be very persuasive. Having established a reputation, such a Commission would be seen as an increasingly popular instrument in the face of proposals for large-scale energy development. However, there is one significant precedent in this context, namely, the Roskill Commission, which investigated proposals for a third London airport between 1969 and 1971. A number of sites were subject to general investigation initially until just four sites were singled out, at which point local inquiries were held at each site and, eventually, one large inquiry was convened at which the arguments for and against each of the sites were heard. The one site which was recommended as a result was rejected following a debate in Parliament, the result of which was that Parliament recommended the site at Foulness which had been included in the final list of four sites. The process took three years, which may be a significant argument against the employment of such a Commission.

3.7.5 The statutory inquiry in future

There have been various proposals for a better modification of the system of statutory inquiries for cases involving complex, controversial issues of national and perhaps international dimensions. Nevertheless, the largely conventional framework has continued to be used for inquiries into proposals to mine coal in the Vale of Belvoir and to build a pressurised water reactor at Sizewell in Suffolk. Given the political and policy controversy which frequently arises from the large scale development proposal, particularly in the context of energy, it is not surprising perhaps that the government should want to maintain a flexibility of response which it can do within the present system with the existing framework of statutory inquiries. A radical modification of the statutory inquiry system through the creation of an expert, investigative body could make it more difficult for a government to resist proposals and recommendations which run counter to its existing policies.

4 Local Authorities

4.1 Status and Functions

Local authorities are statutory corporations established in tiers for the performance of a wide variety of local functions prescribed by statute. Local authorities act through their respective councils comprising democratically elected members. Most of the law relating to the status of local authorities is found in the Local Government Act 1972 which introduced a reorganised system of local government in 1974. That Act defined the main units of local government, the county and district councils, the metropolitan county and district councils and the parish councils (known as community councils in Wales). The metropolitan county councils and the Greater London council were abolished (with effect from 1 April 1986) by the Local Government Act 1985 and their functions transferred to other local authorities such as the metropolitan districts and London boroughs. The Local Government Act 1992 created a Local Government Commission for England. The Commission's functions include the review of local government areas for the purpose of recommending 'structural changes' such as the creation of unitary authorities in non-metropolitan areas by a fusion of certain existing county and district councils.

4.1.1 County councils

County councils' responsibilities include education, personal social services, highways and transportation, town and country planning, the police and consumer protection. Education and personal social services are responsibilities undertaken by the metropolitan district councils.

4.1.2 District councils

District councils' responsibilities include town and country planning, housing, environmental health and the making of bylaws. These principal responsibilities also relate to the metropolitan district councils although it has been seen that these councils have responsibilities for education and personal social services, among others. Although the county councils have responsibilities for planning in addition to those of the district councils, it is the latter which are designated as the principal planning authorities by statute in order to deal with most aspects of this function. In some cases the function is exercised concurrently between the two main tiers of local government, eg in the case of parks and open spaces. On other occasions there is a clear 'dovetailing' of functions, eg in the case of waste management under the Environmental Protection Act 1990, where the county council is normally the waste regulation authority while the constituent district councils are the waste collection authorities. The Environmental Protection Act requires a county council, in connection with its waste management functions, to operate also as a waste disposal authority. In an effort to separate regulatory matters (involving the grant of waste management licences for the deposit, disposal or treatment of 'controlled' waste) and operational matters where, previously a county council would (along with the private sector) provide disposal facilities, the Act imposes important obligations on the waste disposal authority. Any such authority is obliged to 'privatise' its operational waste disposal operations or place them with an 'arm's length company' thereby effectively 'neutralising' local authority control. In a few instances and particularly in the case of sewerage and related services a district council often acts as agent for the sewerage undertaker plcs created under the Water Industry Act 1991. Finally in this context, a number of statutory provisions require that a district council is consulted by a county council before it exercises a function, particularly on those occasions when development plan schemes are being made in order to co-ordinate the making of planning policies in a county.

4.1.3   Local government in Wales

The Local Government (Wales) Act 1994 is the first legislation to deal exclusively with local government in Wales. After 1 April 1996 the eight county councils and 37 district councils established by the Local Government Act 1972 are to be abolished, to be replaced by 22 'principal councils': so-called 'unitary authorities'.

4.1.4   London government

Since the Local Government Act 1985, virtually every function is undertaken by the London borough councils. Before the Act came into force the provision of education was the responsibility of the Inner London Education Authority (ILEA), then a specially constituted committee of the Greater London Council (GLC), in the case of the 12 inner London boroughs. When the Act abolished the GLC the ILEA became a directly elected education authority. Each of the outer London boroughs continues to act as an education authority. With effect from April 1990 the ILEA was abolished under the terms of the Education Reform Act 1988.

4.1.5   Parish councils

Well over 1,000 parish councils in England, and their equivalent community councils in Wales, exercise numerous functions. These elected bodies, usually serviced by a part-time clerk, have limited powers to make bylaws, powers to deal with footpaths, to provide community centres, to acquire land for use as open space, the right to be consulted by the local planning authority in respect of relevant applications for planning permission, the right to issue precepts on the relevant district council to fund its various functions, and so on.

4.2 The Local Authority as a Statutory Corporation

The focal point of a local authority is its council of elected members which is declared by the Local Government Act to be a body corporate under the name of the county or district council concerned. As a corporate entity the council lasts for ever, even though its membership will change from time to time. As a separate legal entity in law, the council can act as an individual in acquiring and disposing of all types of property for the fulfilment of its various functions. In the same way it has the capacity to enter into contracts, again for the fulfilment of its various functions. Finally, and again as an individual corporate entity, the council of a local authority can sue and be sued in its own name. All of this makes for a more efficient discharge of business for the local authority.

4.2.1 The acquisition of property

In order to fulfil its functions a local authority will have to acquire all types of property, from office furniture to land for the building of houses. A large number of statutory powers exist to facilitate these transactions. These powers may be expressed in very broad terms or in very specific terms. As a rule of thumb, the powers will be broadly defined where local authorities can conclude voluntary contracts or similar transactions while the powers will be closely defined where the local authority has to use compulsion, primarily in the area of the compulsory acquisition of land. By way of an illustration of this latter area, s 226 of the Town and Country Planning Act 1990 permits the compulsory acquisition of land for planning purposes. More specifically, the section allows the local planning authority to acquire land in its area which is suitable for and is required in order to secure the carrying out of one or more of the following activities, namely 'development, redevelopment and improvement' or 'which is required for a purpose which it is necessary to achieve in the interests of the proper planning of an area in which the land is situated'. Any compulsory purchase order made under this power has to be submitted to the Secretary of State for the Environment for confirmation. His decision whether to confirm will be taken after a public local inquiry into any objections to the order. By way of contrast, the Local Government Act contains a broadly defined power to acquire land by agreement for the purpose of any function and for the 'benefit, improvement or development' of a local authority's area (s 120). In addition to these statutory powers to acquire land compulsorily or by agreement, the local authority, acting again in its own name, is empowered by s 123 of the Local

Government Act to dispose of land, subject to general consent of the Secretary of State.

These statutory powers may be open to scrutiny by the court which may be invited to decide that they are subject to restriction, usually by reference to what Parliament is said to have intended.

Section 120 referred to above also contains a power whereby a local authority will manage any land so acquired 'for the benefit of their area'. In a case where the local authority purported to use this power in order to ban stag hunting on its land – *R v Somerset County Council, ex p Fewings* (1995) – the Court of Appeal held that the power was exercisable by reference to wider questions of public benefit rather than narrower questions of ethics, animal welfare and social considerations. On the other hand it has been held – in *R v Barnet London Borough Council, ex p Islam* (1991) – that the power of disposal in s 123 must be exercised in good faith, fairly, reasonably and for proper purposes after consideration of all the issues involved.

4.2.2 Contracts

As statutory corporations with functions to fulfil, it is clearly necessary for local authorities to have an effective power to enter into contracts, eg for the supply of goods and services. It would be impossible to define precisely every purpose for which a contract has to be made in the day-to-day discharge of functions which explains the very broad power in s 111 of the Local Government Act. This section empowers a local authority, subject to some limitations, to 'do anything (whether or not involving the expenditure, borrowing or lending of money or the acquisition or disposal of any property or rights) which is calculated to facilitate, or is conducive or incidental to, the discharge of any of their functions'. There are, in addition, a number of specific powers for the making of contracts in some areas, eg where it may not be clear whether s 111 extends to cover the particular transaction. Nevertheless, s 111 is very widely defined and does permit virtually any contract which is in some way reasonably referable to a local authority's function or functions. The powers have not often been challenged in the courts hitherto but in *R v Greater London Council, ex p Burgess* (1978) it was decided that a closed shop agreement between a local authority and a trade union was within the powers of the section. On the other hand, in *R v Wirral Metropolitan Borough Council, ex p Milstead* (1989), the court found that a factoring arrangement where the authority agreed to sell anticipated receipts from council house sales to increase statutory limits on spending powers was not covered by s 111. Such an agreement was not *incidental* to the sale of the council houses. The House of Lords in *R v Richmond-upon-Thames London Borough Council, ex p McCarthy and Stone (Developments) Ltd* (1991) had to deal with the legality of a local authority practice of providing advice on planning matters and the charging for such advice. It was held that, in the absence of any specific power or duty to provide advice, s 111 gives an implied power for this purpose. To provide advice in respect of planning matters is calculated to facilitate or is conducive or incidental to the discharge of the local authority's planning function. On the other hand, it was held that imposition of a charge could not be seen in the same light and was therefore unlawful. The parties to this litigation agreed that a fundamental assumption underpinning the case was the principle in *Attorney General v Wilts United Dairies Ltd* (1921), a case dealt with in Chapter 8. Accordingly a charge may not be imposed unless authorised expressly or by necessary implication in the statute concerned. Because the giving of advice was characterised by the House of Lords as a 'subsidiary' power by virtue of s 111, to charge for the exercise of that power is, at best, 'incidental to the incidental' and not incidental to the discharge of functions.

The useful powers in s 111 may be subject to other statutory requirements which may restrict its coverage. In *North Tyneside Metropolitan Borough Council v Allsop* (1991) it was held that a local authority has no power by statute to pay compensation under a voluntary redundancy scheme in excess of amounts prescribed by statute and subject to approval by the Secretary of State. Similarly, in *Morgan Grenfell and Co Ltd v Sutton London Borough Council* (1995) a local authority used s 111 in order to guarantee and indemnify a loan made to an unregistered housing association. Because s 111 is subject to any 'subsequent enactment' the local authority's action was unlawful and *ultra vires* by virtue of the later Act – the Housing Association Act 1985 – that prohibits the giving of guarantees to unregistered housing associations. On the other hand, in *Credit Suisse v Waltham Forest London Borough Council* (1994) it was held that a local authority acts within its statutory powers when it guarantees the obligations of a company which it had helped to set up and to which it lent money with a view to fulfilling its obligations to house the homeless. However, in *Credit Suisse v Allerdale Borough Council* (1994) it was stressed that although a local authority, in order to execute a statutory function, may establish a company and guarantee any borrowing, that guarantee is unlawful if it is given on the basis of irrelevant and impermissible considerations. Furthermore, the guarantee is void and unenforceable, regardless of the lender's ignorance of the local authority's position here.

The power of a local authority to enter into speculative financial transactions – so-called 'rate swaps' – again focuses attention on s 111 powers. The House of Lords in *Hazell v Hammersmith and Fulham London Borough Council* (1991) has held such transactions to be *ultra vires* in the absence of any express statutory authority to enter into the transactions and the fact that s 111 does not extend to such activity. Furthermore, and although rate swaps are 'part' of the local authority borrowing process, the House of Lords held that Part I of Schedule 13 to the Local Government Act regulating the power of borrowing could not justify rate swaps as being calculated to facilitate or conducive or incidental to, the

44

discharge of the money borrowing function. Lord Templeman was content to conclude that:

> The authorities show that a power is not incidental merely because it is convenient or desirable or profitable. A swap transaction undertaken by a local authority involves speculation in future interest trends with the object of making a profit in order to increase the available resources of the local authorities.

In the context of this important decision it has been held also that one of the banks involved could recover the necessary funds advanced on the basis, *inter alia*, of unjust enrichment as an aspect of quasi-contract and the fact that payments had been made by the bank under a purported contract that was *ultra vires* and void: *Westdeutsche Landesbank Girozentrale v Islington London Borough Council* (1993).

The Local Government Act 1988 introduces new restrictions on contractual powers. Section 17, eg, requires a local authority to exercise its functions without reference to 'non-commercial considerations'. In *R v Islington London Borough Council, ex p Building Employers Confederation* (1989), eg, standard contract clauses requiring contractors to comply with statutory requirements on sex discrimination and health and safety were found to infringe the section. Nevertheless, contracts can promote race relations objectives in conformity with s 71 of the Race Relations Act 1976. Note also that the Act of 1988 introduces new requirements for competitive tendering by authorities.

4.2.3 Extended powers

Beyond the power in s 111, s 137 of the Local Government Act empowers a local authority, again subject to some limitations, to 'incur expenditure which in their opinion is in the interests of and will bring direct benefit to their area or any part of it or all or some of its inhabitants'. This power relates to any transaction which is not already provided for by statute as a particular function and is limited to the product of a statutory formula. Section 137 was in issue in *Manchester City Council v Greater Manchester Council* (1980) when it was decided that the establishment of a trust fund to provide monies for the private education of some children in the Greater Manchester area was within the s 137 powers, even though the council in question was not an education authority. A number of local authorities have used these powers in order to establish and found private companies for the purposes of promoting industrial development in their respective areas. The Local Government Act 1986 now restricts the scope of the section where its powers are used for publicity. The powers can be used only for the production of economic development in a local authority's area where that publicity is incidental to other activities undertaken for that type of promotion. Over-reliance on s 137 in relation to economic development activities is now alleviated by s 33 of the Local Government and Housing Act 1989. This provision now provides a specific power to take 'such steps as they [the local authority] may from time to time consider appropriate for promoting the economic development of their area'.

Because controls like those in s 111 apply to local authorities Parliament has legislated to ensure that similar statutory controls apply to companies influenced or controlled by them. However, the controls – contained in Part V of the Local Government and Housing Act 1989 – focus essentially on the local authorities themselves. According to the type of influence or control a local authority will be subject to differing controls in its conduct of business through a company. Each local authority concerned is subject to a duty to ensure, so far as is practicable, that any company subject to influence or control complies with relevant statutory regulations. Failure is sanctioned through the classification of any expenditure as unlawful expenditure.

4.2.4   Local authorities' contracts and the doctrine of *ultra vires*

Wherever a local authority strays beyond the statutory limits of the various powers prescribing its right to acquire property, make contracts and to enter other transactions, it will be acting *ultra vires* so that the acquisition, contract or transaction will have no effect in law that is, it will be null and void. As an *ultra vires* contract it cannot be enforced so that one of the parties could not seek payment, for example. There was one notable exception to this general rule in the context of the Secretary of State for the Environment's control of local authorities' capital expenditure under the Local Government Planning and Land Act 1980. Where the Secretary of State considered that a local authority had failed or was likely to fail to comply with prescribed limits for capital expenditure he could direct that contractual expenditure should not exceed the limit. If that direction was not adhered to, any contract entered into for this purpose was *ultra vires*, but it would not be null and void as between the local authority and the other party. As a result it would appear that the members of a local authority who sanctioned such contractual expenditure could be surcharged and face other penalties which will be described in section 4.4.2. Finally, it is a fundamental rule of the law that a local authority cannot use a contract or, indeed, any other means in order to fetter or prevent its exercise of functions prescribed by statute (*Stringer v Minister of Housing and Local Government* (1971)).

4.2.5   *Ultra vires* in practice

Although ss 111 and 137 of the Local Government Act bring a useful measure of flexibility to many areas of local government activity, there will be occasions when the more specific statutory powers will be in use and when it will be necessary to decide how far they extend. It is clearly impossible for Parliament to legislate for every detail which is likely to arise from the exercise of such powers. It is equally unrealistic for the law to insist that a local authority should

46

operate strictly within the express limits of the statutory powers. Accordingly, the courts have attempted to apply the doctrine of *ultra vires* so that local authorities can do all those things which are implied from or are incidental to the express statutory powers. In most instances, any other approach would frustrate the working of the legislation. This approach can be illustrated with the case of *Attorney General v Crayford Urban District Council* (1962) where the local authority proposed to introduce a scheme of compulsory insurance for the personal property of its residential tenants. The scheme was introduced under s 111 of the Housing Act 1957 (now s 21 Housing Act 1985) which states that the 'general management, regulation and control of houses provided by a local authority ... shall be vested in and exercised by the authority'. It was decided by the Court of Appeal that the scheme was not *ultra vires* because the statutory powers implied that the local authority could pursue the general social welfare of its tenants.

4.2.6   Challenging local authorities' *ultra vires* acts

There are three methods by which an *ultra vires* act may be challenged:

(a) by an application for judicial review in the Queen's Bench Division or, exceptionally, by an application for a declaration or an injunction in the High Court, topics which are covered in Chapter 13;

(b) indirectly where an individual is prosecuted in a criminal court for an alleged failure to comply with some order, notice or licence: the individual may attempt to avoid conviction by establishing that the order, notice or licence was *ultra vires* so that he could not be convicted for failure to comply with something which does not exist in law;

(c) by means of audit, where the auditor finds that an item in the local authority's accounts is 'contrary to law'. If this finding is confirmed on application to the High Court by the auditor the amounts involved may be surcharged to the members responsible who may also find themselves excluded from membership of the council.

4.3   Legal Control of Local Authorities

Control of local authorities by the court is clearly crucial but the bulk of control occurs outside the courts. In practice, a great deal of control is exerted over local authorities by central government, particularly, in the area of finance. This control is often discrete control where the lever which encourages local authorities to keep within statutory and non-statutory limits is the knowledge that a lot of financial support for their functions comes from central government. It will be seen that central government has many other means of ensuring that local authorities adhere to the law and preferred policies through various powers by which central government can approve schemes, make decisions on appeals, and so on. Each of these areas of control is examined in turn.

4.4 Local Government Finance and its Control

In very broad terms, local authority expenditure falls into two categories: current (revenue) expenditure covering items such as wages, salaries and the cost of running buildings, and capital expenditure, covering the acquisition of assets like roads and buildings. Current expenditure has been financed from various sources including the Council Tax introduced by the Local Government Act 1992, grants from central government as well as from other revenue such as rents and charges.

Some services such as housing attracted specific grants from central government. Much capital expenditure is financed by borrowing within limits set by central government.

4.4.1 Central government control

The statutory control of local government finance by central government is a very complex matter. Much of the statutory control of capital expenditure, eg, is to be found in the Local Government and Housing Act 1989 as well as the Local Government Finance Act 1982, as amended. The Act of 1982 is dealt with, below. The Act of 1989 empowers the Secretary of State to prescribe what is to be regarded as a 'capital receipt'. The Act gives the Secretary of State wide powers to demand information from local authorities. Failure by a local authority to comply further empowers the Secretary of State to make and impose certain 'capital assumptions' and estimates.

4.4.2 Audit

Local authority accounts are subject to audit by an auditor appointed by the Audit Commission. The Commission was created by the Local Government Finance Act 1982 and its membership of not less than 15 but no more than 20 is appointed by the Secretary of State for the Environment in consultation with the local authority associations and the professional accountancy bodies. The Commission is a corporate body. It does not act as an agent of the Crown and its members, officers and employees are not Crown servants. The Secretary of State is empowered to give the Commission directions as to the discharge of its functions whereupon it is the Commission's duty to give effect to those directions. An auditor appointed by the Commission may be an officer of that body or a private accountant. It is the duty of an auditor in examining the accounts to satisfy himself that statutory standards for accounts have been adhered to, that proper practices have been observed in compiling accounts and that the body whose accounts are being audited has made proper arrangements for securing economy, efficiency and effectiveness in its use of resources. He is also required to comply with a code of audit practice, compiled by the Commission, and to consider whether, in the public interest, he should make a report on any matter to the body subject to audit or that such a report should be brought to the attention of the public. In undertaking the audit, the auditor has a right of access to documents and a right to information and explanation for the purpose of that audit. Any person interested has a right to inspect the accounts to be audited and other relevant items such as contracts and receipts. A local government elector for the area has a right to question the auditor about the accounts and a right to object to the audited accounts. A decision of the auditor on an objection must be supported by reasons. Where such an objector is aggrieved by a decision of the auditor not to act in connection with an alleged illegality, any loss due to wilful misconduct or a failure to bring a sum of money into the accounts, he may appeal either to the county court (where the amount in issue is less than the financial limits for this court) or the High Court. However, where the auditor considers that any item of account is contrary to law he is empowered to apply to the court for a declaration to that effect except where it is sanctioned by the Secretary of State. Whoever applies, the court has a power to surcharge any person responsible for incurring or authorising the unlawful expenditure and a power (where the expenditure exceeds £2,000) to disqualify the person responsible from membership of a local authority unless the court is satisfied that the person acted reasonably or believed that the expenditure was authorised by law. It should be noted that where a local government elector makes an application or where the Commission considers it desirable in view of an auditor's report or other reason, the Commission can require that an extraordinary audit of a local authority's accounts is undertaken. The legislation provides a number of other powers of enforcement. An auditor may issue a prohibition order in anticipation of unlawful local authority expenditure. During the currency of the order, the subject action of the local authority is suspended. However, a prohibition may be appealed to the High Court. In addition, an auditor has related powers to seek a judicial review of the legality of local authority action.

More generally, in deciding whether an item of account is contrary to law, the tests to be applied are those in *Giddens v Harlow District Auditor* (1972) where it was stated that the auditor can intervene where the council has:

(a) refused or neglected to take into account matters which it ought to have taken into account; or

(b) taken into account matters which it ought not to have taken into account; or

(c) come to a conclusion so unreasonable that no reasonable authority could ever have come to it.

In effect, the auditor can intervene where an item of account is *ultra vires* and the three grounds for intervention just mentioned are among those which are used in the High Court to review the legality of administrative action generally, as to which, see Chapter 11. Each of the three grounds for intervention by the auditor can be illustrated from cases which have been before the courts. Ground (a) was in issue in *Barnes v District Auditor for No 11 District* (1976) where the council paid excessive wages which were lawfully disallowed by the auditor. The court agreed that the council 'wrongly neglected to take into account the provisions of the Pay Code, the advice of their officers and the National Joint Council, and the interests of the rate payers'. By contrast, in *Pickwell v Camden London Borough Council* (1982) the council settled a pay claim by their striking manual workers at a rate in excess of the later national settlement. It was decided by the court that the council had not incurred an item of account contrary to law, primarily because it had not failed to take into account the legally relevant interests of the rate payers and had balanced the interests and welfare of its workforce, another legally relevant factor. Ground (b) occurred in *Taylor v Munrow* (1960) where expenditure incurred in failing to increase rents, as required by law, was disallowed because the council was influenced by a legally irrelevant consideration, namely, a desire to protect tenants from rent increases under the Rent Act. Finally, ground (c) was in issue in *Backhouse v Lambeth London Borough Council* (1972), another case concerned with a council's attempt to avoid rent increases for many tenants, this time under the Housing Finance Act 1972. In order to avoid such increases, the council took one of its houses and imposed an artificial rent of £18,000 per week, the amount which would have been yielded had the tenants been subject to the increase. It was decided by the court that this was totally unreasonable and so *ultra vires*. In other words, Parliament could never have intended that the provisions of the Housing Finance Act should be used in this way.

4.5 Central Government Control of Local Authorities

It has been seen that there are very comprehensive controls imposed on local authorities in relation to finance, with particular reference to limits on the amounts which can be sought from central government and the purposes for which money can be spent. Other forms of statutory control will be examined in this part of the chapter, with particular reference to the relationship between central and local government as seen in the Town and Country Planning Act. Once again the relationship is defined by law in the Act and although it gives some autonomy to the local planning authorities, central government in the shape of the Secretary of State for the Environment and his department wield great influence. Nevertheless, a good deal will depend on the policies being operated in the name of the Secretary of State at any one time. In the crucially important area of development control, where the local planning authorities are required to determine applications for planning permission if a person intends to undertake 'development' on land, central government policy may be in favour of encouraging as much residential and industrial development as possible. Consequently, if applications for planning permission for such development are ever refused by a local planning authority, an appeal by the disappointed applicant to the Secretary of State is likely to be successful. Indeed, on some occasions the Secretary of State may 'call in' an application for decision before the local planning authority is able to deal with it.

Central government influence may also have been felt where the Secretary of State has imposed his policy preferences in approving the local planning authority's own policies in its development plan, or where the Secretary of State has issued a circular. Government circulars are intended to provide local authorities with guidance on a variety of issues, as well as information. Some local authorities may require guidance on the practical implications of some new piece of legislation which has just come onto the statute book while central government may be anxious to inform local authorities about policy preferences. Both these functions can be performed by circulars; non-statutory channels of communication which have considerable influence over the way that local authorities perform many of their functions. Indeed, where a circular prescribes a policy it is often the case that much time is taken up at a planning inquiry arguing whether the instant case of (say) a refusal of planning permission falls within that policy as described by the words of the circular. This then is the background to a number of statutory controls of local government activity. However, in looking at the important areas of control, some of which have been outlined earlier, it should be remembered that although there are controls available to central government they do not necessarily have to be used and often are not used. It is clearly important that local authorities should be allowed to use their local knowledge and expertise and maintain an effective measure of autonomy. Ideally, therefore, the relationship between the two tiers of government should be defined as a collaborative partnership with ultimate control of many functions residing with central government, with its concern for implementation and co-ordination of national policies. However, the financial arrangements outlined above do compromise very severely local authorities' autonomy.

4.5.1 Statutory control

Some of the more important statutory financial controls affecting local authorities have already been outlined. In the case of the many functions performed by local authorities there is always a need for a statutory framework, effectively defining the terms on which central government will allocate a function. This legislative task will often take place against a background of consultation with, among other organisations, the local authority associations. The statutory framework legislated by Parliament will indicate the nature and scope of any powers given to the local authorities, an issue which will be taken up in Chapter 7, and will indicate the scope of any central government control in the exercise of the function concerned. Section 1 of the Education Act 1993, for example, states that 'The Secretary of State shall promote the education of the people of England and Wales'.

In the area of town and country planning, the Minister of Town and Country Planning Act 1943 (now repealed) states that the minister now responsible for planning, the Secretary of State the Environment, had a duty to secure 'consistency and continuity in the framing and execution of a national policy with respect to the use and development of land throughout England and Wales'. The detailed statutory framework is, of course, to be found in the principal Acts of Parliament. These Acts often contain further powers permitting the Secretary of State or other minister responsible for a function to make rules and regulations and other items of delegated legislation governing the detailed conduct of the local authorities. It has been seen in Chapter 3 that procedural rules have been made for the conduct of public local inquiries into planning appeals, prescribing the steps to be taken by local authorities and others involved in the inquiry process. Another example occurs in the Town and Country Planning (General Development) Order 1995, another item of delegated legislation made by the Secretary of State under the powers conferred on him for this purpose by the Town and Country Planning Act 1990. This order contains a vast amount of detail about the operation of the planning system. Among other things it sets out the procedures to be followed by local planning authorities in dealing with applications for planning permission and those categories of 'development' which are defined as 'permitted development', that is, for which planning permission is deemed to have been granted, eg the extension of a dwelling house by up to 15% of its cubic capacity.

4.5.2   The administrative appeal process

Where a function is conferred on a local authority there may be various reasons why it is deemed appropriate that there should be an appeal against the authority's decision and that the appeal should go to the Secretary of State as opposed to an inferior court or an administrative tribunal. In one of the most frequently used appeal processes, where a local planning authority refuses or grants a conditional planning permission, it is the Secretary of State for the Environment's concern for national planning policy which indicates the need for him to be centrally involved in the planning appeal process. Indeed, he is involved in other planning appeal processes, the two most important of which are appeals against a local planning authority's decision on the question of whether a proposal involves 'development' and requires planning permission, and appeals against enforcement notices served by a local planning authority alleging unlawful development, eg without planning permission. Where such an appeal is undertaken the statutory powers of the Secretary of State are widely defined. In the case of the appeal, eg against a refusal or conditional grant of planning permission, the Secretary of State is able to look afresh at the applicant's proposal and is required to decide at the outset whether a planning permission should be granted or whether any condition or conditions should be deleted from a planning permission. Although many applications for planning permission involving proposals to build single houses, for example, do not involve any policy, it has been seen that in other cases where policy is in issue the appeal decision may permit the Secretary of State's policy preference to be applied.

4.5.3 The approval process

Where a local authority initiates various proposals, which may be administrative or legislative, there is usually a statutory requirement that the Secretary of State approves or confirms them before they become effective or have the force of law. Apart from particular schemes requiring financial sanction, the approval process applies to three very important areas of local authority activity: bylaws, compulsory purchase orders, and (in the area of town and country planning again) development plans. Compulsory purchase orders and bylaws are dealt with in Chapter 8. Suffice it to say in this context that the confirming authority in the appropriate central government department is unlikely to give confirmation where the order or bylaw is considered to be beyond the statutory powers of the local authority. Development plans are the vehicles for local authorities' planning policies under the Town and Country Planning Act. There are two principal varieties of development plan: the structure plan (referred to in Chapter 3) and the local or district plan. It has been seen that the structure plan is prepared by the county planning authority and is essentially a written policy strategy for the county area indicating, eg the likely demand for housing in the next 10 years and the broad areas where that demand may be satisfied. The completed structure plan is submitted to the Secretary of State for the Environment of approval but before arriving at a decision whether to approve the plan, he will convene and eventually consider the report of an Examination in Public. By contrast, the local or district plan is usually made by the constituent district councils within the county and fills out in detail (some of it map-based) the broad policies of the structure plan. This type of development plan can be approved and adopted by the local authority which made it, but the Secretary of State does have a reserve power to call in such a plan for his own and not the local authority's approval. It could be the case that a local or district plan would be 'called in' if it made no attempt to identify any land in its areas for future housing provision where the structure plan has already insisted that the district has the most suitable potential in broad, strategic terms. Once approved, a local planning authority is required to have regard to a development plan in deciding whether to grant planning permission.

4.5.4 Default powers

Reference was made in Chapter 1 to the default powers of the Secretary of State for the Environment in s 164 of the Housing Act 1985 and the Secretary of State for Education in s 68 of the Education Act 1944. It is difficult to generalise about default powers except to say that they facilitate central government intervention on those occasions, eg after a central government inspection, when it is considered that a local authority is not undertaking a proper discharge of its statutory functions. While some default powers require some prerequisite such as an unreasonable act before the Secretary of State can intervene, other default powers operate simply on the basis that the Secretary of State is of the belief that a function will not be performed properly. The default power in s 100 of the Town and Country Planning Act is somewhat different. It states that if it appears to the Secretary of State, after consultation with a local planning authority, that certain action should be taken, he may require that that action be taken, eg that an enforcement notice should be served or that an order revoking planning permission should be submitted to him for confirmation. Default powers in other areas of local authority activity may lead, as in the case of s 164 of the Housing Act 1985, to the Secretary of State taking over the function himself. On the other hand and perhaps more frequently, an exercise of default powers in a statute like the Education Act 1944 requires the Secretary of State to serve a direction. Such a direction might require a local education authority to provide a certain type of educational facility which, hitherto, it had unreasonably failed to provide. Non-compliance with the direction would permit the Secretary of State to apply to the High Court for an order of *mandamus* against the education authority. This remedy, which is dealt with more generally in Chapter 13, comprises an order of the court requiring the authority to comply with any lawful direction. Under the Town and Country Planning Act directions are relatively common and, as such, are not seen as default powers in quite the same way. Some of the more common purposes for which directions are used include the Secretary of State's power to 'call in' an application for planning permission for his own decision and a 'standing' requirement that any proposal to grant planning permission which would be a 'substantial departure' from development plan policies should be advertised and (in some limited cases) referred to the Secretary of State for decision.

4.6 The Council Member

Very little has been said about the membership of the council of a local authority primarily because the law focuses its attention on the legal status of the council as the instrument of administrative action. Consequently, any contract is made by 'the council' and one central question for the law is whether it is within the council's statutory powers. Nevertheless, it has been seen that the individual member is potentially responsible in his own right for any item of account which is found to be contrary to law through the audit process. Other areas of legal significance in relation to the individual member include his right of access to and inspection of documents, the duty to disclose pecuniary interests and the regulation of bribery and corruption.

4.6.1   Right of access to meetings and inspection of documents

Section 228 of the Local Government Act authorises a member's inspection of the local authority's full accounts. As far as other documents are concerned, a member's rights are recognised by the common law which stipulates that he may have access to those documents deemed reasonably necessary for the discharge of his responsibilities as a councillor. This legal right was in issue before the House of Lords in *R v Birmingham City Council, ex p 0* (1983). A council member who was not a member of the social services committee which was dealing with a proposed adoption was entitled to access to documents prepared by the social services department for the committee. The documents covered the proposed adoption and the member was anxious to see them when, as a member of another committee, she had indirect contact with the case which gave rise to some genuine concern. The House of Lords had no hesitation in saying that there is free access to documents for members of the appropriate committee actually dealing with the matter in issue. However, where a member who is not a member of that committee requires access, this is a matter for the council or any person or group exercising powers in this respect delegated by the council. In this particular case access was permitted by the deputy director of social services and not the council and it was the House of Lords' view that he was impliedly authorised to allow access. The conclusion in this important case has been applied in a number of subsequent cases. One of the most significant cases is *R.v Hackney London Borough Council, ex p Gamper* (1985). The High Court concluded that the councillor's right of access to documents and his right of access to meetings (referred to below) depend on whether there is a 'need to know' for the proper discharge of duties as a councillor. The court also raised the question whether the councillor must show a more urgent need to know in the case of attendance at meetings than in the case of access to documents. If the council sets up a working party which is not a committee of that council a councillor who is not a working party member may find that his 'right to know' is outweighed by other considerations such as the need for candid debate: *R v Eden District Council, ex p Moffat* (1988). However, a councillor's exclusion from a committee for party political purposes can never be legitimate: *R v Sheffield City Council, ex p Chadwick* (1985).

4.6.2   Disclosure of pecuniary interests

Sections 94–97 of the Local Government Act state that where a member of a local authority has any pecuniary interest, direct or indirect, in any contract, proposed contract or other matter, and is present at a meeting of the authority at which the contract or other matter is the subject of consideration, he is required to disclose the fact at the meeting and so desist from discussion and voting on that contract, proposed contract or other matter. Non-compliance with this requirement is a criminal offence which can be prosecuted only by the Director of Public Prosecutions or on his behalf. Some interests, such as allowances paid to council chairmen as expenses, are not regarded as 'pecuniary' interests for present purposes. On the other hand, some interests are classified as 'indirect' pecuniary interests as where a member of a local authority is also a member of a company about to make a contract with that authority. An alternative to the method of disclosure mentioned at the beginning of this section allows a member to register a general notice in writing with the proper officer of the authority. A register of such disclosures is maintained for inspection by members. Members' disability in this context can be removed by a district council, in the case of the membership of a parish or (in Wales) a community council, or by the Secretary of State for the Environment, in the case of any other local authority, where it is considered that the number of members disabled by the law is such that council business would be adversely affected or that it is in the inhabitants' interests that disability should be lifted. The member is not affected by a legal disability where an interest in a contract or similar transaction arises by virtue of his status as a Council Tax payer or as a member of the community taking advantage of services normally available. A member's interest will not give rise to a legal disability where that interest is too remote and as such is unlikely to influence his conduct in relation to council business. Nevertheless, the member is regarded as having an indirect pecuniary interest where his beneficial interest in a company or similar organisation does not exceed £1,000 or one-thousandth of the total nominal value of the issued share capital. However, in this situation the member is not disabled from participating in the transaction of relevant council business, but he is obliged to make a disclosure of his interest. More recently, s 19 of the Local Government and Housing Act 1989 has provided for the making of regulations to require a member to give notice to a 'proper officer' of any direct or indirect pecuniary interest, and to keep that information up to date. Failure to comply without reasonable excuse is an offence. More generally, whether a member has a pecuniary advantage or disadvantage, he is subject to the legal disability (*Brown v Director of Public Prosecutions* (1956) and *Rands v Oldroyd* (1959)). The law's coverage has been criticised on occasions, particularly because it does not extend beyond pecuniary and similar interests to other interests which may be equally persuasive, and because a member's legal disability applies only to meetings of a local authority and not private 'party' meetings, for example. Where a member participates in the transaction of council business while subject to the legal disability, any vote of his will be discounted (*Nell v Longbottom* (1894)). Where this is the case the decision of the council may be set aside by the court for the breach of the rule against bias in natural justice, which is dealt with in Chapter 10 (*R v Hendon Rural District Council, ex p Chorley* (1933)). Various recommendations have been made for changes in the law through reports such as the report of the Prime Minister's Committee on Local Government Rules of Conduct published in 1974. These changes have not so far taken place although the Department of the Environment has published recommended standards of conduct for councillors in this context.

4.7 The Council Officer

The officer is a professional employee of the council with day-to-day responsibility for the conduct of council functions. Although there are specific statutory provisions requiring the appointment of certain officers such as senior police officers (eg the chief constable), most appointments are made under s 112 of the Local Government Act. This empowers a local authority to appoint such officers as it thinks necessary for the proper discharge of its functions. Such officers then hold office on such reasonable terms and conditions, including conditions relating to remuneration, as the authority thinks fit. Clearly, any attempt to appoint an officer outside the terms of s 112 would be *ultra vires* and any resulting expenditure on salaries and other related items would be contrary to law and subject to audit sanctions. Officers, like members, are required to disclose certain pecuniary interests, although the relevant provisions in s 117 of the Local Government Act are somewhat different to those relating to members. An officer employed under the Local Government Act or any other Act is obliged to give written notification of a direct or indirect pecuniary interest in a contract or proposed contract with the authority. Unlike the law relating to members' interests, s 117 refers only to contracts and, in addition, there is no requirement of disclosure at a meeting. It was recommended by the Prime Minister's Committee on Local Government Rules of Conduct, referred to in the previous section, that these inconsistencies should be reconciled with the law on members' interests and a register kept in each local authority of interests of chief and deputy officers and such other officers as the authority may require.

The Local Government and Housing Act 1989 in ss 1 and 2, deals with the prevention of those holding a politically restricted post – eg certain chief officers – from standing for election as a local authority member. Furthermore, persons holding a politically restricted post are disqualified from standing for Parliament.

4.8 Bribery and Corruption

Bribery and corruption are criminal offences defined in the Public Bodies Corrupt Practices Act 1889 and the Prevention of Corruption Acts 1906–1916. The Act of 1889 makes it an offence for any person corruptly to give or receive any gift or other advantage as an inducement to influence the conduct of any member, officer or servant of any public body, that is, 'local and public authorities of all descriptions'. The Acts of 1906 and 1916 make it an offence corruptly to provide an agent with or for that agent to receive any gift or consideration as an inducement or reward for influencing the principal's affairs or business.

4.8.1 Coverage of the Acts

The law covers most of the so-called public sector: in general terms, local authorities, public corporations (dealt with in Chapter 6) and Crown servants and agents. However, it is likely that a Crown servant or agent or any other person deemed not to be an employee of a 'local or public authority' would be prosecuted under the Act of 1906. The term 'local authorities' appears to be self-explanatory although s 4 of the Act of 1916 now extends to companies under the control of a local authority. The term 'public authorities' is not defined in the Acts and, unfortunately, very little help is forthcoming from two of the leading cases. In the first, *R v Newbould* (1962), it was decided that the National Coal Board was not a public authority for the purposes of the Act of 1889, whereas in *R v Manners* (1976) it was decided that the North Thames Gas Board was a 'public body'. Despite some uncertainty in this context it is possible that a conviction could be obtained through a prosecution under the Act of 1906, at least on the assumption that the defendant had been acting as an 'agent' on behalf of his principal. All of the offences are punishable with imprisonment and/or a fine while the Act of 1889 provides for subsidiary penalties:

(a) surrender of a corrupt gift to the employer of the recipient;

(b) forfeiture of entitlement to a pension;

(c) disqualification from voting; and

(d) disqualification from holding office as a member or employee of a public body.

The penalties attaching to offences under the Acts of 1889 and 1906 in the case of contracts with public bodies and government departments are more severe than in other cases. Prosecution of offences requires the consent of the Attorney General or Solicitor General.

The ancient common law offence of misconduct in a public office applies to local government. In *R v Bowden* (1995) the Court of Appeal upheld a conviction against an employee of a local authority who had dishonestly caused council employees to carry out works which were not required under the authority's repairing policy. The works in question were executed on the house of the defendant's girlfriend.

4.9 Council Meetings

Meetings are governed by statute and the council's own standing orders. The Local Government Act obliges the principal councils, that is, all those local authorities except parish and community councils, to hold annual meetings and any other meetings as deemed to be necessary for the transaction of business and the performance of functions. While the Act details the various formalities relating to the calling and conduct of meetings, standing orders for each council will detail matters of procedure at meetings where there is no other statutory provision. Similar standing orders can be made by local authorities for the transaction of business by their various committees. Decisions are by a majority of the votes of the members present and in the event of no majority the chairman has a second or casting vote. A minute book must be maintained, copies of which are generally available for public inspection. It is also provided by statute that, as a general rule, meetings are open to the public. Private meetings may be held in special circumstances, usually where it would be contrary to the public interest to disclose the nature of certain confidential business. These rules relating to access to meetings are found in the Public Bodies (Admission to Meetings) Act 1960, an Act which applies to various public bodies including local authorities and which is extended to cover local authority committees. The Local Government (Access to Information) Act 1985, amending the Local Government Act 1972, now provides better legal rights of access to council meetings, agendas, reports and background material but subject to certain restrictions based on confidentiality. Although an individual has free access to council meetings in general, he can be excluded if it is likely that 'exempt' information will be uttered. Such information covers (for example) matters affecting a particular employee of the council or the recipient of financial assistance from the council, together with information about action taken or to be taken in connection with the prevention, investigation or prosecution of crime. The Act also gives additional rights of access to documents to council members. These rights may go some way to meet the law's requirements in *R v Birmingham City Council, ex p 0* (above). It should be noted that a council member may be liable for defamation in respect of what is said, or even written, in the course of council meetings. Defamation covers an oral statement (slander) and a written statement (libel) and any such statement is defamatory where its publication is calculated to injure the reputation of another through exposure to hatred, contempt or ridicule. However, the member may be able to avoid liability if he can establish that his statement was made without any malice. In the leading case of *Horrocks v Lowe* (1974) it was emphasised that a statement is made without malice where it is made with a positive belief as to its truth, ie an honest belief. On this basis, it was stated in *Horrocks* that where the dominant motive for a statement is not a desire to perform the relevant duty or to protect the relevant interest but to give vent to a member's personal spite or ill-will towards the person he defames, the member cannot rely on the defence of an absence of malice. However, depending on the facts of the individual case, the member may be able to rely on two other significant defences: justification and fair comment. As far as the council itself is concerned, the law gives no right to maintain an action for damages for defamation. The House of Lords in *Derbyshire County Council v Times Newspapers* (1993) held that such a right would be contrary to the public interest. It was considered to be a matter of the highest public importance that a governmental body should be open to uninhibited criticism: a right to sue for defamation would place an undesirable fetter on freedom of speech.

4.10 Council Decisions

It is the council of a local authority which is empowered to take decisions for the discharge of functions as prescribed by statute. However, the Local Government Act does empower a local authority to delegate some of its functions. Section 101 in particular states that a local authority may 'arrange for the discharge of any of their functions (a) by a committee, a sub-committee or an officer of the authority or (b) by any other local authority'. It should be noted that there is no reference to the council member. Consequently any attempted delegation to a committee chairman, eg for 'chairman's action' will be unlawful: *R v Secretary of State for the Environment, ex p Hillingdon London Borough Council* (1986). The legal implications of delegation are taken up in Chapter 9. The Deregulation and Contracting Out Act 1994 empowers the minister to make a statutory order to provide for powers delegated to an officer under s 101, to be exercised by an employee or employees of any local authority. However, such a facility is restricted in certain instances, eg if the exercise of such a delegated function would usurp the judicial power of any tribunal or court. More generally, it should be noted that s 101 is an attempt to recognise the need for efficient local government so that every decision need not be taken by the full council itself. The extent of delegation is very much a matter for each council although a comprehensive committee structure is a feature of most local authorities. However, it is not every local authority which allows wide delegated powers to its officers. While the terms of s 101 are drawn quite widely to allow some flexibility to local authorities, there are some statutory provisions which require that particular committees are established, eg social services committees under the Local Authority Social Services Act 1970, and that certain decisions are taken only by the full council, eg s 101(6) of the Local Government Act, which states that a local authority's functions with respect to the levying of a 'rate' shall be discharged only by the full council.

4.11 Legal Liability of Local Authorities

Reference has been made earlier in this chapter to the powers of a local authority to enter a contract. Where the local authority acts in breach of a lawful contract it is generally liable for damages or any other appropriate remedy in the same way as any other individual. The same would be true of public corporations, the subject of Chapter 6. However, where the contract is entered into by or on behalf of the Crown, special rules of law apply and these are outlined in Chapter 14. Apart from contractual liability, it should be remembered that an individual or other corporate body may be liable in tort or criminally liable for its acts or omissions. Criminal liability is a well recognised part of the law. Tortious liability, on the other hand, deserves some explanation. In very general terms, a tort is a civil wrong. Consequently, where an individual or other corporate body can persuade a court that his rights guaranteed by the law of tort have been infringed, he should be able to claim the appropriate remedy which may be damages as compensation for any loss or injury, or (perhaps) an injunction to prevent any repetition of the unlawful conduct in question. Prominent examples of torts, as they are known, include negligence, nuisance, strict liability, trespass, defamation and breach of statutory duty. This final section of the chapter will concentrate on the tortious and criminal liability of local authorities and most of the law here is equally applicable to the public corporations which are dealt with in Chapter 6.

4.11.1   Tortious liability

Although the general rule is that a local authority is liable for its tortious acts or omissions, there are notable exceptions, particularly on those occasions when there is statutory authorisation. By way of an example, the Acquisition of Land Act 1981 empowers a local authority to effect entry to land which is being compulsorily purchased. Consequently, where the requirements of the Act are met the local authority in this case would have the best defence to a civil action for trespass by the landowner, that is, statutory authorisation. One crucial area of tortious liability is that relating to the vicarious liability of an employer for the acts or omissions of his employee. However, where the employee of a local authority also operates in another capacity unrelated to his status as a local authority employee, his employer may not be vicariously liable. This proposition can be illustrated by the case of *Stanbury v Exeter Corporation* (1905) where sheep, allegedly suffering from an infection, were seized negligently by an inspector who, although he was employed by the local authority, was operating as an inspector under the independent statutory authority of the Diseases of Animals Act. By way of contrast, in *Ministry of Housing and Local Government v Sharp* (1970) a local authority was found to be vicariously liable even though the negligent employee had the statutory status of local land charges registrar.

4.11.2   Statutory authority

There has been a reference to statutory authority in the previous section but the area where it has considerable significance is nuisance. A nuisance is some act which interferes with a person's use and enjoyment of his land although the law will not protect a person of peculiar sensitivity. Where Parliament legislates to authorise the construction of large and perhaps controversial undertakings like oil refineries, it will usually authorise all aspects of the construction and use. In so doing the statute takes away the possibility of establishing liability in nuisance against the agency responsible in respect of physical interference arising from construction and use of the undertaking. The courts reinforce this position by saying that the statutory agency in question has authority in respect of anything arising from construction and use which is the inevitable consequence of these activities. In *Allen v Gulf Oil Refining Ltd* (1981), for example, it was decided that noise, smell and vibration were the inevitable consequences of the establishment of an oil refinery. However, where the statutory agency has a discretion, that is, a choice, in deciding where to establish an undertaking, that discretion must be exercised so that a nuisance is avoided (*Metropolitan Asylum Board v Hill* (1881)). In other words, Parliament has not presumed that a particular site is the only one suitable for the purpose so that the statutory agency has to be as vigilant as anybody else in exercising its powers in order to avoid nuisances. In the same way, there is no defence available to the statutory agency that a function is being performed reasonably in the interests of the public (*Pride of Derby and Derbyshire Angling Association v British Celanese Ltd* (1953)). Where there is statutory authority for the establishment of some public or other undertaking such as an oil refinery, motorway or airport, the statutory provisions, having taken away the right to sue for nuisance, usually allow any individual whose land is affected to claim compensation according to criteria set down in those or other statutory provisions.

4.11.3 Negligence

In general terms, negligence indicates a failure to take reasonable care in undertaking some activity. In order to succeed in an action for damages for negligence it is necessary to establish:

(a) that there is a duty on the defendant to take reasonable care, usually because the defendant should have had his victim's interests and welfare in mind;

(b) that there is a breach of the duty; and

(c) as a result the victim has suffered some reasonably foreseeable injury, loss or other damage.

In the case of a local authority performing a statutory duty, the law imposes liability for any negligent exercise of that duty. Consequently, Parliament presumes that every statutory duty will not be performed negligently. Where the authority has a discretion as to the ways and means to be used for the performance of a statutory function there will be liability where the authority chooses to perform it and performs it negligently (*Dutton v Bognor Regis Urban District Council* (1972)). On the other hand, where it is decided not to perform the function or to perform it only partially, liability in negligence arises only where that (policy) decision is *ultra vires* and it is possible to establish the three requirements for negligence mentioned above (*Anns v Merton London Borough Council* (1977)). This approach, however, may now be severely limited by the decision of the House of Lords in *Murphy v Brentwood District Council* (1990). The critical issue in this case was whether the avoidance of economic loss – as opposed to physical damage or injury – fell within the scope of the duty of care owed to the plaintiff by the local authority in its enforcement of the building regulations relating to the health and safety of those using and occupying buildings. Recovery of economic loss must be by reference to remedies in the law of contract. However, if a person suffers physical injury as a result of a breach by the local authority of its duty of care, damages in negligence may well be available.

A local authority may also be liable in respect of a negligent misstatement, in which case a crucial requirement is that the individual concerned, eg an officer of a local authority, holds himself out as having the requisite expertise (*Hedley, Byrne & Co Ltd v Heller & Partners* (1963)). However, the House of Lords in *Murphy* added a further requirement: that there should be evidence of some reliance by the building owner on the local authority. Despite this view the House of Lords did not consider that the 'normal' relationship here would show evidence of any 'reliance', at least in the normal run of tasks involving the approval of plans and the inspection of buildings. Even where there is no negligence the law may impose so called 'strict' liability where a person, for his own purposes, brings onto his land and collects and keeps there anything likely to do mischief if its escapes (*Rylands v Fletcher* (1868)). Where the defendant local authority has brought onto its land some dangerous substance, any damage, loss or injury caused by its escape will bring liability, even though the authority took reasonable care. Nevertheless, there must be reasonable foreseeability of the loss or harm occurring; even in these circumstances there must be control over the offending 'substance' as a pre-requisite for liability *Cambridge Water Co v Eastern Counties Leather plc* (1993). The decision in the *Cambridge Water* case also suggests, *obiter*, that the other pre-requisite for strict liability – a non-natural user of land – may occur in respect of a great many industrial land uses. However, any public authority which functions for the 'public benefit' is not taken to be acting 'for its own purposes' in this context (*Dunne v North Western Gas Board* (1963)). In *Dunne* gas escaped from a main and injured persons and property as a result of a leak from a water main which had removed soil supporting the gas main.

4.11.4   Breach of statutory duty

The House of Lords in a group of cases (*X (Minors) v Bedfordshire County Council*; *M (a Minor) and Another v Newham London Borough Council and Others*; *E (a Minor) v Dorset County Council*; and *Keating v Bromley London Borough Council* (1995)) has held that, normally, a breach of statutory duty does not give rise to a private law cause of action in tort. However, such an action might arise if it could be shown that the statutory duty was imposed for the protection of a limited class of the public and that Parliament intended to confer on members of that class a private right of action for breach of duty. It was suggested that there are various indicators to show the possible existence of such a right of action: in particular the absence of any other statutory remedy in the absence also of any other protection for the limited class in question.

The House of Lords showed great reluctance to allow statutory duties to be subject to a duty of care. In the case of local authority responsibility for the welfare of children in particular it was seen as cutting across an inter-disciplinary system established by statute for the protection of children. If a negligent exercise of a statutory duty is alleged, the plaintiff must be able to show a duty of care as opposed to a mere assertion of carelessness. In drawing a distinction between a duty of care in the exercise of a statutory discretion and a duty of care affecting the manner in which a statutory duty is implemented, the House of Lords stressed that the law cannot interfere with a discretion properly given to the administrative agency. Similarly, there could be no interference where implementation of decisions involves matters of policy. Overall, any common law duty of care that is consistent with or has a tendency to discourage the due performance of statutory duty will not be imposed by the court.

4.11.5   Criminal liability

It is possible for a local authority to be convicted of a criminal offence although there are clear limitations in that an authority cannot be convicted of an offence punishable with imprisonment. Similarly a local authority is subject only to those offences which can be committed vicariously. In *York District Council v Poller* (1975) a builder's skip was hired by the council's housing department. An official intimated to the owner of the skip that there was a 'blanket permission' to leave skips on the highway. The local authority was later (and correctly)convicted of an offence under the Highways Act 1971 since the offence had been committed 'owing to the act or default of some other person', in this case the local authority. In practice, whether the local authority is criminally liable often depends on the extent to which the officer or employee is seen as acting for the authority in the performance of its functions. The legal principle is found in a case involving a company which was acquitted of an offence against the Trade Descriptions Act, *Tesco Supermarkets Ltd v Nattrass* (1971) where Lord Reid in the House of Lords said that:

> [T]he board of directors may delegate some part of their functions of management giving to their delegate full discretion to act independently of instructions from them. I see no difficulty in holding that they have thereby put such a delegate in their place so that within the scope of the delegation he can act as the Company.

As far as local government is concerned, it is clear from this relevant statement of principle that wherever there is in issue a criminal offence which a local authority is capable of committing, the local authority will avoid conviction only where any delegate of that body is clearly acting beyond any express or implied limits of delegated powers, eg as a committee or officer.

5 Administrative Tribunals

5.1 Status

Administrative tribunals might well be referred to as 'administrative courts' since usually their task is to adjudicate disputes which arise from the statutory regulation of a wide variety of situations, some of which will involve decisions or other action by administrative agencies, or the relationship between private individuals. It will be seen later in this chapter that tribunals have been established for many purposes, including the adjudication of disputes between landlord and tenant about the payment of rent and between an individual and a local authority about the payment of compensation for the compulsory acquisition of land. They have been established also in order to decide appeals from decisions of other tribunals and administrative agencies on issues such as statutory entitlement to certain welfare benefits. The Council on Tribunals, described below, has defined a tribunal (in the absence of any statutory definition) as 'any person or body (other than a court of law) exercising judicial or quasi-judicial functions which are provided by or under statute' (Annual Report, 1993–94). Annually tribunals deal with more than a quarter of a million cases.

5.1.1 Tribunals and inquiries distinguished

The tribunals differ from the statutory inquiries which operate in the context of ministers' decision-making responsibilities in central government. This difference was described by the Council on Tribunals in its Annual Report for 1960 where it was observed that:

.   Tribunals, generally speaking, exercise an independent jurisdiction: they decide particular cases by applying rules and regulations and sometimes by using their own discretion. Inquiries, on the other hand, form part of the process by which a minister exercises his discretion – discretion for which he is answerable to Parliament.

Because tribunals are not generally concerned with policy-oriented decisions, normally associated with ministers in central government departments, it is of greater relevance to compare tribunals with courts of law. In simple terms, tribunals and courts of law are concerned with the application of the relevant law to the facts of a particular case in a judicial spirit. However, the court is a truly independent entity whereas the tribunal is created by the relevant government department to adjudicate disputes arising under a statutory provision. Although it is the objective of the law to see that the independence of the tribunals is effectively safeguarded, there is responsibility in many cases for expert adjudications arising from disputes relating to the department's legislation. Indeed, the Franks Report considered it a matter of principle 'that a decision should be entrusted to a court rather than to a tribunal in the absence of special considerations which make a tribunal more suitable'. Apart from the fact that judges in courts of law are generalists whereas tribunal members are specialists in the relevant field of activity, there are various other reasons why the administrative tribunal has advantages over the court of law, and these are examined below.

5.1.2 Tribunals as 'court substitutes'

The Franks Report emphasised that tribunals:

> ... are not ordinary courts, but neither are they appendages of Government Departments ... tribunals should properly be regarded as machinery provided by Parliament for adjudication rather than as part of the machinery of administration. The essential point is that in all these cases Parliament has deliberately provided for a decision outside and independent of the Department concerned ... and the intention of Parliament to provide for the independence of tribunals is clear and unmistakable.

In most cases, this accurately reflects the status of the tribunal and it is now referred to frequently as the 'court substitute' tribunal. However, there are a few odd exceptions where the tribunal is more closely associated with the relevant government department. Because these few tribunals are more closely associated with particular government departments and their policies, they are referred to frequently as 'policy-oriented' tribunals. The latter category of tribunal will be dealt with in the following section.

5.1.3 Policy-oriented tribunals

The policy-oriented tribunal cuts across the sentiments about the independence of tribunals expressed in the Franks Report because, in one way or another, it is obliged to take notice of and perhaps implement the policy pronouncements of the relevant government department. One prominent example concerns the Civil Aviation Authority which, as a tribunal, is responsible for the licensing of civil air transport. By virtue of the Civil Aviation Act 1971, the Secretary of State for Trade was empowered to give policy guidance to the Authority whose responsibility was then to perform its licensing functions in such manner as it considered to be in accordance with that guidance. In this way, the Department of Trade is able to maintain an influence in policy terms over what is an area of importance for government. Rather more detailed directions are permitted under the later Civil Aviation Act 1982 in s 6. A similar example occurs in the Goods Vehicles (Licensing of Operators) Act 1995 where the minister is empowered to give policy directions to the traffic commissioners dealing with licence applications from goods vehicle operators. Such guidance is in turn carried forward to the Transport Tribunal which deals with appeals arising from the decisions of traffic commissioners.

5.2   Characteristics

The fact that most tribunals come within the category of 'court substitutes', provides one characteristic, but there are, of course, reasons why the comparison with ordinary courts of law cannot be carried too far. Such reasons emerge from an examination of the advantages of tribunals compared with courts of law. The Franks Report concluded that:

> [T]ribunals have certain characteristics which often give them advantages over the courts. These are cheapness, accessibility, freedom from technicality, and expedition and expert knowledge of their particular subject. It is no doubt because of these advantages that Parliament, once it has decided that certain decisions ought not to be made by normal executive or departmental processes, often entrusts them to tribunals rather than to the ordinary courts.

The advantages of tribunals will be seen in more detail later in this chapter. In more general terms, however, one of the outstanding advantages must be the first one, cheapness. The main emphasis of this advantage depends chiefly on the comparison of costs for the litigant who has to use the ordinary courts of law. For him there is the greater likelihood of considerable costs incurred through the need to engage a solicitor and possibly a barrister as well. The second characteristic mentioned above, accessibility, refers to the fact that in the case of the more popular tribunals there is a greater likelihood that they are organised with relative informality on a regional or local basis so that it can be said that the particular tribunal, such as an Industrial or a Social Security Appeal Tribunal, does operate within easy reach of most people. This, however, is not always the case. The Council on Tribunals, in a discussion about the proper forum for the resolution of disputes about rights of access to neighbouring land, pointed to the importance of local fora for the handling of such disputes. Its preference here was for the county court, rather than the Lands Tribunal, which has no formal, local organisation. Freedom from technicality means that in the case of most tribunals there are no technical rules of procedure or evidence to be observed as in an ordinary court of law. Such freedom from technicality means that hearings are shorter than in the case of a full trial before a court of law with a resultant saving of time and money. This characteristic shades in to the next advantage relating to expedition and expert knowledge. The tribunal system permits an efficient disposal of many cases by a body which has the relevant expertise in the area of the dispute or matter being dealt with. Accordingly, one of the most convincing arguments in favour of the system of tribunals is that it enables a large body of cases to be disposed of efficiently in a way which, given the present judicial system, is not possible as far as the ordinary courts of law are concerned. A graphic example occurs in the

case of the Industrial Tribunals which deal with a large number of matters, the most frequent cases relating to unfair dismissal and redundancy payments. The dramatic increase in industrial tribunal activity is seen in the number of applications received. The figure stood at 39,000 in 1990–91. Thereafter applications have risen to 62,000 in 1991–92, 67,000 in 1992–93, reaching 72,000 in 1993–94. Nevertheless, an expanding jurisdiction continues to add to the workload. Recent additions to jurisdiction include employment agencies, employee rights under the Sunday Trading Act 1994 and disputes about refusal of employment on grounds of union membership, a recent addition to the Employment Act 1980. In one annual report, the Council on Tribunals comments that:

> The organisation of the Industrial Tribunals could be described as one classic pattern for tribunals: a strong presidential and regional organisation, a tribunal composed of a legally qualified chairman with two lay members expert in industrial practice and representative of (but not representing) employers and employees respectively, and comprehensive modern rules of procedure designed to provide a firm structure but encouraging informality and expedition in the proceedings.

The further development of this profile is to be seen in revisions to and consolidation of rules of procedure. In its Annual Report for 1993–94, the Council on Tribunals points to the prospect for a more inquisitorial approach in Industrial Tribunal procedure. One example of such a trend is seen in the ability of the tribunal to summon witnesses at its own initiative. Furthermore, a recent addition to the Employment Protection (Consolidation) Act 1978 permits the chairman of an Industrial Tribunal to sit alone (without two additional members representative of both sides of industry) in certain circumstances, for example where the parties consent. Another addition to the same Act provides for pre-hearing reviews as a means of settling cases without those cases necessarily reaching the tribunal.

5.3   Varieties of Tribunal and their Functions

Tribunals fall into four categories according to their various functions, which are:

(1) to decide appeals from decisions taken by government departments;

(2) to determine various claims at first instance;

(3) to decide disputes arising as between individuals; and

(4) to undertake various other functions.

Each of these categories will be examined in turn.

5.3.1   Tribunals and appeals from departmental decisions

Some of the best-known tribunals dealing with appeals from decisions of government departments are the so-called Social Security Appeal Tribunals. These tribunals (which are described in more detail later) deal with a wide variety of social security disputes, eg about benefit. Another area where appeals go to a tribunal from a governmental decision is income tax. Decisions on liability to tax go to either the General Commissioners of Income Tax or the Special Commissioners of Income Tax, according to the technical nature of the dispute. General Commissioners are required to have some knowledge of income tax legislation and are usually appointed from the ranks of magistrates, solicitors and accountants. The Special Commissioners constitute a tribunal of two or three members. They are appointed by the Treasury from among barristers and solicitors in the Inland Revenue and once appointed, sever any links with that department. Nevertheless, these adjudicators have attracted considerable criticism, eg by reference to their close links with the Inland Revenue, which undertakes organisation of appeals. A similar criticism was voiced by the Council on Tribunals in its Annual Report for 1993–94, in relation to Valuation Tribunals which deal with appeals about liability and valuation in relation to the Council Tax and non-domestic rating. In this case the criticism is aimed at the preponderance of representatives of county councils (as the 'billing' authorities) on the tribunals. A third example in this first category are the six Vaccine Damage Tribunals which deal with disputes arising from claims to the Secretary of State for Health for compensation arising from severe disablement caused by vaccination. These tribunals are covered in more detail later in this chapter. Another tribunal which is covered in detail is the Transport Tribunal. Although it does not deal with decisions of a central government department, it has been seen that the local licensing body is susceptible to policy guidance from the Secretary of State for Transport.

5.3.2   Tribunals and 'first instance' claims

Some tribunals deal with claims at first instance. Reference has been made already to the Civil Aviation Authority and its responsibility for the licensing of civil air transport. The Authority deals with the licence applications initially and its decision may be appealed to the Secretary of State for Trade. Consequently, this opportunity and any earlier opportunities which may have been taken through policy guidance enable the Secretary of State to influence the direction of decisions. Another tribunal in this limited category is the Foreign Compensation Commission which adjudicates claims for compensation from British subjects, usually where their property has been requisitioned or damaged in another country. Where the government of that country agrees with the British government that compensation is payable, the sum agreed will be distributed to claimants according to the decisions of the Commission.

5.3.3 Tribunals and disputes between individuals

The main feature of the tribunals whose task is to decide disputes between individuals is that their decision relates to some statutory right or entitlement. Perhaps the best-known tribunals in this context are the Industrial Tribunals, referred to previously in this chapter. Most of their work arises from disputes about unfair dismissal and redundancy payments as between employer and employee. Such disputes arise primarily by reference to the relevant employment legislation which prescribes a general right not to be dismissed unfairly and a general right to compensation where an employee is dismissed by reason of redundancy. It is the tribunal's task to decide whether or not a claimant comes within the terms of the statutory scheme or is excluded from protection and entitlement. Where the claimant is found to be within the terms of the statutory scheme it is the tribunal's task to decide on the amount of redundancy payment or compensation for unfair dismissal or, exceptionally, whether an unfairly dismissed employee should be reinstated. Other important tribunals in this category are the Rent Assessment Committees and Rent Tribunals whose tasks include the resolution of rent disputes between landlord and tenant or the parties to a restricted tenancy contract.

5.3.4 Additional functions of tribunals

The final category of tribunals includes those which have various other functions over and above their other, normal functions. This does raise the question: what are those 'normal' functions? Is it possible to characterise tribunals as undertaking judicial functions similar to those of an ordinary court of law, or are they essentially investigatory bodies? Reference back to the definition at the opening of this chapter may be useful. Some tribunals, notably the Lands Tribunal and the Transport Tribunal, function like ordinary courts of law. Even where the formality of tribunal procedures does not permit this comparison, it is possible to conclude that most of such bodies are judicial and not investigatory so that they act as impartial adjudicators of evidence presented to them by the respective parties. Beyond such a normal judicial function, some tribunals do undertake additional functions. The Mental Health Review Tribunal, comprising a number of separate tribunals throughout England and Wales, has operated as part of the scheme of the Mental Health Acts in order to review decisions whereby compulsory powers have been used to detain people for the treatment of mental disorder. Another facet of this tribunal has been its function in giving the Home Secretary advice on the recall to hospital of restricted patients who have been conditionally discharged or given leave of absence. A second example here is the Civil Aviation Authority, a regulatory authority which is responsible for air transport licensing, together with the maintenance and enforcement of safety standards. Beyond its judicial, tribunal function, the

Authority also exercises important rule-making functions and this legislative function in the interest of air safety involves enforcement functions as well.

5.4 Allocation of Functions to Tribunals

Reference has been made earlier in this chapter to the advantages of using a tribunal as opposed to an ordinary court of law for the adjudication of disputes and it has been said that most tribunals can be regarded as 'court substitutes'. However, it is still necessary to determine why the various adjudicatory functions have been given to tribunals in the first place. Apart from the supposed advantages of tribunals previously listed, what is it about the adjudicatory functions which make them appropriate subjects to be dealt with by tribunals?

5.4.1 The policy element in administrative decisions

As a general rule, it appears that any function involving an element of policy will not be conferred on a tribunal and is most likely to be conferred on a minister in central government who will be democratically accountable for any such policy to Parliament. This is well illustrated in the context of a licensing system which was aimed at encouraging industry to develop in the depressed areas of the UK. Although the system has now been suspended and is unlikely to be resurrected, the Town and Country Planning Act specifies that any application for planning permission for industrial development within certain categories and areas shall be of no effect without an industrial development certificate granted by the Secretary of State for Industry. In deciding whether to grant such a certificate, the Secretary of State is obliged to satisfy himself that the development can be carried out consistently with the proper distribution of industry. Such a decision is bound to involve the weighing of the applicant's case, not against some fixed or measurable criteria against the background of which tribunals normally operate, but against a judgment of the national distribution of industry and employment. Apart from the fact that such a matter is likely to be a sensitive issue of a government's economic policy, it is unlikely that any government would be willing to give away an important decision like this to a tribunal which is unlikely to be able to respond to shifts in economic conditions and economic policy. When the Hunt Committee investigated some of the issues in this area in 1969, it was suggested that there should be an appeal against the Secretary of State's refusal of an industrial development certificate. The committee's report observed that:

> [T]he flexibility and sensitivity with which the policy is operated ... means that there is a lack of permanent and readily applicable criteria which would guide an independent appeal tribunal.

Accordingly, the Secretary of State's decision remains final.

5.4.2   The Civil Aviation Authority and the Transport Tribunal

It has been seen that some significant policy-based decisions may occur away from central government in these tribunals. It must be remembered in these cases that the responsible minister is not without influence in view of the statutory powers conferred on him to give so-called policy 'guidance'. Furthermore, the licensing function of the Civil Aviation Authority was undertaken by a central government department until the early 1970s and with a transfer of the responsible staff to the Authority there was little adverse effect on the government's influence over policy. In addition, where there is an adverse decision of the Authority the appeal lies to the Secretary of State, so providing the best opportunity for emphasising any policy. In the case of the Transport Tribunal there was, before privatisation of road and passenger transport undertakings, a considerable reduction in the significance of goods vehicle licensing given the influence of the nationalised transport undertakings. Indeed, in 1981 the Transport Tribunal dealt with 29 cases only in this context. Subsequently legislation like the Transport Act 1982 has resulted in greater interest in licensing. For example statutory objectors (but not other objectors) have a right of appeal to the Transport Tribunal on environmental grounds, among others.

5.4.3   Objective decisions: tribunals or courts?

A further factor in favour of allocating a decision-making function to a tribunal is the likelihood that a person's rights, interests or even his very livelihood may be affected. Where this is the case and there is a need for objective decision-making with clear safeguards there is likely to be an option: either to allocate the function to an ordinary court or to a tribunal. If it is likely that many cases will be generated by the statutory scheme in question then it is unlikely that the ordinary courts could cope. However, where the issue or dispute to be adjudicated is, for example, a matter of some sensitivity or importance in a wide context, a court may be the more appropriate forum. Indeed, when the Race Relations Act 1968 was being legislated it was the county court system which was chosen to deal with race relations disputes where conciliation between the parties had failed. In one of the Parliamentary debates on the Race Relations Bill it was observed that tribunals might not be regarded as instruments of law in quite the same way as the courts and might come to be regarded as conferring special rights on minority groups.

5.4.4   Immigration appeals

The need for some clearly objective decision-making occurs in the field of immigration. This was an important theme of the Wilson Committee Report on Immigration Appeals in 1967 where it was said that:

> However well administered the present law may be, it is fundamentally wrong and inconsistent with the rule of law that power to take decisions

affecting a man's whole future should be vested in officers of the executive, from whose findings there is no appeal.

It was also emphasised that a system of appeals to tribunals from immigration decisions is necessary in order 'to check any possible abuse of executive power but also to give a private individual a sense of protection against oppression and injustice and of confidence in dealings with the administration'. In 1985 the Home Office undertook a review of immigration control procedures and confirmed its view that effective procedures here depended on the finality and expedition of appeals provisions. Since 1969 there has been a two-tier system of appeals involving in the first tier adjudicators appointed by the Home Secretary, and the Immigration Appeal Tribunal. Again to illustrate a recent baseline for an expanding jurisdiction a chief adjudicator, 15 adjudicators and 61 part-time adjudicators disposed of nearly 12,000 cases in 1981 while the Tribunal disposed of nearly 450 appeals from the adjudicators who themselves deal with appeals from the decisions of the immigration authorities, for example, refusing entry to the UK. In some instances there is no appeal from a decision of the immigration authorities, in particular where the Home Secretary has himself directed that a person should not be permitted to enter on the ground that his presence in the UK is not conducive to the public good. This is an important illustration of the fact that there are some decisions which are more sensitive than others from a political point of view and so are reserved for central government whose view it would be, no doubt, that tribunals should not be arbiters of matters such as national security and the public interest.

5.4.5 Tribunals and local authority decisions

While there are broad guidelines to indicate the likely circumstances in which an adjudicatory function will be conferred either on a tribunal or a central government department, can the same be said as between tribunals and local authorities? Local authorities, like central government, are democratically accountable bodies and it has been seen in Chapter 4 that they are also responsible for many policy-based decisions. Once again, the presumption is that any policy-based decision of a local authority will be subject to appeal to or be reappraised by the appropriate central government department. The exercise of powers of compulsory purchase is subject to confirmation of the necessary compulsory purchase order by the relevant government minister, usually the Secretary of State for the Environment. A similar situation exists in the case of local authority decisions on applications for planning permission, where any adverse decision affecting the applicant can be appealed by him to the Secretary of State for the Environment. There are, however, two notable areas of local authority action which involve recourse to tribunals. The first area of recourse arises from a dispute between a local authority and an individual on the amount of compensation payable for the compulsory acquisition of land. This is one of the more important matters dealt with by the Lands Tribunal. The second area relates to Council Tax valuations and assessments in respect of which there is an appeal to a local valuation tribunal.

5.4.6   Tribunals and inferior courts

Where there is no significant policy element in administrative action taken by local authorities there may be facilities for an appeal to a court rather than a tribunal. Where an appeal is permitted in these circumstances the choice of a court may be explained in historical terms by the fact that the statutory scheme in question was created some years ago before the advent of tribunals on a large scale. The choice might also be explained by the fact that, even if a tribunal was an option, a local court might still provide convenient, local expertise, so avoiding the need to create an entirely new system of tribunals.

The county courts and the magistrates' courts provide good examples in the present context of inferior courts, that is, courts below the Supreme Court of Judicature. Among the tasks of the magistrates' courts is that of deciding appeals against notices served under s 215 of the Town and Country Planning Act 1990 by local authorities where it is considered that the condition of open land is seriously injurious to the amenity of an area. One of the appeals dealt with by the county courts relates to repair notices served under the Housing Act 1985. One of the housing repairs notices which can be served by a local authority requires the person having control of the dwelling to undertake necessary repairs where the authority is satisfied that it is unfit for human habitation and that repair is the most satisfactory course of action. In the case of these and many similar appeals to such inferior courts the courts in question usually have wide powers to deal with the matters in issue and may be able to substitute their own conclusions, eg by confirming a notice and substituting certain terms of any notice or order served.

5.5   Tribunals and Inquiries Act 1992

It has been seen in Chapter 3 that the Tribunals and Inquiries Act is an important element in the control of many of the more important inquiry-based decisions taken under statutory powers by various ministers in central government. The Act is also of great significance in organising and controlling the many administrative tribunals which function as an important element in dispensing administrative justice. Most of the recommendations from the Franks Report were implemented and it will be seen that these recommendations have found their way into the Tribunals and Inquiries Act where they seek to uphold the important idea that procedures and processes in this context should once again manifest 'openness, fairness and impartiality'. Reference has been made to the Council on Tribunals in Chapter 3. Having been established by the Tribunals and Inquiries Act, its principal function in relation to tribunals is to:

... keep under review the construction and working of the tribunals specified in Schedule 1 to the Act and, from time to time, to report on their constitution and working; [and] to consider and report on such particular matters as may be referred to the Council under the Act with respect to tribunals other than the ordinary courts of law, whether or not specified in Schedule 1 to the Act ...

Most of the tribunals are listed in Schedule 1 to the Act and this, of course, means that they are under the scrutiny of the Council. According to the Annual Report of the Council on Tribunals for 1993–94, 70 tribunals were at that time subject to the Council's supervision. Their inclusion here also means that they are subject to the various safeguards built into the provisions of the Tribunals and Inquiries Act, which will be examined below. All of the tribunals so far mentioned are 'Schedule 1' tribunals. Bodies excluded from Schedule 1 include the Parole Board, the Gaming Board and local legal aid committees.

5.6 Tribunals and Inquiries Act Safeguards

Whether a tribunal falls within the Act and its provision of safeguards, including supervision by the Council on Tribunals, depends on whether a statutory order (an item of delegated legislation) has been made and approved. Consequently, when a new tribunal or system of tribunals is created there will be some interest in the question of whether they are to be 'Schedule 1' tribunals. However, a particular tribunal may not be subject to all the provisions and safeguards in the Act so that the relevant statutory order may specify which parts of the Tribunals and Inquiries Act apply. The safeguards in the Act are concerned primarily with tribunal membership and procedure, and they are now dealt with in turn.

5.6.1 Tribunal membership

On matters of membership in relation to tribunals, the Act in s 5 empowers the Council to make general recommendations to the appropriate minister on the subject of appointments to Schedule 1 tribunals and panels from which tribunal membership is drawn. However, the minister is obliged only 'to have regard to' any such recommendations. Where s 6 applies, the minister is required to select tribunal chairmen from a panel maintained for this purpose by the Lord Chancellor. Although this provision applies to Social Security Appeal Tribunals, chairmen are selected instead by the President of these tribunals. Where s 7 applies, a minister is unable to terminate a person's membership of a tribunal without the consent of the Lord Chancellor.

The power to make general recommendations about membership has been used on several occasions by the Council. In recent years the Council's concern about membership has focused on a number of issues including a policy of the Department of Social Security prior to the creation of the Social Security Appeal

Tribunals not to allow chairmen of National Insurance Local Tribunals and Supplementary Benefit Appeal Tribunals to serve on the panels of both tribunals at the same time. Other issues have included the need for more legally qualified chairmen of the former Supplementary Benefit Appeal Tribunals and (in Scotland) the need for more women to serve as members of these tribunals.

5.6.2 Rules of procedure for tribunals

In relation to procedure, the Council exercises a very important consultative function since under s 8, no power of a minister to make, approve, confirm or concur in procedural rules is exercisable without consultation with the Council in the case of Schedule 1 tribunals. Section 10 deals with the giving of reasons for tribunal decisions and stipulates that where any Schedule 1 tribunal gives a decision there is a duty to furnish a written or oral statement of reasons on request. The section goes on to say that a statement of reasons may be refused or restricted on grounds of national security and that a tribunal may refuse to furnish the statement to a person not primarily concerned with the decision if of the opinion that to furnish it would be contrary to the interests of any person primarily concerned. In practice rules of procedure for tribunals will normally stipulate an obligation to provide reasons for a decision.

Although not strictly a matter of procedure, it should be noted that in the case of some of the Schedule 1 tribunals there is an appeal on a point of law to the High Court from their decisions. This is provided for by s 11 which contains an alternative whereby the tribunal can be requested to state and sign a case for the opinion of the High Court. It is difficult to generalise about this facility in s 11. On some occasions, as with decisions of the Immigration Appeal Tribunal, s 11 did not formerly apply so that any challenge to the legality of a decision had to be by means of judicial review in the High Court as described in Chapter 13. The Asylum and Immigration Appeals Act 1993 now provides for an appeal directly to the Court of Appeal. On the other hand, s 11 does apply to decisions of Rent Tribunals and Rent Assessment Committees. Finally, in the case of a few tribunals, such as the Lands Tribunal, the Immigration Appeal Tribunal and the Transport Tribunal, any appeal on a point of law will go directly to the Court of Appeal, leap-frogging the High Court. This facility for an appeal directly to the Court of Appeal is undoubtedly a reflection of the tribunals' high legal reputation and specialist expertise. Where s 11 applies to a tribunal this will not exclude recourse to other remedies in the High Court where it is alleged that a decision is *ultra vires* and should be quashed. This matter is dealt with in Chapter 13.

5.7   Aspects of Tribunal Procedure and Organisation

Whether a tribunal operates effectively will necessarily depend on its membership and their ability to deal with the powers and procedures in question. The tribunal system permits the appointment of members by the relevant minister in the government department concerned. It has been seen previously that, with the exception of Social Security Appeal Tribunals, in some instances the relevant minister is required to appoint tribunal chairmen from a panel maintained by the Lord Chancellor, which is usually an indication that such chairmen are to be legally qualified. Legal qualifications are regarded as being particularly relevant for the chairmen of appellate tribunals. As far as general tribunal membership is concerned, the relevant statute constituting the tribunal will usually specify desirable qualifications. In practice, most tribunals comprise a chairman and two other lay members with assistance from a clerk.

5.7.1   The presidential system in tribunals

The position of the tribunal clerk is often a matter of concern. In its Annual Report for 1981–82, the Council on Tribunals reported on a complaint concerning the independence of the former National Insurance Local Tribunals. The complainant thought it wrong that anyone wishing to raise a matter with the tribunal by telephone had to speak to the department as the tribunal appeared to have no independent staff working in independent premises directly approachable by a claimant or representative. Although recognising the need for an employee of the department to act as tribunal clerk in some instances, eg where the volume of work did not justify the tribunal employing its own full-time staff, the Council 'entirely accepted that it would be desirable for tribunals to be administered completely independently from Government departments'. Although departmental administrative arrangements for tribunals are closely monitored by the Council to ensure that their independence is not compromised, there is one measure which is probably more effective than most: the 'presidential' system. This system exists in some areas, notably the Industrial, Social Security Appeal and Immigration Tribunals, and depends on a president who is responsible for the operation of the tribunals in question and stands between the tribunal and the responsible department. Because it is the president to whom reference is made for most purposes of tribunal operation, the system, according to the Council on Tribunals, 'fosters a desirable spirit of independence and properly emphasises a feeling of separation between the tribunals and the administration of the responsible Government department'.

5.7.2   Openness in tribunal procedure

The requirement of 'openness' emphasised by the Franks Report provides the basis for the general rule that tribunal proceedings are in public. There are notable exceptions, eg in the case of the Mental Health Review Tribunal, although it is general practice in most tribunals to read the evidence prior to the hearing so that there is not always the same public airing of evidence as in a court of law. Furthermore, it is generally the case that tribunals do not follow strict rules of evidence observed by the courts, eg so that 'hearsay' evidence may be admitted. Although there are differences in the rules of procedure for the various tribunals, one fairly typical example of procedural flexibility enjoyed by tribunals comes from the Industrial Tribunals: the tribunal conducts the hearing in such manner as it considers most suitable to the clarification of the issues before it and generally to the just handling of the proceedings. It seeks to avoid formality in its proceedings and is not bound by an enactment or rule of law relating to the admissibility of evidence in proceedings before the courts of law.

Very largely, therefore, the procedure before the tribunal will be at the discretion of the chairman although, as will be seen in Chapter 10, this does not absolve him from observing the rules of natural justice. These common law rules would, for example, require a tribunal chairman to disclose most documents submitted by one of the parties to the proceedings, to the other party. Failure to observe this and the other requirements of natural justice would probably lead to a quashing of the tribunal's decision.

5.7.3   Tribunal representation

Parties to most tribunal proceedings are able to rely on representation whether in the form of legal or lay representation. Many welfare tribunals such as the Social Security Appeal Tribunals see a great deal of representation by the various voluntary agencies whose expertise before these tribunals is considerable. Indeed, there are those who would argue that lawyers are out of place in tribunals and tend to introduce a measure of formality and technicality which is alien to administrative tribunals.

5.7.4   Legal aid, advice and assistance

In order to prepare a case for presentation to a tribunal it may be possible to rely on the free services of one of the voluntary agencies. In practice, many cases before the Industrial Tribunals are prepared and presented by officers of workers' trade unions as a service to the membership. In other cases where such assistance is not available to parties to tribunal proceedings legal advice and assistance is available from solicitors in the preparation of a case. However, legal aid to cover further expenses in pursuing or defending a case before a tribunal is not available except before the Lands Tribunal, the Employment Appeal Tribunal and the Commons Commissioners. This latter tribunal deals with disputes about the designation of land as common land. Assistance by way of representation may also be available before the Mental Health Review

Tribunals. This matter of legal aid was dealt with by the Lord Chancellor's Advisory Committee on Legal Aid in 1974. Although it was recognised that different persons have different needs before different tribunals, the Committee concluded that financial help should be extended to those voluntary agencies already operating in the tribunal system. Nevertheless, it was also recognised that legal aid before tribunals would lead to too much formality in their proceedings and the possibility that the proceedings would become too lengthy. The Council on Tribunals has also added its weight to the controversy in calling for legal aid to be made available before those tribunals under its supervision where legal representation is available.

5.7.5   Legal immunity for tribunal proceedings

Where judicial proceedings are being conducted in a court of law the judges enjoy an immunity from legal liability in tort. In other words, they cannot be liable for civil wrongs such as libel and slander, a matter which is dealt with again in Chapter 14. One of the big problems in the present context is whether this immunity extends to and protects the members of tribunals. In one of the leading cases, *Royal Aquarium and Summer and Winter Garden Society Ltd v Parkinson* (1892), the court was concerned with a case of slander in respect of words spoken at a meeting of London County Council while it was acting as a licensing body for music and dancing licences. The defendant, Parkinson, claimed that his allegedly slanderous statements were protected by absolute privilege of the sort accorded to judges in judicial proceedings. However, it was decided that absolute privilege did not apply because the licensing body did not have the characteristics of a court even though it was obliged sometimes to act judicially. As a result Parkinson, it was decided, could rely only on 'qualified' privilege so that he could claim immunity from tortious liability for slander if he could prove that the offending words were spoken without malice.

While tribunals are obliged to act judicially, there must be some doubt about the legal immunity of their membership. This doubt is emphasised in relation to proceedings for contempt of court where there is a failure to comply with some order or some interference with the functioning of a court. One important aspect of the law relating to contempt permits an order for committal for contempt to be made by a Divisional Court of the Queen's Bench Division (part of the High Court) where the contempt is committed in connection with proceedings in an 'inferior' court. It was decided in *Attorney General v British Broadcasting Corporation* (1981) that a local valuation court did not come within this description. As a result, it may now be the case that only those tribunals which are described as 'courts' in their statutory definition will be regarded as deserving immunity in certain areas of tortious liability and as being within the care of the Queen's Bench Division for the punishment of contempt.

5.7.6   Precedent in tribunals

One final area of interest in this context of procedure and organisation concerns precedent. By means of judicial precedent the common law has been developed through a system which requires a court to follow a decision of a court above it where the facts are similar. In theory there is no similar requirement for tribunals although in practice a system of precedent has developed in most cases. In particular, where there is an hierarchy of tribunals culminating with an appeal tribunal as with the Social Security Commissioners and the Immigration Appeal Tribunal, the lower tribunals will follow similar decisions of the appeal tribunals. However, this system does depend on an effective publication of significant previous decisions.

5.8   Specific Tribunals

In order to show the tribunal system in action and some of the foregoing principles in practice, the remaining section of this chapter is devoted to a description of the nature and purpose of some particular tribunals. The tribunals which are covered are the Transport Tribunal, the Vaccine Damage Tribunals, Rent Assessment Committees and Rent Tribunals, the Social Security Appeal Tribunals and the Social Security Commissioners.

5.9   The Transport Tribunal

The Goods Vehicles (Licensing of Operators) Act 1995 states that: '... no person ... shall use a goods vehicle on a road for the carriage of goods (a) for hire or reward; or (b) for or in connection with any trade or business carried on by him, except under a licence.' Applications for such licences are made to the local licensing authority. Before granting a licence, such a traffic commissioner has to be satisfied about a number of matters, eg that the applicant is a fit and proper person to hold an operator's licence and that there will be satisfactory facilities and arrangements for maintaining the authorised vehicles in a fit and serviceable condition. The disappointed applicant is entitled to appeal against an adverse decision to the Transport Tribunal. The Tribunal has High Court status which means that it has the power to compel the attendance and examination of witnesses, to secure the production and inspection of documents, to enforce orders and to enter and inspect property.

5.9.1   Composition

The Tribunal comprises a president who is an experienced lawyer and four other members, of which two are required to be persons of experience in the transport business, one a person of experience in commercial affairs and one a person of experience in financial matters or economics. The membership is appointed by Her Majesty on the joint recommendation of the Lord Chancellor and the Minister of Transport. When the Tribunal is dealing with a licensing appeal of the type previously described, it comes before the Road Haulage Appeals Division which comprises at least two members of the Tribunal. Decisions of the Tribunal are by a majority and there is an appeal on a point of law, not to the High Court, but to the Court of Appeal, whose decision is stated to be final.

5.9.2 Procedure

Procedural requirements are governed by the Transport Act 1985 which indicate the considerable status of this body. Bearing in mind that the Tribunal has High Court status for various purposes and is designated as a statutory court of record, the Act stipulates that: 'Where not inconsistent with these Rules the general principles of practice or any particular practice of the superior court may be adopted and applied as the Tribunal may think fit.' Two other requirements stipulate that a party may be heard in person or by counsel or a solicitor and that reasons shall be given for a decision.

5.9.3 Status

The Tribunal is a 'Schedule 1' tribunal under the Tribunals and Inquiries Act but the foregoing requirement for reasons in the Transport Act supersedes the requirement of reasons on request under s 10 of the Act of 1992. In the same way, the facility for an appeal on a point of law to the High Court in s 11 is superseded by a specific provision for a similar appeal to the Court of Appeal. As a tribunal under the supervision of the Council on Tribunals, the Transport Tribunal is subject to the Council's general recommendations about membership and the Council's concurrence is required for the removal of any member of the Tribunal. Finally, the Council has to be consulted in respect of any changes to rules of procedure.

5.10 The Vaccine Damage Tribunals

The Vaccine Damage Payments Act 1979 provides for a lump-sum payment to be made to any person whom the Secretary of State for Health is satisfied has suffered severe disablement as a result of vaccination. Certain conditions have to be satisfied, for example, in general the vaccination must have been before the age of 18 and the person concerned must have suffered 80% or greater disability as a result. Where it is decided that there is no entitlement, the written notification must state the grounds for the decision. Where the written notification states that the Secretary of State is not satisfied that the claimant is severely disabled as a result of vaccination, it must specify arrangements for the matter to be referred to an independent medical tribunal, that is, one of the Vaccine Damage Tribunals. Decisions of any such tribunals are conclusive and binding on the Secretary of State. In some circumstances, for example, where there is a material change of circumstances, the Secretary of State is empowered to reconsider a decision within six years of that decision.

5.10.1 Procedure

The Vaccine Damage Payments Regulations 1979 contain the procedural and other details governing the operation of the tribunals. The tribunals each comprise a chairman and two medical practitioners, each chairman being nominated by the President of the Social Security Appeals Tribunals. In common with most other tribunals, hearings are in public 'except in so far as the chairman may for special reasons otherwise direct'. Apart from the specific statutory procedural requirements, the procedure is at the discretion of a tribunal. The Secretary of State and the claimant have a right to be heard before a tribunal so that they can call witnesses, question any witnesses and address the tribunal. For this purpose, any person having a right to be heard can be represented at the hearing by another person whether or not that person has professional qualifications. Where in the opinion of the chairman it would be undesirable in the interests of the claimant or the disabled person to disclose to them medical advice or medical evidence which is before a tribunal, such advice or evidence need not be disclosed but may be taken into account in making a decision.

5.10.2 Status

The tribunals came under the supervision of the Council on Tribunals in 1979. Apart from the Council's power to make recommendations about the tribunal's membership and the need for chairmen to be selected from a panel maintained by the Lord Chancellor, the Council has to be consulted in respect of procedural rules and the tribunals are bound to give reasons for decisions by virtue of s 10 of the Tribunals and Inquiries Act. However, s 11 of the Act does not apply so there is no appeal on a point of law to the High Court from decisions of the Vaccine Damage Tribunals. Consequently, tribunal decisions are subject only to judicial review in the High Court, (the implications of this will be examined in Chapter 13). Six tribunals have been established and they disposed of 230 cases in 1981.

5.11 Rent Assessment Committee and Rent Tribunals

These tribunals, organised locally throughout the country, are concerned with disputes arising under the Rent Acts, that is, disputes relating to private residential tenancies and similar arrangements. Rent Assessment Committees are responsible for fixing rents under 'assured and other types of tenancy on an appeal from a decision of a rent officer. Rent Tribunals are responsible for the fixing of rents in respect of 'restricted contracts', eg where rented accommodation is situated in property which is also being occupied by the landlord or the rent includes an amount for the provision of furniture or services, and for awarding 'security of tenure' whereby a person may be able to stay on in the accommodation. The statutory provisions in question stipulate that a Rent Assessment Committee, when constituted to carry out these latter functions, shall be known as a Rent Tribunal! Considerable changes confronted the jurisdiction of these tribunals under the Housing Act 1988, eg through the restrictions on the creation of new restricted contracts. The fact that there is a close relationship between these tribunals is reflected in their membership arrangements. The Secretary of State for the Environment maintains a panel of persons to act as chairmen and members of the Rent Assessment Committees established in various areas of the country. Each area has a panel containing a list of persons appointed by the Lord Chancellor who are capable of acting as chairmen, and a list of persons appointed by the Secretary of State in consultation with the Council on Tribunals who can sit as members. Rent Tribunals are constituted from the same source. Each Rent Tribunal comprises a chairman and two members while each Rent Assessment Committee comprises a chairman and one or two members.

5.11.1   Rent Assessment Committees

Hearings are in public unless, for special reasons, it is decided to meet *in camera*. The conduct of the hearing is at the discretion of the Committee and any of the parties has a full right to be heard. The Committee may inspect a dwelling subject to the proceedings and must inspect it if requested to do so by one of the parties. Most Rent Assessment Committee work is concerned with the task of resolving disputes about the fixing of 'fair' rents: in 1981 they disposed of over 13,000 cases. A rent assessment committee may now act as a Leasehold Valuation Tribunal for the purposes of the Landlord and Tenant Act 1987. This Act gives tenants of blocks of flats 'first refusal' where a landlord is disposing of his interest. Disputes here may be resolved by the Leasehold Valuation Tribunal.

5.11.2   Rent Tribunals

Reference of restricted contracts for a tribunal's consideration is in writing. After a consideration of the reference, any such inquiry as the tribunal may think fit and any oral or written representations from the parties, the tribunal will fix a 'reasonable' rent. Any party may appear in person, be legally represented or be accompanied by any person. Hearings are usually in public but again, as is often the case with many tribunals, 'special reasons' may justify a hearing *in camera*. In 1981 the tribunals disposed of nearly 3,000 cases.

5.11.3   Status

It was seen previously that the membership of the tribunals is regulated by the Act to the extent that the Secretary of State is obliged to involve the Lord Chancellor and the Council on Tribunals. In addition, the Lord Chancellor's consent is required for the termination of a person's membership of one of the tribunals. Beyond the membership provisions of the Act, the tribunals are subject to s 10 (reasons for a decision to be given on request) and s 11 (appeal on a point of law to the High Court), as well as being under the supervision of the Council of Tribunals.

5.12   Social Security Appeal Tribunals

In 1983 the National Insurance Local Tribunals were merged with the Supplementary Benefit Appeal Tribunals to form the unified Social Security Appeal Tribunals. The starting point is a claim for benefit or entitlement which is made to an adjudication officer. Decisions on many such claims are subject to an appeal to a Social Security Appeal Tribunal. An exception worthy of note occurs under the Social Security Act 1986. Many supplementary benefit payments are replaced by discretionary loans and grants from the Social Fund, decisions on which are not subject to appeal to a tribunal but only a review by another departmental official.

The social security tribunals are headed by a president. Membership (including the chairmen) of the tribunals is no longer appointed by the Department of Social Security: appointments are now made by the president. The presidential system has the following merits: (a) it reinforces the independence of the tribunals from government; (b) the president can be pro-active in training and is able to maintain consistency in decision-making approaches; (c) the president is able to improve communications within the tribunal network.

The chairman of one of these tribunals will be a barrister or solicitor of at least five years' standing. Two additional members of the tribunal are drawn (by the president) from a panel of persons appearing to have knowledge or experience of conditions in the area and who are representative of persons living or working there.

Public, oral hearings are required although the chairman has the discretion to require a private hearing, eg where delicate financial evidence may be in issue. The members of the tribunal have an investigatory function so that issues can be determined without strict adherence to the parties' contentions. The tribunal is empowered to refer questions for examination and report by an expert. This facility is used particularly in relation to specialist medical matters. Prior to presentation of the appeal the case is referred back to the adjudication officer for reconsideration. If there is no movement as a result, the appeal proceeds. On completion of the appeal, reasons are required for the decision. A further appeal, on matters of law, goes to a Social Security Commissioner.

5.13   Social Security Commissioners

There are 13 Social Security Commissioners who are barristers or solicitors of at least 10 years' standing. Before an appeal can be accepted, leave (or consent) of the chairman of the tribunal or the commissioner must be obtained. This filter is aimed at eliminating unmeritorious appeals. Hearings are normally in public and reasons have to be given for decisions. An appeal on a point of law from a Commissioner's decision goes to the Court of Appeal.

6 Public Corporations, Executive and Privatised Agencies

6.1 Status

Public corporations are bodies with their own legal entity created by statute in most instances, normally without the status of Crown servant or agent, to undertake functions of concern to and subject to some control by government. While a good deal of what follows relates to public corporations some reference is made to the process of privatisation and the development of so-called 'Next Step' executive agencies. A well-known example of privatised industry is included in the reference to the privatised British Steel. While this example relates to what may be described as 'total' privatisation through the flotation of a conventional company, some examples may be referred to as 'qualified' privatisations. The privatisation of the water industry through the Water Act 1989 (now provided for through the Water Industry Act 1991) is notable on two counts. First, those companies that are chosen as the new water and sewerage undertakers have to comply with fairly extensive statutory requirements relating (for example) to prices and quality of service. Secondly, the law on insolvency in the Insolvency Act 1986 is modified in order to provide a rather more generous safety net for the companies that may find themselves in financial difficulty in providing this fundamental commodity. The same insistence on a strict statutory framework is seen in the coverage of the privatised electricity industry, described below.

The case of the 'Next Step' executive agencies is rather different. In this case government policy since the end of the 1980s has sought to separate out the 'service delivery' element of central government and to place it in the hands of 'quasi-independent', 'quasi-corporate' agencies. Nevertheless, each of the foregoing categories involves corporate status of some sort, against a well-defined statutory framework.

6.1.1 Statutory corporations

Like local authorities, most public corporations are created by statute, in which case the corporation is referred to as a 'body corporate'. As an artificial individual in law, the public corporation may be able to undertake transactions in its own name, acquire, hold and dispose of property in its own name, and sue and be sued in its own name. The one notable exception to the general rule that public corporations are statutory corporations is the British Broadcasting Corporation, which was created by charter under prerogative powers. In *British*

Broadcasting Corporation v Johns (1965) (referred to in Chapter 2), it was decided that the Corporation was not a Crown servant or agent so that there could be no Crown immunity from the payment of taxes. In the case of most public corporations, the relevant statute will define any Crown status. The usual practice is to include a statement that the corporation is not a Crown servant or agent. However, in some cases it may have been decided that a corporation should have Crown status for a particular purpose, eg in relation to the payment of rates on land in its ownership.

6.1.2 Public corporations and functions of concern to government

There may be many reasons why government decides to create a public corporation. These reasons are best reflected in the categories of corporation which will be examined in the next three sections. It has been noted that public corporations are not totally independent of government. Why, then, should government decide not to incorporate a particular function in a government department? The answer is not a simple one. From a political point of view, government may not want to be identified too directly with sensitive or potentially embarrassing areas of social regulation, for example. On the other hand, it may be considered that there is insufficient expertise in a government department for the purpose of some area of regulation or that the nature and scale of a commercial operation is such that it cannot be undertaken by a government department. In this context it has been seen that government policy has been very much in favour of a separation out of 'service' functions from central government departments under the 'Next Steps' initiative, outlined below. As to the types of function undertaken by public corporations, there seem to be three broad categories, although there is always the possibility of an overlap between the categories in some cases. In the first category, one finds the commercial and industrial organisations many of which have been or are in the process of being privatised. The second category covers the organisations concerned with economic, social and welfare regulation, while the third category covers those organisations whose concern is with social standardisation. Each of the three categories is now examined after a description of the 'Next Steps' initiative.

6.1.3 'Next Steps'

The intention of this initiative, launched in the late 1980s by the government, is to rationalise the Civil Service and reorganise government departments by reference to a separation (in broad terms) of service provision and policy-making. Gradually since then there has been an emergence of semi-autonomous, 'quasi-corporate' agencies employing civil servants enjoying some freedom particularly in relation to day-to-day departmental supervision. The agencies are characterised as executive bodies. Within approximately two years of the launch of the initiative, over 30 executive agencies had been created including the Driver and Vehicle Licensing Agency, the Land Registry and the Vehicle Inspectorate. More recent creations include the Contributions Agency and the Parole Board. The Criminal Justice and Public Order Act 1994 incorporated the Parole Board with full, non-departmental public body status. Prior to 1991 the Board was empowered only to make recommendations to the Home Secretary. The Board now has executive powers, eg to review and finally decide on the release of life prisoners serving discretionary life sentences. Accordingly, the Criminal Justice Act 1991 is amended by the Act of 1994, indicating that the Board shall not be regarded as the servant or agent of the Crown, or as enjoying any status, immunity or privilege of the Crown, and that the Board's property shall not be regarded as property of, or held on behalf of, the Crown. The chairman and membership of the Board continue to be appointed by the Home Secretary.

6.1.4 Industry, commerce and public utilities

Where there was a need for governmental intervention in economic activity, eg because of a perceived need for monopolistic supply of a particular commodity or because of the importance of effective price control, a public corporation could be created either for the purpose of taking over an enterprise or group of enterprises or for the purpose of starting some undertaking right from the start. It is in this context that one finds the better-known public corporations like British Coal. However, it must be recognised that government policy over quite a substantial period has stressed a need for competition in the context of privatisation. This theme underpins much of the remainder of this chapter. Privatisation of the major public utilities supplying water, gas and electricity in particular is a major theme for present purposes. Electricity privatisation is described more fully, below.

6.1.5 Economic, social and welfare regulation

Public corporations in this category may be seen as agents of government in the fulfilment of some area of public policy, although this observation in no way suggests that such corporations are 'Crown' agents. As regulatory corporations, the bodies in this category are concerned to ensure that particular policies of the government are implemented. Health authorities, for example, are concerned with implementing the policies of successive governments which have provided the National Health Service. Among other tasks, the health authorities act as providers as well as regulators of health care in each area of the country. When it comes to economic regulation, public corporations in this category should be contrasted with those in the first category. Corporations in this second category are regulatory agencies: they are not usually the initiators of the economic activity itself. A prominent example in this area of economic regulation is any one of the agricultural marketing boards which facilitate the marketing of commodities provided by the various producers. In the case of social regulation, again the task of any public corporation is to implement government policies. One striking example here is the Housing Corporation which is organised regionally for the purpose, among other purposes, of regulating and financing the activities of housing associations. Consequently, housing rehabilitation can be effected by a fusion of these important elements in one body which for many financial purposes acts as an agent of government.

6.1.6   Social standardisation

This category, like the one above, is almost always the product of some area of public policy and, again, there are probably many comparisons with the public corporations in the second category. However, in this third category it often appears that the public corporations are concerned particularly with the enforcement of standards of social behaviour. Prominent examples are the Commission for Racial Equality, the Equal Opportunities Commission, the Nature Conservancy Council for England and the Advisory, Conciliation and Arbitration Service (ACAS). Social standardisation by these public corporations may involve a variety of techniques, eg licensing, criminal prosecution or conciliation.

6.1.7   Government control

A clear point of distinction between the public corporation and the private company lies in the statutory facility for control of the public corporation by the minister, who is, in turn, responsible to Parliament. Examples of this control and its scope will be examined below where specific types of public corporation are dealt with. Apart from this area of control there are four other areas of control: Parliamentary control, control by means of the Companies Act, 'consumer' control and judicial control by the courts. Parliamentary control is achieved through debates, questions and scrutiny by Select Committees either in general terms or on those occasions when some specific financial item is questioned, as a result of auditing, for example. Control by means of the Companies Act may be available through government investment in what is referred to as a 'golden' or 'master' share. Provision for such a share in a newly privatised corporation's articles of association allows the government to enforce certain defined (government) shareholder's rights restricting (for example) sale of the company to foreign interests without its consent. Of course the government may be free to renounce its rights at a point that is considered to be politically or economically appropriate. So-called 'consumer control' is available in some cases, usually where consumer or consultative councils are established in relation to the commercial activities of some of the nationalised industries. Finally, there is judicial control, which is outlined in the next section.

6.1.8   Judicial control

In the case of most public corporations, and the nationalised industries in particular, there appear to be few opportunities to challenge their acts as being *ultra vires*. It is difficult to identify precisely why this should be the case but there are some broad indications. In the first place, the statutory powers and responsibilities of many public corporations are quite widely drawn so that proof of an *ultra vires* act could be quite difficult. Secondly, government control, eg in the context of financial sanction for various projects, programmes or schemes, may provide a filter to guard against anything which might be *ultra vires*. Finally, where the functions of a public corporation are undertaken mainly through contracts, it is that contractual forum which is the focus of attention so that the main concern is with the law of contract and whether the terms of any contract have been fulfilled. These three observations relate mainly to the small number of so-called nationalised industries in industry and commerce. However, in the case of many other of the public corporations with statutory powers of regulation and social standardisation, there have been greater opportunities for challenge by reference to *ultra vires*. Individuals or organisations subject to administrative action by these public corporations have not always been slow to challenge that action as being *ultra vires* action. Whether it has been a case of the Commission for Racial Equality taking action to require a person to desist from allegedly unlawful discrimination contrary to the Race Relations Act or a case of ACAS acting to require a company to recognise a trade union in collective bargaining (prior to the statutory restriction on formal recognition machinery), the fact that an individual or organisation has considered that legal rights are affected by administrative action has been sufficient to give rise to a challenge in the High Court. One of the responsibilities of ACAS under a now repealed provision of the Employment Protection Act 1975 was to facilitate union recognition. ACAS was under a statutory duty to 'ascertain the opinions of workers to whom the issue relates by any means it thinks fit'. It will be seen in Chapter 9 that action by ACAS was challenged successfully by one employer in this context on the ground of procedural *ultra vires*. A number of other challenges to the exercise of these powers were mounted, but not always with similar success.

6.1.9   Legal liability of public corporations

Many of the legal principles mentioned in relation to the legal liability of local authorities in Chapter 4 are relevant to public corporations. The one crucial difference occurs where a public corporation is, in law, a Crown servant or agent, in which case the Crown's legal privileges referred to in Chapter 14 may apply. However, because most public corporations do not enjoy this status, this matter is of little significance here. Nevertheless, it was seen in Chapter 2 that some public corporations are closer to government than others, in which case they are likely to have the status of Crown servant or agent, eg the health authorities.

Apart from this issue of Crown status, the legal liability of the public corporation will depend in many cases on whether there is sufficient statutory authority to protect the corporation, eg in respect of action which is alleged to be a tortious nuisance. The public corporation's legal liability may depend also on the scope of any statutory duty which prescribes the functions it is expected to perform. In many instances, particularly in relation to the public utilities like the former regional water authorities, the statutory duty was defined very broadly. The Water Act 1973 s 11 indicated, for example, that it was the duty of a water authority to supply or secure the supply of water for its area. Very similar, broadly defined duties are to be found in the Water Industry Act 1991, defining the duties of the water and sewerage undertaker companies. It is the case that such widely drawn statutory duties cannot be enforced in law directly by a person who complains that he has no water supply, a point which is taken up in Chapters 11, 12 and 13. Because the fulfilment of these important duties depended on all sorts of financial and policy issues affecting water companies, the law requires any complaint to be taken directly to the administrative framework established by statute, in this case the Water Industry Act 1991. Only as a last resort would the matter be subject to enforcement by the courts and, even here, only at the instance of the Secretary of State. In this latter context of statutory duties therefore, it may be possible to generalise by saying that such duties are not usually intended to be legally enforceable in the courts but they do underline the scope of government control of many public corporations and privatised companies. The remainder of the chapter contains a brief description of some of the different public corporations which fall within the foregoing categories together with one example of a privatised corporation: British Steel.

6.2 The Independent Television Commission

A White Paper published in 1988, entitled 'Broadcasting in the 90s', stressed the importance of competition, choice and quality. The White Paper emphasised further a greater diversity of services in a market context, involving less supervision and regulation but more 'consumer choice'. The Broadcasting Act 1990 sought to implement the ideas behind the White Paper. The essence of the Act is the regulation of the electronic media within the independent broadcasting sector: the private rather than the public sector. Two major agencies are created by the Act of 1990, the Independent Television Commission and the Radio Authority. The Commission is an independent agency subject to certain areas of accountability to the Secretary of State. Otherwise, the Commission is to achieve financial independence through fees to be charged for its services.

6.2.1 Membership and status

The Commission comprises a chairman and deputy chairman together with not less than eight but no more than 10 members, appointed by the Secretary of

Commission is a body corporate but is not a body exercising func-
ehalf of the Crown for the purpose of enactments relating to privileges
of the Crown.

6.2.2   Powers, duties and functions

The essential function of the Commission is regulation of television services in
the independent sector, regardless of technology. Licences may be granted only
to 'fit and proper persons'. A wide power to impose conditions is available and
may include requirements about good taste and decency as well as the fulfilment of promises made in any bid for a licence. There are statutory restrictions
on licence-holding, eg by certain foreign interests and anti-competitive organisations. It is a fundamental duty of the Commission to determine whether programmes meet the standards set out in the Act: eg that news is accurate and
impartial.

6.3   British Steel

The British Steel Act 1988 provided the vehicle for privatisation of the former
British Steel Corporation. The Act transferred the assets and liabilities of the old
corporation to a new public limited company nominated by the Secretary of
State and provided for dissolution of the British Steel Corporation. Initially the
statutory requirement was for shares to be issued to the Crown in a nominated
company so that the company was wholly owned by the Crown. Thereafter a
Stock Exchange flotation enabled private investors to purchase the shares. For
all purposes the company is a conventional corporate entity registered under
the Companies Act in the normal way.

6.4   The Electricity Generating and Supply Companies

The privatisation of the electricity industry was foreshadowed by the White
Paper 'Privatising Electricity' published in 1988. Ultimately the government's
proposals were incorporated in the Electricity Act 1989. The assets of the electricity industry were transferred to 'successor companies' in the context of a regulatory system designed to encourage competition.

6.4.1   The regulatory regime

The two main actors in the regulatory regime of the Act of 1989 are the
Secretary of State and the Director General of Electricity Supply. The issuing
and monitoring of licences to generators, transmitters and suppliers of electricity is undertaken by the Secretary of State. A central feature of the Electricity

Act, therefore, is the requirement for a licence to authorise key supply and related functions. The unlicensed supply of electricity is a criminal offence. Where a licence is issued subject to conditions, those conditions are enforceable either by the Secretary of State or, (more usually) by the Director General. Once issued, a licence empowers the recovery of charges as well as the acquisition of land, according to the requirements of the Act. Additionally, the Secretary of State's consent is required for the construction, extension and operation of generating stations. The Act also empowers the Secretary of State to require public electricity suppliers to make arrangements to secure that a specified proportion of supply is obtained from non-fossil fuel generating stations.

6.4.2   General duties

There are certain general statutory duties defined by the Electricity Act that are binding on the Secretary of State and the Director General. The duties are three fold: first, to secure all reasonable demands for electricity; secondly, to secure that licence-holders are able to finance their activities and, thirdly, to provide competition in the generation and supply of electricity.

6.4.3   The Director General's powers

The Electricity Act empowers the Director General to secure compliance with licence requirements. In addition the Act facilitates the use of provisional and final orders for enforcement purposes against licence-holders. A licence may be modified, with the consent of the licence-holder. There is a discretion to refer relevant matters to the Monopolies and Mergers Commission under the Fair Trading Act. Thereafter the Commission is subject to certain duties in reporting on a reference in this context and the Director General is subject to a duty to modify a licence following any adverse report from the Monopolies and Mergers Commission. Two other powers are worthy of inclusion: the power to publish information and advice considered to be 'expedient' for the benefit of customers or potential customers, and the power to set standards for overall performance.

6.4.4   Powers of direction

The Secretary of State is empowered to give general directions to the Director General on two issues. The first issue relates to priorities for any review by the Director General of the performance of his duties while the second relates to those considerations to be taken account of in the exercise of his functions.

6.5   The Housing Corporation

The Corporation has various functions, the more important of which are promotion and assistance in the development of registered housing associations, the registration of housing associations, supervision and control of the associations and the processing of applications for housing development funds from such bodies. In order to achieve these objectives the Corporation has the capacity to do such things and enter into such transactions as are incidental to the exercise or performance of the above functions. The Corporation is not a Crown servant or agent for any purpose.

6.5.1   Government control and membership

The Corporation is subject to general directions from the Secretary of State, a particularly important element of control in the case of this and other public corporations with statutory responsibilities for the distribution of public money. The Secretary of State again has the responsibility for appointing members of the Corporation, in this case 15 members.

6.6   The British Wool Marketing Board

This Board is one of a number of agricultural marketing boards which are now governed by the Agricultural Marketing Act 1958. Schemes for the market regulation of an agricultural product may be submitted to the minister by persons who are substantially representative of the producers of that product. The minister is required to publicise a scheme, indicating that there are facilities for objections. Any objections which are made are examined at a public inquiry and the minister is obliged to consider the inspector's report before deciding whether the scheme should be implemented. If a scheme is to be implemented, a board is appointed to administer that scheme. The minister has a power to give directions where it appears to him that any act of a board will be contrary to the public interest. However, the board must receive notice of any such direction and can require that the matter be referred to a committee of investigation. The Wool Marketing Board comprises 10 regional members, two 'special' members and three persons appointed by the minister. Each regional member is elected by the registered producers in his area. The Board maintains a register of producers. Any producer who is neither registered nor exempt from registration is prohibited from selling wool, although the Board can grant exemptions. No registered producer can sell wool except through the agency of the Board which has wide powers in connection with matters such as the condition of wool to be sold. Valuation decisions are conclusive unless a valuation appeal tribunal is set up under the scheme. Contravention of the scheme by a registered producer attracts financial penalties levied by a disciplinary committee under the scheme. It should be noted finally in this context that this and other agricultural marketing boards now operate against a broader background of EC law and the Common Agricultural Policy. As a result, there is always a possibility that an agricultural marketing scheme will be contrary to certain EC legal rights and safeguards such as the provision in the Treaty of Rome which requires the free movement of goods between the Member States. The status of EC law in relation to administrative law is outlined in Chapter 8.

6.7   The Nature Conservancy Council for England

The Environmental Protection Act created three nature conservancy councils, albeit with difference names, for England, Scotland and Wales. The Nature Conservancy Council for England, often referred to as 'English Nature' has a variety of functions. In the first place it has an advisory function in indicating, for example, the categories of plants and animals to be protected under the Wildlife and Countryside Act 1981. Secondly, there are licensing functions, eg in permitting the taking of animals for scientific purposes, an act otherwise unlawful under the Act of 1981. Thirdly, the Council has executive functions, including the identification of land considered to be of special interest by virtue of its flora, fauna or other similar characteristics. After notifying the land-owner, local planning authority and the Secretary of State, the Council can enforce any restrictions on the use of the land and pay compensation therefor. Fourthly, the Council has a loan and grant-giving function for nature conservation, and fifthly, there is a legislative function in making bylaws for marine nature reserves.

6.7.1   Membership and status

The Council is a body corporate, subject to directions from the Secretary of State. There are not less than 10 members of the Council and not more than 14, all appointed by the Secretary of State. The Council is not a servant or agent of the Crown and enjoys no status, immunity or privilege of the Crown. The Council's property is not regarded as the property or property held on behalf of the Crown.

6.8   The Advisory, Conciliation and Arbitration Service

The Service, usually referred to as ACAS, is governed by the Employment Protection Act 1975 and has a general duty of promoting the improvement of industrial relations, and providing conciliation and arbitration in trade disputes. ACAS has six functions:

(1) the provision of conciliation in industrial disputes;

(2) the provision of conciliation officers to promote the settlement of complaints made to industrial tribunals;

(3) the reference of matters in dispute to arbitration;

(4) the presentation of advice to the parties to industrial relations problems;

(5) inquiries into industrial relations problems; and

(6) the preparation and publication of codes of practice for the promotion of good industrial relations.

Because ACAS has to be seen to be a truly independent body in the often sensitive area of industrial relations, the Act of 1975 states that 'the Service shall not be subject to directions of any kind from any minister of the Crown as to the manner in which it is to exercise any of its functions'. The Act also designates ACAS as a body performing its functions on behalf of the Crown and goes on to emphasise that it enjoys the Crown's special legal position in civil proceedings as defined in the Crown Proceedings Act 1947, a subject dealt with in Chapter 14. ACAS is governed by a council whose membership is appointed by the Secretary of State from both sides of industry, with the addition of a minority of 'independent' members.

7 The Nature and Characteristics of Administrative Powers

7.1 Statutory Powers

The principal characteristic of most administrative powers is that they arise from and can be used by virtue of legislation. It will be seen in Chapter 8 that there are different varieties of legislation and that they each relate to different areas of administrative powers. However, the most important variety of legislation is the so-called public general Act which affects the law across the country as a whole. It was seen in Chapters 3 and 5 that the Tribunals and Inquiries Act 1992 governs some of the important requirements to be observed by most administrative tribunals and statutory inquiries. In addition to defining the general legal standards to be observed in this context, the Act also permits the making of statutory orders to bring a tribunal under the Act and statutory rules to set down rules of procedure for some statutory inquiries. It will be seen in Chapter 8 that such orders and rules are items of subordinate, or delegated, legislation since they are made under the authority of a principal Act of Parliament by a delegate, in this case, a minister of the Crown. In some instances, the Crown relies on prerogative powers, as described in Chapter 1. It was seen that these are recognised by and may be enforced by the courts. The rarity of such decisions indicates the predominance of legal powers in the present context and, in particular, statutory powers.

Reference must be made finally to the common law, that is, the case law developed by the courts. The common law has been developed where the courts have had to make the law for a situation which is not governed by statute and where it is necessary to interpret Parliament's words in a statute. It is this second situation which has characterised the development of so much administrative law. Most administrative powers are statutory, so that it has been the case on frequent occasions that the High Court in particular has been called upon to interpret the statutory words of an Act of Parliament or some other item of legislation, primarily by reference to the doctrine of *ultra vires* as described in Chapter 1 and Part 3. As a result of judicial decisions in the courts, it has been possible for all sorts of administrative agencies to appreciate the scope of their various statutory powers. In matters of substance and procedure the courts' decisions have had a very persuasive influence on the way in which many administrative powers are used as well as the purposes for which they are used. Such matters are addressed more fully in Part 3.

7.2   The Law of the European Union

Chapter 8, which deals with the sources of administrative powers, includes a reference to the law of the European Union, the EU. When the UK became a member of the EC (the pre-Maastricht name for the collection of Member States which recognised the Treaty of Rome), it was agreed that the Treaty of Rome would apply to and be observed in the UK. It will be seen in Chapter 8 that the Treaty of Rome provides the basis for the constitutional and legal framework of the EU. This is now recognised by the European Communities Act 1972 by which Parliament accepts that EU law is superior to UK law and will apply to the exclusion of the latter whenever there is an overlap. The European Communities (Amendment) Act 1986 now extends the scope of the Community following the signing of the Single European Act in February 1986, creating a new single market. Moreover, the European Communities (Amendment) Act 1993 has incorporated the Treaty on European Union (the so-called 'Maastricht Treaty'), into UK national law and has hence arguably made it a little more likely that the original Treaty of Rome's goal of an 'ever closer union among the peoples of Europe' will be achieved. Consequently, it is necessary to identify three things:

(1) the object of the EU for the purpose of indicating the areas of law where the UK Parliament has accepted the superiority of EU law;

(2) the nature of EU law; and

(3) the characteristics of administrative law and administrative powers as they are affected by EU law.

7.2.1   The object of the EU

Article 2 of the Treaty of Rome specifies that the EU is an economic and monetary union of Member States. In general terms, this means that EU law must relate in some way to the economic relationship between Member States. Accordingly, the more important areas of EU law relate to economic competition, the free movement of goods and the free movement of workers. An example of EU law in operation is seen in its environmental protection policy and various items of law which have been legislated since 1973 by reference to Articles 2 and 100 of the Treaty, among others. Environmental protection is now recognised explicitly as an area of competence in the Union. Article 100 provides for the harmonisation of such legislation among Member States as affects the establishment or functioning of the Union. The apparent intention behind the EU law in this area is the harmonisation or reconciliation of the pollution laws in the Member States in order to reduce or eliminate disparity between their respective laws in this field. In this way, it is less likely that there will be great disparity in the costs of industrial production in Member States according to the relative laxity of their respective pollution laws. EU law deals with the pollution problem both specifically, in relation to particular problems, and generally. In this latter context of general EU laws, the UK has promoted much legislation in recognition of the numerous directives from the Union on the subject of environmental protection. For example, the Directive on Assessment of the Environmental Effects of Major Developments was legislated as regulations under the Town and Country Planning Act.

7.2.2   The nature of EU law

The outstanding characteristic of EU law is that it sets legal standards which are to be observed by and, sometimes, enforced against, governments of Member States, individuals and organisations. In some instances, EU law gives legally enforceable rights and it is often the case that such rights can be enforced in the UK courts, whether the matter is civil or criminal. In pursuing their duty to recognise and implement EU law, the UK courts may find problems in interpreting that law. The Treaty of Rome states that in these circumstances any such court may, or, in circumstances where there is no judicial remedy under national law against the decision of the court, shall refer the problem of interpretation to the European Court of Justice. EU law as interpreted by the Court of Justice will be applied to the facts of the case by the court dealing with the case in the UK. By way of an illustration of the essential nature of much of EU law, one can turn to Article 48 of the Treaty of Rome. Among other things, Article 48 stipulates that there shall be freedom of movement for workers as between the Member States and that there shall be no discrimination for this purpose in relation to employment, remuneration and conditions of employment. This important area of EU law would be infringed where an organisation in one of the Member States has a requirement that its employees shall be nationals of that Member State, for example. Any national of a Member State excluded from employment by such an organisation could well claim a legal right to challenge the legality of the organisation's employment restriction as being contrary to Article 48 of the Treaty of Rome. There are exceptions to Article 48, and one EU Directive states that it does not apply in various situations, eg where a person is expelled from a Member State and the expulsion is referable to his personal conduct in relation to matters of public policy, public security or public health. Consequently, a deportation order served by the Home Secretary against a national of a Member State under his powers in the Immigration Act 1971 will be perfectly lawful as long as it can be justified under any of the exceptions to Article 48. If the order was challenged in the High Court, it would be found to be *ultra vires* as contrary to Article 48 if one or more of the exceptions could not be established. The Immigration Act 1988 now ensures that domestic immigration law is fully consistent with EU law. This is achieved through a statement in the Act that a person shall not require consent to enter or remain in the UK where he has an entitlement to do so by virtue of an enforceable Union right.

7.2.3 Administrative law, administrative powers and EU law

From the previous section it can be seen that an exercise of statutory administrative powers may be subject to the limitations of EU law. Where statutory administrative powers are conferred on any administrative agency and are exercisable for purposes which overlap with EU law then those powers must be exercised consistently with EU law. An example from the Immigration Act and Article 48 was given in the previous section and in one of the leading cases, *van Duyn v Home Office* (1977), the issue related to those immigration powers which permit an immigration officer to refuse entry to the UK. Miss van Duyn was a member of the Church of Scientology which was regarded by the UK government as being an undesirable organisation, for a number of reasons. The government's attitude to the Church had been made known publicly as had its intention to take steps to curb its activities. As a Dutch national, ie a national of a Member State of the EU, Miss van Duyn sought to enter the UK in order to take up employment at the Church's college in Sussex. Entry was refused, whereupon Miss van Duyn applied to the High Court for a declaration that she was lawfully entitled to enter the UK to take up employment with the Church. Following a referral on a matter of interpretation to the European Court of Justice by virtue of Article 177 which was alluded to in the previous section, the basis of the domestic court's decision to refuse to grant the declaration was that Miss van Duyn's exclusion came within the 'public policy' exception to the legal rights conferred by Article 48. As a result, a government of any Member State can lawfully discriminate against the nationals of another Member State in relation to Article 48, even though the same action might not be taken lawfully against one of its own nationals. Another example goes back to what was said in Chapter 6 about public corporations and, in particular, the agricultural marketing boards. It was seen in Chapter 6 that the various agricultural marketing schemes are approved by the Minister of Agriculture and operated by the boards concerned. It was suggested in *Potato Marketing Board v Robertsons* (1983) that the potato marketing scheme was contrary to certain provisions of EU law. The issue arose when the Board sued Robertsons, a registered potato producer, for payment of a levy which was due under the scheme. In answer to Robertsons' claim it was decided by the court that, among other provisions of the Treaty of Rome, the scheme (which provided for quantitative marketing restrictions) did not contravene Article 34 which provides that quantitative restrictions on exports, and all measures having equivalent effect, shall be prohibited between Member States. One of the technical reasons for this part of the decision was that the relevant parts of the scheme did not have as their specific object the restriction of patterns of exports.

A final, more recent example of a case in which it was argued that the exercise of statutory administrative powers was subject to the limitations of EU law was the decision in *R v London Boroughs Transport Committee, ex p Freight Transport Association Ltd* (1991). In this particular case, the applicants, transport associations and operators, sought judicial review of a condition contained in delegated legislation which required the holder of a permit to drive goods vehicles in excess of 16.5 tonnes in restricted areas to minimise the noise emitted by the vehicle's air brake system by the fitting of a noise level suppresser where such a device was capable of being fitted. It was contended on behalf of the applicants that the condition was unlawful since it was, *inter alia*, incompatible with the requirements of two EU directives on vehicle brake devices and sound levels with which their vehicles complied. However, it was held by the House of Lords that the condition was not unlawful since it did not conflict with either of the Directives which were in fact concerned with matters other than the regulation of traffic. Moreover, the condition was lawful under EU law since it reflected the EU's wider policy of seeking to ensure the protection of the environment.

7.3   The Nature of Statutory Administrative Powers

In Part 1 the various administrative agencies were examined together with their various functions. In the remainder of this chapter it will be seen that some generalisations can be made about the nature and characteristics of the powers conferred on these agencies to enable them to perform their various functions. As to the nature of administrative powers, there is a simple distinction between discretionary and non-discretionary powers. This distinction is one which relates to whether an administrative agency has an opportunity to make choices in performing its statutory functions. In general, this opportunity to make discretionary choices is one which goes to ministers of the Crown and local authorities. Both of these are democratically accountable, to Parliament and councils respectively, for a large number of policy-based decisions in relation to functions which require a flexibility or response. Some public corporations, and the so-called nationalised industries in particular, also enjoy a large measure of discretion for the purpose of being able to fulfil an effective commercial or industrial role. However these bodies are only indirectly accountable to Parliament through the minister responsible and the system of Parliamentary Select Committees. Administrative tribunals, on the other hand, are characterised by non-discretionary powers conferred by statute. As was seen in Chapter 5, the 'court-substitute' tribunals usually operate in order to adjudicate some statutory entitlement. In general terms, therefore, as long as any claim, dispute or similar matter can be isolated within the statutory formula by reference to which the tribunal operates, there is no discretion for the tribunal to do anything but deal with it within the terms of the statutory scheme concerned.

7.3.1   The nature of discretionary powers

It often appears that any discretionary powers conferred on a minister of the Crown are wider than those conferred on any other administrative agency. There may well be some substance in this observation, particularly in areas such as national security and economic regulation. As to national security, the Prevention of Terrorism (Temporary Provisions) Act 1989 states that:

> The Secretary of State may exercise the powers conferred on him ... in such way as appears to him expedient to prevent acts of terrorism ...

The Act goes on to confer wide powers on the Home Secretary to make exclusion orders under the Act. As to economic regulation, s 7 of the Industrial Development Act 1982 states that for various purposes such as the promotion of the development or modernisation of an industry:

> [T]he Secretary of State may ... provide financial assistance where, in his opinion –
>
> (a) the financial assistance is likely to provide, maintain or safeguard employment in any part of the assisted areas ...

Each of these examples of discretionary powers indicates that within the broad limits of the statutory powers the Secretary of State responsible enjoys an important flexibility in his choice of action. As long as the particular Secretary of State has some grounds for an opinion under the Act of 1982 and is able to justify the expediency of his use of the powers under the Act of 1989, the law considers that he is acting *intra vires*, that is, within his statutory powers, and will not interfere on the basis that the task being performed is his task, conferred by Parliament. More particularly, the law is concerned only with the question of whether the Secretary of State has strayed beyond the limits of his powers, eg where, in an unlikely event, the powers in the Act of 1989 were to be used to prevent non-violent political acts in the UK. Clearly, it would be difficult and often controversial for the High Court to deal with questions as to whether it was 'expedient' for a Secretary of State to act in order to prevent acts of terrorism or whether the economy of the UK would be benefited by financial assistance to industry. The limits of the doctrine of *ultra vires* in areas like this are dealt with more fully in Chapter 11.

7.4   Characteristics of Administrative Powers

Administrative powers are characterised by many different forms, according to a variety of different requirements, such as the need to allocate scarce financial resources for the fulfilment of important national needs and the need to control some potentially dangerous activity. Although it is not an easy task to characterise and categorise the various forms of administrative powers, six categories seem to provide an effective picture of the way in which statute confers these powers:

(1) the initiation of administrative action;

(2) licensing;

(3) financial regulation;

(4) contractual regulation;

(5) regulation by the criminal law; and

(6) disciplinary regulation.

While it is recognised that there may be overlaps between these categories, each one will be examined in turn.

7.4.1   The initiation of administrative action

The initiation of administrative action is usually the responsibility of democratically accountable administrative agencies acting under the umbrella of statutory discretionary powers. The initiation of administrative action is most clearly associated with central government departments, as where the Home Secretary decides to exclude a person from the UK under the Immigration Act on the ground that his presence is not conducive to the public good. While this example relates to a single, individual case, there are many instances where all sorts of large, important schemes can be initiated under various statutory powers such as the Industrial Development Act 1982, s 7 of which was mentioned earlier in the present chapter. The initiation of administrative action often occurs against a background of policy for which a minister is responsible to Parliament.

In the case of local government, the initiation of administrative action can be illustrated by reference to the various statutory powers which permit the compulsory purchase of land for all sorts of different purposes. Although some local authorities may be reluctant, as a matter of policy, to allow a use of these powers, where they are used, any order made will be subject to confirmation by the appropriate minister, usually the Secretary of State for the Environment. Such a power to make a compulsory purchase order is strictly a legislative function, not an administrative function, but there are many other examples of purely administrative action being initiated by local authorities, eg where a local authority serves a repair notice in respect of a dwelling house which is unfit for human habitation but repairable at reasonable expense, under the power conferred by s 189 of the Housing Act 1985.

7.4.2   Licensing

Licences are required for a wide variety of different purposes. Licensing therefore represents one of the most important types of administrative action. The various licensing agencies usually operate under discretionary powers which should permit effective control of the activities concerned. Many such activities are prohibited by statute which goes on to provide that they may be permitted where a licence or consent is granted by the particular licensing agency. Liquor licensing by magistrates is one of the better-known examples. One of the more important licensing functions relates to town and country planning where the Town and Country Planning Act 1990 states that the development of land requires planning permission, that is, a 'land use licence'. Local authorities have many other licensing functions in addition, covering activities such as the operation of pleasure boats and lotteries, and the use of firearms. Bodies such as the Civil Aviation Authority may undertake relatively limited licensing functions compared with central government. Central government is usually concerned with licensing in so far as any proscribed activity has some broad, national significance, as in the case of industrial development certificates mentioned in Part 1.

7.4.3   Financial regulation

Administrative powers conferred in this area are usually related to central government statutory control of local authorities' finances and to other grant-making activities undertaken by all types of administrative agency. The Housing Corporation, for example, distributes grants to housing associations. In the same general area, local authorities are responsible for the payment of housing renovation grants for the repair and improvement of substandard housing. A third example comes from the Water Industry Act 1991 and its mechanisms for controlling the prices that can be charged for water supply by the privatised water companies.

7.4.4   Contractual regulation

This area of administrative action provides what is often effective regulation from the point of view of the administrative agency although it is a fundamental legal restriction that any such agency cannot extend its statutory powers by the use of contractual powers. It was seen in Chapter 6 that the Independent Television Commission undertakes its statutory functions primarily by reference to the contracts made with companies providing programmes by virtue of the Broadcasting Act 1990. One of the most far-reaching statutory powers permitting the making of contracts appears in the Town and Country Planning Act 1990 and some related statutory provisions. These powers permit local planning authorities to make planning agreements with developers, usually in conjunction with grants of planning permission. These contractual agreements allow a far more effective, detailed control of development than is normally available through the conventional 'land use licence' comprising a planning permission and any conditions attached to it.

7.4.5 Regulation by the criminal law

The criminal law tends to be used as a means of regulation where an activity has potentially serious consequences. Some of the best examples occur in the general context of pollution. Section 1 of the Clean Air Act 1993, for example, stipulates that it is a criminal offence to emit dark smoke from the chimney of any building. The law operates against the occupier of the building, the categories of which include dwelling houses in addition to the more obvious industrial buildings. There are some exceptions to the coverage of the criminal law in this area, as well as certain defences, eg that the failure of a furnace was not reasonably foreseeable. The law is enforced by local authorities in the districts and the Clean Air Act prescribes a maximum fine in respect of dark smoke emitted from a private dwelling house and a maximum fine in respect of any other building. Local authorities tend to use the criminal law in this and similar areas as a last resort, preferring to persuade occupiers to comply with the law voluntarily.

In other areas, the criminal law may be used as a means of regulation but less immediately than in the case of the Clean Air Act and similar statutes. The Town and Country Planning Act, for example, empowers a local planning authority to serve an enforcement notice requiring development without or in breach of planning permission to be discontinued. Only where the requirements of the notice are not complied with is there an opportunity for the authority to prosecute the offender in the magistrates' court.

7.4.6   Disciplinary regulation

This variety of regulation usually occurs within non-statutory domestic organisations such as trade unions, clubs, societies and professional organisations. Such organisations are of interest in administrative law particularly where the rules of natural justice are concerned. As far as statutory administrative agencies are concerned, disciplinary regulation is a matter of interest in two particular areas: the police and the agricultural marketing boards. In both areas there is some statutory regulation of discipline according to the respective requirements of these organisations which are therefore amenable to the doctrine of *ultra vires*.

8 The Sources of Administrative Powers

8.1 The Range of Administrative Powers

It was seen at the beginning of Chapter 7 that most administrative powers have their source in legislation, ie they are statutory powers. As a general rule it can be said that such powers must have the force of law because they affect, or may affect, the rights of individuals or organisations. The impact of this general rule is seen in another dimension in the fundamental rule of law that where an administrative agency acts beyond or outside its statutory powers, the resulting action is regarded as being *ultra vires*, that is, no action at all in law. The general nature of this fundamental source of administrative powers will be outlined later in this chapter.

Reference has been made to the common law in Chapter 7. The common law is clearly a secondary though important source of administrative powers. As was seen in Chapter 7, the courts' interpretation of the statutory powers provide valuable guidance for many administrative agencies. Many of the rules of law developed by the courts in the context of the doctrine of *ultra vires* occur in Part 3 where it will be seen that it is the task of the courts to interpret and apply Parliament's intentions in relation to the statutory powers governing the functions of the administrative agencies. As these rules are developed under the umbrella of the doctrine of *ultra vires*, so they become an important influence in relation to much administrative action.

While Part 3 deals with the common law and the doctrine of *ultra vires*, the present chapter deals also with EU law, not so much as a source of administrative powers but rather as a source of law and legal restrictions in relation to the functions and activities of administrative agencies as they fall within the objectives of the Union.

Finally, reference should be made to the prerogative as a source of administrative powers. It was seen in Chapter 1 that it is the government of the day which exercises the Crown's remaining prerogative powers. In many (though not all) instances, prerogative powers do not impinge directly on the individual's rights, eg in the broader regulation of government monetary and economic policy. Consequently, in the absence of any statutory regulation, there appears to be some considerable flexibility of action available to the government within what is an ill-defined source of administrative powers. It is only on the rare occasion that a use of powers said to have their source in the prerogative may come under the scrutiny of the courts. In these circumstances the court may wield considerable influence in terms of being able to dictate where prerogative regulation ends and legal regulation begins and in being able to determine whether an exercise of such powers is justiciable.

It was said at the outset of this chapter that most administrative powers have their source in legislation as statutory powers. Accordingly, the remainder of this chapter is taken up with an examination of such powers and the other major source – EU law.

8.2 Legislation

Any government will use its (albeit temporary) control of Parliament to legislate measures in fulfilment of its various policies. Such legislation may, for example, set out a statutory scheme, its substantive and procedural requirements and the nature of any relationship between the administrative agency dealing with the scheme and the minister responsible.

8.2.1 The advantages and disadvantages of legislation

In a modern, complex society there is often a need for a precise definition of the law as it governs administrative powers and their implementation. It is often said that the common law has developed from 'accidents of litigation' between individuals and organisations, so that this area of the law is clearly unsuited for the provision of precisely defined, complex schemes governing areas like the social security system. However, even the major legislation like the Social Security and Housing Acts are subject to some limit on the amount of detail that can be incorporated. It is for this reason that many such Acts contain a power conferred on the minister responsible to make delegated, or subordinate, legislation specifying details for the operation of the statutory scheme. Most legislation operates in advance: exceptionally, a statute may be retrospective and operate against events in the past, eg creating or removing legal liability. One of the most widely recognised examples of a piece of retrospective legislation is the War Damage Act 1965 which was passed in order to abolish rights to compensation arising under the common law where the property of an individual or company had been damaged or destroyed on the authority of the Crown during or in the contemplation of the outbreak of war. This very brief Act was passed solely for the purpose of overruling the decision of the Privy Council in *Burmah Oil Co v Lord Advocate* (1965) where such a right to compensation had been held to exist. Thus this episode neatly demonstrates the ultimate authority that Parliament is capable of asserting over the courts. However, the questionable constitutional propriety of legislating retrospectively ensures that a 'court will not ascribe retrospective effect to new laws affecting rights unless by express words or necessary implication it appears that such was the intention of the legislature' (*per* Willes J in *Phillips v Eyre* (1870)).

The recent decision of the House of Lords in *Plewa v Chief Adjudication Officer* (1994) involved a consideration of s 53 of the Social Security Act 1986 and whether the provision in question had retrospective effect. Section 53, prior to its repeal by the Social Security (Consequential Provisions) Act 1992, enabled the Secretary of State to recover overpayment of both means tested and non-means tested benefits from either the recipients or from third parties. As such, it replaced s 119 of the Social Security Act 1975, which applied to non-means tested benefits, and s 20 of the Supplementary Benefits Act 1976 which applied to means tested benefits. The question for the House of Lords was thus whether overpayment of benefit made prior to the date on which s 53 came into force could be recovered under the 1986 Act, or alternatively, whether recovery would have to be in accordance with the earlier statutory provisions. During the course of the leading judgment, Lord Woolf stated with approval the words of Lord Brightman in the Privy Council decision in *Yew Bon Tew v Kenderaan Bas Mara* (1982) where his Lordship observed that:

> ... there is at common law a *prima facie* rule of construction that a statute should not be interpreted retrospectively so as to impair an existing right or obligation unless that result is unavoidable on the language used. A statute is retrospective if it takes away or impairs a vested right acquired under existing laws, or creates a new obligation, or imposes a new duty, or attaches a new disability, in regard to events already past.

Examining the relevant statutory provisions in the light of the Interpretation Act 1978, a unanimous House of Lords held that since s 53 created a new obligation to make repayment where overpayment had occurred due to the recipient's misrepresentation or failure to disclose relevant information, it therefore followed that the presumption against retrospectively applied in this case. It would be unfair to hold otherwise especially since s 53 imposed potential liability on a third party for making a misrepresentation or failing to disclose information where such liability had not been capable of arising under the old statutory machinery relating to non-means tested benefits. The effect of this House of Lords decision is to overrule the earlier decision in *Secretary of State for Social Services v Tunnicliffe* (1991) where the Court of Appeal held that the new regime under s 53 rather than the old statutory regime applied in relation to the recovery of overpayment of benefits. In addition, *Plewa* emphasises the general reluctance on the part of the judiciary to accord statutory provisions retrospective effect unless it is clear that that was what Parliament intended at the time of enactment.

Most legislation is complex and not easily understood (even by lawyers on some occasions!). This difficulty is eased on those occasions when various items of legislation are consolidated in one Act. The Merchant Shipping Act 1995, for example, consolidated a great many enactments relating to Merchant Shipping including the Merchant Shipping Act 1894. However, it is not always the case that a consolidating enactment is able to tidy up the statute book quite as thoroughly as was originally intended. This was certainly the case with regard to the predecessor of the Town and Country Planning Act 1990, the 1971 Town and Country Planning Act which consolidated the Town and Country Planning Acts of 1962 and 1968. Unfortunately, it was not long before the legislation was being amended once again in the Town and Country Planning (Amendment) Act 1972, the Local Government Act 1972 and various other Acts. Although it is true to say that the central scheme of the law may well remain the same in such an event, there are considerable difficulties in having to look at other Acts to find answers to detailed questions where the law has been modified and amended or even repealed in some respects. In some other countries this problem is solved by amending the principal Act as soon as changes are legislated, so that there is no need to go beyond that Act.

8.2.2 The Renton Committee on the Preparation of Legislation

This Committee reported in 1974 and made four broad criticisms of legislation. First, it was said that the language of legislation was obscure and complex, its meaning elusive and its effect uncertain. Secondly, legislation is subject to over-elaboration, often in order to avoid uncertainty. Thirdly, the internal structure of legislation is illogical. Finally, and returning to the point canvassed at the end of the previous section, existing legislation is not amended by reference to new legislative provision.

8.2.3 The categories of legislation

Before a Bill can become an Act of Parliament, it requires the approval of Parliament and the Royal Assent. Bills fall into four categories:

(1) Public Bills;

(2) Private Bills;

(3) Hybrid Bills; and

(4) Private Members' Bills.

Most administrative powers conferred on the administrative agencies originate in Public Bills which become Public Acts of Parliament, such as the Education Act 1944, the Industrial Development Act 1982 and the Housing Act 1985, to name but three. As Public Acts, each of these statutes has effected a change in the general law in pursuance of a government's public policy. Private Bills, on the other hand, deal with the position of some individual, organisation or group of individuals on a matter of their private, personal or local interest. Hybrid Bills fall between Public and Private Bills because, as Public Bills, they nevertheless deal with some private interest, for which reason they are subject to special legislative procedures. As to the procedural differences between the Public and the Private Bill, *Erskine May*, the authoritative source on Parliamentary procedure states that:

[T]he essential difference in procedure ... is that, whereas a public bill is either presented direct to the House or introduced on motion by a Member of Parliament, a private bill is solicited by parties who are interested in promoting it ...

The Private Members' Bills, as their name suggests, are introduced by private members and can deal with any matter except the authorisation of expenditure. The Abortion Act of 1967, for example, was the result of a Private Members' Bill since it was felt at the time, and indeed it remains the case today, that abortion is so sensitive a matter of conscience for an individual MP that it would be inappropriate for the issue to form part of a government's legislative programme.

8.2.4   The legislative procedure for Public Bills

When a Bill has been drafted, it is presented to Parliament for a first reading. Thereafter, the second reading sees a discussion of the broad principles and structure of the proposed legislation. Some Bills will be regarded as non-controversial Bills while others will be unopposed. In the case of these Bills, where time on the floor of the House is short, they will be referred to a Second Reading Committee of the House. Following the second reading, the Bill is referred to a Standing Committee for what is appropriately described as the 'committee stage'. This is followed by the report stage where there is a report to the House on the Bill and any amendments to it. The third reading is usually a formality after the report stage and precedes reference of the Bill to the House of Lords where procedures are broadly similar to those in the House of Commons. Any amendments made in the House of Lords will be returned to the House of Commons. Subject to some restrictions, Bills can be and occasionally are introduced in the House of Lords. Whatever the sequence, following a Bill's approval by both Houses, it goes for the Royal Assent whereupon it has the force of law, although the new Act or parts of it may not come into force until an order (an item of delegated legislation) is made by the minister responsible and approved by Parliament.

An example of this procedure in action is the legislation of the Control of Pollution Act 1974 which was foreshadowed in the Queen's Speech on 12 March 1974 anticipating measures for 'the protection and improvement of the environment'. The Control of Pollution Bill started its passage in the House of Lords with the first reading on 30 April 1974 and a second reading on 7 May. Thereafter, the Bill went to a Committee of the whole House, an alternative to a Standing Committee and usually an indication of a Bill's importance, bearing in mind that all members can participate in the deliberations. The committee stage took place on 14 and 16 May, followed by the report stage and third reading on 21 May. The Bill went to the House of Commons on 17 June for a second reading and reference to a Standing Committee. The report stage and third reading were dealt with on 19 July. The Bill went back to the House of Lords subject to amendments made by the House of Commons. The amendments were dealt with on 25 July whereupon the Bill was agreed and received Royal Assent on 31 July. The Bill was introduced in the House of Lords as 'a development of existing legislation in the waste disposal, water pollution, noise and air pollution fields'. As such, it received considerable support from the Opposition which undoubtedly speeded its progress through Parliament. The Act comprised 109 sections in six parts and contained four schedules. Many provisions in the Act operate only when a commencement order is made by the Secretary of State for the Environment. In large part this seems to be explained by the cost of implementing the statutory provisions for monitoring and enforcing the requirements for solid waste disposal, among others. Part 2 of the Act, for example, was introduced in phases over a period of many years.

8.2.5 The legislative procedure for Private Bills

The initial stages of the procedure require the promoter to give public notice of the Bill. A petition is then presented for permission to introduce the Bill, copies of which have to be deposited by 27 November in each Parliamentary session. The Bill is scrutinised for compliance with various Parliamentary formalities, after which it is decided whether the Bill should proceed. This initial stage is followed by a second reading when the broad principles of the Bill are examined. Thereafter, one of the most important stages occurs when the Bill is subject to the committee stage where much depends on whether the Bill is opposed or unopposed. Where there is no opposition or objection to the Bill the promoter is normally obliged to demonstrate formally that the Bill is an expedient measure in the circumstances. An opposed Bill is examined by an *ad hoc* committee before which the promoter and objectors are represented by lawyers in most cases. Although opponents may register their various objections, the promoter may challenge their *locus standi*, that is, their status or standing to raise objections, eg because of remoteness of their interest in a project to be authorised if the Bill is approved. The atmosphere at this committee stage is essentially judicial with the committee having to make decisions on preliminary points like *locus standi*, and having to hear the evidence and witnesses presented by both sides to the argument and the necessary examination and cross-examination. This committee stage procedure will apply also to a Bill which, although regarded initially as unopposed, is to be treated as an opposed Bill by virtue of its importance or controversial nature. Following this committee stage in the House of Lords, a Private Bill goes for a third reading whereas in the House of Commons there is a report stage unless there have been no amendments at the committee stage. Thereafter, a Bill will go for Royal Assent.

8.2.6 The status of Private Bills

Although a Bill is introduced as a Private Bill, there may be factors which indicate that it should be dealt with as a Public Bill. These factors are set out in *Erskine May* and are concerned with whether:

111

(1) public policy is affected;

(2) the proposal is to repeal or amend Public Acts of Parliament;

(3) public matters are at the heart of the Bill;

(4) the Bill's provisions apply to a large area and affect a multiplicity of interests; and

(5) safeguards exist to deal with these foregoing matters.

At the outset it is the Department of the Environment which undertakes the examination of most Private Bills, usually by reference to a strong presumption that private, local powers are not necessary. This element of control prior to presentation is reinforced by Standing Orders in Parliament, one of which calls on a committee dealing with a local authority Private Bill to consider, among other things, 'whether the Bill gives powers relating to police, sanitary or other local government matters in conflict with, deviation from, or excess of, the provisions or powers of the general law'. Further control appears in the Local Government Act 1972, s 70 of which prevents the promotion of a Private Bill for the purpose of changing a local government area, its status or electoral arrangements.

8.2.7 The scope of Private Acts

Even though the promoters have succeeded in persuading Parliament that additional statutory provision is required through a Private Act, the courts still insist that the statutory provisions are strictly interpreted against those promoters. In order words, any ambiguity will not be interpreted in the promoter's favour. The promotion of such legislation is not restricted to local authorities: various other public corporations and private organisations seek powers by means of Private Acts. Indeed, it appears that this method of acquiring powers is less popular than it used to be in the case of local authorities: in recent years, local authorities have promoted no more than about 30–40% of all Private Bills. This matter will be taken up again in the next section of the chapter. It is of more immediate interest to give some examples of the Private Acts which have found their way to the statute book. First, a Private Act obtained by a private company, Gulf Oil Refining Ltd. The Act – the Gulf Oil Refining Act 1965 – authorised the construction and operation of an oil refinery at Milford Haven, in Dyfed. The second example comes from one of the many Private Local Acts promoted by local authorities over the years. The Act – the Leicestershire County Council Act 1970 – contains a number of provisions of local interest. One such provision, in s 6, empowers the county council to enter into legally binding agreements with developers of land for a variety of purposes such as the phasing of any development of the land and the maintenance of open spaces. As such, this provision adds to broader powers in Public Acts, but it has been the case that local authorities have obtained Private Local Act powers to undertake functions normally outside their competence or to enlarge the scope of existing functions, or even to provide powers to deal with some matter or characteristic which is peculiar to their areas, eg in the area of support for industrial development. The county authorities have usually promoted Private Local Bills under the statutory powers given for this purpose by s 239 of the Local Government Act 1972, at the same time accommodating the requirements of constituent district authorities.

One final point concerns those occasions when some inconsistency may arise as between a Private and Public Act provision. Section 182 of the Housing Act 1985, for example, states that the Secretary of State may by order repeal or amend any provision of a Local Act passed before the Act where it appears to him that the provision is inconsistent with any provision of the Act.

8.2.8 Private Local Acts and reorganisation of local government

There was a reorganisation of local government in 1974 by virtue of the Local Government Act 1972. One of the most obvious alterations related to the boundaries of the local authority areas so that for present purposes the crucial question was whether Private Local Acts should continue to apply in the redrawn areas or whether the area of their application should be amended. Section 262 of the Local Government Act appears to adopt the former solution, providing as it does that Private Local Acts in force on 1 April 1974 shall remain in force unless subject to an order made by the Secretary of State extending the Act to the whole of a new, redrawn local authority area. The Local Government Act also required that Local Acts in the non-metropolitan areas cease to be operative at the end of 1986. Local authorities are now obliged to consider the status and importance of their Local Acts and, where necessary, prepare new legislation for four purposes, covering:

(1) matters of general concern where the general law may not be sufficiently extensive;

(2) local matters;

(3) the updating of legislation governing the functions of local undertakings such as transport; and

(4) any further requirements requiring statutory authorisation.

With the advent of these important transitional provisions, local authorities may be seen to rely less and less on the Private Local Acts for the acquisition of their powers. Instead, there may be an increasing reliance on the regular Local Government (Miscellaneous Provisions) Acts which pass through Parliament, and the various adoptive Acts by which some areas of law apply in a local authority area only after a council's formal adoption of provisions from such Acts.

8.2.9 Miscellaneous Provisions Acts and Adoptive Acts

In one of the most recent Local Government (Miscellaneous Provisions) Acts one finds a considerable range of topics, including facilities for the control of the sale of food by hawkers, take-away food shops and the control of acupuncture, tattooing, ear-piercing and electrolysis. This Act of 1982 deals also with the control of 'sex establishments', defined to include sex cinemas and sex shops. In this context the Act of 1982 is an adoptive Act since a local authority is at liberty to decide whether the statutory provisions are to apply in its area. If this part of the Act is to apply to the area of a local authority then it is a requirement that any person wishing to use premises as a sex establishment should have a licence for that purpose from the local authority. The local licensing authority is empowered to refuse applications on certain fixed grounds and any adverse decision is subject to an appeal to a magistrates' court. Failure to comply with the licensing provisions is a criminal offence.

8.2.10 Provisional Orders

These orders are a means of avoiding the sometimes long-winded procedures for Private Bills. In practice, these orders tend to be used for the removal of Private Local Acts from the statute book by virtue of s 262 of the Local Government Act, dealt with previously. A local authority is required to apply to the appropriate minister for a Provisional Order, giving public notice of the application. If any objections to the proposed Order arise, they will be heard at a public inquiry convened by the minister, after which a decision is made whether to make an order. If it is decided to make an Order, a Provisional Order Confirmation Bill is presented to Parliament by the minister. Where the Bill is opposed in Parliament it will be dealt with as though it was a Private Bill.

8.2.11 Special Procedure Orders

These orders are governed by the Statutory Orders (Special Procedure) Act 1945 to 1965 and are subject to a special Parliamentary procedure. Once again, as with Provisional Orders, a local authority makes an application to the minister for the order. With the minister's agreement, the proposal is publicised and any objections are dealt with by a public inquiry. Where the minister decides to make the order it is laid before Parliament. Thereafter, objectors may petition Parliament and a joint committee of both Houses will deal with objections so made by persons with sufficient *locus standi*. Where the order is not approved by Parliament its contents can acquire the force of law only through an Act of Parliament. In practice there are very few objections so that the procedures are not as cumbersome as they might at first appear.

8.3 Delegated Legislation

Much of what has been said in this chapter so far has related to what is often referred to as 'primary' legislation, that is, Acts of Parliament. However, from time to time reference has been made to 'delegated legislation' which is a process by which different types of law are made under the authority and within the terms of an Act of Parliament. Accordingly, the Act delegates this law-making function to the administrative agency such as the appropriate minister or a local authority, usually in those cases where the Act itself cannot contain a large amount of detail or where some flexibility of response is required in order to deal with unforeseen contingencies. From what has been said, then, it can be appreciated that delegated legislation is sometimes referred to as 'subordinate' or 'secondary' legislation, although for the purpose of this chapter references will be to delegated legislation.

8.3.1 Primary and delegated legislation in action

Section 83 of the Housing Act 1985 states that the county court shall not entertain proceedings by a local authority for possession of a council house unless the authority has served a notice on the tenant. The section goes on to state that a notice must be in a form prescribed by regulations made by the Secretary of State and must specify the ground, eg non-payment of rent, on which the court will be asked to make a possession order as well as giving particulars of that ground. Elsewhere the Act states that: 'Any power of the Secretary of State to make an order or regulations under this Act shall be exercisable by statutory instrument'. The regulations actually made are called the Secure Tenancies (Notices) Regulations 1987.

The relationship between primary and delegated legislation was neatly demonstrated in *Kent County Council v Peter Thompson Poultry* (1989) where the respondent company was charged with marketing poultry that had an excess water content contrary to regs 11(1) and (2)(a) of the Poultry Meat (Water Content) Regulations 1984. At first instance, the respondents had been acquitted on account of the fact that the information was out of time since the statutory time limit of two months from the date on which the sample was taken, as specified by s 95(2)(b) of the Food Act 1984, had in fact expired. It was argued on appeal by the prosecutor that the regulations amounted to a self-contained code independent from the provisions of the 1984 Act and that accordingly, the time limit specified in the statute was irrelevant to a prosecution under the regulations. However, this argument was rejected by the High Court. The regulations were not a self-contained code. It was necessary for the Act and the regulations to be read in conjunction with one another. Therefore, the magistrates had been right to apply the provisions of s 95 of the 1984 Act to the present case with the consequence that the information failed since it had been laid out of time.

8.3.2   Statutory instruments

In any description of delegated legislation there has to be a reference to statutory instructions. In the example above, the wording of the 1985 Housing Act suggests that there is some importance attached to the term 'statutory instrument'. The status and importance of the statutory instrument emerges from the Statutory Instruments Act 1946. Where, after the passing of this Act, any Act empowers Her Majesty in Council (by Order in Council) or a minister of the Crown (by statutory instrument) to make, confirm or approve orders, rules, regulations or other delegated legislation, any resulting document is referred to as a 'statutory instrument' to which the provisions of the Act of 1946 applies. The Act itself contains provisions for the numbering, printing, publishing and laying before Parliament of statutory instruments: particularly important safeguards, bearing in mind the amount and complexity of delegated legislation which is generated each year.

8.3.3   The classification of delegated legislation

There are three items of delegated legislation which are of particular interest to local authorities, namely, bylaws, compulsory purchase orders and standing orders. These items will be described in the following sections of this chapter. Most other delegated legislation comes within the Statutory Instruments Act under the following categories: (a) regulations, (b) rules, and (c) orders. Regulations are concerned with the substantive detail of the law, as in the case of the Secure Tenancies (Notices) Regulations mentioned previously. The regulations require any notice served on a secure council tenant to state that the council is required to obtain a court order before a tenant can be evicted, and that he can obtain advice from a Citizen's Advice Bureau, Housing Aid Centre, Law Centre, or solicitor. Rules are concerned with procedural requirements, as was seen in Chapter 3 where reference was made to the Town and Country Planning (Inquiries Procedure) Rules 1992. Orders are divided into two categories: prerogative orders and statutory orders. Prerogative orders are not statutory instruments and can be used only to the limits of the Crown's prerogative powers. Statutory orders are used for a variety of purposes but particularly for the purpose of bringing new statutory and certain EU legal provisions into force. Where just one department of government is affected, it is usually the minister responsible who is empowered to make the order. On the other hand, where a number of departments or governmental functions are affected, it is usually the practice that the power to make the order will be conferred on Her Majesty in Council.

One further category should be mentioned here: directions. It has been seen previously that there are various statutory powers which allow a minister to give directions to various administrative agencies which are directly or indirectly within his responsibilities. In some instances a direction must be given by means of a statutory instrument as was the case in s 4 of the Water Act 1973 by which the Secretary of State for the Environment was empowered to give directions to the National Water Council requiring that Council to discontinue any of its activities. On the other hand, any direction to the Council concerning national water policy was not subject to the same requirement.

8.3.4 Bylaws

Although various administrative agencies are empowered by statute to make bylaws, these items of delegated legislation are more often associated with local authorities. Their outstanding characteristic is that they apply in a specific area. Section 235 of the Local Government Act 1972 (as amended) sets out the general power which permits the making of most bylaws: 'The council of a district the council of a principal area in Wales and the council of a London borough may make bylaws for the good rule and government of the whole or any part of the district principal area or borough ... and for the prevention and suppression of nuisances therein'. The section goes on to say that the confirming authority for a bylaw is the Secretary of State for the Environment, representing an important measure of control in this process of creating delegated legislation. In practice model bylaws are maintained and it is highly unlikely that a local authority bylaw would be confirmed where it did not adhere to any such model. Bylaws are essentially local laws which regulate some unique local situation not already covered by some other form of statutory provision and may be enforced through the imposition of a fine by a court as a result of criminal prosecution. The Local Government Act stipulates the procedures to be observed in the making of a bylaw, eg the need to make a copy of the proposed bylaw available for public inspection for at least one month before seeking confirmation. Because bylaws are subject to confirmation and usually adhere to model bylaws, it is very unusual to find that a bylaw has been struck down by a court as being legally invalid. Nevertheless, the validity of a bylaw can be challenged in two ways, either:

(1) directly, eg through an application for a declaration in the High Court that a bylaw is *ultra vires* the empowering provision in the primary legislation, ie the Act of Parliament allegedly authorising the bylaw; or

(2) indirectly, usually where a person is prosecuted for a breach of a bylaw whereupon he argues that there can be no conviction for breach of a bylaw which is legally invalid: *R v Crown Court at Reading, ex p Hutchinson* (1988).

Whatever the form of challenge, there are various grounds on which the legal validity of a bylaw may be challenged:

(1) *ultra vires*, as previously indicated;

(2) uncertainty;

(3) inconsistency with the general law; and

(4) unreasonableness.

As to a challenge based on *ultra vires*, the Act in *R v Wood* (1855) required occupiers of premises to remove dust, ashes, rubbish, filth, manure, dung and soil. The bylaw in this case was found to be *ultra vires* in requiring occupiers to move any snow from the footpaths adjacent to their premises. The Divisional Court has prescribed an interesting but controversial approach to situations where bylaws are found to be *ultra vires*. If a court is modifying or severing the affected part of a bylaw it is altering or severing a measure created under statutory powers. The court suggested that this should be done only where it is clear that this approach is the one that would have been taken had the bylaw maker known of the limitation. In the present case – *DPP v Hutchinson* (1988) – it was found that, had the bylaws been drafted within the powers of the enabling Act, a conviction would still have resulted. Arguably, this approach provides a dangerous blurring of the fundamental distinction between the functions of the courts and those of the law-makers. On appeal (*DPP v Hutchinson* (1990)) the House of Lords reversed the earlier decision of the Divisional Court by holding that parts of the relevant bylaws were *ultra vires* and that it was not possible to sever the remainder therefrom. Their Lordships were anxious to stress that as a basic principle, an *ultra vires* enactment such as a bylaw is void *ab initio* and thus of no legal effect whatsoever. However, the so-called 'blue pencil test' as severing is sometimes known, represents a concession to practicality and is therefore acceptable provided that the courts do not in effect legislate by altering the original meaning of the enactment. The second ground of challenge – uncertainty – occurred in *Staden v Tarjanyi* (1980) where the bylaw prohibited any person using a park to 'take off, fly or land any glider'. The defendant in criminal proceedings for an alleged breach of the bylaw was a hang-gliding enthusiast who had twice flown over the park in his hang-glider. It was decided by the court that he should not be convicted because the bylaw was uncertain in failing to explain how and in what respect a hang-glider could act in breach of the bylaw and in failing to set a lower limit below which a hang-glider should not fly. Inconsistency with the general law, the third ground for challenge, occurred in *Powell v May* (1946) where the bylaw prohibited betting 'in a public place' when two other Public General Acts permitted such activities. In connection with a challenge based on unreasonableness, in the leading case of *Kruse v Johnson* (1898) the bylaw in question was found not to be unreasonable in prohibiting any person 'playing music or singing in any place within fifty yards of any dwelling house after being requested to desist'. The court set down four tests for the unreasonableness of a bylaw where it is:

(1) partial and unequal in its operation as between different classes, eg where controls are imposed on members of sporting clubs for a purpose totally unconnected with their social and sporting activities;

(2) manifestly unjust, eg in imposing a heavier obligation on a person than is reasonably justified;

(3) made in bad faith, eg where the motive is clearly contrary to the need for 'the good rule and government' of an area; and

(4) oppressive or involves gratuitous interference with the rights of a person subject to the bylaw, eg where the privacy of the individual is subject to unjustified interference.

In the recent case *Bugg v DPP* (1993), which, like *DPP v Hutchinson* concerned bylaws made under the Military Lands Act 1892, the High Court addressed the issue as to the legal grounds on which bylaws may be the subject of challenge before a court during the course of criminal proceedings. The court drew a distinction between bylaws which were substantively invalid, that is to say those which were *ultra vires* or patently unreasonable, and, those bylaws which are procedurally invalid because of non-compliance with a procedural requirement in the actual making of the bylaw, eg where there has been a failure to consult. The distinction is an important one since in criminal proceedings for the alleged contravention of a bylaw, it would seem possible to raise the substantive invalidity of the bylaw as a defence whereas it would not be possible to do likewise in relation to the procedural invalidity of the bylaw. The reason for this relates to the jurisdiction of the court. Whilst a court in criminal proceedings would be able to determine the *vires* of a bylaw simply by reference to the terms of the primary and delegated legislation, to suggest that a bylaw is procedurally invalid would require examination of evidence from the body responsible for making the bylaw. This is not possible where that body is not party to the criminal proceedings. Thus it would seem that so far as procedural invalidity is concerned, the correct approach is to regard bylaws as legally valid until they have been set aside by a court with the jurisdiction to do so.

8.3.5   Compulsory purchase orders

Although they serve distinctly different purposes, as another item of delegated legislation, the compulsory purchase order is very similar to the bylaw with regard to the process by which an order attains the force of law. Many Acts of Parliament contain statutory powers which permit local authorities and, to a lesser extent, other administrative agencies to make compulsory purchase orders for the acquisition of land. Once made an order only becomes operative when it has been confirmed by the Secretary of State. The legal validity of an order can be challenged in the High Court on a limited basis, eg that it is *ultra vires* the enabling Act, as will be seen in Chapter 13. The process of compulsory purchase is now very much more streamlined than it used to be, particularly in the 19th century when it was normal practice to seek an Act of Parliament as a means of acquiring land compulsorily. The modern procedures are to be found mainly in the Acquisition of Land Act 1981 whereas the specific powers are in the appropriate Acts such as the Housing Act 1985 authorising the acquisition of land for the provision of housing accommodation by local authorities.

8.3.6 Standing orders

The Local Government Act 1972 authorises a local authority to make standing orders for the regulation of its proceedings and business. Standing orders are concerned with the internal workings of local authorities and will regulate matters like the making of contracts, the operation of the committee structure within the council and the procedure for disclosure of members' pecuniary interests. Standing orders are extremely flexible and can be changed very easily so that any non-compliance would be difficult to enforce in law.

8.3.7 The publication of statutory instruments

Publication of statutory instruments is one of the most important safeguards in a system which permits the making of delegated legislation. Once it is made, the statutory instrument is sent to the Queen's Printer or the Controller of the Stationery Office where it is numbered and printed and arrangements are made for its sale. Some statutory instruments are not subject to the requirement of printing and sale:

(1) 'local' statutory instruments;

(2) statutory instruments of limited application where measures are taken for their publicity;

(3) statutory instruments whose size or nature make it unnecessary or undesirable they should be published, a matter which has to be certified by the appropriate minister; and

(4) statutory instruments whose publication would be contrary to the public interest, as certified by the appropriate minister.

Each year about 2,000 statutory instruments are issued, two-thirds of which are published. The Act of 1946 requires Her Majesty's Stationery Office to publish lists indicating the date of issue of statutory instruments which have been printed and sold: such lists serve as conclusive evidence of the date on which an instrument was first issued. This is a matter of great importance because the Act of 1946 provides a defence for the person prosecuted for non-compliance with the terms of a statutory instrument, to the effect that although made at the date of the offence, the instrument had not been issued. Nevertheless, such a defendant could be convicted of the offence where it is proved that reasonable steps had been taken at the date of the offence to bring the instrument to the attention of the public, anyone likely to be affected or the person charged with the particular offence. The courts have insisted that any statutory instrument should have been adequately publicised to those affected by it. In *Simmonds v Newell* (1953), for example, the court quashed a conviction, even though steps had been taken to publicise the substance of a schedule to a statutory instrument, because there was no evidence before the court of such publicity. By way of contrast, in *R v Sheer Metalcraft Ltd* (1954) the Crown was able to prove to the court's satisfaction that reasonable steps had been taken to notify those affected so that on this occasion the conviction stood.

8.3.8 Parliamentary control of delegated legislation

Delegated legislation normally requires the direct approval of Parliament except in some cases, as with bylaws and compulsory purchase orders previously discussed. On those occasions when such approval is required it is usually the case that delegated legislation is subject either to an affirmative resolution or a negative procedure. In either case, an item of delegated legislation will be laid before Parliament for 40 days. In the case of the affirmative procedure, a resolution is required within 40 days to bring the item of delegated legislation into force, whereas the negative procedure sees the delegated legislation in force after 40 days when no challenge has been made in that time. The more popular procedure is the negative procedure. Parliamentary control also occurs through the facilities for scrutinising delegated legislation for the purpose of making Parliament aware of any areas of concern. In general terms, there is usually some concern about delegated legislation which is not clearly defined and which may give administrative agencies unduly wide powers. There is similar concern where delegated legislation attempts to give a power to levy taxation, to alter or amend statutory provisions, or to preclude the judicial control of any statutory powers and their use. The scrutiny is undertaken principally by the Joint Select Committee on Statutory Instruments, drawn from the House of Commons and the House of Lords, the House of Commons' Select Committee on Statutory Instruments, the House of Commons' Select Committee on European Secondary Legislation and the House of Lords' Select Committee on the European Communities. These committees do on occasions examine draft statutory instruments where drafts are required to be submitted.

One example of the scrutiny process comes from the Eleventh Report of the Joint Committee on Statutory Instruments in the Parliamentary Session 1993 to 1994. The Committee drew attention to the Environmental Protection (Non-Refillable Refrigerant Containers) Regulations 1994. The Committee noted that in one place the Regulations required elucidation and in another, they were defectively drafted giving rise to doubt as to whether they were *intra vires*. Regulation 8(2) creates a number of offences. It appeared to the Committee that reg 8(2) was made under s 140(9) of the Environmental Protection Act 1990 which stipulates that:

> Regulations under this section may provide that a person who contravenes or fails to comply with a specified provision of the regulations or causes or permits another person to contravene or fail to comply with a specified provision of the regulations commits an offence and may prescribe the maximum penalty for the offence.

In the opinion of the Committee, if reg 8(2) was made under this provision certain of the sub-paragraphs of the regulation would appear to be *ultra vires* since the actions described in the sub-paragraphs did not contravene specified provisions of the Regulations. The Department of the Environment contended that the relevant sub-paragraphs were made under a different provision of the Environmental Protection Act, s 140(3)(d), which provides that regulations made under s 140 may:

> ... include such other incidental and supplemental, and such transitional provision, as the Secretary of State considers appropriate.

In the opinion of the Committee, there was 'grave doubt' whether the power to include incidental and supplemental provision could be construed as authorising the creation of criminal offences. This argument was reinforced by the fact that there was already express power to create criminal offences in the same section of the 1990 Act. The appropriate course of action would have been for the Regulations to have contained substantive provisions prohibiting the actions covered by the relevant sub-paragraphs. Accordingly, the Committee reported the instrument for defective drafting giving rise to doubt as to whether the sub-paragraphs were *intra vires*.

8.3.9 Delegated legislation and the courts

While the courts have a crucial role to play in ensuring that delegated legislation is within the limits of the enabling Act, they are in no way able to challenge the validity of primary legislation, that is, Acts of Parliament (*Pickin v British Railways Board* (1974)). So, in the case of delegated legislation, the courts have to ensure that the doctrine of *ultra vires* is adhered to. It is unusual for there to be a direct challenge to the legal validity of delegated legislation, eg through an application to the High Court for a declaration that a regulation is *ultra vires* its enabling Act. However, this is precisely what did happen in *R v Secretary of State for Social Security, ex p Britnell* (1991) where the applicant sought to challenge the *vires* of a regulation made pursuant to s 89(1) of the Social Security Act 1986 which entitled the Secretary of State to make deductions from the applicant's supplementary benefit in order to recover the balance of an overpayment which had been made in respect of unemployment benefit. As in the case of *Plewa v Chief Adjudication Officer* (1994) discussed earlier in this chapter, the House of Lords was required in the present case to examine s 53 of the 1986 Act which provides for the recovery of overpaid benefits. In particular, it was necessary to consider the nature and scope of the regulation which made transitional provisions for the recovery of overpaid benefits in accordance with s 53. A unanimous House of Lords in dismissing the applicant's appeal concluded that the regulation was a transitional provision, that it is to say a legal instrument whose function it is 'to make special provision for the application of legislation to the circumstances which exist at the time when that legislation comes into force.' Such a finding was in part based on the fact that the regulation was expected to be of temporary effect even though it was considered that it may be some time before it would no longer be required. Furthermore, the House of Lords were of the opinion that the power contained in s 89(1) of the 1986 Act to make regulations which modified 'any enactment contained in this or any other Act' was such that the modification made by the regulation in question to s 53 of the same Act was 'not so radical as to be an excess of power'. Accordingly, the regulation was not *ultra vires*.

More usually the issue of the legal validity of delegated legislation will arise indirectly, eg in criminal proceedings for an alleged breach of a regulation. In *Chester v Bateson* (1920) the Defence of the Realm Act 1914 empowered the making of regulations 'for securing the public safety and defence of the realm'. A regulation made under this power enabled the Minister of Munitions to declare an area in which munitions were manufactured a 'special area'. The intended effect was to prevent any person, without the minister's consent, taking proceedings to recover possession of any dwelling house in the area if a munitions worker was living in it and paying rent. It was decided that Parliament had not deliberately deprived the individual of access to the courts but that the regulation was *ultra vires* because it could not be shown to be a necessary or even a reasonable manner of securing the public safety or defence of the realm. In *Attorney General v Wilts United Dairies Ltd* (1921) the New Ministers and Secretaries Act 1916 imposed a duty on the Food Controller to 'regulate the supply and consumption of food in such manner as he thinks best for encouraging the production of food'. The Controller attempted to impose a charge of 2 pence per gallon as a condition of issuing licences for the supply of milk. It was decided by the court that the charges were *ultra vires*. It was stated by one of the judges that the charges were not justified by the express powers in the enabling Act: 'all the powers given appear capable of performance without any power to levy money'. Another case is *Customs and Excise Commissioners v Cure and Deeley Ltd* (1962), which is dealt with in Chapter 11. In deciding that the regulation in this case was *ultra vires*, the court took the view that it sought to prevent the taxpayer proving in a court of law the amount of tax actually due and substituted for the tax authorised by Parliament some other amount to be calculated arbitrarily by the Commissioners. Another example is the case of *McEldowney v Forde* (1971), involving the Special Powers Act in Northern Ireland, an Act which is now repealed. By virtue of the Act the government of the Province was empowered to make regulations 'for preserving the peace and maintaining public order'. One of the regulations made created a criminal offence to be a member of an organisation describing itself as a 'republican club' or of 'any like organisation howsoever described'. Relying very heavily on the feeling that the regulation was not made in bad faith, the House of Lords, by a slim majority of three to two, decided that the regulation was not *ultra vires* the Act. Lord Hodson, for example, stated that:

> ... the word 'republican' is capable of fitting the description of a club which in the opinion of the minister should be prescribed as a subversive organisation of a type akin to those previously named in [a] list of admittedly unlaw-

ful organisations ... On this matter, in my opinion, the court should not substitute its judgment for that of the minister ...

As to the words 'any like organisation howsoever described', the same member
of the court considered that the minister's regulation, although vague, did not
affect the legal validity of the whole and emphasised that these words were not
in contention in this case. A similar issue arose in *Dunkley v Evans* (1981) where
the court was concerned with a statutory order covering an area, part of which
it could not cover under the terms of the enabling Act. The West Coast Herring
(Prohibition of Fishing) Order 1978 was made under the Sea Fish (Conservation)
Act 1967, which Act did not apply to certain waters adjacent to the coast of
Northern Ireland which were nevertheless included in the Order. The master of
a trawler and its owner were prosecuted under the Order for illegal fishing in
an area to which it lawfully applied. It was decided by the court that there
should be a conviction since the invalid part of the Order could be severed from
the remainder since it was not inextricably connected to the remainder of the
Order.

8.4   EU Law

It was said at the outset of this chapter that EU law was to be dealt with, not so
much as a source of administrative powers but rather as a source of law and
legal restrictions in relation to the functions and activities of the administrative
agencies in the UK, as they fall within the objectives of the Union. This framework of EU law and its impact on administrative law in the UK was illustrated
in the previous chapter. In the remainder of the present chapter it is proposed to
outline the institutions of the Union, including the European Court of Justice,
and the sources of EU law and their effect. In this latter area reference back to
the relevant sections of the previous chapter will be helpful. Before these items
are examined it is as well to appreciate that EU law provides the administrative
powers necessary for various agencies of the Union such as the Commission to
implement and enforce their functions in Member States.

8.4.1   The EU institutions

The Commission is responsible for the co-ordination of national policies, and
the formulation of EU policies and their administration. Governments of the
Member States appoint the Commissioners. The Council consists of delegates
from the governments of the Member States and is responsible for decisions on
policy and various other legal acts. The European Parliament represents the
Union's population and acts mainly as a consultative body in relation to acts
and proposals generated by the Council and the Commission, although it does
have significant powers in relation to the Union's budget and in its power to
force the resignation of the Commission. The important decision of the
European Court of Justice in *European Parliament v Council of the European*

Communities (1987) shows that the Parliament may have important influence over the Council in relation to some aspects of policy creation. On this occasion the Parliament was successful in proceedings for failure to act under Article 175 of the Treaty when the Council failed to formulate a Common Transport Policy. The broad framework for decision-making in the EU involves a proposal for action from the Commission being notified to the Parliament for consultation with a final decision being taken by the Council.

8.4.2   European Court of Justice

The functions of the Union's Court can be divided into four:

(1) to enforce and interpret EU law;

(2) to adjudicate disputes between Member States and the EU;

(3) to adjudicate disputes between the Union's institutions; and

(4) to protect individual legal rights and interests against infringement by the institutions, particularly through the power of annulment which is examined in Chapter 13.

8.4.3   Sources of EU law

The principal source of EU law is the Treaty of Rome itself. Beyond this principal source, there are various other sources, often referred to as EU secondary legislation:

(1) regulations;

(2) directives; and

(3) decisions.

Regulations set down general rules which are binding within the Union and its Member States. In the previous chapter reference was made to Article 48 of the Treaty of Rome and the free movement of workers. One aspect of this area of EU law is that there shall be no discrimination based on nationality as between the workers of Member States. Equality of treatment for workers is defined in detail in Regulation 1612/68 which covers a worker's eligibility for employment, equality of treatment in employment and his right to bring his family to a Member State for these purposes. Directives do not have a general binding effect but are binding only on the Member States to which they are directed and in relation to the objective to be realised so that it is up to the Member State to decide the means and methods by which that objective may be achieved. A convenient example can again be taken from Chapter 7 where Article 48 was described. The directive in question – 64/221 – contains exceptions to the coverage of the law in Article 48 by reference to matters of public policy, public security or public health. Decisions also do not have a general binding effect but bind only the individual or Member State to whom they are addressed, eg a decision of the Commission that a company had been acting in breach of the law on competition in the Union. In the case of regulations, directives and decisions it is a requirement of Article 190 of the Treaty of Rome that in undertaking such acts the Council and the Commission 'shall state the reasons on which they are based'. Two other possible sources should be mentioned: recommendations and opinions. However, because these are usually concerned with hypothetical situations in many cases they are not legal acts and are not therefore binding. More generally, it was seen previously that the European Court of Justice has as one of its functions the interpretation of EU law. Article 177 of the Treaty of Rome permits any court in the UK and other Member States to make a preliminary reference to the European Court of Justice for a conclusive interpretation of EU law as it affects a case before that court. Whether a reference is made depends on the criteria set out by the High Court in *Customs and Excise Commissioners v ApS Samex* (1983). The starting point is the question whether a decision on the meaning of a provision of EU law is necessary. In deciding that question the court has to consider the advantages enjoyed by the Court of Justice in having a detailed knowledge of the workings of the Union. A reference is not required on every occasion that a litigant raises a serious point of EU Law: the court has to consider whether the point is conclusive and determinative of the litigation. Has the Court of Justice considered the point previously? Is the point clear and free from doubt? If the point has been considered previously by the Court of Justice, that decision should be followed. However, the national court also has to consider the length of time that may elapse before a decision, the undesirability of overloading the court, the need to formulate points clearly, the difficulty and importance of the point, the wishes of the parties and whether the point is raised *bona fide* or as a means of obstruction.

8.4.4 The direct applicability and direct effect of EU law in Member States

It has been seen previously that the European Communities Act 1972 permits the introduction of EU law to the UK where it is superior to the UK's national law in areas of overlap. A provision of EU law which is said to be directly applicable is incorporated automatically into the national law of a Member State. This is the case with EU regulations and all regulations are accepted into the law of this country by virtue of s 2(1) of the European Communities Act either by Order in Council or by departmental regulations as described previously in this chapter. EU laws which are not directly applicable are given effect to in this country by the same means but subject to various restrictions by which the orders or regulations proposed cannot increase taxation or operate retrospectively, for example. These items of delegated legislation are scrutinised by the specialised scrutiny committees of the two Houses of Parliament referred to previously in this chapter.

A provision of EU law said to have direct effect gives individuals in the Member States enforceable legal rights in national courts: for example Article 48 on the free movement of workers. The concept of direct effect is essentially the product of the jurisprudence of the European Court of Justice since it is not mentioned in the Treaty of Rome. Whilst it is relatively uncontroversial that both Treaty articles and regulations should be capable of giving rise to legal rights enforceable before national courts, controversy has surrounded the issue of direct effect as it applies to directives. Consequently a distinction has developed, partly in order to appease some of the Member States, between the notion of vertical direct effect, whereby an individual seeks to enforce rights against a public body or 'emanation of the state', and horizontal direct effect whereby an individual seeks to enforce rights against another individual. Treaty articles and regulations may be both vertically and horizontally directly effective; directives can only be vertically directly effective (*Marshall v Southampton and Southwest Hampshire Area Health Authority (No 1)* (1986)). In part the reason for this approach is based on the belief that a Member State should not be able to plead its own failure to implement a directive as a defence in proceedings where an individual seeks to rely on a right enshrined in EU law. Furthermore, it would be inequitable for an individual to suffer adversely at the suit of another individual where a Member State has failed to implement a directive which was addressed to it since the individual is not at fault; the responsibility for the implementation of a directive is, by virtue of Article 189 of the Treaty of Rome, vested in the Member State, not the individual.

The concept of direct effect is arguably now of less significance in the light of the decisions in *Von Colson v Land Nordrhein Westfalen* (1984) and *Marleasing v La Commercial Internacional De Alimentacion SA* (1990). In *Von Colson*, the European Court of Justice stressed that a Member State has an obligation under a directive to achieve the result envisaged by the directive. Moreover, the general duty under Article 5 of the Treaty of Rome to take all appropriate measures to ensure the fulfilment of that obligation was binding on all the authorities within the Member State, including the courts. Accordingly, in applying the provisions of national law which have been introduced in order to implement the terms of a directive, it is incumbent on the national court to interpret their national law in the light of the wording and purpose of the directive. In *Marleasing*, this duty of interpretation was extended still further by the European Court of Justice so that it is now necessary to interpret national law in the light of a directive irrespective of whether the national law was made before or after the directive.

In the recent case of *Francovich v Italian Republic* (1992), the European Court of Justice established that a Member State may be liable to compensate those who have been adversely affected by its failure to implement a directive provided that: the right prescribed by the directive entails the grant of rights to individuals; the content of those rights can be identified from the directive; and, a caused link exists between the breach of the State's obligation and the loss suffered by the plaintiff.

9   Procedural *Ultra Vires*

9.1   Statutory Procedures

In conferring various powers on administrative agencies by statute, Parliament will usually find it necessary to prescribe various procedures which should be observed in the exercise of those powers. Procedural requirements will be found either in the statute itself or perhaps in statutory rules or regulations made under the authority of the statute or some other related statutory provision. On some occasions the court may prescribe that where the statute is silent on matters of procedure or where there is an inadequate procedure, common law rules of natural justice will be implied. These are essentially rules of fair procedure which, if broken, may render the resulting administrative action *ultra vires*. The rules of natural justice have also been applied to the non-statutory procedures of purely domestic organisations like trade union disciplinary committees.

In general, statutory procedures fall into two categories, those prescribed for the guidance of the administrative agency concerned and those prescribed for the benefit and guidance of the individual in his dealings with that administrative agency. The latter procedures provide an important measure of the extent to which the system of administrative justice provides any facilities for public participation in the process of bureaucracy. However, there is usually very little if any guidance in the statute concerned on the legal consequences if any of a failure to comply with the procedural requirements; does non-compliance render the administrative action *ultra vires* in a particular case?

9.1.1   Mandatory and directory procedures

Guidance on the legal effect of a failure to comply with procedures comes from *Howard v Bodington* (1877) where Lord Penzance said that 'In each case you must look to the subject-matter; consider the importance of the provision that has been disregarded, and the relation of that provision to the general object intended to be secured by the Act ...'. In applying this test the court will be seeking to ascertain whether a statutory procedural requirement is either mandatory or merely directory. If the requirement is mandatory, non-compliance renders the administrative action *ultra vires*, while non-compliance with a directory requirement generally has no effect except, perhaps, where there is a need for 'substantial compliance' with a particular requirement, eg a requirement that an administrative agency provides some description of a prescribed activity in using statutory powers to regulate that activity. Whether a procedural requirement is mandatory or directory depends partly on the court's interpretation of the relevant words of the statutory provision, although consideration is often given to the consequences of that interpretation both by reference to the supposed requirements of the 'public interest' as well as the individual interests of the person affected by the administrative action. There is a considerable spectrum of possibilities here. It has been said that:

> ... what the courts have to decide ... is the legal consequence of non-compliance on the rights of the subject viewed in the light of a concrete statement of facts and a continuing chain of events. It may be that what the courts are faced with is not so much a stark choice of alternatives but a spectrum of possibilities in which one compartment or description fades gradually into another ... (T)hough language like "mandatory", "directory", "void", "voidable" ... may be helpful in argument, it may be misleading in effect if relied on to show that the courts, in deciding the consequences of a defect in the exercise of power, are necessarily bound to fit the facts of a particular case and a developing chain of events into rigid legal categories ...

These words were spoken by Lord Hailsham in a case before the House of Lords, *London and Clydeside Estates Ltd v Aberdeen District Council* (1979), where a local authority's decision, contained in a certificate delivered to the applicant, omitted any reference to the applicant's statutory right of appeal. This was held to be a breach of a mandatory requirement, meaning that the certificate had to be set aside.

In *Secretary of State for Trade and Industry v Langridge* (1991), the Court of Appeal was required to consider a procedural irregularity that occurred in relation to s 16(1) of the Disqualification of Directors Act 1986. By virtue of s 6 of the same Act, an application to the High Court for a disqualification order in respect of a company director cannot be made, without leave of the High Court, in excess of two years from the date on which the company became insolvent. The effect of s 16 of the 1986 Act is to require that the individual in respect of whom the application is made is given at least 10 clear days' notice of the intention to make the application. In the present case, the Secretary of State for Trade and Industry gave the respondent nine days' notice of his intention to apply for a disqualification order in respect of the respondent. Thus the issue for the Court of Appeal to determine was whether the application should be struck out on account of the procedural irregularity. Put another way, was the giving of nine rather than the statutorily prescribed 10 days' notice such as to render the application void or voidable? In order that this question could be answered, it was necessary for the Court of Appeal to consider whether the 10 days time limit was a mandatory or a directory requirement. Whilst the court was anxious to stress that there should, in the normal course of events, be a strict compliance with the requirement of s 16 of the 1986 Act, it was nevertheless felt that the notice was only of limited importance on account of the deficiencies in the protection that it afforded to a person against whom a disqualification order was sought. For example, there were circumstances where no notice was required, there was no need to stipulate the grounds on which the application was made in the notice, and, the 10-day period was considered by Balcombe LJ to be 'too short for the recipient to be able to do much' other than produce evidence of mistaken identity or seek to challenge the decision to apply for a disqualification order by way of judicial review. These factors coupled with the general object of the 1986 Act, which was to ensure the protection of the public, lead the majority in the Court of Appeal to conclude that the 10-day limit was directory rather than mandatory. Accordingly, the failure to satisfy this directory procedural requirement did not render the Secretary of State's application either void or voidable.

9.1.2   Public functions

In practice the court is reluctant to categorise a procedural requirement as mandatory, even though it is stipulated that the agency 'shall' undertake certain action, where this would severely prejudice the performance of public functions. In the New Zealand case of *Simpson v Attorney General* (1955) the Governor General failed to authorise the issue of writs required by legislation as a pre-requisite to a general election as a result of which it was unsuccessfully alleged that the result of the election was nullified so that any legislation by the newly elected Parliament was of no effect. It was recognised that there was neglect of a public duty.

> ... but the case is clearly such that to hold null and void the acts which were done would work serious general inconvenience, and at the same time would not promote the main object of the Electoral Act 1927. The main object of that Act I conceive to be to sustain; not to destroy the House of Representatives; and I am satisfied that those provisions ... which relate to the times when the warrant and the writs shall be issued are directory and not mandatory; and that neglect ... cannot invalidate the election.

9.1.3   Individual rights and interests

Where the public interest in preserving public functions is not paramount and the statutory requirement is sufficiently clear, the individual's rights and interests can be recognised. For example, the Coast Protection Act 1949 stipulates that a local authority is required to communicate to relevant property owners the charges due for coast protection work not later than six months from completion of the work. In *Cullimore v Lyme Regis Corporation* (1962) details of the charges were communicated nearly two years after completion of the work: this, it was decided, was in breach of a mandatory time limit of six months so that the notification was *ultra vires* and had no effect. Again, s 14 of the Employment Protection Act 1975 stated that: 'In the course of its inquiries into a recognition issue ... the [Advisory, Conciliation and Arbitration] Service shall ascertain the opinions of workers to whom the issue relates by any means it thinks fit ... '. The issue for the court in *Grunwick Processing Laboratories Ltd v Advisory, Conciliation and Arbitration Service* (1978) was whether the Service was subject to a mandatory duty to consult those involved in a trade union recognition dispute or whether the Act prescribed a mere discretion, as though the words of the above provision were merely directory. In finding that there was a mandatory duty, the court's decision was summarised in the following observation, that:

> If ACAS makes a recommendation and the employer fails to comply with it, that may mean ... that terms and conditions may be written into an employee's contract of employment without further reference to the employee himself, whether or not the employee is a member of the union in question or of a union at all and whether or not the employee desires to have his interests represented by the particular or any union ... these powers given to ACAS are very large and ... the court should ensure that the obligation and safeguards are strictly observed. [There is] no doubt that the requirement in s 14(1) [is] mandatory ... In the context of this part of the Act it is unthinkable that Parliament should have left it to the discretion of ACAS whether they should or should not consult those to whom the issue relates before coming to their conclusion.

It is usually quite clear that a procedural requirement is incorporated in a statutory provision for the benefit of the individual. To that extent it is also clear that the provision confers a legally enforceable right, eg where the administrative agency is obliged to notify a person of proceedings affecting his interests or of his right of appeal against a decision of that administrative agency. Failure to comply with such mandatory requirements would render any subsequent administrative action *ultra vires*. However, there may be occasions when the court feels that the individual's interests require protection in the present context but where the words of the statutory provision provide no options to enable such protection. In the Housing Act 1985, for example, it is stipulated that once a demolition order has been served on a house the local authority shall forthwith serve a notice on the occupants of the house requiring them to vacate the premises. Even though a local authority delays serving a vacation notice for the best motive of enabling the occupants to find alternative accommodation, the duty to serve the notice has been found to be mandatory and, as such, enforceable by the freehold owner of the house in question through an order of *mandamus* which compels the administrative agency (in this case, the local authority) to undertake its (mandatory) duty according to law (*R v Epsom and Ewell Corporation, ex p RB Property Investments* (1964)).

9.1.4 Individuals' procedure obligations

It is not uncommon to find that procedural requirements have to be observed by individuals as well as by administrative agencies. For example, applications for grants and licences may have to conform to certain requirements as to form and content, appeals from certain decisions may have to be notified within a certain time limit and in a certain form, and objections to various proposals for administrative action may have to comply with certain requirements as to form and content. Again the court has to determine whether a procedural requirement is mandatory or directory and in general there is an attempt to interpret the various requirements as liberally as possible in favour of the individual.

9.1.5 Application requirements

Statutory provisions will often make it abundantly clear what is the requirement in relation to an application, for example. By way of illustration, the Goods Vehicles (Licensing of Operators) Act 1995 states quite explicitly that:

A separate application for the grant of an operator's licence shall be made in respect of each traffic area in which the applicant has an operating centre but no operator's licence ... An applicant shall not include in any application –

(a) a vehicle specified in a current operator's licence ...

Every application shall be signed –

(a) if made by a body corporate, by a person duly authorised in that behalf by such a body corporate ...

Nevertheless, there is a tendency for the court to regard such application requirements as being directory, at least to the extent that an application may be accepted as such as long as there is substantial compliance with the statutory requirements so that the necessary details of the application are made known. The practice of many administrative agencies is to use standard forms for all types of application so that the defective application may be a rarity. On those occasions when the administrative agency deems an application to be deficient, statutory provisions may enable 'such further information as may be specified ... to be given ... in respect of an application'. This is a provision from the Town and Country Planning legislation relating to applications for planning permission. This legislation also requires an applicant for planning permission in respect of another person's land to inform that other person of his application and to certify to the local planning authority that this has been done when the application is submitted. In order to reinforce this protection for the landowner, the Act also stipulates that in the absence of a certificate for present purposes, the authority 'shall not entertain' an application for planning permission (s 65 of the Town and Country Planning Act 1990 as substituted by s 16 of the Planning and Compensation Act 1991; s 65 should be read in conjunction with art 8 of the Town and Country Planning (General Development Procedure) Order 1995, SI 1995/419). Although these words would seem to import a clear mandatory requirement, the court will (as was seen previously) take account of a number of variables. In *Main v Swansea City Council* (1984) a third party sought to quash a decision granting an outline planning permission where a s 27 certificate (a predecessor of s 65 of the 1990 Act) was defective in that the unknown owner of a small part of the subject site had not been notified, as required by the section. Although the Court of Appeal considered that the defects were sufficient to strike down the planning permission, the circumstances suggested that this should not happen. In particular the court was influenced by the fact that the third party had not previously objected to a grant of outline planning permission, that development would not occur on the land owned by the unknown person and that (in any event) the application was too late. Presumably a prompt challenge by the land owner affected would have sufficed.

9.1.6 Appeal requirements

Statutory provisions frequently provide for appeals from many decisions of administrative agencies. For example, as seen in Chapter 4, adverse local authority decisions on applications for planning permission are subject to appeal to the Secretary of State for the Environment (s 78 Town and Country Planning Act 1990). It is usually necessary to stipulate with some certainty the time limit within which any such appeal should be lodged. Accordingly, it is generally the case that notice of any such appeal must be notified, usually to the appeal body concerned, before the expiration of the appropriate time limit which means that in law the time limit is mandatory (*Howard v Secretary of State for the Environment* (1974)). As a mandatory requirement, any failure to observe the time limit means that the appeal body is legally entitled to reject any purported notice and to refuse to determine the appeal. However, it is generally the case that the need to communicate the facts and grounds for an appeal is a mere directory procedural requirement (*Button v Jenkins* (1975)). Consequently, the facts and grounds do not generally need to be communicated within any time limit for appeals although there will be a mandatory requirement for their submission if eventually the appeal body requires them to be given. Again, failure to comply with this later requirement would be a breach of a mandatory requirement and entitle the appeal body to proceed to determine the appeal in the absence of the facts and grounds.

9.1.7 Objections

Some statutory administrative schemes provide a facility for objection to proposals for administrative action, particularly where such proposals, eg to grant various liquor and gaming licences, might affect members of the public. Such objections will arise from the advertisement of the proposals, for example, to grant a licence, although in many cases the advertisement will simply relate to details of a particular application for a licence. Where this advertising obligation is prescribed by statute it is usually regarded as a mandatory requirement although in some areas of licensing there is no clear indication of the legal consequences of a failure to comply (*R v Pontypool Gaming Licensing Committee, ex p Risca Cinemas Ltd* (1970)). In other areas there is a clear indication of the possible consequences of a failure to comply: s 65 of the Town and Country Planning Act 1990 (as substituted by s 16 of the Planning and Compensation Act 1991; s 65 should be read in conjunction with the Town and Country Planning (General Development Procedure) Order 1995, SI 1995/419), for example, stipulates that a local planning authority 'shall not entertain' an application for planning permission for 'undesirable development' (which might include the establishment of, among other things, casinos and cemeteries) without proof of publicity for the application. Following the advertisement of licence applications and other administrative proposals, the submission of any objection or (perhaps) other representations is seen as a directory requirement. This is a reference to the fact that the law does not generally stipulate that an objection or representation should accord strictly with any mandatory requirement as to form and content. Consequently, in *Re L (AC) (An infant)* (1971) an official of a local authority had led a party to child care proceedings to assume that an objection to a resolution of that authority need not be put in writing. In fact, the statute concerned required objections to be in writing but nevertheless the local authority was prevented from alleging that no written objection had been issued within the prescribed time limit.

9.1.8 Specific areas of procedure

In the remaining sections of this chapter the legal status of some more important areas of procedure will be examined. These areas of procedure relate to consultation, delegation of decision-making and other administrative action, the communication of decisions and obligation to give reasons for decisions and other administrative action.

9.2 Consultation

Consultation is one means by which public participation can be achieved in administrative action whether in relation to the making of policy, or in the making of actual decisions. It is not the only method of involving the public in administrative policy and decision-making: the public inquiry is an important example of the wider involvement of the public in many areas of decision-making. Consultation is usually required either where a person or a group may be affected by some administrative action or where they have some expert contribution to make to proposed administrative action. The statutory machinery for consultation tends to be less formal than that relating to the public inquiry and it is often the case that the administrative agency has a discretion as to who is consulted. In *Lee v Department of Education and Science* (1967), for example, the court was concerned with s 17(5) of the Education Act 1944 which required that the Secretary of State for Education, before varying the articles of government of a school, should afford 'to the local education authority and to any other persons appearing to him to be concerned with the management or government of the school' an opportunity to make representations. The court decided that a governor and a teacher had a legal right to be consulted under this provision, but not a parent. The court was also willing to define the limits of the discretion in *Agricultural, Horticultural and Forestry Industry Training Board v Aylesbury*

Mushrooms Ltd (1972) where, under the Industrial Training Act 1964, the minister was obliged to consult any 'organization or association or organizations appearing to him to be representative of substantial numbers of employers engaged in the activities concerned'. Because the minister had failed to consult the Mushroom Growers' Association, the court declared that part of the Board's order relating to the Association was *ultra vires*. Where, on the other hand, the authority has a very broad discretion as to whom should be consulted and exercises that discretion fairly and reasonably, the court may be reluctant to specify who should be consulted (*R v Post Office, ex p ASTMS* (1981)). Even where there is no express statutory provision for consultation the court may be able to prescribe a limited common law obligation to consult, as in *R v Liverpool Corporation, ex p Liverpool Taxi Fleet Operators' Association* (1972). In this case the Corporation undertook not to increase the number of taxi licences until a Private Act was legislated controlling the operations of mini-cabs in the city. The Corporation sought to act in breach of this undertaking, as a result of which the court decided that although the undertaking was not binding, there was an obligation on the Corporation to act fairly and to consult the Association to hear its views before increasing the number of licences, even though the Private Act controlling mini-cabs was not yet on the statute book.

The court's prescription of a limited common law obligation to consult is often characterised as a legitimate expectation from the point of view of the beneficiary of that duty. This was very much the emphasis of events in the GCHQ case examined previously. It seems that although 'high' prerogative decisions on national security will not be interfered with by the court mere procedural matters may be open to judicial scrutiny. This was the case in *R v Director of GCHQ, ex p Hodges* (1988) where security clearance for an employee at the government establishment was withdrawn when he admitted his homosexuality. A summary of the interview with his employers was provided but not a full note. The employee was unsuccessful in claiming a breach of natural justice because the summary was regarded as sufficient. Nevertheless there may have been circumstances in which the court might have found this decision procedurally unfair.

In pursuing a requirement to consult, the authority must ensure that the purpose of that consultation is reflected in the issues put forward for consultation. In *Legg v Inner London Education Authority* (1972) an injunction was granted by the court in order to prevent the implementation of a scheme for comprehensive education because the proposals sent by the education authority to the Secretary of State differed from the proposals in the statutory notice which invited objections. Not only must the issues for consultation relate to the purposes of that exercise, the authority must supply sufficient information to the other party or parties to enable any advice to be tendered and must allow a reasonable amount of time for the consultation process. In *R v Secretary of State for Social Services, ex p Association of Metropolitan Authorities* (1993), one of the issues to be determined by the court was whether regulations were valid where the Secretary of State had failed to comply with a statutory duty under the Social Security Act 1986 to consult the Association of Metropolitan Authorities before making amendments to certain housing benefit regulations. The duty to consult contained the proviso that consultation was not necessary where the urgency of the matter made it inexpedient to do so. However, in the opinion of Tucker J, the Secretary of State could not be allowed to take advantage of the proviso where it ought to have been apparent at an early stage that consultation was necessary before amending the relevant regulations. Accordingly, the applicants succeeded in their contention that there had been a failure to consult and a declaration was made to this effect. Finally, it has been said in one of the leading cases (*Rollo v Minister of Town and Country Planning* (1948)) that the authority 'with a receptive mind, must by such consultation seek and welcome the aid and advice which those with local knowledge may be in a position to proffer in regard to a plan which [the authority] has tentatively evolved'. However, it appears that the existence of a policy in favour of a particular course of action does not necessarily mean that any consultation will not be undertaken without a receptive mind.

9.2.1 Legal effect of a failure to consult

In general, consultation is mandatory although the court may prescribe a directory obligation if the statutory provision seems to indicate a sufficient discretion, particularly in relation to those who are to be consulted, or where a person's interests are not prejudiced by a failure to consult in some respect. Two cases relating to statutory requirements for consultation in relation to the introduction of comprehensive education illustrate the contrast between the effects of mandatory and directory requirements in the present context. In *Bradbury v Enfield London Borough Council* (1967) the court was concerned with various provisions of the Education Act 1944, one of which, s 13, stipulated that after proposals for comprehensive reorganisation (involving an intention to 'cease to maintain' schools and to establish new schools') had been submitted to the Minister of Education:

> ... the authority ... shall forthwith give public notice of the proposals in the prescribed manner, and the managers or governors of any voluntary school affected by the proposals or any ten or more local government electors ... may within three months after the first publication of the notice submit to the minister objections to the proposals ...

This was a major prerequisite before any approval could be given by the minister to a scheme for comprehensive reorganisation, hence the court's decision that the requirement was mandatory. Failure to comply rendered the relevant resolutions of the education authority *ultra vires*. Following this decision the Education Act 1968 was passed whereby the 's 13' procedure would now apply to a 'significant change in the character, or significant enlargement of the premises' of a school: whether a particular change is 'significant' was to be determined by the Secretary of State for Education, not the court. The second, contrasting case is *Coney v Choyce* (1975) where the notice requirements of s 13 were regarded by the judge as being merely directory because the relevant regulations – the County and Voluntary Schools (Notices) Regulations 1968 – intended 'that notice should be published in a manner designed to show a representative number of people what their rights are'. The Regulations required notice to be given in a local newspaper, in some conspicuous place or places, at or near any main entrance to the school in question, and in such other manner as appeared to be desirable for giving publicity to the notice. In the case of two schools no notice was posted at or near the main entrance although notices were well publicised elsewhere and no person had suffered any substantial prejudice. Overall, therefore, non-compliance with the requirements did not affect the legality of the authority's action.

Whether the court intervenes to quash or declare administrative action a nullity may be uncertain. The High Court – in *R v Gwent County Council, ex p Bryant* (1988) – considered that any failure by the local authority in that case was remedied by the Secretary of State's consideration of the case. Perhaps more controversially, the High Court has also refused to quash new social security regulations even though the Secretary of State had failed to consult properly when very little time was given for a response from the Association of Metropolitan Authorities. In this case – *R v Secretary of State for Social Services, ex p Association of Metropolitan Authorities* (1986) – the court was clearly influenced by the fact that the regulations were already in force and being administered by the local authorities. In a later case involving the same applicants referred to in the previous section, Tucker J was also not prepared to quash the regulations in question where the Secretary of State had failed to comply with a mandatory requirement to consult by not consulting with anyone. As a general proposition, it was not in the public interest to upset regulations in the absence of a good reason for doing so since to do otherwise would be disruptive in that it would give rise to uncertainty and delay. In the present case, the fact that the regulations had only been in force for a short time and that by quashing them the court 'would not be opening the flood gates to great rebate or payment' did not amount to a sufficiently good reason for granting an order of *certiorari*.

9.3 Delegation

An important element in many types of administrative action is the need to expedite the procedures and the need to recognise that many of the administrative and judicial functions cannot be undertaken 'personally' by the minister at the head of a government department, the council of a local authority or the nominated board of a public corporation. A number of administrative and judicial functions may be and often are delegated by these agencies, at least to the extent that the law permits such delegation.

Whether the law permits delegation of functions depends on the maxim *delegatus non potest delegare*: an administrative agency with statutory responsibility for an exercise of powers cannot delegate them without statutory authorisation. However, the maxim *delegatus non potest delegare* applies strictly to judicial functions. But it is different with a body which is exercising administrative functions or which is making an investigation or conducting preliminary inquiries, especially when it is a numerous body (*per* Lord Denning in *Selvarajan v Race Relations Board* (1976)). Even where the function is administrative its delegation may be expressly prevented by an appropriate statutory provision (*per* Lord Somervell in *Vine v National Dock Labour Board* (1957)). Whether delegation is permitted, therefore, depends on the terms of any statutory powers and, in general, on whether a particular function is 'administrative' or 'judicial'. A judicial function arises where 'any body of persons [have] legal authority to determine questions affecting the rights of subjects': *R v Electricity Commissioners, ex p London Electricity Joint Committee* (1924)). Only where there is clear statutory authorisation can this type of function be delegated.

One of the clearest examples of a judicial function relates to disciplinary functions which were in issue in *Barnard v National Dock Labour Board* (1953) where Lord Denning observed, no facts which showed that Barnard had been suspended from his employment as the result of a decision taken by a tribunal which had no power to take such action, that:

> [t]he Board are put in a judicial position between the men and the employers; they are to receive reports from the employers and investigate them; they have to inquire whether the man has been guilty of misconduct ... and if they find against him they can suspend him without pay, or can even dismiss him summarily. In those circumstances they are exercising a judicial function ... No judicial tribunal can delegate its functions unless it is enabled to do so expressly or by necessary implication.

Similarly, consideration of an information laid before a magistrate or a magistrates' clerk alleging a criminal offence is a judicial rather than an administrative function. Consequently, if such an information is considered by anyone else who is not authorised by statute for this purpose, any subsequent conviction would be quashed (*R v Gateshead Justices, ex p Tesco Stores Ltd* (1981)).

Administrative functions are less easily defined although by their very nature they tend to cover ministerial tasks such as the collection of information and the preparation of that information and other material for submission to a deciding body whose task would normally be seen as a judicial function. Where such a task of collecting information is lawfully delegated it is usually necessary for the delegate to submit all the information to the deciding body, failing which it might be said that there was a breach of the rules of natural justice inasmuch as any person submitting information or evidence might allege that a mere summary thereof could amount to a denial of a legal right to a reasonable opportunity for his case to be heard by the deciding body (*Jeffs v New Zealand Dairy Production and Marketing Board* (1967)).

9.3.1 Government departments and local authorities

Special attention needs to be given to the position of central government departments and local authorities. In the case of central government departments, a fundamental concept involves the idea that the civil servant is the minister's *alter ego* so that in law anything done by the civil servant is done in the name of and is binding on the minister. It was seen in Chapter 4 that local authorities enjoy a special position because the Local Government Act 1972 states in s 101 that:

> Subject to the express provisions contained in this Act or any Act passed after this Act, a local authority may arrange for the discharge of any of their functions –
>
> (a) by a committee, a sub-committee or an officer of the authority; or ... by an other local authority.

Normally, any decision or other similar administrative action taken by the local authority only becomes a legally effective decision when passed in a resolution of the whole council. If the power to delegate in s 101 is used, the decision of the delegate committee, officer or other authority is legally the decision of the council. If this power to delegate is used, it is usually for the purpose of expediting the decision-making processes of the council. In practice the council will usually require a report from the delegate indicating details of delegated decisions actually taken. Those councils who make very little use of this facility tend to the view that the full, democratic process should apply to every decision or other administrative action of the council. It has been seen previously in Chapter 4 that s 101 does not permit delegation to a number, thereby eliminating the facility for chairman's action!

In the case of central government departments, it is generally recognised that the minister at the head of the department is not legally obliged to direct his mind to each case. In the leading case of *Carltona Ltd v Commissioners of Works* (1943) it was observed that:

> In the administration of government in this country the functions which are given to ministers (and constitutionally properly given to ministers because they are constitutionally responsible) are functions so multifarious that no minister could ever personally attend to them ... the duties imposed upon ministers and the powers given to ministers are normally exercised under the authority of the ministers by responsible officials of the department ... Constitutionally, the decision of such an official is, of course, the decision of the minister. The minister is responsible. It is he who must answer before Parliament for anything that his officials have done under his authority.

Applying this principle in *R v Skinner* (1968), the court was concerned with a statutory prerequisite that the Home Secretary should approve for use any breathalyser device before any person could be convicted of a drinking/driving offence under the Road Traffic Act. It was decided by the court that approval could quite lawfully come from an Assistant Secretary in the Home Office Police Department. Again, in *Re Golden Chemical Products Ltd* (1976) the court was concerned with the Secretary of State for Trade's statutory power to present a winding-up petition to the High Court where it appears to him to be necessary in the public interest as provided for by s 35 of the Companies Act 1967 (now s 124A of the Insolvency Act 1986 as substituted by s 60 of the Companies Act 1989). Such a requirement, it was decided, did not have to be undertaken personally by the Secretary of State.

An exception to the *'alter ego'* principle occurs where statute expressly or, perhaps impliedly, prohibits anybody but the minister making a particular decision. Section 13(5) of the Immigration Act 1971, for example, states that:

A person shall not be entitled to appeal against a refusal of leave to enter, or against a refusal of an entry clearance, if the Secretary of State certifies that directions have been given by the Secretary of State (and not by a person acting under his authority) for the appellant not to be given entry on the ground that his exclusion is conducive to the public good ...

The above statutory limitation on delegation was considered in *R v Secretary of State for the Home Department, ex p Oladehinde* (1991) where the principal issue for the consideration of the House of Lords was whether an immigration inspector, acting on behalf of the Secretary of State, was entitled to decide that the appellants should be deported where they had, in the first case, contravened a condition restricting the taking of employment whilst residing in the UK as a student, and in the other, overstayed the period for which leave to enter the UK had been granted. A unanimous House of Lords decided that the initial decision to deport could indeed be taken by an immigration inspector. The *Carltona* principle, referred to earlier in this section, was a recognition of the fact that the devolution of responsibility amounted to a practical necessity in the administration of government. Moreover, whilst the 1971 Immigration Act contained a number of instances where the power to delegate was restricted, such as s 13(5), there was no such limitation in respect of the decision to deport and the court would be 'very slow to read into the statute a further implicit limitation'. Lord Griffiths, who gave the leading judgment in the case, succinctly stated the position thus:

The immigration service is comprised of Home Office civil servants for whom the Secretary of State is responsible and I can for myself see no reason why he should not authorise members of that service to take decisions under the *Carltona* principle providing they do not conflict with or embarrass them in the discharge of their specific statutory duties under the Act and that the decisions are suitable to their grading and experience.

9.3.2 Implied authority

In local government it appears that the effect of s 101 of the Local Government Act is that any delegation of powers must be express, leaving no room for any implied delegated authority. As far as central government is concerned, again there appears to be no room for the concept of implied delegated authority simply because administrative action is not regarded as being legally delegated: all action is taken theoretically by and in the name of the appropriate minister. In the case of any other administrative agency, including local government before the advent of express powers of delegation in the Act of 1972, implied delegated authority is sometimes recognised and provides a means by which administrative action taken without express statutory powers may be saved from being declared *ultra vires*. In *Nelms v Roe* (1969), for example, the issue related to the Road Traffic Act 1960 and the fact that under the Act information could be sought in relation to an alleged traffic offence 'by or on behalf of a chief officer of police'. The court found that there was no written authority from the Commissioner of Metropolitan Police either to the inspector concerned with the case of his superintendent. It was decided that the *'alter ego'* principle did not extend to the case but there was implied authority delegated to the superintendent with the power further sub-delegated to the inspector dealing with the case.

In practice, implied authority may be used by the court in order to save what would otherwise be seen to be an *ultra vires* delegation of powers. To that extent the court may be using a rather tenuous legal concept in order to fill a gap left in the relevant statutory powers in order to avoid a conclusion that the ultimate decision or other administrative action is *ultra vires* and that therefore the administrative agency is not bound by that action. Inevitably the court has to be able to conclude that Parliament must have intended that the particular statutory powers should be capable of being impliedly extended. In this task the court must be aware of the need to interpret the statutory powers, so far as is possible, as a workable entity. Consequently, it might be possible in some cases for the court to find that an administrative agency is legally able to establish a general policy and overall guidelines for the exercise of particular statutory responsibility, leaving an officer of that agency with implied authority to process the administrative details relating to individual cases. Nevertheless, there can be no substitute for a comprehensive definition of statutory powers which avoids any recourse to implied powers, thereby putting beyond doubt the scope of an administrative agency's powers.

9.3.3 Legal effects of delegation

If there is lawful delegation, the agency retains concurrent powers (*Huth v Clarke* (1890)). Consequently, a delegate's decision may have no effect in law where it is taken after a decision on the same issue by the delegating authority. Furthermore, the delegating authority is able to revoke the delegated powers at any time (*Manton v Brighton Corporation* (1951)). However, where the powers have not been revoked the delegating authority is bound by the delegate's decision, as long as that decision is made within the terms of the delegated authority, that is, as long as the decision is not *ultra vires* the delegate's powers. The best illustration of this proposition comes from the local government context where the council of a local authority resolves to delegate certain powers to one of its chief officers, for example. Any decision of that officer within his delegated powers which is not revoked will be binding on that authority (*Lever (Finance) Ltd v Westminster London Borough Council* (1970)).

9.4 Estoppel

Closely related to the foregoing principles relating to delegation is the doctrine of common law estoppel. The doctrine applies where an officer or other representative of an administrative agency:

(1) makes an adequate statement of fact or fact and law which is

(2) within his delegated or other lawful authority where

(3) the person dealing with that officer or representative relies on the statement to his detriment.

Where all these requirements are satisfied the administrative agency will be bound by and cannot deny the validity of the officer's statement. However, the doctrine applies to statements and representations as opposed to decisions. The law was fully developed through some fairly bold pronouncements, from the Court of Appeal in particular. Since the high point – in *Lever (Finance)* – was reached, the courts have spent a lot of time seeking to limit this form of estoppel, as will be seen later. Where a decision is made by a delegate officer acting within his express authority in local government, for example, that decision is legally the council's. Where the officer makes a statement or representation short of a decision, for example to the effect that no licence is required for a particular activity or that a person is entitled to a grant for a particular purpose, these are the circumstances in which common law estoppel may apply.

A striking example of common law estoppel in action occurs in *Lever (Finance)* where a planning officer working for the local planning authority indicated to an architect in a telephone conversation that the resiting of a house shown on plans for which planning permission had been granted was an 'immaterial variation' not requiring a fresh planning permission. After the building work was commenced the planning authority threatened to serve an enforcement notice requiring the allegedly unlawful development to be discontinued because there was no planning permission. The company applied successfully to the court for a declaration that they were entitled to complete the house on the amended site, and for an injunction to prevent service of the enforcement notice. In the Court of Appeal Lord Denning observed that:

If the planning officer tells the developer that a proposed variation is not material, and the developer acts on it, then the planning authority cannot go back on it ... If an officer, acting within the scope of his ostensible authority, makes a representation on which another acts, then a public authority may be bound by it ...

Subsequently it was suggested that when a developer 'acts' on the representation he should be acting to his detriment. This suggestion was made in the High Court in *Norfolk County Council v Secretary of State for the Environment* (1973) where the council resolved to refuse planning permission for a factory extension. In error the officer sent a notification to the developer indicating that planning permission had been granted. It was decided that the notification was not binding on the council since the officer had no authority to send the wrong notification with the consequence that the council was not bound, that is, estopped or prevented from denying the validity of the notification, so that in law no planning permission had been granted.

9.4.1 Requirements for common law estoppel

To be bound by a representation or statement of an officer then the three requirements for common law estoppel previously listed must be satisfied. The first of these requirements is that there should be an adequate statement of fact or of fact and law. In the most likely situation where a person seeks a determination of the question of whether he requires a licence for a particular activity or whether he is entitled to a grant for a certain purpose, the authority's statement or representation will relate the legal position concerning licences or grants to the facts of the inquirer's situation. Whether there is an adequate statement may depend on the court's satisfaction that adequate information was given to the authority's officer in the first place. In *Re Suruk Miah* (1976) it was decided that a letter from the Department of Employment indicating that a work permit would be granted to a person wishing to come to the UK to work was not an adequate representation: the law required that person to present a work permit on arrival if he was to be allowed to enter the country. In other words, the letter was not binding on the Department. Similarly, in *Wells v Minister of Housing and Local Government* (1967) deletion of words (on a form indicating the local authority's approval of plans under the Building Regulations) indicating that planning permission might also be required for the proposed development covered by the plans was not an adequate representation by the authority that planning permission was not required. Consequently and because the authority was not estopped or prevented from denying the validity of the representation, it could serve a legally effective enforcement notice on the developer requiring him to remove the building on the ground that it required but did not have planning permission. The court also decided that any such enforcement notice would not have been legally effective where the local authority responded to an application for planning permission by saying that in the circumstances no planning permission was, in fact, required. Even though such a determination can normally be made only on a formal basis following a specific application for such a determination, the informal response in this case would have been regarded as an adequate representation. It was argued in the case that the authority could only have been bound, that is, estopped, by a formal determination that planning permission was not required. This argument was rejected by the court and Lord Denning said that, ' ... a public authority cannot be estopped from doing its duty, but I do not think it can be estopped from relying on technicalities'.

The second of the requirements for common law estoppel is that the relevant statement or representation should be made within the delegated or other lawful authority of the officer. This is a fundamental requirement, bearing in mind that no statutory authority can be bound by an *ultra vires* act or representation. In *Princes Investments Ltd v Frimley and Camberley Urban District Council* (1962) planning permission was granted for the building of houses, subject to a condition that the council should approve the sewerage arrangements. In fact, the council's engineer approved the arrangements but it was decided that his statement of approval was not binding on the council which could only fulfil its statutory responsibilities by formal resolution of the whole council at a time when local authorities had no facilities for the formal delegation of functions. The same conclusion occurred in *Southend-on-Sea Corporation v Hodgson (Wickford) Ltd* (1962) where an officer represented that no planning permission was necessary for a proposed development of land as a builder's yard. The council disagreed and it was decided by the court that it was not bound by the officer's representation, which was made without any delegated authority, so that the council was free to exercise its statutory discretion to serve an enforcement notice to prevent the land's use as a builder's yard. Equally, if the authority in question is obliged to exercise a statutory duty, it cannot be estopped or prevented from so doing by a representation or statement of an officer acting without or outside any delegated powers (*Maritime Electric Co. Ltd v General Dairies Ltd* (1937)). This conclusion clearly upholds the essential requirements of the doctrine of *ultra vires* but this requirement is seemingly ignored in the case of *Robertson v Minister of Pensions* (1949). Colonel Robertson, an army officer, received a determination from the War Office that a disability was attributable to military service. The injury in question occurred in December 1939 but War Office responsibility for making these determinations only extended to claims for injuries incurred up to 2 September 1939: thereafter responsibility was transferred to the Ministry of Pensions. The Ministry subsequently determined that the colonel's disability was not attributable to military service. This decision was upheld by the Pensions Appeal Tribunal but the High Court decided that the Ministry was bound by the War Office determination. Denning J (as he then was) stated that:

> ... if a Government department in its dealings with a subject takes it upon itself to assume authority upon a matter with which it is concerned, he is

entitled to rely upon it having the authority which it assumes. He does not know, and cannot be expected to know, the limits of that authority.

Although the just result was undoubtedly achieved in this case, it does indicate that the Ministry of Pensions was being bound by an *ultra vires* determination of the other ministry, the War Office. Subsequently it was stated in the House of Lords, in a reference to the *Robertson* decision, that there was no such principle in the law: 'The illegality of an act is the same whether or not the actor has been misled by an assumption of authority on the part of a government officer, however high or low in the hierarchy' (*Howell v Falmouth Boat Construction Co* (1951)).

The third requirement in the present context relates to the need for detrimental reliance on the officer's statement or representation. In *Robertson* the detrimental reliance occurred when, having received a determination from the War Office, the colonel took no further steps to obtain an independent medical opinion in relation to his injury and disability. In the *Norfolk County Council* case previously referred to, the court decided that there was no detrimental reliance in so far as the developer was able to cancel contracts for the purchase of machinery for the factory extension without incurring any contractual penalties. In the course of his judgment in this case, Lord Widgery observed that 'What one hopes to achieve in a situation like this, where there is an honest mistake, is that everybody shall end up in the position in which they would have been if no mistake had been made'. It could be argued that this perceived need to restore the status quo was a significant influence in the court's finding that the 'detriment requirement' for common law estoppel was not satisfied.

9.4.2 Restriction of estoppel

That there is a reluctance to find an estoppel against an administrative agency is seen in another judgment of Lord Widgery in *Brooks and Burton Ltd v Secretary of State for the Environment* (1977). Here he observes that:

> Any attempt to expand the doctrine of estoppel expressed in *Lever* ... is to be deprecated, because it is extremely important that planning authority officers should feel free to help applicants without having the shadow of estoppel hanging over their heads and the possibility of immobilising the authority by some careless remark.

The court certainly has a great deal of room for manoeuvre in this respect in determining whether, for example, any representation was 'adequate' or any reliance 'detrimental'. However, there is always the possibility that a person quite innocently relies on a statement or representation by an officer of an administration agency only to find that in law there is no estoppel against that authority: it is bound by the officer's statement. That person, having suffered some loss, will find that, legally, there is no remedy: a considerable gap in the law which would be well filled if the law recognised that damages were available for an *ultra vires* act or statement. In Chapter 15 it will be seen that the giving of misleading advice could well amount to 'maladministration' enabling an investigation by one of the ombudsmen according to whether the complaint relates to a central government department or a local authority and assuming that the alleged 'maladministration' has caused injustice. A successful complaint in this context could in some cases secure an *ex gratia* compensation payment to cover any loss which is suffered.

The court's attempt to cut down the application of estoppel, in local government at least, is seen in suggestions made by Megaw LJ in delivering the Court of Appeal's judgment in *Western Fish Products Ltd v Penwith District Council* (1978). He first re-emphasised that: 'An estoppel cannot be raised to prevent the exercise of a statutory discretion or to prevent or excuse the performance of a statutory duty.' He then indicated that there are two kinds of exception:

> If a planning authority, acting as such, delegate to its officers powers to determine specific questions ... any decisions they make cannot be revoked ... *Lever (Finance)* ... is an application of this exception ... In the court's opinion [the] principle laid down by Lord Denning was not authority for the proposition that every representation made by a planning officer within his ostensible authority binds the planning authority ... For an estoppel to arise there has to be some evidence justifying the person dealing with the planning officer for thinking that what the officer said would bind the planning authority ... The second exception is that if a planning authority waives a procedural requirement relating to any applications made to it for the exercise of its statutory powers, it might be estopped from relying on lack of formality. This is supported by *Wells* ... There is other than these two exceptions no justification in extending the concept of estoppel ...

In re-emphasising the fact that any determination made under lawfully delegated powers is binding on the authority, Megaw LJ is also suggesting that an estoppel is available only where there is 'some evidence' justifying the person dealing with the officer in thinking that the officer had the requisite delegated powers. If this is eventually accepted as part of the law, estoppel would effectively become a dead letter since no individual dealing with an officer of an administrative agency could be expected to realise that he should ascertain the scope of any of that officer's delegated powers. As to the second 'exception' referred to by Megaw LJ this relates to any situation in which an officer of an administrative agency represents that there is no requirement for compliance with an inconsequential procedural requirement, as in the case of *Re L (AC) (An infant)*, dealt with previously. Where, on the other hand, the officer indicates that a mandatory requirement may be waived, that *ultra vires* statement could not be binding on the administrative agency in question, eg a statutory provision which stipulates that a licence application 'shall be of no effect' or 'shall not be determined' in the absence of a certain certificate. Clearly, any statement indicating that a certificate need not accompany the application could not create an estoppel against the authority in question.

It may be significant that the courts appear to be developing a far more flexible approach to problems in this area. This is seen most clearly in the decision of the House of Lords in *R v Inland Revenue Commissioners, ex p Preston* (1985) where it was said that an abuse of statutory powers could include an unfair exercise of powers where an agency's decision or act is equivalent to a breach of contract or breach of a representation giving rise to an estoppel. On the facts, however, it was found that the commissioners had not agreed or represented that they would desist from raising tax assessments against the taxpayer. This more flexible approach does again suggest that the courts have a good deal of leeway in deciding what amounts to an agreement or representation.

9.4.3 Estoppel and government policy

It was decided in *Laker Airways Ltd v Department of Trade* (1977) that an estoppel could not operate against the government in view of the government's previous conduct, albeit the conduct of a predecessor government. The issue arose following the government's attempt to withdraw the designation of Laker Airways as one of the airlines recognised as an operator on an air route between the UK and the United States, despite encouragement from a predecessor government as a result of which designation had been obtained, albeit subject to final confirmation. Although the members of the Court of Appeal had slightly different grounds for their conclusion, the main emphasis of this area of the decision (which, as will be seen later in Chapter 11 also related to other matters concerning statutory powers for air traffic licensing under the Civil Aviation Act 1971) was that an estoppel against a government would effectively hinder its ability to act for the public good. Lawton LJ for example, suggested that: 'Estoppel cannot be allowed to hinder the formation of Government policy.'

9.5 Communication of Decisions

Wherever there is a statutory responsibility requiring an administrative agency to make a decision or take similar administrative action, a time limit will normally be imposed within which any such action shall be taken. In general such a time limit – a period of two months is a fairly common stipulation – is regarded in law as being merely directory (*James v Minister of Housing and Local Government* (1966)). This is in contrast to the time limits for appeals within an administrative system, eg an appeal against the decision of a local authority to the Secretary of State for the Environment, where (as have been seen previously) the time limit for the notice of appeal is regarded as being mandatory. In the case of the typical decision on an application for a licence or grant, the status of the time limit as a directory requirement may be explained by the fact that many decisions would be *ultra vires* even as the result of the shortest delay beyond the prescribed time limit. If the time limit was normally mandatory, this could also provide an opportunity for the individual to escape his obligations under any conditions, eg by alleging at the later time for compliance with those conditions, that the original decision was out of time and therefore *ultra vires*.

In practice, the individual does often have a legal right to press against any administrative agency which is at all dilatory in notifying a decision. That right will be prescribed by the appropriate statutory provision indicating (for example), that, 'Every decision shall be notified in writing to the applicant'. Such a provision tends to suggest that the decision is contained in the relevant resolution of the authority so that the above provision is in the nature of a ministerial requirement ensuring that the decision is promptly communicated to the applicant. This conclusion is certainly suggested by the decision in the *Norfolk County Council* case where it was decided that the council had resolved to refuse a planning permission and that a notification to the contrary could not override that original refusal. More recently the High Court has said that, as long as proposals remained confidential, they were revocable: *R v Secretary of State for Education and Science, ex p Hardy* (1988). The proposals (to close a school under the powers conferred for that purpose by the education legislation) did not become irrevocable merely because they were disclosed, mistakenly, to an outside organisation. All of this, though, had to be seen in the context of the Education legislation which requires a formal, precise, published decision. This may suggest that the law requires a clear, statutory indication that a decision has full, legal status in the absence of which (outside central government departments) the internal resolution carries the decision's final legal status. This approach would confirm the view that final, written communication is a mere ministerial requirement which is at odds with the House of Lords decision in *Epping Forest District Council v Essex Rendering Ltd* (1983) which indicates that the requirement of consent in writing for the purpose of the Public Health Act is mandatory. Consequently, the local authority's alleged connivance in the operation of a plant without formal permission was no defence to an operation without consent.

9.6   Reasons

English law provides no universal obligation for reasons to be given for administrative action. The most comprehensive requirement for reasons appears in s 10(1) of the Tribunals and Inquiries Act 1992 which covers decisions of administrative tribunals listed in Schedule 1 to the Act and decisions of any minister of the Crown either following a statutory inquiry or where a person concerned could have required the holding of a statutory inquiry. In this context '... it shall be the duty of the tribunal or minister to furnish a statement, either written or oral, of the reasons for the decision if requested, on or before the giving of notification of the decision'. Tribunals and inquiries were dealt with previously in Chapters 3 and 5.

Under the same Act it has been seen that the Lord Chancellor is empowered to make procedural rules for certain types of inquiry. Such rules related mainly to inquiries into compulsory purchase orders and planning appeals and contain a stipulation requiring reasons to be given, not merely on request, but as a matter of course. Accordingly, the Town and Country Planning (Inquiries Procedure) Rules 1992 indicate that 'The Secretary of State shall notify his decision on an application or appeal, and his reasons for it, in writing ...'. Apart from the two foregoing categories, the existence of any legal obligation to give reasons for administrative action can only be discovered by a perusal of particular Acts of Parliament or regulations made under such Acts. By way of an example, s 510 of the Housing Act 1985 requires a local authority to state the reasons for any refusal of an improvement grant.

In view of the foregoing situations where there is an obligation in law to give reasons, it is a matter of the first importance to ascertain those areas of administrative action where there is no legal obligation to give reasons. Until recently, a local authority was subject to no obligation to give reasons for evicting a tenant from council housing accommodation (s 21 Housing Act 1985). A statutory inquiry into a compulsory purchase order made for slum clearance under Part 3 of the Housing Act 1957 is not covered by the procedural rules for inquiries into compulsory purchase orders and the rules' requirement of reasons for the minister's eventual decision. Finally, s 20C(3) of the Taxes Management Act 1970 (as amended by s 146 of the Finance Act 1989) does not oblige an Inland Revenue officer to give reasons for a seizure of documents from an individual. The Tribunals and Inquiries Act also contains exemptions from the general obligation to give reasons imposed on tribunals and ministers. Reasons may be refused on grounds of national security and refused to any person not primarily concerned with the decision where such reasons, if furnished, would be contrary to the interests of any person primarily concerned (Tribunals and Inquiries Act 1992 s 10(3)). Reasons need not be given in connection with any decision of a minister relating to any matter of a legislative character (Act of 1992 s 10(5)). Reasons need not be given where some other statutory provision governs the giving of reasons. Where it appears expedient to the Lord Chancellor and the Lord Advocate, following consultation with the Council on Tribunals, that the giving of reasons for certain decisions taken by tribunals and ministers is 'unnecessary and impracticable', an order may be made excluding the duty to give reasons in these cases (Act of 1992 s 10(7)).

9.6.1 The purpose of reasons

What purpose is served by the requirement that reasons should be given for decisions and other administrative action? Perhaps the most important purpose of giving reasons is to enable the individual concerned to know the basis of a decision so that he can effectively challenge that decision either by way of appeal or review, as the case may be. Consequently, reasons will be of interest for a variety of purposes in order to show how the facts and evidence were treated, together with the relevant law in relation to its application to the issues in the case. One of the leading statements of principle occurs in *Re Poyser and Mills' Arbitration* (1964) where Megaw J states that:

> Parliament having provided that reasons shall be given ... [means] that proper, adequate reasons must be given; the reasons that are set out, whether they are right or wrong, must be reasons which not only will be intelligible, but also can reasonably be said to deal with the substantial points that have been raised ... I do not want it to be thought for a moment that I am saying that any minor or trivial error, or failure to give reasons in relation to every particular point that has been raised at the hearing would be sufficient to invoke the jurisdiction of this court.

In the leading case *Save Britain's Heritage v Secretary of State for the Environment* (1991) which was referred to in Chapter 3, it was necessary for the House of Lords to consider whether the Secretary of State had given adequate reasons for his conclusion, in agreement with a planning inspector, that the appellant's proposals to demolish a number of listed and unlisted buildings in a conservation area to make way for a new modern building should be approved. In allowing the appeal, the House of Lords held that the requirement in r 17(1) of the Town and Country Planning (Inquiries Procedure) Rules 1988 that the Secretary of State should give notification of the reasons for his decision had been satisfied where his singling out of the landmark points in the inspector's reasoning process in his own decision letter demonstrated his acceptance of the substance of the inspector's judgment. Lord Bridge, who delivered the leading judgment, remarked that the statutory requirement to give reasons for their decisions imposed on both inspectors and the Secretary of State alike by the planning legislation:

> ... is a statutory safeguard to enable interested parties to know that the decision has been taken on relevant and rational grounds and that any applicable statutory criteria have been observed. It is the analogue in administrative law of the common law's requirement that justice should not only be done, but also be seen to be done.

In some cases it may be all too easy to expect too much of a statement of reasons, particularly where there are two conflicting opinions arising from the evidence before the tribunal or other administrative agency. In these circumstances, it may not be possible to explain why one opinion is preferable to the other: 'Such explanations are not possible. They are matters of judgment, impression and sometimes even instinct, and it is quite impossible to give detailed reasons to explain how the system of decision has worked.' (*per* Lord Widgery CJ in *Guppys (Bridport) Ltd v Sandhoe* (1975)). Accordingly, it is necessary that decision letters 'should not be construed as statutes and should be read as a whole' in order to avoid the possibility of 'excessive legalism' turning the requirement to give reasons 'into a hazard for decision-makers in which it is their skill in draftmanship rather than the substance of their reasoning which is put to the test' (*per* Lord Bridge in the *Save Britain's Heritage* case).

Although the court is often reluctant to define the major issue in a particular administrative decision, there are various instances where that reluctance is forgotten in a conclusion that there are no adequate reasons. Consequently, in *Mountview Court Properties Ltd v Devlin* (1970) it was found by the court that a Rent Assessment Panel had failed to deal with 'substantial' arguments and facets relating to one of the flats referred. Again, in *French Kier Developments Ltd. v Secretary of State for the Environment* (1977), Willis J concluded that the reasons given were:

> ... so vague, inadequate and unintelligible as to leave anyone reading the letter of decision from the Secretary of State quite unable to understand why, when so much of the factual conclusions were accepted by the Secretary of State, the inspector's recommendation was rejected.

Finally, in *Kent Messenger Ltd v Secretary of State for the Environment* (1977) Phillips J considered that the reasons in issue were not proper and adequate ' ... simply because they omit any reference whatever to what was an important material argument ... and one indeed which had played a substantial and influential part in the mind of the inspector in leading him to the recommendation which he made'.

9.6.2 Legal effect of a failure to give reasons or adequate intelligible reasons

Any failure to fulfil these important procedural requirements where they apply has to be examined against the background of the remedy which is available to the person challenging the decision in question. Generally, a failure to give reasons does not render any administrative action *ultra vires* (*Brayhead (Ascot) Ltd v Berkshire County Council* (1964), so that an order of *mandamus* might be available from the High Court to compel reasons, or adequate, proper reasons to be given. However, where the legislation by which a minister takes a decision specifies the terms on which the High Court may review the legality of that decision, eg a decision on a planning appeal, the court may be empowered to quash a decision for failure to comply with the legal obligation relating to reasons (*Givaudan v Minister of Housing and Local Government* (1967)). Where the legislation prescribes only an appeal on a point of law, usually from a tribunal's decision, failure to give adequate, proper reasons, might indicate an error of law so justifying the court in referring the case back to the tribunal for reconsideration in this respect (*Mountview Court Properties Ltd v Devlin* (1970)).

Where there is no legal obligation to give reasons, any failure in that respect cannot be remedied in law. However, it was suggested by the House of Lords in *Padfield v Minister of Agriculture* (1968) that this might not always be the case. In this case the minister gave reasons voluntarily but Lord Upjohn thought that if no reasons had been given, ' ... it may be, if circumstances warrant it, that a court may be at liberty to come to the conclusion that he [the minister] had no good reason for reaching [his] conclusion'. Lord Reid equally did not consider that a decision of the minister could be immune from challenge in the court if no reasons are given in the absence of any legal obligation to give reasons if this refusal to give reasons appeared to frustrate the policy and objects of the Act. A good example of this approach in practice appears from the New Zealand case of *Fiordland Venison Ltd v Minister of Agriculture and Fisheries* (1978) where the company applied to the minister for a game packing licence. Under the appropriate legislation there was a duty on the minister to grant a licence if he was satisfied on five matters. The minister refused the application, 'having regard to the criteria for new licences' set out in the legislation: no other reasons were given. The court examined the available evidence and concluded that the minister must have rejected the application on a ground which was not authorised by the legislation. He had not submitted an affidavit to the court indicating his reasons for the decision and a declaration was granted to the effect that the company was entitled to a licence. This approach by the court seems to be possible only where the statutory powers prescribe well-defined pre-requisites to be satisfied before a licence can be granted or any other similar decision made. If the administrative agency has a very discretionary decision to make involving a large measure of policy, for example, it would be difficult for the court to speculate about the real reasons for the decision as they did in *Fiordland Venison*.

10 Natural Justice

10.1 Background to Natural Justice

Whereas Chapter 9 was concerned with the scope and legal implications of procedures defined by statute, the present chapter is concerned with common law rules of fair procedure. These rules are developed by the courts and applied to certain functions of statutory administrative agencies and non-statutory domestic organisations. In broad terms, the rules of natural justice require that no person should be judge in his own cause (the rule against bias) and that a person whose rights may be affected shall have a reasonable opportunity of being heard.

10.2 Exclusion or Limitation of Natural Justice

At the outset it must be emphasised that the rules of natural justice do not necessarily apply to all exercises of powers. It will be seen subsequently that the court has previously drawn a distinction between 'administrative' and 'judicial' functions, applying the rules of natural justice to the latter. This distinction is now less frequently drawn so that even where a function might have been defined as 'administrative' there may now be a limited duty to observe some aspect of natural justice, ie a duty to act fairly. It has been seen that the rules are in two categories: the rule against bias and the rule that no person shall be condemned without being given reasonable opportunity for his case to be heard. Before these two rules are examined, it is necessary to determine the broad circumstances in which the law may exclude natural justice, to define the legal distinction between 'administrative' and 'judicial' functions, and to examine the meaning of the rather nebulous duty to act 'fairly'.

In *Gaiman v National Association for Mental Health* (1971) Megarry J observed that '... there is no simple test, but there is a tendency for the court to apply the principles [of natural justice] to all powers of decision unless the circumstances suffice to exclude them'. On those occasions when the court has excluded natural justice the circumstances have usually involved (1) express or implied statutory limitations, or (2) the absence of any rights meriting protection.

10.2.1 Statutory provisions

Expressly or impliedly, some statutory procedures may seek to exclude or limit the rules of natural justice. The Town and Country Planning Act 1990 contains many examples. In convening an Examination in Public of a structure plan, the Secretary of State for the Environment is empowered to nominate those objectors who are to be permitted a hearing at the Examination and to define the issues to be examined by the participants (Town and Country Planning Act 1990 (as amended)). In determining an application for planning permission the Act indicates a limited category of applications which must be publicised (s 65, which ought to be read in conjunction with the Town and Country Planning (General Development) Order 1995). Any person making objections in response to such a publicised application is legally entitled to have his written objections taken into account by the local planning authority (Act of 1990 s 71). This clearly excludes any right to an oral hearing before the authority prior to a decision being taken and also excludes any legal right to make representations for any person in respect of applications which fall outside a category requiring publicity. In practice, many authorities advertise most, if not all, applications and voluntarily take account of the written representations made. Finally, the statutory rules of procedure governing public local inquiries into planning appeals (and compulsory purchase and highway proposals) expressly exclude any questions being raised as to the merits of government policy. This exclusion of discussion about the merits of government policy was in contention at an inquiry into highway proposals in *Bushell v Secretary of State for the Environment* (1980). Somewhat surprisingly the House of Lords decided that the inspector's refusal to permit cross examination on traffic flow forecasts was justifiable since these forecasts are facets of government policy relating to criteria for motorway construction. The courts may be increasingly sympathetic to the idea that, in so far as inquiries are involved in the consideration of objections or recommendations and reporting to the relevant minister, any refusal of cross-examination of witnesses does not amount to a breach of natural justice. This conclusion is based on the observation that such inquiries are concerned with non-justiciable issues: *R v London Regional Passenger Committee, ex p London Borough of Brent* (1985).

10.2.2 Absence of rights

An absence of rights has usually given rise to a presumption that the rules of natural justice do not apply. A good illustration of the court's attitude comes in *McInnes v Onslow-Fane* (1978). McInnes applied to the British Boxing Board of Control for a boxing manager's licence, demanding an oral hearing of his case together with notice of any case against him so that he could disabuse the Board of any allegations which might appear in such a case. His application was refused without reasons being given, whereupon McInnes applied to the court for a declaration that the Board had acted unfairly and in breach of the rules of natural justice. The court refused to grant the declaration on the basis that the Board had discharged its necessarily limited obligations in relation to natural justice by reaching an honest conclusion, without bias, without reference to any capricious policy. It was suggested by the court that all the facets of natural justice would apply where a licence or other right was being forfeited or renewed whereas a 'first time' applicant for a licence would not have any legitimate expectation of a licence being granted so that in law he would have no right to notice of any case against him and no opportunity to be heard. Where the licensing body is not a 'domestic' organisation like the British Boxing Board of Control but a statutory body, the relevant statutory provisions governing its licensing responsibilities will (as in the example of the local planning authority) tend to indicate that the rules of natural justice are either excluded or limited. The present case is one of a long line of decisions where the court has drawn a distinction between 'rights' and mere 'privileges' although even in this latter instance where no rights are at issue the court will usually insist that, as in *McInnes*, there is a measure of fairness in the procedures. That limited measure of fairness may involve the need to recognise either the rule against bias, as in *McInnes*, or the rule that no person shall be condemned without a reasonable opportunity for his case to be heard, as in *R v Liverpool Corporation, ex p Liverpool Taxi Fleet Operators' Association* (1972). By way of contrast, in *R v Secretary of State for the Home Department, ex p Gunnell* (1983), the granting of parole was characterised as a privilege, not a right. Furthermore, the fact that the Parole Board was performing an administrative judicial function meant that the applicant could not claim that material on the case should be disclosed to him or that he should have an oral hearing. The position in relation to procedures before the Parole Board has now altered somewhat since *Ex p Gunnell* was decided due to a change in Home Office policy which has been reflected both in case law and statutory developments. In *R v Parole Board, ex p Wilson* (1992), the Court of Appeal upheld the applicant's appeal against an earlier High Court refusal to disclose to him adverse information relating to his request for release from prison. It was felt that in order for the applicant, a discretionary life sentencer, to be in a position to make effective representations to the Parole Board so as to disabuse them of the view that he was unacceptably dangerous to the public, it was necessary that he should be made aware of what had been said against him. The Court of Appeal considered that a further justification for their finding was afforded by the fact that provisions of the Criminal Justice Act 1991, which were shortly to come into force at the time of the decision, would give the applicant a statutory entitlement to disclosure subject to any public interest immunity that could be established (see also *Doody v Secretary of State for the Home Department* (1993) discussed below).

10.2.3 Preliminary processes

There has been resistance to the application of natural justice where the process in question has not led immediately to a final decision, prejudicing any rights. In other words, where there is something in the nature of a two-stage process, the first stage involving a preliminary investigation may not affect the individual's rights. This is frequently the case where a suspension takes place pending the outcome of a disciplinary investigation. In *Lewis v Heffer* (1978) the National Executive of the Labour Party suspended the local committees and officers of a constituency Labour Party, pending the result of an inquiry by the Executive. A local officer sought an injunction to prevent the suspension on the ground that the Executive had acted unlawfully and in breach of natural justice. Similar grounds were used subsequently by the plaintiff and another officer when they found that the Executive had it in mind to suspend them from Labour Party membership pending the result of the same inquiry. In refusing injunctions in both cases, the court considered that suspension as a temporary measure may be a matter of 'good administration' pending investigation so that natural justice ought not to apply. A further example of a finding that the rules of natural justice had not been breached occurred in *Herring v Templeman* (1973), where it was held that there was no implied obligation for an academic board to accord a hearing to a student who was facing the prospect of being expelled from a teacher-training college since the board only had power to make recommendations. It was the governing body which was charged with the responsibility of making a final decision, and hence it was they who owed the student a duty to act fairly by affording him an adequate opportunity to explain before them why the recommendations of the academic board should not be accepted. Nevertheless, the House of Lords has taken the view that even in the course of preliminary proceedings, any provisional finding in the establishment of a *prima facie* case could significantly prejudice a person's rights and interest to the extent that a hearing ought to be given to that person (*Wiseman v Borneman* (1971)). In *Re Pergamon Press* (1970) Board of Trade inspectors appointed under the Companies Act to investigate and report on the affairs of a company were under a duty to act fairly and to give anyone whom they proposed to condemn or criticise a fair opportunity to answer what was alleged against them. It was claimed by the company's directors that they had a legal right to see transcripts of witnesses' evidence against them and to cross-examine those witnesses. This claim was rejected by the court where Lord Denning indicated that there was no need to quote chapter and verse so that a mere outline of the charge will usually suffice. Further proceedings in the case led to the court's conclusion that there was no legal obligation requiring the inspectors to indicate their tentative conclusions for comment by the parties prior to publication of their report (*Maxwell v Department of Trade and Industry* (1974)).

10.2.4   Absence of contractual or similar relationships

The absence of any contractual of similar relationship with a non-statutory domestic organisation such as a trade union or professional association may indicate that natural justice does not apply to its transactions with individuals (*Byrne v Kinematograph Renters Society* (1958)). The main justification for this proposition is that the absence of a contractual or similar relationship means that the individual has not associated himself with the organisation and any express or implied obligation on its part to comply with natural justice. Nevertheless, the cases are unpredictable in this context. For example, in *Nagle v Feilden* (1966) the stewards of the Jockey Club failed to persuade the court to strike out Nagle's claim for a declaration that the Club's policy of refusing trainers' licences to women was contrary to public policy on the ground that the plaintiff's right to work was in issue. It is difficult to reconcile this decision, indicating the relevance of natural justice to a licence application, with the statement of principle in *McInnes* to the effect that the rules do not apply to an initial licence application but would apply to a revocation or renewal.

10.2.5   Professional advice

The rules do not apply to professional advice although there is an exception where a person's rights may be affected. This is seen clearly in *R v Kent Police Authority, ex p Godden* (1971). A police doctor and a consultant concluded that Godden, a police officer, was mentally ill but the court required that their reports be produced to Godden's own consultant when the police authority sought to employ the same police doctor in order to certify Godden as permanently disabled for the purpose of the police pensions regulations. Had the authority chosen a different police doctor for this latter purpose then no doubt natural justice would not have applied in this doctor-patient relationship on the ground that Godden's rights might not have been prejudiced. The general absence of natural justice from the professional relationship can also be seen in *Hounslow London Borough Council v Twickenham Garden Developments Ltd* (1970). Under a contract of the Royal Institute of British Architects an architect gave appropriate notice that a contractor had failed to proceed 'regularly and diligently'. It was decided that the notice was not void for want of natural justice since although an architect must retain his independence when exercising his skilled professional judgment, there was nothing in the nature of a 'judicial' determination requiring application of the rules.

10.2.6   Disciplinary proceedings

In some cases, disciplinary proceedings can occur without reference to natural justice, usually where no rights of the individual are liable to be prejudiced. Whether the rights of the individual are in issue seems sometimes to depend on the severity of any punishment which may result from the disciplinary proceedings: a rather uncertain basis for the law. Accordingly, in *Ex p Fry* (1954) a fireman was punished for disobeying an order. He alleged that the hearing was unfair but at first instance the court decided that the law could not interfere with the exercise of a disciplinary power in a service such as the fire service. Such cases would suggest that natural justice should be excluded from disciplinary proceedings in institutions and organisations where discipline is perhaps the sole responsibility of the person in charge, such as a headmaster. In referring for present purposes to the governor of a prison, Lord Denning stated in *Becker v Home Office* (1972) that a governor's life would be intolerable if the courts were to entertain actions for breaches of natural justice from disgruntled prisoners. The Court of Appeal in *R v Deputy Governor of Camphill Prison, ex p King* (1985) repeated these sentiments, referring to the possible weakening of a governor's authority. The prisoner's remedy lay in a complaint to the board of visitors and then (if necessary) a petition to the Home Secretary. Only thereafter might there be a legitimate challenge before the court. By way of contrast, it has been held that in *R v Hull Prison Board of Visitors, ex p St Germain* (1979) that natural justice did apply to disciplinary functions in prisons carried out by boards of visitors. Megaw LJ emphasised a difference between the disciplinary functions of the governor and those of the board, acting as a 'judicial' tribunal:

> While the governor hears charges and makes awards his position in doing so corresponds to that of a commanding officer or a school master. Both good sense and the practical requirements of public policy make it undesirable that his exercise of this part of his administrative duties should be made subject to *certiorari*. The same, however, does not apply to the adjudications and awards of boards of visitors who are enjoined to mete out punishment only after a formalised inquiry and/or hearing.

There are difficulties in defining material differences between the disciplinary functions of the board and the governor, eg outlined in the same case by Shaw LJ in relation to the levels of punishment to be administered, so that the law really seems to rest on judicial policy. The House of Lords acknowledged the reality of this position in their important decision in *Leech v Parkhurst Prison Deputy Governor* (1988) which served to clarify the law by removing the distinction between prison governors and boards of visitors so that the adjudications of both became subject to judicial review. In *Leech*, the appellants had been found guilty of offences contrary to the Prison Rules 1964 and accordingly they had been punished by having awards of a number of days' loss of remission made against them. Following a careful examination of the authorities, the House of Lords came to the conclusion that the reasoning underpinning the decision in *Ex p King* could no longer be supported and hence the decision should be overruled. Lord Bridge considered that the views expressed in *Ex p King* as to why judicial review should be refused were 'based on subjective judicial impression' and whilst he acknowledged that his own views were 'no less speculative', he was nevertheless of the opinion that:

> ... if the social consequences of the availability of judicial review to supervise governors' disciplinary awards are so detrimental to the proper functioning of the prison system as *King's* case predicts, it lies in the province of the legislature not of the judiciary to exclude the court's jurisdiction.

It is worth noting that since the decision in *Leech*, boards of prison visitors have in fact lost their disciplinary functions following a recommendation of the Woolf Report, *Prison Disturbances*, April 1990, Cm 1456 (1994). Finally, in the context of an employment relationship, the court may be prepared to imply natural justice, eg for the purpose of defining a procedure for dismissals, but only where the employee enjoys a statutory status or office in public employment or service (*Malloch v Aberdeen Corporation* (1971)). Consequently, a private employer is able to dismiss an employee without a hearing at common law (*Hill v CA Parsons & Co* (1972)).

10.3   Judicial and Administrative Functions

The distinction between 'judicial' and 'administrative' functions has been of fundamental importance in determining whether natural justice applies in any particular case. However, in restricting the rules to 'judicial' or 'quasi-judicial' functions, the common law has perhaps failed to do justice in cases where an individual's rights and interests may be affected, albeit incidentally, in the context of what seems to be an administrative function. The possibility that such a situation could arise is in itself an indictment of this rather nebulous distinction between judicial and administrative functions. Nevertheless, it will be seen subsequently that it is a distinction which is still used by the court from time to time, in which case there will probably be reliance on the leading statement of principle from the House of Lords in *Ridge v Baldwin* (1963). In this case Ridge, the Chief Constable of Brighton, had been acquitted of a conspiracy to obstruct the course of justice but two officers from the Brighton police force had been convicted. The judge, in passing sentence, referred to an absence of professional and moral leadership on the part of their Chief Constable. Following Ridge's acquittal, the Brighton Watch Committee (as the police authority) dismissed him from office without notice and without hearing any case he may have wanted to present. Subsequently, Ridge's solicitor was allowed to appear before the Committee but the dismissal was confirmed. The Home Secretary later dismissed an appeal by Ridge against the decision of the Watch Committee. Thereafter, Ridge, being anxious to protect his pension rights in the police service, sought a declaration from the court that he had been wrongfully dismissed. The House of Lords granted the declaration on the basis that natural justice applied to the Watch Committee's function and that Ridge had no adequate opportunity of knowing the case against him so that he had no reasonable opportunity to put his case against dismissal. The important statement of principle is that a 'judicial' function arises wherever action is taken by any body or persons having legal authority to determine questions affecting the rights of subjects (*per* Atkin LJ in *R v Electricity Commissioners* (1924)). Such a function presupposes a dispute between the parties where they present their respective cases, perhaps by adducing evidence on disputed facts and/or by advancing legal argument on disputed points of law, as a result of which a decision finally disposes of the case. By contrast, the quasi-judicial function involves a decision on the parties' cases but also covers other matters such as policy and the public interest.

10.3.1 The duty to act judicially

The duty to act judicially applies to trade union disciplinary committees (*Taylor v National Union of Seamen* (1967)), academic institutions exercising disciplinary functions (*Glynn v Keele University* (1971)), and various other domestic organisations (*John v Rees* (1969)), among others. Prior to these modern cases it had been decided in *Cooper v Wandsworth Board of Works* (1863) that the Board of Works, a statutory body, was not empowered to demolish property without affording the owner an opportunity of putting his case against such action. In contemporary times, many statutes empowering action to be taken by an administration agency like a local authority will prescribe the terms on which any representations may be made. For example, the Housing Act 1985 ss 264 (as substituted by Schedule 9 of the Local Government and Housing Act 1989), 268 and 275 (as amended), require a local authority to provide an opportunity for an owner to discuss the condition of a house before a demolition order is executed so that the authority can then be satisfied that the premises are unfit for human habitation and incapable of repair at reasonable expense. Because there is a statutory prescription expressly applying a relevant aspect of natural justice in these circumstances, it may be argued that no common law right to a hearing can be implied into a statutory power enabling a local authority to take emergency action to demolish any structure which is regarded as being dangerous. Accordingly, the need to identify judicial functions may now often be overridden by the express or implied terms of specific statutory provisions either limiting or excluding natural justice. Nevertheless, in some areas the definition of judicial and administrative functions may still be important in determining whether there has been a breach of natural justice, for example, in cases like *Gunnell* (above) and on the part of a minister in the statutory context of deciding whether a compulsory purchase order submitted by a local authority should be confirmed. This area of activity has produced some of the leading cases on the identification of judicial and administrative functions where a minister is often charged with making a policy decision. Such a 'policy' decision frequently requires the minister to consider all manner of questions relating to the public interest and in law, he cannot be prevented from attaching more importance to the fulfilment of his policy than to the fate of individual objectors.

Against this background it was stated by Greer LJ in *Errington v Minister of Health* (1934) that a minister, in dealing with objections to a compulsory purchase order, was 'exercising quasi-judicial functions' because 'the decision of the minister is a decision relating to the rights of the objecting parties'. In another of the leading cases, *B Johnson & Co (Builders) Ltd v Minister of Health* (1947), it was found that natural justice did not apply to require a minister, in considering whether to confirm a compulsory purchase order, to divulge information put before him before he considered objections, that is, before he assumed a quasi-judicial role. Lord Greene MR observed that the 'administrative' process in the present context:

... may begin in all sorts of manners – the collection of information, the ascertainment of facts, and the consideration of representations from all sorts of quarters ... long before any question of objections can arise under the procedure laid down by the Act ... The administrative character in which [the minister] acts reappears at a later stage because, after considering the objections, which may be regarded as the culminating point of his quasi-judicial functions, there follows something which again ... is purely administrative, *viz* the decision whether or not to confirm the order. That decision must be an administrative decision, because it is not based purely on the view that he forms of the objections *vis-à-vis* the desires of the local authority, but is to be guided by his view as to the policy which in the circumstances he ought to pursue ...

10.3.2   Reliance on the distinction between functions

The distinction has been relied on in a number of important cases but not without considerable criticism in some instances. In *Franklin v Minister of Town and Country Planning* (1947) the minister was responsible for making orders designating sites for new towns. At a public meeting preceding a proposal to designate Stevenage as a new town, the minister insisted that he would discharge his statutory duty in this context despite any obstructive behaviour by the public. When an order was subsequently made under the New Towns Act 1946, an attempt was made to quash it on the ground that the minister had been acting unlawfully in breach of natural justice as a judge in his own cause. The House of Lords decided that there was no breach of the rule against bias: the minister's responsibilities were administrative: to appoint a person to hold a public inquiry and to consider that person's report. In *Nakkuda Ali v Jayaratna* (1951) the Controller of Textiles in Ceylon was empowered by statute to cancel textile licences where he had reasonable grounds to believe that any dealer was unfit to be allowed to continue as a dealer. The Controller dealt with some objections to a proposed licence cancellation by correspondence but it was decided that the Controller's function here were administrative, not judicial, so that he was not obliged to afford a hearing prior to revoking the licence. The facts of the third case, *R v Metropolitan Police Commissioner, ex p Parker* (1953) are similar to those of *Nakkuda Ali*, and involved the Commissioner's statutory power to revoke taxi licences. It was decided that Parker, whose licence was subject to revocation, was not entitled to produce witnesses to make representations on his behalf before the Commissioner prior to the decision being made. Finally, in *Essex County Council v Minister of Housing and Local Government* (1968) it was decided there was no right to be heard before the minister in respect of the making of a statutory Special Development Order designating Stansted Airport as the third London airport on the ground that a legislative function was involved.

The decision in *Franklin* emphasises the nebulous basis for the distinction between administrative and judicial functions. However, the decision together with those in *Nakkuda Ali* and *Parker* may be explained by the courts' post-War reluctance to question the legality of many exercises of executive power. A more satisfactory basis for the decision in *Franklin* would have been the statutory 'authorisation' for the minister's actions, recognising that by the very scheme of things he would be 'judge in his own cause'. Nevertheless it was suggested in the Report of the Committee on Ministers' Powers (1932) that a strong and perhaps sincere conviction as to public policy of the sort that seems to have pervaded the situation in *Franklin* may operate as a more serious disqualification than some pecuniary interest in a decision. More recently, in *R v Secretary of the Environment, ex p Brent London Borough Council & Others* (1981) it was held that a policy formulated by the Secretary of State by which he would reduce the rate support grant payable to councils which had overspent was unlawful, not on the ground of bias, but because he refused to hear representations from councils whose financial rights would be affected by a reduction in grant. Finally, the facts and decision in *Nakkuda Ali* and *Parker* would no doubt be seen in a different light if they had occurred more recently. In view of the legal recognition of rights in relation to the renewal and revocation of licences from cases like *McInnes v Onslow-Fane*, there can be little doubt that in both cases the court would have decided that there was a judicial function being exercised, attracting at least the right for the licensee to be heard.

Although reliance on the definition of administrative and judicial functions has declined for the purposes of natural justice, it can be seen that it has not been abandoned entirely. In *Hibernian Property Co Ltd v Secretary of State for the Environment* (1974) the court expressed its approval of the decision in *Errington* in quashing the Secretary of State's decision to confirm a compulsory purchase order on the ground of a breach of natural justice. The breach occurred when an inspector conducted a site visit following the close of the inquiry in the absence of any representative of one of the chief objectors to the order and when the residents of certain houses expressed their views about whether their houses should be demolished or improved. The court was willing to quash the decision because there was a risk that the transaction might have prejudiced the chief objector's interests. In *R v Barnsley Metropolitan Borough Council, ex p Hook* (1976) the court was concerned with the revocation of a market trader's licence originally granted by the local authority. An allegation of misconduct and a breach of market rules was made by the market manager who was also present while Hook was excluded on the two occasions when the case was adjudicated by committees of the local authority. This was found to be a breach of both rules of natural justice by virtue of the fact that the trader's legal rights to use the market were subject to adjudication, a clear case of a judicial function, even though the local authority's control of the licensing of market stalls was essentially in other respects an administrative function. More recently, the House of Lords was concerned with the legality of the Secretary of State's order approving a motorway scheme in *Bushell v Secretary of State for the Environment* (1980). It was decided that objectors could not make representations on new traffic flow criteria adopted by the Department of the Environment following the close of the inquiry when the Secretary of State's function was essentially administrative. Not long before it had been decided that the Secretary of State was obliged to act fairly to the extent that he should have allowed representations from objectors in relation to evidence obtained by an inspector following the close of an inquiry into a compulsory purchase order for slum clearance (*Fairmount Investments Ltd v Secretary of State for the Environment* (1976)). In this latter case there was no reference to the distinction between administrative and judicial functions.

It is very difficult if not impossible to reconcile the foregoing decisions although a great deal does seem to depend on the judicial policy of the court in relation to the facts of each case. Consequently, the court's reluctance to admit the rules of natural justice into the final stages of a minister's decision, particularly where it seems to involve significant areas of government policy, may explain the decision in *Bushell*. The facts in *Fairmount*, on the other hand, could have confronted the court with a dilemma if the definition of administrative and judicial functions from the other leading cases on compulsory purchase orders had been adopted. Had the definition of functions from *Errington* and *Johnson* been adopted, the 'post-inquiry' stage might have been seen as the administrative function which excludes natural justice in a case where the rights of the landowner were clearly still in issue. The decision in *Hibernian Property* may be reconciled with the function definition of the earlier cases by saying that the site visit following the inquiry is still very much the focus of the objectors' rights, as is the inquiry itself. From the foregoing discussion it can be appreciated how rigid the definition of functions can be in many cases, eg in failing to recognise that even in what may have been seen to be an administrative function rights may be at issue. Such difficulties may now be largely avoided through the adoption of the more flexible duty to act 'fairly' which is examined in the next section. It may be argued, therefore, that the definition of functions as the basis for natural justice tends to be used wherever the court is anxious to exclude natural justice, perhaps as a matter of 'judicial policy', as in *Bushell* or *Gunnell*, where the court is confronted by a clearly defined judicial or quasi-judicial function as in *Hook*, or where the case in hand involves the rule against bias which can only arise in the context of a judicial function.

10.4   The Duty to Act Fairly

The adoption of a flexible duty to act fairly has enabled a very much more sensitive reconciliation of the common law requirements of fair procedure with the many different bureaucratic functions and their requirements. One of the most significant cases in this area of the common law is *Re H K (An Infant)* (1967) where an immigration officer refused entry to a boy on the ground that he was over 16. The boy said that he was only 15, in which case he would have had a right of entry to the UK. Lord Parker CJ doubted whether the officer was:

... acting in a judicial or quasi-judicial capacity... But at the same time, I myself think that even if an immigration officer is not in a judicial or quasi-judicial capacity, he must at least give the immigrant an opportunity of satisfying him of the matters in the subsection, and for that purpose let the immigrant know what his immediate impression is so that the immigrant can disabuse him. That is not, as I see it, a question of acting or being required to act judicially, but of being required to act fairly. Good administration and an honest or *bona fide* decision must, as it seems to me, require not merely impartiality, nor merely bringing one's mind to bear on the problem, but acting fairly; and to the limited extent that the circumstances of any particular case allow, and within the legislative framework under which the administration is working, only to that limited extent do the so-called rules of natural justice apply, which in a case such as this is merely a duty to act fairly.

The duty to act fairly seems to connote an obligation to observe some aspect of the rules of natural justice, according to the circumstances and background of the particular case. Accordingly, there may be an obligation to make a decision impartially even though there is no legal obligation to provide a person concerned with that decision a reasonable opportunity of being heard. This variety of the duty to act fairly is illustrated by Megarry J in *Leary v National Union of Vehicle Builders* (1971) where he refers to a situation in which a student has no right to be heard by examiners dealing with his work although he is entitled to have his case '... duly considered by whatever bodies have the power of decision'. Disciplinary proceedings, on the other hand, might well attract both rules of natural justice, in other words the right to be heard and the rule against bias (*Glynn v Keele University* (1971)). The duty to act fairly may well require observance of the requirement that a person is given a reasonable opportunity for his case to be heard, albeit on a limited basis. This was seen in Chapter 9 in *R v Liverpool Corporation, ex p Liverpool Taxi Fleet Operators' Association* (1971) where the Corporation had a statutory power to license taxis. Discussions took place between the Corporation and the Association during which an undertaking was given by the Corporation that no further taxi licences would be granted until private legislation was enacted to regulate mini-cabs. Subsequently and without consulting the Association, the Corporation proposed to increase the number of licences before the legislation concerning mini-cabs was enacted. An order of prohibition was granted by the court to the Association requiring the Corporation to grant a hearing before deciding whether to depart from the undertaking. Although the Association's rights were not in issue, the taxi owners were clearly affected by the Corporation's proposal to grant further licences which seems to account for the court's willingness to require limited consultation. The courts now rely considerably on so-called 'legitimate expectations' in this context. In *Attorney General of Hong Kong v Ng Yuen Shin* (1983) an immigration officer had publicly announced that each case of illegal immigration into the colony would be considered on its merits. The court granted the applicant a remedy requiring compliance with a duty to act fairly by adhering to the promised procedure, in the interests of good administration. However, the limited, procedural enforcement of this legitimate expectation had to be consistent with the exercise of the authority's statutory duty.

By way of contrast, in *Re H K* the immigrant's rights were in issue and this was sufficient for the court to suggest that the immigration officer should determine the case impartially, having given notice of possible disqualification from entry and having provided a reasonable opportunity for that person to reply. In *Schmidt v Home Secretary* (1969), on the other hand, an alien applied unsuccessfully to remain in the UK beyond the period stipulated in his permit. He was not given a hearing and the court decided that the Home Secretary had not acted unfairly because Schmidt had no right to remain and no legitimate expectation of remaining. Had there been an attempt to exclude him before the expiration of his permit then, it was suggested, the duty to act fairly would have prescribed a hearing in defence of the legitimate expectation that he would be permitted to remain in the country for the duration of his permit. The decision in a case like *Schmidt* does raise a comparison with *R v Liverpool Corporation*. It seems that a very limited duty to act fairly may occur where, short of the circumstances creating a legally binding estoppel against a statutory authority, some promise or undertaking is made on which another person or organisation relies. Such a promise or undertaking may not be broken except where a reasonable opportunity is given for any objections or other representations, beyond which that promise or undertaking may be broken. Where, for example, a licence has expired, an undertaking may be given to the licensee by the licensor that the activity covered by the licence may continue informally for a certain period of time. Although that undertaking is not strictly binding in law, the court might be prepared to restrain any sanctions against the licensee's continuation of the activity until he is given a reasonable opportunity of making representations to the licensor, eg in favour of a continuation of the 'informal' permission.

10.5   The Rule Against Bias

The first of the rules of natural justice – *nemo judex in causa sua* – stipulates that no man can be a judge in his own cause. This rule against bias is clearly consistent with the characteristics and requirements of a judicial function as seen previously in *R v Barnsley Metropolitan Borough Council, ex p Hook*. Many cases concern magistrates, as in *R v Altrincham Justices, ex p Pennington* (1975), where a magistrate was also a member of the county education committee. Consequently, she had an active connection with the 'victims' of an offence committed against the county council when short supplies of vegetables were delivered to two of its schools. The farmer in question had also supplied vegetables to a school of which the magistrate was a governor. Overall, therefore, the magistrate's interests were sufficient to disqualify her from hearing the criminal charges. The rule against bias applies also to statutory authorities (*R v Hendon Rural District Council, ex p Chorley* (1933)) and to domestic organisations (*Roebuck v NUM (Yorkshire Area) (No 2)* (1978)).

10.5.1   Application of the rule against bias

The rule applies:

(1) where there is some direct interest in the matter to be adjudicated and

(2) where, short of a direct interest, there is some reasonable suspicion, appearance or likelihood of bias.

In the first case there are few problems, eg where there is some direct financial interest in proceedings as in *R v Hendon Rural District Council* where the local planning authority's decision granting planning permission was quashed by the court because a member of the authority was an estate agent appointed to deal with that land. This separate category was alluded to in the judgment in *R v Camborne Justices, ex p Pearce* (1955), where it was observed that:

> ... any direct pecuniary or proprietary interest in the subject matter of a proceeding, however small, operates as an automatic disqualification. In such a case the law assumes bias.

A further example of a case in which a person sitting in an adjudicative capacity had a pecuniary interest in the outcome of the proceedings is the well known case of *Dimes v Proprietors of Grand Junction Canal* (1852). In this case, decrees were affirmed by Lord Cottenham LC in favour of a canal company in which he had a considerable shareholding. In setting aside the decrees, the House of Lords were not concerned whether there was in fact bias, or, whether there was some reasonable suspicion, appearance or likelihood of bias. It was enough that the nature of Lord Cottenham's interest was such that public confidence in the administration of justice demanded that his decision be set aside. Lord Campbell summarised the position thus:

> No one can suppose that Lord Cottenham could be, in the remotest degree, influenced by the interest that he had in this concern; but, my Lords, it is of the last importance that the maxim that no man is to be a judge in his own cause should be held sacred.

In the case of the more indirect type of bias, (2), the generally accepted rule was that:

> ... in considering whether there was a real likelihood of bias, the court does not look at the mind of the justice himself or at the mind of the chairman of the tribunal or whoever it may be, who sits in a judicial capacity. It does not look to see if there was a real likelihood that he would, or did in fact favour one side at the expense of the other. The court looks at the impression which would be given to other people. Even if he was as impartial as could be, nevertheless if right-minded persons would think that, in the circumstances, there was a real likelihood of bias on his part, then he should not sit. And if he does sit, his decision cannot stand. Nevertheless there must appear to be a

real likelihood of bias. Surmise or conjecture is not enough. There must be circumstances from which a reasonable man would think it likely to probable that the justice, or chairman, as the case may be, would, or did, favour one side unfairly at the expense of the other. The court will not inquire whether he did, in fact, favour one side unfairly. Suffice if that reasonable people might think he did (*per* Lord Denning in *Metropolitan Properties Co (FGC) Ltd v Lannon* (1969)

In this case the court quashed the decision of a Rent Assessment Committee by which the rent of certain flats was reduced. The solicitor chairman of the Committee lived with his father and had dealt with disputes between the father and his landlord, a company which was a member of the group of companies to which Metropolitan Properties belonged.

Although there is a strong presumption that the rule against bias applies in the context of a judicial function, there are occasions when the court has regarded it as inappropriate to apply the law concerning a suspicion of bias. For example, the membership of an expert tribunal will not be disqualified by reference to their pre-existing knowledge and impressions. Any suggestion that a tribunal is affected by an unlawfully biased predetermination in a particular case is dealt with in the leading statement of principle by Lord du Parcq in *R v Westminster Assessment Committee* (1940) where he stated that:

> ... the experience of an expert tribunal ... is part of its equipment for determining the case. Litigants must take that experience as they find it, and because the tribunal is assumed to be impartial they have no grievance if they cannot test it by cross-examination.

Nevertheless, even in these circumstances, evidence of some overtly prejudicial views of a particular case by a member of the tribunal would amount to a reasonable suspicion of bias. Similarly, previously expressed views in respect of a particular case may suggest prejudgment sufficient to amount to unlawful bias (*R v Kent Police Authority, ex p Godden* (1971)). However, where any administrative agency appears to be unlawfully prejudging a case by reference to a policy the court may well conclude that at that stage there is an administrative function in which case the rule against bias cannot apply (*Franklin v Minister of Town and Country Planning* (1947)). Whenever a policy affects a decision it is a factor which may prevent a wholly impartial adjudication of the competing rights and interests, hence the law's acceptance of the proposition that the rule against bias can only operate in relation to a truly judicial function. The policy of a government department, for example, may be to encourage local authorities in a time of chronic housing shortage to buy land for house building even though some of the land is not wholly suitable for that purpose. Accordingly, any compulsory purchase order submitted to the Secretary of State by a local authority would probably be confirmed even though in normal circumstances any strong, well-founded objections based on the suitability of the land would normally lead to an adjudication in favour of the landowner and against the local authority.

10.5.2 The test for bias

The test has recently been the subject of consideration by the House of Lords in *R v Gough* (1993), a case which involved an appeal against conviction for conspiracy to rob on the ground that a member of the jury was the next door neighbour of the appellant's brother. Originally, it had been the intention of the prosecution to also proceed against the brother, but the case against him had been dropped at the committal stage on the grounds of insufficient evidence. In order for the House of Lords to determine the matter before them, it was necessary to conduct a review of the authorities which were, in the opinion of Lord Goff, 'not only large in number, but bewildering in their effect'. Since the decision in *Lannon*, the court had tended to set aside any decision by reference to the objective test of a reasonable suspicion of bias. This case was however distinguished by the High Court in *R v Sevenoaks District Council, ex p Terry* (1985) where the council had accepted a tender for the lease of a site in its ownership from a development company. Thereupon the council granted planning permission for the agreed development before a formal agreement was struck between the parties. The decision to grant planning permission was challenged unsuccessfully. The court concluded that administrative decisions, if they were subject to challenge on the *Lannon* test, would lead to an administrative impasse where the local authority owned the land in question. The test was whether the authority had exercised a proper discretion: remarkably the court found that a proper discretion was exercised, prior to the formal agreement.

Another test was expounded by the court in *R v Barnsley Licensing Justices, ex p Barnsley and District Licensed Victuallers' Association* (1960) where Devlin LJ considered that the members of the court had to satisfy themselves that there was a real likelihood of bias. Compared with the test defined by Lord Denning in *Lannon*, this test is concerned essentially with the subjective estimation of bias by the members of the court. Another version of the objective test occurred in *R v Sussex Justices, ex p McCarthy* (1924) where Lord Hewart CJ said that it is '... of fundamental importance that justice should not only be done, but should manifestly and undoubtedly be seen to be done'. Applying the test of a real likelihood of bias in the *Barnsley Licensing Justices* case, the court found that Justices who were members of the Co-operative Society which was applying for a spirits off-licence were legally disqualified. However, it was decided that *certiorari* would not lie to quash the decision since there was no real likelihood of bias. It is probably the case that there was very little if any difference in the result of applying the two tests. Interestingly, Lord Goff was of the opinion in *R v Gough* that whilst Lord Denning in *Lannon* purported to differ from the remarks of Lord Justice Devlin in the *Barnsley Licensing Justices* case, what he in fact said differed very little from that which had been said by the latter. To an extent the point is of academic interest only since *R v Gough* has now clarified the position with regard to the 'reasonable suspicion test' and the 'real likelihood test'. In all cases of apparent bias, whether they involve justices or members of other inferior tribunals, or, as in the present case, jurors or alternatively arbitrators, the test is now that if there is a real danger of bias on the part of the decision-maker then justice requires that the decision should not be allowed to stand. In so finding, the House of Lords applied the 'real danger' test laid down in *R v Spencer* (1987). The preference for the statement of the test in terms of 'real danger' rather than 'real likelihood' reflects a deliberate attempt by the House of Lords 'to ensure that the court is thinking in terms of possibility rather than probability of bias'. Lord Woolf summed up the view of their Lordships when he concluded his judgment with the observation that:

> The real danger test is quite capable of producing the right answer and ensure that the purity of justice is maintained across the range of situations where bias may exist.

Since the decision in *Gough*, the real danger test for bias has been applied in a number of cases. In *R v Bailey* (1994), for example, an appeal against conviction was not upheld where a juror had accidentally sighted the defendant at a tube station during the course of the trial since although the jury had collectively discussed the sighting and the juror's fear, the incident had not coloured their decision; in the circumstances, there was no real danger of bias. By contrast, in *R v Khan* (1995), there was held to be a real danger of bias where a juror knew one of the witnesses called on the defendant's behalf as well as the victim of the crime and the victim's mother. Accordingly, the appeal against conviction was allowed and a retrial was ordered at a Crown Court where the likelihood of witnesses and jurors knowing one another would be reduced.

10.5.3   Modification or exclusion

The rule can be modified or excluded by statute. Equally, the common law may exclude or modify the rule, eg on the ground of necessity or by reference to a party's waiver of his legal right requiring observance of the rule as in *Thomas v University of Bradford (No 2)* (1992). Necessity might well be pleaded where no other suitable adjudicator is available while waiver requires that the party knows of the adjudicator's disqualification (*R v Essex Justices, ex p Perkins* (1927)). The statutory exclusion or modification of the rule usually relates to some governmental function where the particular administrative agency is necessarily judge in its own cause in the absence of any other statutory machinery securing independent facilities for the performance of relevant functions. In *Wilkinson v Barking Corporation* (1948) the relevant legislation provided that a person's entitlement to a superannuation allowance was to be determined initially by his local authority employer with an appeal to the Minister of Health, even though both parties contributed to the relevant fund. In *Jeffs v New Zealand Dairy Production and Marketing Board* (1967) it was also decided that there could be no legal objection on the matter of bias to an order of the Board which allocated areas of supply among various companies, even though the Board had made large loans to one of the companies and so had an interest in its prosperity, since these were functions expressly conferred on the Board by statute. Statute may also expressly clarify areas of difficulty in relation to the rule against bias. Section 3 of the Justices of the Peace Act 1949, as re-enacted in 1979, prohibited a magistrate from hearing an action brought by a local authority of which he is a member. However, s 130 of the Licensing Act 1964 stipulates that a magistrate is not disqualified from hearing a licensing application merely because he is a member of the licensing planning committee. Nevertheless, s 193 of the Act states that:

> No justice shall act for any purpose under this Act in a case that concerns any premises in the profits of which he is interested ... Provided that a justice shall not be disqualified under this provision by reasons only of his having vested in him a legal interest only, and not a beneficial interest, in the premises concerned or the profits of them.

The section goes on to state that no act done by any justice disqualified by the section shall be invalid by reason only of the statutory disqualification.

10.6 The Right to Be Heard

The second of the rules of natural justice – *audi alteram partem* – states that no person shall be condemned without being given a reasonable opportunity for his case to be heard. There are two aspects to this rule requiring that adequate prior notice is given of any case, charge or allegation and that the person concerned should have a reasonable opportunity to put his case against the same. It has been seen previously that natural justice is generally presumed to be excluded in a number of circumstances. Nevertheless, the court may prescribe a duty to act fairly in these circumstances, to the extent that the context of any decision-making process may suggest that one aspect only of natural justice applies. Where, for example, a minister is conducting a preliminary inquiry into a company's affairs under the Companies Acts, there may be a duty to act fairly to the extent that prior notice may have to be given of any potentially contentious finding (*Re Pergamon Press* (1971)). However, where it appears that any administrative agency is obliged to act judicially then there is a presumption that all aspects of the rules apply, in which case the court would require clear statutory words in order to justify any exclusion of natural justice (*R v Housing Appeal Tribunal* (1920)).

10.6.1 Prior notice

The first requirement of the rule is that adequate prior notice should be given of any charge or allegation. Accordingly, in *Fairmount Investments Ltd v Secretary of State for the Environment* (1976) it was found by the court that there was no notice given to the owner of the building subject to a compulsory purchase order in respect of the inspector's findings on the condition of the structure. These findings had not been in issue at the inquiry but were made following the close of the inquiry and used by the Secretary of State as the basis for his decision, without any opportunity being made available for the owner to rebut them. Furthermore, in *R v Trafford Magistrates' Court, ex p Riley* (1995), a conviction for an offence under the Dangerous Dogs Act 1991 together with a destruction order made under the same Act were quashed, in part due to the fact that there had been a denial of natural justice by not giving the owner of the dog notice of the hearing at which magistrates made the destruction order. The unusual circumstances of the case were that at the time that the applicant's dog bit a policeman, another woman was holding the dog's lead and accordingly it was this other woman rather than the owner who was proceeded against on the basis that she was the person for the time being in charge of a dog dangerously out of control in a public place. In the opinion of the court, the owner of the dog should be given notice of any further hearing so that she would be able to attend and make such points as were open to her. Nevertheless, in some cases the facts may suggest that the substance of a charge or allegation is, in fact, known to the plaintiff so that the absence of any further information thereon does not amount to a breach of the rules (*Sloan v General Medical Council* (1970)). Statutory provisions may expressly require clear notice to be given of proposed action by an administrative agency as well as providing in many cases a definite opportunity for any person affected to be heard. For example, s 73 of the Planning (Listed Buildings and Conservation Areas) Act 1990 requires a local planning authority to publicise any application for planning permission affecting land in a conservation area. Thereafter, in determining such an application the authority is obliged by s 29 to 'take into account' any representation made in response to the publicity. In practice, such representations are made in writing and there is no legal obligation on the authority to permit oral representations (*Local Government Board v Arlidge* (1915)).

In theory, the requirement relating to prior notice must extend to every person who is actually or potentially affected by any charge, allegation or other administrative action (*R v Kensington and Chelsea Rent Tribunal, ex p MacFarlane* (1974)). Statutory provisions like s 73 of the Planning (Listed Buildings and Conservation Areas) Act 1990 recognise that the local planning authority cannot ascertain precisely who may be affected by development in conservation areas. In a slightly different vein, s 176 of the Town and Country Planning Act 1990 allows the Secretary of State for the Environment, in an appeal against an enforcement notice requiring that unlawful development of land without planning permission should be discontinued, to disregard failure to serve the notice on everyone affected if there has been no substantial prejudice to interests as a result.

The notice actually served must contain sufficient detail to enable the person concerned to know the substance of any charge, allegation or action to be taken against him. Where, as in the case of an enforcement notice, statutory provisions stipulate the need to specify the details of any allegation of unlawful development, there may be few problems. In other, non-statutory cases the adequacy of the notice, eg in relation to the time allowed to respond or the definition of the allegation, will be a question of fact and degree for the court (*R v North, ex p Oakey* (1927)).

10.6.2 The opportunity to be heard

The second requirement of the *audi alteram partem* rule, that there should be a reasonable opportunity for a person's case to be heard, is capable of applying to a justiciable issue between two parties. In this case it was stated by Lord Loreburn in *Board of Education v Rice* (1911) the respective parties must be able to exercise a fair opportunity to put their case and to correct or contradict any relevant prejudicial statement. Equally, the requirement can apply where an issue relates to the rights or other interests of one party (*Ridge v Baldwin* (1963)). It has been seen that there is no general obligation in law to accord an oral hearing so that this area of natural justice might be complied with, eg where written representations were permitted. However, if an oral hearing is given it is generally required that the case shall both be heard and decided by the same person (*Jeffs v New Zealand Dairy Production and Marketing Board* (1967)). Nevertheless, in the case of decisions taken in the name of a minister within a government department, there is no right to be heard by the person taking the decision or to know his identity. An inquiry may be conducted by one of the minister's inspectors but the ultimate decision may be taken by another member of the department (*Local Government Board v Arlidge*). The common law exclusion of the right to be heard before the person taking a decision in the name of a minister is considerably modified by contemporary legislation prescribing rights to be heard before the minister's inspector at a statutory public inquiry, previously referred to in Chapter 3.

10.6.3 Scope of the rule

Subject to statutory procedures administrative agencies (including statutory tribunals and inquiries) in complying with the rules of natural justice are not required to adopt and observe the various technical rules of evidence associated with courts of law (*R v Deputy Industrial Injuries Commissioner, ex p Moore* (1965)). Accordingly, it will not be contrary to natural justice where hearsay evidence is accepted (*Miller v Minister of Housing and Local Government* (1968)). Any information acted upon must have some probative value and there must be a preparedness to hear both sides, according to the type of hearing granted, and to allow comment and contradiction to both sides in respect of any information obtained (*R v Hull Prison Board of Visitors, ex p St Germain (No 2)* (1979)). It must be emphasised that the *audi alteram partem* rule requires only a reasonable opportunity to be granted: eg there is no requirement that there should be an adjournment where a party absents himself from a hearing without explanation

(*Glynn v Keele University*). On the other hand, the refusal of an adjournment to a party who reasonably requires additional time for the preparation of his case could be seen as a breach of the *audi alteram partem* rule (*R v Thames Magistrates' Court, ex p Polemis* (1974)).

10.6.4   Legal representation

Whether the rule permits legal representation is by no means easy to determine. In *Pett v Greyhound Racing Association (No 1)* (1968) the Court of Appeal was concerned with proceedings for an interlocutory injunction to prevent an inquiry by the Association into suspicions that one of Pett's dogs was drugged before a race. The injunction was granted on the ground that Pett was entitled to legal representation at the inquiry. Lord Denning, who gave the leading judgment of the court, was of the opinion that not every person has the ability to either defend themselves or cross-examine witnesses during the course of a hearing. Accordingly he considered that:

> If justice is to be done, he ought to have the help of someone to speak for him; and who better than a lawyer who has been trained for the task? I should have thought, therefore, that when a man's reputation or livelihood is at stake, he not only has a right to speak by his own mouth. He has also a right to speak by counsel or solicitor.

Subsequently in a claim by Pett for a declaration that the Association was acting *ultra vires* in refusing legal representation, it was decided that there was no facet of natural justice requiring the provision of legal representation (*Pett v Greyhound Racing Association (No 2)* (1969)).

Whereas the rules of the Greyhound Racing Association did not exclude legal representation, the rules of the Football Association in contention before the Court of Appeal in *Enderby Town Football Club Ltd v Football Association Ltd* (1971) did exclude such representation. On this occasion an injunction to prevent the hearing of an appeal without legal representation was refused. Although difficult issues of law arose in the appeal, the court considered that they might be adequately dealt with on an application to the court for a declaration. In the meantime, the Association rules had to be observed. Consequently, it may now be the case that if the rules of an association do exclude legal representation, such an exclusion can be enforced except that, in its discretion, the association may be required to allow representation to any person who seems to be in need of such a facility, eg because of difficulties with language or by virtue of a particularly serious charge or allegation. In *Manchanda v Medical Eye Centre Association* (1987) the court considered that a domestic disciplinary tribunal had a duty to allow legal representation if the issue concerned an allegation of unbecoming conduct. Any police officer appearing before the chief constable in respect of an alleged breach of discipline is not entitled to legal representation (*Maynard v Osmond* (1976)). The Court of Appeal justified this conclusion by reference to the requirement of the Police (Discipline) Regulations 1965 that representation be provided by a police officer, not a lawyer, which was found to be *intra vires*. Similarly, in *Fraser v Mudge* (1975) it was decided, again by the Court of Appeal, that a prisoner had no right in law to legal representation for the purpose of appearing before the board of visitors on a disciplinary charge.

This latter decision has been followed in *Hone v Maze Prison Board of Prison Visitors* (1988) where the House of Lords considered for the first time the question whether a prisoner was entitled as of right to legal representation during disciplinary proceedings. In dismissing the appeal against the decision of the prison visitors not to grant the appellant legal representation, Lord Goff declared himself to be:

> ... unable to accept ... that any person charged with a crime (or the equivalent thereof) and liable to punishment is entitled as a matter of natural justice to legal representation. No doubt it is true that a man charged with a crime before a criminal court is entitled to legal representation ... No doubt it is also correct that a board of visitors is bound to give effect to the rules of natural justice. But it does not follow that, simply because a charge before a disciplinary tribunal such as a board of visitors relates to facts which in law constitute a crime, the rules of natural justice require the tribunal to grant legal representation.

Thus it would seem to be the case that whether or not an individual may be legally represented at a hearing is very much a matter of discretion for the tribunal. In exercising that discretion, especially in the context of prison disciplinary proceedings, the following factors may be taken into account: the seriousness of the charge and of the potential penalty; whether any points of law are likely to arise; the capacity of a particular prisoner to present his own case; any likelihood of procedural difficulties arising; the need for reasonable speed in the making of an application; and, the need for fairness as between prisoners and as between prisoners and prison officers (*R v Secretary of State for the Home Department, ex p Tarrant* (1985)).

10.6.5 Duty to give reasons

A duty to give reasons for an administrative decision has the appearance of a logical and desirable aspect of the general duty to act fairly. When a decision has an adverse affect upon the rights of an individual, it seems only just that he should be informed of the reasons which influenced the decision-maker and which therefore underpin the decision itself. However, despite the desirability of giving reasons for decisions which have been made in that in addition to the argument advanced above, such an approach also ensures a degree of openness in the administrative process, it is not entirely clear whether English law as it stands at present recognises a general duty to give reasons.

There have been a number of recent cases in which this issue has exercised the minds of the courts, but it is important to note that the approach taken by the courts has, to a large extent, been influenced by the circumstances of the case before them. As a general proposition, it seems to be the case that the courts are more inclined to impose an obligation to give reasons on a decision-maker where the impugned decision has a serious affect upon the individual to whom it relates. For example, in *R v Secretary of State for the Home Department, ex p Duggan* (1993), the Divisional Court held that a high security risk category A prisoner ought to be informed of the reasons for any decision not to change his category A status. The justification for this finding was that such a decision had important consequences for the liberty of the prisoner since category A prisoners are those who are considered to present grave danger to the public in the event of an escape, and accordingly, to remain classified as a category A prisoner would lessen the likelihood of being released on parole. By contrast, in *R v Higher Education Funding Council, ex p Institute of Dental Surgery* (1994), it was held that reasons need not be given by the Higher Education Funding Council for its decision not to award the Institute the research rating which the Institute itself believed that it merited.

The leading authority in this developing area of administrative law is the decision of the House of Lords in *Doody v Secretary of State for the Home Department* (1993). The applicants in this case were all convicted murderers who had received mandatory life sentences for their crimes. By virtue of s 35 of the Criminal Justice Act 1991, the Home Secretary has a discretion whether to refer the case of such a prisoner to the Parole Board for review. Before so doing, it is Home Office procedure for the Home Secretary to consult both the trial judge and the Lord Chief Justice with regard to the issues of retribution and deterrence as they apply to the sentence which was originally imposed, and then the Home Secretary himself decides upon the penal element of the sentence. The applicants in the present case sought, among other things, a declaration that the Home Secretary was obliged to give reasons for his decision where that decision departed from the period recommended by the trial judge and the Lord Chief Justice. In granting the relief sought by the applicants, Lord Mustill stated the current position of the law thus:

> I accept without hesitation ... that the law does not at present recognise a general duty to give reasons for an administrative decision. Nevertheless, it is equally beyond question that such a duty may in appropriate circumstances be implied.

Thus although there is currently no general duty to give reasons for an administrative decision, it would seem that whether reasons are in fact given in practice, or alternatively, whether they are demanded by the courts in judicial review proceedings before them, will depend very much upon what is required in the interests of fairness. It may be that the views expressed in *McInnes v Onslow Fane* (1978), to the effect that a board is under no obligation to inform an applicant of the reasons why his application has been unsuccessful, represent a line of thinking for which there is still solid support since in such a situation, the applicant has not lost anything; he has simply not been granted that for which he applied but to which he was not entitled as of right. However, in the more serious cases, such as those involving the liberty of the individual as discussed above, it seems only right and proper that the decision-maker should be required to give reasons for his decision.

10.7 The Effect of Breaches of Natural Justice

The effect in law of a failure to comply with the rules of natural justice seems to be that any decision or other administrative action is null and void (*Ridge v Baldwin*). There are also dicta to this effect in *Anisminic v Foreign Compensation Commission* (1969) where Lord Pearce, for example, observed that:

> Lack of jurisdiction may arise in various ways ... the tribunal ... while engaged in a proper inquiry ... may depart from the rules of natural justice ... thereby it would step outside its jurisdiction. It would turn its inquiry into something not directed by Parliament and fail to make the inquiry which Parliament did direct. [This] would cause its purported decision to be a nullity.

If any breach of natural justice is to render a decision null and void it is because statutory powers and the rules of private organisations are impliedly subject to the rules of natural justice. There are also *dicta* in *Dimes v Grand Junction Canal Proprietors* (1852) to the effect that a breach of the rule against bias renders a decision merely voidable but since this case involved a decision by a judge of a superior court the term 'voidable' may simply mean that the decision is 'appealable' to the next court in the hierarchy of superior courts. The same approach could apply to decisions of inferior courts such as magistrates' courts except that here there is the possibility of seeking review of the decision. In the case of statutory administrative agencies and voluntary domestic organisations there may also be an appeal available within the statutory scheme or rules of the organisations so that again there will be a similar choice as in the case of a decision by an inferior court. Generally, the court will entertain an application to set aside such a decision affected by a breach of natural justice, subject to any express restrictions in the scheme or rules of an organisation, as the case may be (*Leigh v National Union of Railwaymen* (1970)).

However, until a decision is declared null and void by the court, it may have some existence in law (*per* Lord Wilberforce in *Calvin v Carr* (1979)). Where, within the rules of a voluntary domestic organisation, a subsequent hearing is conducted by an appellate body, the decision may still be open to challenge in the court on the ground that the person aggrieved has not enjoyed a proper initial hearing and an appellate hearing (*Leary v National Union of Vehicle Builders* (1970)). It was suggested by the Judicial Committee of the Privy Council in *Calvin v Carr* that the principle in *Leary* was too widely expressed. It was decided in *Calvin* that the result of a stewards' inquiry in New South Wales was affected by a breach of natural justice. The jockey in question was disqualified for one year but it was also decided that the original breach could be remedied by a subsequent hearing before the appeal committee of the Jockey Club which did comply with natural justice. It was suggested that the principle in *Leary* would apply only in cases where, for example, the rules of the organisation required observance of a natural justice at every stage of the relevant procedures. As an alternative to the above situations, it is always possible that a failure to comply with natural justice may be made good by a fresh hearing, leading to a legally valid decision (*De Verteuil v Knaggs* (1918)). In *Ridge v Baldwin*, Ridge's solicitor was not fully informed of the charges against the Chief Constable of Brighton and the Watch Committee did not annul the decision which they had already published and proceed to a new decision: an inadequate substitute for a full rehearing.

11   Substantive *Ultra Vires*

11.1   The Nature of Substantive Powers

Chapter 7 dealt with the nature and characteristics of administrative powers while Part 1 described the various administrative agencies which use those powers. Whereas the statutory procedures described in Chapter 9 and the rules of natural justice described in Chapter 10 determine the steps to be taken in pursuing the exercise of administrative powers, the present chapter is concerned with the rules of administrative law as they are developed and applied for the purpose of defining the scope of any functions conferred on an administrative agency.

11.2   Judicial Review of Substantive Powers

It was seen in Chapter 1 that the High Court sets the limits of statutory substantive powers on any occasion when uncertainty about those limits has given rise to litigation. Through its inherent power to review the legality of administrative action, the High Court is able to ascertain whether an administrative agency or inferior court has exceeded or abused the legal limits of the substantive powers governing its functions. Any excess or abuse of those powers means that the decision or other administrative action is *ultra vires* and may be dealt with through a range of remedies, which are described in Chapter 13. However, merely because the High Court disagrees with a decision and considers it to be wrong on the merits of the case in question does not mean the decision is *ultra vires*. To be *ultra vires* a decision has to be proved to have exceeded the express or implied statutory limits of the powers given to the administrative agency, ie to have gone beyond the jurisdiction of that agency. The *GCHQ* case contains an important statement by Lord Diplock about the qualifying requirements for judicial review. He considered that:

> ... the decision must have consequences which affect some person (or body of persons) other than the decision-maker, although it may affect him too. It must affect such other person either: (a) by altering rights or obligations of that person which are enforceable by or against him in private law; or (b) by depriving him of some benefit or advantage which either (i) he had in the past been permitted by the decision-maker to enjoy and which he can legitimately expect to be permitted to continue to do until there has been communicated to him some rational grounds for withdrawing it on which he has been given opportunity to comment; or (ii) he has received assurance from

the decision-maker will not be withdrawn without giving him first an opportunity of advancing reasons for contending that they should not be withdrawn.

It will be seen that this formula encompasses procedural and substantive shortcomings as well as those that fall under the heading of natural justice.

11.3   The Limits of Statutory Powers

The law prescribes various rules or tests for the limits of substantive powers. In general, these rules are applicable according to whether or not the powers are discretionary and whether matters of fact or law are in issue. However, before these rules are examined, it must be re-emphasised very strongly that merely because the reviewing court considers a decision to be wrong on the merits, ie matters within the limits of statutory powers, does not render it *ultra vires*. The law recognises here that an administrative agency should have some opportunity to exercise its expert skill or judgment in particular cases. Hypothetically, a furnished rent tribunal might have the power '... to determine disputes between landlord and tenant in respect of the payment of rent for furnished premises'. If the tribunal is to avoid an *ultra vires* decision it would probably have to decide correctly at the outset and to the satisfaction of a reviewing court that a case referred to it involved what is in fact a dispute on what in law is a rent payment as between parties who are in law landlord and tenant concerning premises which are, as a fact, furnished premises (*R v Fulham, Hammersmith and Kensington Rent Tribunal, ex p Zerek* (1951)). Thereafter, any expert conclusions arrived at by the tribunal about the physical condition of the premises and that, for example, the rent should be reduced by 10% in recognition of those conditions is a decision on the merits of the case and therefore generally beyond review for *ultra vires*. However, if Parliament had prescribed an appeal from the tribunal's decisions, the appeal court or tribunal would be able to re-examine the merits of the tribunal's decision in order to substitute its own decision, eg by reducing the rent by 20%. Accordingly, there is a fundamental distinction between review, which is concerned to ascertain whether a decision should be quashed or declared a nullity as being in excess or abuse of statutory limits, and appeal.

The need for any administrative tribunal or agency to determine correctly the limits of its powers is well illustrated in *R v Blackpool Rent Tribunal, ex p Ashton* (1948), where the tribunal had statutory responsibility for determining disputes in relation to furnished premises. The tenancy of a flat was referred to the tribunal where the flat contained a clock, curtains in two rooms, a gas cooker and a water heater. The court quashed the tribunal's decision: the first two items were regarded by the court as being *de minimis* while the other items were not 'furniture'. The fact that certain matters have nothing to do with the limits of statutory powers but relate entirely to the merits of a case, to be weighed and dealt with entirely by the agency itself, is seen in *Dowty, Boulton Paul Ltd v Wolverhampton Corporation (No 2)* (1973). The corporation decided to discontinue the provision of its municipal airport by virtue of the powers in s 163 of the Local Government Act 1933 which stipulated that '... a council may appropriate for any purpose for which the council are authorised ... to acquire land ... any land which belongs to the council and is no longer required for the purpose for which it is held immediately before the appropriation'. It was found by the court that a decision of the corporation under these powers by which the land's use could be discontinued in order to permit the building of houses was entirely a matter within their powers, that is, a matter for their judgment on the merits of the competing claims to the land. Even if the court sympathised with the merits of the airport user's claim, this could not have rendered the corporation's decision *ultra vires*.

The fundamental distinction between on the one hand, the merits of an administrative decision, which is not a matter which is appropriate for the supervisory jurisdiction of the courts, and on the other, the legality of that same decision which is, was highlighted in *Save Britain's Heritage v Secretary of State for the Environment* (1991) referred to in Chapters 3 and 9. The developers' proposals to demolish listed and unlisted buildings in a conservation area and build in their place a modern building designed by a leading architect had aroused much public controversy. Indeed, the local planning authority, English Heritage and non-statutory organisations such as Save Britain's Heritage were all opposed to the scheme. However, the House of Lords made it abundantly clear that aesthetic judgments were for the Secretary of State to make, not the court. Accordingly, the issue for the court was whether or not the Secretary of State had complied with the statutory requirement to give reasons for his decision to approve the scheme. Lord Bridge, echoing earlier judicial sentiments, stated that the concern of the court in the context of judicial review proceedings 'is solely with the legality of the decision-making process, not at all with the merits of the decision'.

11.3.1 Defining the limits

The task of identifying the limits of powers depends on the definition of matters of fact and/or law which are considered to be fundamental to the powers of any administrative agency. If such matters of fact and/or law are considered by the court to be fundamental, this is an indication of Parliament's supposed intentions in relation to the limits of an administrative agency's powers. In *R v Hillingdon London Borough Council, ex p Puhlhofer* (1986), for example, the House of Lords emphasised that under the Housing (Homeless Persons) Act 1977 the local authority was obliged only to provide 'accommodation'. This fundamental requirement was not qualified by any requirement that the accommodation was fit for human habitation, for example, any failing in the quality of the accommodation would not be capable of rendering action *ultra vires*. The legislation has now been amended by the Housing and Planning Act 1986 which stipulates that a person shall not be treated as having accommodation unless it is accommodation which it would be reasonable for him to continue to occupy. Failure to interpret correctly a legal requirement which is fundamental to the limits of powers renders a decision *ultra vires*. Equally, failure to find evidence for a matter of fundamental fact is a prerequisite for an *ultra vires* decision (*Coleen Properties Ltd v Minister of Housing and Local Government* (1971)).

11.3.2 Fundamental matters of law

In *Padfield v Minister of Agriculture* (1968) the House of Lords dealt with the minister's refusal to refer a complaint about differentials in milk prices paid by the Milk Marketing Board to farmers in different regions of the country to a committee of investigation under s 19 of the Agricultural Marketing Act 1958. Section 19 stipulated that the minister shall appoint a committee of investigation which 'shall ... be charged with the duty, if the minister in any case so directs, of considering and reporting to the minister on ... any complaint made to the minister'. It was decided by the House of Lords that the minister had misconstrued the legal requirements of the Act which indicated that he was obliged to refer the complaint made if the objects and intentions of the legislation were to be realised. Although the minister had a discretion, there was a fundamental legal requirement that complaints be referred to a committee in order to provide protection for those affected by milk marketing schemes. In *Pearlman v Keepers and Governors of Harrow School* (1978) the court quashed the decision of a county court in respect of a determination relating to the rateable value of a dwelling for the purposes of the Leasehold Reform Act. Under the Act certain requirements have to be satisfied before a long leaseholder can purchase the freehold of his property, one of which is a rateable value limit. Normally, any improvement or alteration to a property would have the effect of pushing up the rateable value beyond the limit so that the long leaseholder would no longer qualify for a purchase of the freehold. Accordingly, it is provided by the Act that in some circumstances such as where there is a 'structural alteration' to property, the rateable value should be subject to a notional reduction. Any long leaseholder is permitted by the Act to apply to a county court for a determination whether certain improvements amount to a 'structural alteration': any such determination is stated to be 'final and conclusive'. In this case the county court decided that the installation of central heating was not a 'structural alteration', a decision which was quashed by the Court of Appeal as being an *ultra vires*, fundamental error of law.

11.3.3 Inferior courts

The House of Lords in *Re Racal Communications Ltd* (1980) concluded that there is something akin to a presumption that errors of law by inferior courts like the county court are not generally fundamental, primarily by reference to the need to recognise the expertise of the judges in those courts. Consequently, decisions of inferior courts affected by errors of law will usually be, at most, voidable decisions (legally effective decisions unless quashed by the court) by virtue of there being a less than fundamental error of law on the face of the record of the decision. This concept is examined below. It will be noted that the principle in *Re Racal Communications Ltd* applies to inferior courts as opposed to other administrative agencies, including tribunals, where the House of Lords' decision in *Anisminic Ltd v Foreign Compensation Commission* (1969) remains the leading authority.

11.3.4 Administrative agencies

In *Anisminic* the British government received from the Egyptian government a sum of money in respect of outstanding claims following the sequestration of British property in Egypt. By virtue of the Foreign Compensation Act 1950, it has been seen that the Foreign Compensation Commission has statutory responsibility for the determination of claims made in respect of the money received from any foreign government. A claim would be 'established' according to an Order in Council if certain requirements were met, one of which was that a claimant had to be British. In rejecting Anisminic's claim the Commission found that the company, although British, had not satisfied another requirement, ie that a claimant's successor in title should also have been British. It was found that the Commission had misinterpreted the Order in Council defining the limits of its powers. The Commission had made a fundamental error of law by taking into account the need for a claimant to prove that a successor in title was also British, something that amounted to an additional requirement which had not been specified in the Order in Council. Despite the words of s 4(4) of the Foreign Compensation Act to the effect that any decision on an application made to the Commission 'shall not be called in question' in any court of law, the House of Lords was willing to grant a declaration that the Commission's decision was *ultra vires*. Lord Pearce emphasised that it is possible to exceed or abuse statutory powers in various ways:

> There may be an absence of those formalities or things which are conditions precedent to the tribunal having any jurisdiction to embark on an inquiry. Or the tribunal may at the end make an order that it has no jurisdiction to make. Or in the intervening stage, while engaged in a property inquiry, the tribunal may depart from the rules of natural justice; or it may ask itself the wrong questions; or it may take into account matters which it was not directed to take into account. Thereby it would step outside its jurisdiction. It would turn its inquiry into something not directed by Parliament and fail to make the inquiry which Parliament did direct. Any of these things would cause its purported decision to be a nullity.

The decisions in *Anisminic* and *Re Racal Communications Ltd* indicate that virtually any error of law committed by an administrative agency such as a local authority or an administrative tribunal will be regarded by the High Court as a fundamental error of law rendering any resulting decision or other administrative action *ultra vires*. The accuracy of this view has recently been confirmed by the House of Lords in *R v Hull University Visitor, ex p Page* (1993) where Lord Browne-Wilkinson in the leading judgment observed that '... Parliament had only conferred the decision-making power on the basis that it was to be exercised on the correct legal basis: a misdirection in law in making the decision therefore rendered the decision *ultra vires*'. In *Pearlman*, Lord Denning and the majority of the court considered that such a principle should extend to all administrative agencies and inferior courts. Lord Denning stated that: 'No court or tribunal has any jurisdiction to make an error of law on which the decision of a case depends. If it makes such an error, it goes outside its jurisdiction.' In his important dissenting judgment, which was subsequently approved by the House of Lords in *Re Racal Communications Ltd*, Geoffrey Lane LJ considered that the inferior court should have some leeway in which to make wrong determinations of law without any eventual decision being regarded as *ultra vires*. Clearly, expert judges are capable of arriving at differing views of the law on many occasions. Although the High Court may consider a county court judge's interpretation of the law to be wrong in a particular case, that does not necessarily mean that it is so wrong as to offend the fundamental limits of powers prescribed by Parliament in order to render a decision *ultra vires*.

11.4   Error of Law on the Face of the Record

It was noted previously from the case of *Re Racal Communications Ltd* that decisions of inferior courts affected by errors of law will usually be regarded, not as *ultra vires* for excess or abuse of some fundamental legal requirement of their powers, but as merely voidable decisions. A voidable decision is a legally effective decision until it is quashed by the court, in contrast to an *ultra vires* decision which is null and void *ab initio*, that is, a decision which has never existed in law. Because an error of law on the face of the record does not render a decision *ultra vires*, the error is not, therefore, made in respect of some fundamental requirement defining the limit of statutory powers. Accordingly, some incidental misconstruction of a statutory provision appearing on the face of the record of a decision by an inferior court is the most likely occurrence where the court would be invited to quash a voidable decision. In *R v Crown Court at Knightsbridge, ex p International Sporting Club (London) Ltd* (1981) the court quashed a decision of the Crown Court, dismissing appeals from decisions of the justices, to the effect that companies' licences to operate casinos should be cancelled on the ground that there had been serious contraventions of the Gaming Act 1968 in the operation of the premises. The error of law appearing in the record of the judgment related to the judge's conclusion that the question whether the companies were 'fit and proper persons' for the purpose of the Gaming Act could only be judged by their past conduct. This conclusion failed to take into account the legally relevant fact that the original companies had sold their interests and shareholdings to new owners: this failure to take into account company restructuring was an error of law appearing on the face of the record of the decision.

11.4.1 Error of law on the face of the record and the doctrine of *ultra vires*

Historically, error of law on the face of the record provided the basis for the High Court's control over inferior courts and other administrative bodies. Nevertheless, a decision could be quashed as being *ultra vires* if additional evidence beyond the record of a decision could be produced. Gradually in the case of error of law on the face of the record, *certiorari* would issue to quash even the most trifling, technical errors of law. Parliament responded by legislating that in many cases *certiorari* would not be available to quash certain decisions. Accordingly, efforts were made by the court to admit evidence more freely for the purpose of establishing that decisions may have been made in excess of powers conferred, that is, *ultra vires*. Thereafter, the doctrine of *ultra vires* became the real basis of judicial review and error of law on the face of the record was virtually forgotten until the Court of Appeal decision in *R v Northumberland Compensation Appeal Tribunal, ex p Shaw* (1952).

Mr Shaw lost his job as clerk to the West Northumberland Joint Hospital Board when the National Health Service Act 1946 was passed. As a result he was entitled to claim compensation and he claimed in turn that his previous employment in local government should have been taken into account in computing the payment. Being dissatisfied with the amount of compensation awarded, Shaw appealed to the tribunal which rejected his claim that previous employment should have been taken into account. Shaw made a successful application to the court for an order of *certiorari* to quash the tribunal's decision on the ground that an error of law resulting from the misinterpretation of statutory regulations relating to compensation appeared on the face of the record of the tribunal's decision. The error of law in misconstruing the statutory compensation regulations was not a fundamental error affecting the very limits of the tribunal's powers. As an error of law which appeared on the face of the record it merely rendered the decision voidable and quashable by *certiorari*. As for the record of the tribunal's decision, the error was admitted in open court and incorporated as reasons for the decision. Denning LJ considered that:

> ... the record must contain at least the document which initiates the proceedings; the pleadings, if any; and the adjudication; but not the evidence, nor the reasons, unless the tribunal chooses to incorporate them. If the tribunal

does state its reasons, and those reasons are wrong in law, *certiorari* lies to quash the decision.

Although the availability of *certiorari* to cure error of law on the face of the record once assumed considerable importance, the remedy in this context is of increasingly less significance. First, the Tribunals and Inquiries Act 1992 provides an appeal on a point of law from many administrative tribunals to the High Court in an area which was previously dominated by *certiorari* where a tribunal's decision was affected by an error of law on the face of the record. Secondly, the House of Lords' *dicta* in *Re Racal Communications Ltd*, as seen previously in the present chapter, seem to restrict error of law on the face of the record to the decisions of inferior courts, as opposed to tribunals and other administrative agencies.

11.5   Ouster Clauses and the Doctrine of *Ultra Vires*

It is sometimes the case that an Act of Parliament will attempt to prevent any challenge to an administrative decision, usually by attempting to oust the jurisdiction of the court. In *R v Medical Appeal Tribunal, ex p Gilmore* (1957) the legislation provided that decisions of the tribunal should be 'final'. It was decided by the Court of Appeal that in the absence of any other clearer statutory words, the decisions of the tribunal were subject to *certiorari* either in respect of decisions beyond the limits of the statutory powers or for an error of law on the face of the record. The court considered, therefore, that although a decision might be final as to the facts and (presumably) any expert conclusions drawn from those facts, it would not be final in respect of any matter of law. Therefore, the finality clause in the Act could be effective only to prevent any appeal against the facts and merits of the decision. Nevertheless, it is at least arguable that Parliament actually intended to exclude any challenge to the tribunal's decisions, including review.

Another significant ouster clause arose for the court's consideration in *Anisminic*. It was seen previously that the ouster clause here related to decisions of the Foreign Compensation Commission. The Act stated that the '... determination by the Tribunal of any application made to them under this Act shall not be called in question in any Court of Law'. It was decided by the House of Lords that this ouster clause would not exclude any challenge by the court in respect of any decision which involved any error which took the tribunal beyond the limits of its statutory powers, that is, an *ultra vires* decision. In the event, a fundamental error of law rendered the Commission's decision *ultra vires*. The basis of the court's decision is that a reference in the ouster clause to a 'determination' or a 'decision' implies a legally effective decision, as opposed to an *ultra vires* decision. While the ouster clause protects any determination or decision which exists as a legally valid decision, including a merely voidable decision, it cannot be taken to protect from review by the court a determination or decision which does not exist in law, ie an *ultra vires* decision. Accordingly, in *Anisminic* the court was prepared to declare that the decision was null and void as an *ultra vires* decision because the fundamental error of law had taken the Commission beyond the limits of its statutory powers. A similar approach is seen in the Court of Appeal decision in *Pearlman* where the court was concerned with s 107 of the County Courts Act 1959 which states that: 'No judgment or order of any judge of County Courts, nor any proceedings brought before him or pending in his court, shall be removed by appeal, motion, *certiorari* or otherwise into any other court whatever.' Despite these words in s 107, it has been seen previously that the court was prepared to grant *certiorari* to quash a county court decision, following the reasoning in *Anisminic*.

Another ouster clause of considerable scope was before the Judicial Committee of the Privy Council in *South-East Asia Fire Bricks v Non-Metallic Mineral Products Manufacturing Employees Union* (1980). This clause appeared in the Malaysian Industrial Relations Act 1967 and stipulated that: '... an award of the (Industrial) Court shall be final and conclusive, and no award shall be challenged, appealed against, reviewed, quashed or called into question in any court of law.' Again, following the approach in *Anisminic*, it was decided that although these words would protect any voidable decision affected by an error of law on the face of the record from review by the court, they did not prevent the court reviewing a decision of the Industrial Court which was found to be *ultra vires* and void.

The foregoing ouster clauses can be distinguished from other clauses which do permit the High Court to review the legality of decisions but only where an application for that purpose is made to the court within six weeks of that decision. Such clauses are examined in the context of judicial remedies in Chapter 13. These clauses are to be found primarily in legislation governing town and country planning and compulsory purchase. In both cases a decision of the Secretary of State for the Environment, for example, on an appeal from a refusal of planning permission by a local authority or in respect of a local authority's invitation to confirm one of its compulsory purchase orders, may be challenged, but only within the strict limit of six weeks (*Smith v East Elloe Rural District Council* (1956)). It is clear, therefore, that these statutory ouster clauses differ from the other varieties previously examined, particularly in so far as six weeks are allowed for a challenge in the High Court. It is probably this factor which has influenced the court more than any other in resisting an application of the principle in *Anisminic* so that any application to the court after six weeks would still be refused (*R v Secretary of State for the Environment, ex p Ostler* (1977)).

In *R v Cornwall County Council, ex p Huntington* (1992), the Divisional Court ruled that the court had no jurisdiction to grant judicial review of an order made under the Wildlife and Countryside Act 1981 where the statutorily prescribed time limit of 42 days for such a challenge had been exceeded. In a passage which was cited with approval by the Court of Appeal when they later upheld the Divisional Court's decision (*R v Cornwall County Council, ex p Huntington* (1994)), Mann LJ stated the position in relation to ouster clauses and time limit clauses in the following terms:

> The intention of Parliament when it uses an *Anisminic* clause is that questions as to validity are not excluded. When paragraphs such as those considered in *ex parte Ostler* are used, then the legislative intention is that questions as to invalidity may be raised on the specified grounds in the prescribed time and in the prescribed manner, but that otherwise the jurisdiction of the court is excluded in the interest of certainty.

11.6 The Limits of Discretionary Powers

Reference has been made to the general practice of conferring discretion on the initiators of administrative action to determine the limits of their statutory powers whereas the adjudicators – tribunals in particular – usually operate with reference to such discretionary powers. Where an administrative agency's powers are discretionary so that it is able to make choices before acting, those choices must be made by reference to lawful factors which are expressly or impliedly recognised by and within the statutory limits under which the powers are exercised. Equally, any policy which is made by the administrative agency in order to guide the exercise of these discretionary choices must be within the same statutory limits.

Before these principles are explained and illustrated, reference must be made to the leading statement of principle by Lord Greene MR in *Associated Provincial Picture Houses Ltd v Wednesbury Corporation* (1948). He stated that when a discretion is granted:

> ... the law recognises certain principles upon which that discretion must be exercised, but within the four corners of those principles the discretion ... is an absolute one and cannot be questioned in any court of law. What then are those principles ... The exercise of such a discretion must be a real exercise of the discretion. If, in the statute conferring the discretion, there is to be found expressly or by implication matters which the authority exercising the discretion ought to have regard to, then in exercising the discretion it must have regard to those matters. Conversely, if the nature of the subject-matter and the general interpretation of the Act make it clear that certain matters would not be germane to the matter in question, the authority must disregard those irrelevant collateral matters ... [A] person entrusted with a discretion must ... direct himself properly in law. He must call his own attention to the matters which he is bound to consider. He must exclude from his consideration matters which are irrelevant to what he has to consider. If he does not obey those rules, he may truly be said ... to be acting 'unreasonably'.

A good example of a statutory discretion is to be found in s 8 of the Education Act 1944 by which the council of a local education authority is obliged '... to secure that there should be available for their area sufficient schools for providing full-time education' suitable to the requirements of pupils. It was decided in *Meade v Haringey London Borough Council* (1979) that this discretion does not permit the council simply to provide school buildings. Through an interpretation of the Act the Court of Appeal decided that the discretion also required the provision of teachers and other essentials if the object of the Act – to secure the education of children – was to be realised. In other words, these wider requirements mark the limits of the council's statutory powers, emphasising the fact that it is the court which is the judge of the legal limits of discretionary powers. It was further suggested in *Meade* that the council would have been acting *ultra vires* had it been established that its schools had remained closed during a caretakers' strike as a result of political influences and considerations. In the event, the injunction sought by parents against the council to restrain any further breach of duty under s 8 and to require the reopening of the schools was not granted when, during the litigation, the strike was ended. From the foregoing principles it can be seen that any discretion, whether it relates to the limits of statutory powers (as in *Meade*) or to a determination of the merits of any case by an administrative agency within those limits, can only be influenced by considerations which are legally relevant to the legislation containing the powers. Hence from *Meade* political reasons for keeping the schools closed were regarded as being legally irrelevant to and *ultra vires* the Education Act powers. The same is true of the hypothetical furnished rent tribunal mentioned at the beginning of the present chapter. Where that tribunal, in the course of dealing with the merits of any claim by a tenant within its powers, takes into account some consideration which is regarded as alien to the Act conferring the powers, eg that the tenant is an immigrant, its eventual decision will again be *ultra vires*. The same conclusion would be possible upon proof that the administrative agencies in question had used their various statutory powers for improper purposes, that is, unlawful purposes beyond the defined statutory limits.

Assuming that an administrative agency has correctly determined the scope of its statutory powers at the outset, either for the purpose of initiating administrative action or for the purpose of adjudicating some claim or dispute, then it will be action *intra vires*, that is, within the limits of its statutory powers. Thereafter, the agency, in dealing with the merits of different alternatives for administrative action or the merits of competing claims, as the case may be, has to avoid the foregoing irrelevant considerations or improper purposes. If it does then its eventual decision or other action will not be *ultra vires* as long as that decision or other action is expressly or impliedly permitted by the empowering legislation. In so avoiding any review of the legality of its decision or other action, the administrative agency is free, within these legal constraints, to exercise its expertise, judgment and opinion in relation to the problem to be dealt with. Accordingly, and by way of illustration, the way in which educational facilities are provided by virtue of s 8 of the Education Act is entirely a matter for the responsible council acting as local education authority. If, therefore, it is felt that more resources are required for the provision of educational facilities to benefit particularly deprived members of the community, that is a matter entirely for the council acting within its powers: any such decision cannot be *ultra vires* where it is motivated by educational considerations.

The point is also illustrated in *Eckersley v Secretary of State for the Environment* (1978) where the Secretary of State confirmed a compulsory purchase order for the acquisition of land to permit the clearance of slum properties, by virtue of powers contained in Part 3 of the Housing Act 1957 now contained in the consolidating Housing Act 1985. It was decided that the confirmation was *ultra vires* on the ground that there was a failure to take into consideration comparative costs of demolition and rebuilding. Had the Secretary of State lawfully taken these fundamental factors into consideration, his conclusions on cost would not generally have been of any concern to the court. He may have had a policy to aid him in the exercise of his discretionary powers. The policy may have been in favour of saving houses where possible. Accordingly, any decision not to confirm a compulsory purchase order, even though renovation of the housing might cost £500,000 more than demolition and redevelopment, is entirely a matter for the Secretary of State acting within his statutory powers, ie it is a matter going to the merits of the decision, which cannot be challenged as an *ultra vires* decision.

11.6.1 The problem of subjectively worded discretionary powers

It has been emphasised that the High Court must be the final arbiter of the outer limits of any discretion conferred on an administrative agency. One of the leading statements of principle comes from the judgment of Sachs J in *Customs and Excise Commissioners v Cure and Deeley Ltd* (1961). By virtue of s 33 of the Finance (No 2) Act 1940 the Commissioners were empowered to '... make regulations providing for any matter for which provision appears to them to be necessary for the purpose of giving effect to the provisions of this Part of this Act and of enabling them to discharge their functions thereunder'. In a set of regulations made in 1945 it was stated that: 'If a person fails to furnish a return as required by these regulations the Commissioners may ... determine the amount of tax appearing to them to be due from such person ... which amount shall be deemed to be the proper tax due.' In a claim for purchase tax against the company it was decided that this regulation was *ultra vires* the empowering Act. In so deciding, Sachs J rejected the view that the words 'appear to them to be necessary' when used in a statute conferring powers on a competent authority:

> ... necessarily make that authority the sole judge of what are its powers as well as the sole judge of the way in which it can exercise such powers as it may have. It is axiomatic that ... 'the paramount rule remains that every statute is to be expounded according to its manifest or expressed intention'. It is no less axiomatic that the application of that rule may result in phrases identical in wording or in substance receiving quite different interpretations

according to the tenor of the legislation under consideration. As an apt illustration of such a result it is not necessary to go further than *Liversidge v
Anderson* (1942) ... and *Nakkuda Ali v Jayaratne* (1951) ... in which the words
'reasonable cause to believe' and 'reasonable grounds to believe' received
quite different interpretations.

In *Liversidge* the Home Secretary was empowered by Defence Regulation 18B to
make order for the detention of persons where he had reasonable cause to
believe that they were of hostile origin or association. In an action by a detainee
for false imprisonment against the Home Secretary it was found by the House
of Lords that there could be no inquiry by the court into the question of whether
there were reasonable grounds for the Home Secretary's belief that a person
should be detained, except on proof of bad faith. In exercising his considerable
discretion the Home Secretary was responsible only to Parliament, not the
court. By contrast, in *Nakkuda Ali* it has been seen in the chapter on natural justice that a Controller of Textiles in Ceylon was empowered by a regulation governing his powers to cancel textile licences where he had reasonable ground to
believe that any dealer was unfit to continue in that capacity. In giving judgment the Judicial Committee of the Privy Council sought to emphasise that
Liversidge was a decision referable to its own peculiar wartime context. As to the
words in the present case, Lord Radcliffe giving judgment considered that:

> ... they must be intended to serve in some sense as a condition limiting the
> exercise of an otherwise arbitrary power. But if the question whether the
> condition has been satisfied is to be conclusively decided by the man who
> wields the power the value of the intended restraint is in effect nothing ...
> Their Lordships therefore treat the words in [the] regulation ... as imposing a
> condition that there must in fact exist such reasonable grounds, known to the
> controller, before he can validly exercise the power of cancellation.

Decisions like that in *Liversidge*, where the court was effectively saying that it
could not define any statutory limits surrounding the minister's powers, are
rare. Indeed, the case is most frequently remembered for the dissenting judgment of Lord Atkin who desired that an objective construction be placed on the
terms of Defence Regulation 18B. In what was a truly remarkable judgment,
Lord Atkin was unashamedly critical of '... judges who on a mere question of
construction when face to face with claims involving the liberty of the subject
show themselves more Executive-minded than the Executive'. However, the
trend is very much in a direction where the court will not often find that a complete discretion has been granted to a minister or any other administrative
agency. In *Secretary of State for Employment v ASLEF (No 2)* (1972) the court
found that the Secretary of State's decision to order a strike ballot under the
Industrial Relations Act 1972 was not *ultra vires* his powers under the Act.
Nevertheless, and despite the fact that he could take action 'where it appeared'
to him that irregular industrial action had begun or was likely to begin, this did
not mean, according to Lord Denning that:

... the minister's decision is put beyond challenge ... [I]f the minister does not act in good faith, or if he acts on extraneous considerations which ought not to influence him, or if he plainly misdirects himself in fact or in law, it may well be that a court would interfere; but if he honestly takes a view of the facts or of the law which could reasonably be entertained, then his decision is not to be set aside simply because thereafter someone thinks that his view was wrong. After all, this is an emergency procedure, it has to be set in motion quickly, when there is no time for minute analysis of facts or of law.

Further important examples in the present context of the court's concern about discretionary powers are found in *Norwich City Council v Secretary of State for the Environment* (1982), referred to in Chapter 1, *Congreve v Home Office* (1976) and *Secretary of State for Education and Science v Tameside Metropolitan Borough Council* (1977). In *Congreve* a large number of television licence holders had prematurely renewed their licences in order to avoid paying an increased fee when it came into force subsequently. They were told by the Home Office that unless they paid the balance between the cost of the old licence and the increased cost for new licences, their licences would be revoked. This action was taken under s 1(2) and s 1(4) of the Wireless Telegraphy Act 1949. Section 1(2) states that: 'A licence ... may be issued subject to such terms, provisions and limitations as the minister may think fit.' Section 1(4) states that a licence: '... may be revoked ... by a notice in writing served on the holder.' It was found by the Court of Appeal that the powers were not unlimited and could only be exercised to revoke a licence for good reason and the Home Office's dislike of 'overlapping' licences was not a good reason so that the threatened revocation was *ultra vires*. In the *Tameside* case a Conservative-controlled education authority refused to implement proposals for the introduction of comprehensive secondary education which had been approved by the Secretary of State for Education when the Labour Party had controlled the authority. Section 68 of the Education Act 1944 empowers the Secretary of State to serve a direction against an education authority if he '... is satisfied ... that any local education authority ... have acted or are proposing to act unreasonably with respect to the exercise of any power conferred or the performance of any duty imposed by or under this Act'. In the face of the refusal to implement the proposals for comprehensive education, the Secretary of State served a direction and now sought an order of *mandamus* to enforce observance of that direction. It was decided by the House of Lords that the direction was *ultra vires* because there were no grounds for concluding that the authority has acted 'unreasonably'. Following the dicta of Lord Denning in the *ASLEF* case, it was considered that although the Secretary of State might legitimately take the view that the authority's proposal to retain grammar schools and to implement selection procedures for certain schools was misguided or wrong, there were no grounds which could justify a conclusion that the proposal was such that no education authority, acting reasonably, would carry it out.

A similar conclusion to that in *Tameside* was reached by the Court of Appeal in *Coleen Properties Ltd v Minister of Housing and Local Government* (1971), using the so-called 'no evidence' rule. Once again the court was confronted by a minister's statutory powers which appeared to confer a considerable discretion. The Housing Act 1985 empowers the minister to confirm a local authority's compulsory purchase order which includes land which is 'reasonably necessary', either for the purpose of securing a slum clearance area of convenient shape and dimensions or to secure the satisfactory development or use of the area (s 290(2)). The court concluded that what is 'reasonably necessary' is a fundamental question of fact so that if land is to be included in a confirmed order, the minister should have evidence to justify its inclusion. On this basis, the 'grounds' which were lacking in the Secretary of State's action in *Tameside* could have been provided had there been some evidence that the education authority had acted 'unreasonably' (a question of fact) in refusing to implement the proposals for comprehensive education.

11.7 Policy and the Exercise of Discretionary Powers

It has been seen previously that where statute confers a discretion on an administrative agency, that agency has an opportunity to make a choice in determining what action to take or decision to make. In order to guide the making of any such discretionary choice, the administrative agency may adopt a policy. A policy will often be made where the administrative agency is charged with the responsibility of distributing scarce resources in order to achieve what seems to be the most equitable distribution of that resource. A local authority, for example, may adopt a policy in relation to the payment of grants for the repair and improvement of houses by reference to the high priority needs of certain areas of urban decay. Whatever the policy adopted by an administrative agency, that policy must be within the limits of the powers of the Act in question (*Cumings v Birkenhead Corporation* (1972)).

11.7.1 Lawful and unlawful policies

If a policy is *ultra vires* the Act under which an administrative agency is discharging its functions, that agency nevertheless acts unlawfully where the policy prevents consideration of the merits of each case. The essence of this legal requirement has been expressed in a number of cases. The requirement was dealt with by Lord Reid in *British Oxygen Co Ltd v Minister of Technology* (1971):

> The general rule is that anyone who has to exercise a statutory discretion must not 'shut his ears' to an application ... There may be cases where the Board should listen to argument against the policy. What it must not do is to refuse to listen at all ... a large authority may have had to deal already with many similar applications and then it will almost certainly have evolved a

policy ... There is no objection to that provided it is always ready to listen to new argument.

In another leading statement of principle, Bankes LJ in *R v Port of London Authority, ex p Kynoch* (1919) expanded this all important distinction between lawful policies and unlawful, preclusive policies. Referring to a licensing function of the Authority, he observed that:

> There are on the one hand cases where a tribunal in the honest exercise of its discretion has adopted a policy, and, without refusing to hear the applicant, intimates to him what its policy is, and that after hearing him it will in accordance with its policy decide against him, unless there is something exceptional in his case ... If the policy has been adopted for reasons which the tribunal may legitimately entertain, no objection could be taken to such a course. On the other hand there are cases where a tribunal has passed a rule, or come to a determination, not to hear any application of a particular character by whomsoever made. There is a wide distinction to be drawn between these two cases.

The basis of these legal requirements relating to policy is that the statutory responsibilities of administrative agencies cannot be fettered or frustrated. Wherever Parliament has specified by statute that administrative action should be initiated, that administrative disputes should be adjudicated or that applications should be processed, any attendant duty or discretion should be exercised according to law. In R *v Secretary of State for the Environment, ex p Brent London Borough Council & Others* (1982) the court was concerned with the Secretary of State's policy to reduce the rate support grant payable to local authorities affected by this policy. Because their rights were adversely affected by the potential loss of grant it was decided that the Secretary of State had not acted fairly towards the local authorities and in so doing had used his policy unlawfully to fetter any genuine exercise of his statutory discretion under the Local Government, Planning and Land Act 1980. As a result, the court quashed the decision to reduce the local authorities' rate support grant.

In the same way that an unlawful policy may preclude or fetter the lawful exercise of a statutory duty or discretion, these statutory responsibilities may also be affected by contracts and other similar transactions. In *Ayr Harbour Trustees v Oswald* (1883) the trustees were subject to a statutory duty to acquire such land as was required for the construction of harbour facilities. Having purchased land, it was agreed that no construction would take place on that land which would injuriously affect other neighbouring land retained by the vendor. It was decided that this restriction in the agreement was *ultra vires* the trustees' statutory duty. Similarly, in *William Cory & Son Ltd v Corporation of London* (1951) the court refused to imply a term in a contract between the parties that the local authority would not make a bylaw which was inconsistent with the contractual terms. However, there can be no such objection to such a contract or other similar transaction which is consistent with statutory duties or discretions. It was seen in Chapter 4 that local authorities have wide statutory powers to undertake a large range of functions involving the making of contracts of all sorts. That such contracts are usually compatible with underlying statutory powers is illustrated by *Birkdale District Electricity Supply Co Ltd v Southport Corporation* (1926). It was agreed between the parties that the company would not charge higher prices for electricity than those charged by Southport Corporation. Subsequently, the corporation sought an injunction to restrain the company charging higher prices in breach of the agreement. It was found by the court that the agreement was not *ultra vires*: it was an agreement which was compatible with the corporation's statutory power to determine the rates for electricity supply. That some contracts and agreements are not incompatible with statutory powers may be represented as a tenuous conclusion, as seen in *Terry* in the previous chapter. Finally in this context there seems to be a general presumption in the law that where the Crown is concerned, the court, in order to preserve freedom of executive action, will find that a contract or any other similar transaction cannot lawfully fetter the exercise of appropriate statutory or prerogative powers (*Crown Lands Commissioners v Page* (1960)).

11.7.2 Acts under dictation

There is resort to what is in effect an unlawful policy where an act is performed under dictation. This problem has occurred previously where local authorities in undertaking their statutory film licensing responsibilities have been prepared to grant licences to films approved by the British Board of Film Censors without themselves adjudicating the merits of each film (*Ellis v Dubowski* (1921)). In *H Lavender & Son Ltd v Minister of Housing and Local Government* (1970) the minister, in determining a planning appeal in respect of a proposal to extract minerals from high-grade agricultural land, indicated that it was his policy not to permit such extraction in such areas unless the Minister of Agriculture was not against the proposal. The court quashed the minister's decision on the ground that the policy precluded an exercise of the minister's statutory discretion so that in failing to determine the appeal himself, he had acted *ultra vires*. An opinion from the Secretary of State confirming that he would grant planning permission on appeal in conformity with a department circular is *ultra vires* when it influenced the local planning authority's decision: *R v Worthing Borough Council, ex p Burch* (1983). Even in the absence of a policy an administrative agency may act unlawfully under dictation. In *Laker Airways Ltd v Department of Trade* (1977) which was previously dealt with in Chapter 9 under the heading of 'Estoppel', the Civil Aviation Authority had to review Laker Airways' licence to operate 'Skytrain', acting under dictation from the Department of Trade. It was decided that any withdrawal of the licence was *ultra vires* because the Department had no power to give 'directions' to the Authority which, under the Civil Aviation Act 1971, was subject only to 'guidance' from the Department. Whether a policy is unlawfully preclusive is a matter of fact in each case. In *Attorney General, ex rel Tilley v Wandsworth London Borough Council* (1981) the local authority adopted a policy that whenever any case of an intentionally homeless family was before the social services committee it would not provide accommodation by virtue of s 1(1) of the Children and Young Persons Act 1963 which allows 'assistance in kind' (including the provision of accommodation) as part of the local authority's statutory duty to promote children's welfare. There was evidence before the court that exceptions to the policy could be made in appropriate cases. However, it was decided by the court that the policy was unlawful: the committee would be much influenced by the policy to an extent that there would be doubts as to the fairness of decisions made. The mere existence of the policy meant that in operating s 1(1) there would be differentiation between children according to the conduct of their parents.

Tilley was distinguished by the House of Lords in *Re Findlay* (1984) where the Home Secretary's parole policy was in issue in proceedings where prisoners claimed that they had suffered loss of expectation of parole. The policy here was regarded as a complex one but perfectly lawful in so far as the merits of cases in particular categories could still be considered.

11.7.3   The interpretation and application of policy

Where an administrative agency indicates reliance on a policy for the purpose of making a decision or taking any other administrative action, the law may require a correct interpretation and application of that policy. The precise requirements were set out in *Niarchos v Secretary of State for the Environment* (1978) where it was considered to be:

> ... trite law that the Secretary of State is entitled to have a policy and to change it from day to day, and accordingly he is not bound to apply (although he must have regard to) the policy ... However ... when he expresses himself to be deciding a case under a stated policy, it must follow that if he decides the case other than in accordance with the policy he misdirects himself ... where there are no other considerations. Accordingly, ... if he misdirects himself as to the provisions of the policy he acts in excess of his power.

Although this case related to the Secretary of State's determination of a planning appeal, where the Town and Country Planning Act 1971 s 29 (the predecessor of s 70 of the Town and Country Planning Act 1990) required him to have regard to the policy in the appropriate development plan and to any other material considerations, the principle could be applicable elsewhere in other statutory contexts.

11.8   Relevant Considerations

Whether or not a policy is being employed by an administrative agency in order to guide its exercise of discretion, the court will require that it avoids being influenced by irrelevant considerations. Equally, the administrative agency must not fail to take into account any relevant considerations. According to Lord Greene MR in *Associated Provincial Picture Houses*, if:

> ... in the statute conferring the discretion, there is to be found expressly or by implication matters which the authority exercising the discretion ought to have regard to, then in exercising the discretion it must have regard to those matters. Conversely, if the nature of the subject-matter and the general interpretation of the Act make it clear that certain matters would not be germane to the matter in question, the authority must disregard those irrelevant collateral matters ...

Failure to adhere to any of these requirements will usually render any decision or other administrative action *ultra vires*. However, where the administrative agency is responsible for a purely administrative function which does not affect a person's rights, the court will not apply these requirements (*R v Barnet and Camden Rent Tribunal, ex p Frey Investments Ltd* (1972)).

Where statute prescribes the relevant or material considerations which can influence a discretionary decision there will be few problems for the court in determining the limits of the statutory powers in question. However, it is not uncommon to find that Parliament has merely stipulated, as in s 70 of the Town and Country Planning Act 1990 relating to the determination of applications for planning permission by local authorities and (on appeal) the Secretary of State, that there shall be regard for 'the development plan' and 'any other material considerations'. In *Stringer v Minister of Housing and Local Government* (1971) it was decided that the minister, in determining a planning appeal, was able to take into consideration possible interference with Jodrell Bank telescope by a proposed new residential development nearby. Looking at the overall objects of the Act, Cooke J concluded that 'material' considerations:

> ... have to be 'planning' considerations ... In principle ... any consideration which relates to the use and development of land is capable of being a planning consideration'.

Whatever the identity of a consideration which is legally relevant to a discretionary decision, the weight and significance to be given to that consideration is entirely a matter within the powers of the administrative agency. Accordingly, in *Sovmots Investments Ltd v Secretary of State for the Environment* (1976) it was decided at first instance that cost is a legally relevant consideration for the Secretary of State in deciding whether to confirm a compulsory purchase order for the acquisition of land for the provision of housing accommodation under the Housing Act. Forbes J went on to emphasise '... that the weight to be given to cost ... is also a matter for the minister and not one in respect of which the court is entitled to substitute its opinion'.

Two leading cases in the present context relate to local government finance. First, in *Roberts v Hopwood* (1925) the court was concerned with s 62 of the Metropolis Management Act 1855 by which Poplar Borough Council was empowered to pay employees '... such salaries and wages as ... [the Council]

196

may think fit'. The district auditor disallowed part of the wages paid by the council. The council had continued to pay a minimum wage of £4 per week in 1921–22 as in the previous year despite a fall in the cost of living. The auditor found that the payments were not wholly wages but were in part contrary to law as gratuities. The disallowance was upheld by the House of Lords on the ground that the discretion in s 62 had not been exercised reasonably, more particularly because there had been no regard for factors like existing labour conditions and other ordinary economic considerations.

The second case, *Bromley London Borough Council v Greater London Council* (1982), was concerned with the legality of a supplementary rate levied by the GLC on constituent councils in order to finance a 25% reduction of fares on London Transport. It was decided by the House of Lords that the rate was *ultra vires* the Transport (London) Act 1969. The basis of the decision was that the GLC had failed to take into account the need for the London Transport Executive to avoid a deficit by disregarding their legal duty to operate 'economic' transport facilities. This occurred through the acceptance of the scheme to reduce fares which placed an undue burden on ratepayers in breach of a legal duty to ensure that, so far as was practicable, outgoings were met by revenue. In many cases involving local government finance the court has accepted the broad proposition that a local authority should have due regard for the interest of its rate payers, as was seen in the section of Chapter 4 dealing with audit.

11.9 Improper Purposes

Closely related to the above requirements relating to relevant considerations is the requirement that a statutory power can be used only for the purposes expressly or impliedly indicated in the legislation. In many instances it may be the case that a decision or other administrative action may be *ultra vires* by reference to either of these legal requirements. Indeed, on those occasions when a decision is quashed as being *ultra vires* by reference to improper purposes, the likelihood is that the administrative agency has either taken account of irrelevant considerations or failed to take into account relevant considerations.

A further, final example of a case in which the issue of relevant considerations was central to the decision of the court is *R v Secretary of State for the Home Department, ex p Asif Khan* (1985). In this case, the Secretary of State had issued a circular in which he had set out the criteria that would be applied in relation to the admission of children into the UK for adoption. The applicant complied with the published criteria but nevertheless the Secretary of State refused to admit a relative's child that he wished to adopt on the basis of a ground that was not present in the published criteria. Accordingly on an application for judicial review, the court of Appeal quashed the refusal of entry clearance. The circular had created a legitimate expectation that entry would be allowed provided that the criteria were complied with. The Secretary of State had in effect made his own rules by stating those matters which were relevant to his decision, but the fact that he had decided the matter on the basis of a consideration not stated in the circular, an irrelevant consideration, ensured that in the opinion of the court, he had 'misdirected himself as to his own criteria and acted unreasonably'.

Whether a statutory power has been used lawfully for the express or implied requirements or purposes of the particular legislation is again a matter of statutory interpretation for the court. In *Sydney Municipal Council v Campbell* (1925) the council was empowered to purchase compulsorily any land required for 'carrying out improvements in or remodelling any portion of the city'. Without any proposal or intention to improve or remodel any area, the council resolved to purchase land, including land in the ownership of the respondent. It was found that the council's intention was to obtain the benefit of an increase in land values following a highway extension into the area, a proposal which was not related, directly or indirectly, to the objects and purposes of the statutory powers. Similarly in *Webb v Minister of Housing and Local Government* (1965) it was decided that a power to acquire land for the provision of coast protection could not lawfully be used for the purpose of providing a promenade. However, in *Hanks v Minister of Housing and Local Government* (1963) it was decided that general highway and planning purposes were lawfully incidental to the prime purpose of powers in the Housing Act by which land can be acquired for the provision of housing and, more particularly in this case, a housing estate. Where the purposes for which statutory powers are conferred are not clearly and expressly indicated, the court will look to the overall policy and objects of the relevant Act or section of the Act (*Padfield v Minister of Agriculture* (1968)). Section 120(1) of the Local Government Act 1972 states that:

(1) For the purposes of –

...

(b) the benefit, improvement or development of their area, a principal council may acquire by agreement any land, whether situated inside or outside their area.

It was decided in *Costello v Dacorum District Council* (1983) that these powers are widely drawn. As a result the council was found not to have used these and other powers under the Open Spaces Act 1906 for an unlawful, improper purpose when a lease was taken of land in order to enable the eviction of gipsies. This was despite a temporary planning permission given to the Secretary of State for the Environment under the Town and Country Planning Act enabling the gipsies to stay on the land. However, in *R v Somerset County Council, ex p Fewings* (1995), the principal issue for the court was whether the councillors moral objections to the practice of stag-hunting were capable of justifying the prohibition of hunting on land that they owned as a measure achieving the purpose of s 120 of the 1972 Act. The Divisional Court held that the council's resolution to ban stag-hunting was *ultra vires* since it amounted to the use of its statutory powers for an improper purpose as well as the taking of irrelevant considerations into account, namely the ethical perceptions of the councillors as to the rights and wrongs of hunting.

Where there appears to be a plurality of motives for administrative action the court will seek to identify the dominant purpose for which the powers are exercised. In *Westminster Corporation v London and North Western Railway Co* (1905) the court was concerned with a statutory provision which stated that: 'Every sanitary authority may provide and maintain public lavatories ... in situations where they deem the same to be required.' The corporation used this power to build lavatories underneath the middle of a street and provided access by means of a subway from either side. Consequently, the subway could be used as a means of crossing the street by persons with no desire to use the lavatories. It was argued that the corporation had unlawfully abused its powers. This argument was rejected by the court and in delivering judgment, Lord MacNaughton observed that:

> It is not enough to show that the Corporation contemplated that the public might use the subway as a means of crossing the street ... it must be shown that the Corporation constructed this subway as a means of crossing the street under colour and pretence of providing public conveniences which were not really wanted at that particular place.

It seems, therefore, that as long as the corporation considered that the lavatories were genuinely required at the point in question, it mattered not that some consideration may have been given to the need to provide a subway street crossing.

It is sometimes the case that an administrative agency is confronted by a number of different courses of action, any one of which could be adopted for the purpose of dealing with a particular problem. This was the case in *Asher v Secretary of State for the Environment* (1974) where local councillors refused to increase council house rents, as required by the Housing Finance Act 1972. The Secretary of State had four possible alternative options in order to deal with this situation. He could appoint a Housing Commissioner to take over the council's statutory housing responsibilities, require the district auditor to undertake an extraordinary audit of the council's accounts, reduce the council's housing subsidy, or apply to the High Court for an order of *mandamus* requiring the council to undertake its statutory housing responsibilities according to law. The Secretary of State chose an extraordinary audit of the accounts as a result of which the councillors were surcharged and disqualified. The court rejected an argument that the Secretary of State was motivated by an unlawful, improper motive, to see the councillors punished. It was emphasised that ministers frequently have to balance one course of action against another and in the absence of any proof of bad faith the court would not interfere. The court did interfere in *Wheeler v Leicester City Council* (1985) when the council purported to use its statutory powers to ban the use of a public park for practice by Leicester Rugby Football Club. The ban occurred after the club refused to condemn a rugby tour to South Africa in which members of the club would participate. In essence the House of Lords decided that the powers could not be used to punish the club when it had done no wrong. Similarly, in *R v Lewisham London Borough Council, ex p Shell UK Ltd* (1988), the court upheld an application for judicial review of a decision by the council to boycott the company's products due to its links with South Africa. Whilst the council was entitled to take into account the need to promote good race relations in the exercise of its functions, its attempt to induce Shell to sever its trading links with South Africa amounted to the exercise of a power for an improper purpose.

Finally, where statutory powers overlap so that it may be apparent that either power may be used by an administrative agency, it may be unlawful to use one power to the exclusion of the other, particularly if a person's rights are affected as may have been the case in *Costello*. However, statute may prescribe that the administrative agency may lawfully use particular powers, even though a person's rights may be prejudiced by the use of these but not the other overlapping powers. This was the case in *Westminster Bank Ltd v Minister of Housing and Local Government* (1970) where proposed development involving an extension to a bank could be restrained either by refusing planning permission under the Town and Country Planning Act or by imposing an 'improvement' line under the Highways Act. The latter powers involved a payment of compensation whereas a refusal of consent under the Planning Act powers did not attract compensation. It was decided by the House of Lords that in refusing consent under the planning powers, there had been no *ultra vires* decision motivated by any unlawful desire to avoid compensation primarily because the Town and Country Planning Act expressly permitted other powers to be ignored. The section in question stipulates that:

> ... the provisions of this Act ... apply ... in relation to any land notwithstanding that provision is made by any enactment in force at the passing of the Act ... for statutory 'immunity' in relation to improper purposes only extends to 'competing' powers in an Act in force at the passing of the Town and Country Planning Act where the authority is concerned with the 'regulation' of any development of land.

11.10   Total Unreasonableness

Lord Greene MR in *Associated Provincial Picture Houses* characterised any administrative act as having been performed 'unreasonably' in law where, for example, there is a failure to take account of relevant considerations. The same description would apply to any act motivated by unlawful, improper purposes. However, Lord Greene goes on to say such unreasonableness in law can also cover a situation where '... a decision on a competent matter is so unreasonable that no reasonable authority could even come to it'. Clearly, any such decision will be regarded in law as being *ultra vires* not because it is affected by irrelevant considerations, failure to take into account relevant considerations or improper purposes, but because it is such an extreme decision that the court will assume that Parliament could never have intended that any reasonable authority would use the statutory powers in that way. In the *GCHQ* case, Lord Diplock chose to use the term 'irrationality' to denote 'unreasonableness' in the *Wednesbury* sense. In his Lordship's opinion, an irrational decision is 'a decision which is so outrageous in its defiance of logic or of accepted moral standards that no sensible person who had applied his mind to the question to be decided could have arrived at it'.

There are very few authentic examples of the court's use of this ground for the review of discretionary powers. One of the best examples is the Court of Appeal decision in *Hall & Co v Shoreham-by-Sea Urban District Council* (1964). The local planning authority granted planning permission subject to a number of conditions, one of which was that the developer should construct a road on his land to be dedicated to the public, as and when required by the authority. This condition was held to be totally unreasonable and therefore *ultra vires* on the basis that there was interference with the developer's property rights without a payment of compensation. There was no suggestion that the condition was influenced by irrelevant considerations since the provision of roads is clearly relevant where planning powers are exercised. Consequently, it is the extreme requirements of the condition alien to the presumed limits of the powers in the Act that render it totally unreasonable. *In R v Hillingdon London Borough Council, ex p Royco Homes Ltd* (1974) planning permission was granted for the construction of flats subject to conditions which included the requirements that they should first be occupied by persons who had been on the housing waiting list for 12 months and that such persons should have security of tenure for 10 years from the date of occupation. These conditions were found to be totally unreasonable and *ultra vires*, again on the grounds advanced in *Hall*. However, Royco Homes is not as clear an example of unreasonableness as *Hall* if it is accepted that the local planning authority was influenced at the outset by an irrelevant consideration, ie the provision of housing. In other words, if the provision of housing is not a legally relevant consideration for the purpose of a planning decision that would have been the simpler ground on which to base the conclusion about the legality of the conditions.

Accordingly, total unreasonableness is a ground for the review of discretionary decisions, eg wherever they are beyond challenge by reference to irrelevant considerations or improper purposes. Total unreasonableness may also apply to any decision which cannot reasonably be justified on the evidence so that no other reasonable authority would have come to that decision (*Banks Horticultural Products Ltd v Secretary of State for the Environment* (1979)). Again, such a conclusion must be justified only on the ground that Parliament could not have intended that the powers should be exercised except by reference to a certain minimum 'quantity' or 'quality' of evidence. This variety of total unreasonableness serves to emphasise the great difficulty in using and applying this ground for review. Indeed, of the few cases apparently decided by reference to total unreasonableness, it is clear that they could have been decided, as perhaps is the case in *Royco Homes*, eg by reference to irrelevant considerations or improper purposes. A prime example is *Backhouse v Lambeth London Borough Council* (1972), previously seen in the section of Chapter 4 dealing with audit. Although it was decided that the resolution containing the proposal to increase the rent of one council house was totally unreasonable, the case could have been decided quite easily by reference to a failure to take into account some relevant consideration contemplated by the Housing Finance Act.

11.11 Proportionality

Whilst the discussion in this chapter has, in part, focused on the accepted grounds for review of administrative decisions, it is worth emphasising that such grounds rarely exist in isolation; it is by no means uncommon for a decision to be susceptible to review for more than one reason as was indicated when improper purposes and relevant considerations were discussed above. In addition, it would appear that the grounds for review are by no means closed. This point was made by Lord Diplock in the *GCHQ* case where his Lordship observed that:

> That is not to say that further development on a case by case basis may not in course of time add further grounds. I have in mind particularly the possible adoption in the future of the principle of 'proportionality' which is recognised in the administrative law of several of our fellow members of the European Community.

The principle of proportionality is, as Lord Diplock implied, a general principle of EU law and as such, it has been relied upon where the legality of an EU measure has been contested, or alternatively, in relation to a challenge against a national measure seeking to implement an EU provision. Proportionality as a ground for review does not question the objective or the end sought, rather, it alleges that the means of achieving the objective were disproportionate; they were in excess of what was necessary to bring about the intended result. Put more colloquially, it could be argued that a disproportionate administrative decision gives rise to the same effect that would occur were a sledgehammer used to crack a nut. The status of the principle of proportionality in domestic administrative law is not entirely settled at present.

In the leading case of *R v Secretary of State for the Home Department, ex p Brind* (1991), where journalists sought judicial review of directives issued by the Home Secretary which had the effect of placing a ban on the direct broadcasting of statements made by terrorists and the supporters of terrorism, the House of Lords rejected proportionality as a separate ground for review. Concern was expressed at the perceived constitutional dangers inherent in the acceptance of the principle. It was felt by Lord Roskill and Lord Ackner that if the courts showed a willingness to review administrative decisions on the basis of proportionality, there was every likelihood that they would become involved in an inquiry into the merits of the decision which is of course beyond the remit of the court in judicial review proceedings. However, such sentiments do not mean that proportionality will not ultimately become part of English administrative law. Lord Bridge in *Brind* felt that incorporation will eventually take place some time in the future, and then of course there are the remarks of Lord Diplock in *GCHQ* referred to earlier. In addition, there have been cases where the principle of proportionality has been either expressly or implicitly referred to, the most notable of these being *R v Barnsley Metropolitan Borough Council, ex p Hook* (1976) where a market stallholder had his licence revoked after he had been caught urinating in a side street by two council workmen after the closure of the public lavatories. Whilst the case was decided on the basis that the principles of natural justice had not been complied with during the course of an appeal hearing conducted in relation to the revocation of the licence, two of the three members of the Court of Appeal were prepared to discuss the facts in terms of 'proportionality' during the course of their judgments. Sir John Pennycuick felt that the loss of the licence amounted to a too severe punishment for what was an isolated and trivial incident. Lord Denning went still further and contended that the decision of the corporation could be quashed solely on the basis of the disproportionate nature of the punishment since a review of the authorities revealed that a court 'can interfere by *certiorari* if a punishment is altogether excessive and out of proportion to the occasion'. Subsequent judicial decisions have not embraced the principle of proportionality with quite the same vigour as did the majority of the Court of Appeal in *Hook*, but it is possible to discern traces of the principle in decisions such as *Wheeler v Leicester City Council* (1985) and *R v Lewisham London Borough Council, ex p Shell UK Ltd* (1988) where it tends to co-exist with other, more widely accepted grounds for review. If proportionality does ultimately achieve judicial acceptance as a separate ground for review, as seems likely, it will have to be treated with caution by the courts so as to avoid any suggestion that they are flagrantly exceeding the bounds of their supervisory jurisdiction.

12   Administrative Remedies

12.1   Administrative and Judicial Remedies Contrasted

A remedy can be described as an administrative remedy where it is provided for by statute and does not involve recourse to a court of law. Whatever the status of the remedy, be it administrative or judicial, the law provides such a facility for the purposes of enabling an individual to challenge administrative action. The nature and effect of any such challenge allowed by a remedy will depend on a wide range of factors. In the case of the administrative remedy, it is usual to find that the challenge available through the remedy permits a complete re-examination of a decision or some other administrative action. In the case of judicial remedies, which are the subject of the next chapter, the law seeks to ensure that administrative action takes place according to the requirements of the law. If it does not then the individual who is aggrieved and has a sufficient interest in the matter, eg as the person directly affected by a decision, should be able to apply to the appropriate court for one of the judicial remedies. Such a judicial remedy is likely to be available once any administrative remedies have been exhausted. Where, for example, a local planning authority has served an enforcement notice under the Town and Country Planning Act alleging unlawful development without planning permission there is an appeal against the notice to the Secretary of State for the Environment and a further appeal on a point of law to the High Court against his appeal decision. Sometimes there may be a limit placed on any challenge to the validity of a decision taken by an administrative agency on an appeal through the use of an ouster clause of the sort described in Chapter 11. Such a clause might state that: '... the validity of any decision shall not be questioned in any proceedings whatsoever' and appears to make the decision final and conclusive. However, important decisions in cases like *Anisminic v Foreign Compensation Commission* (1969) which are dealt with in Chapter 11 show that the decision of the administrative agency concerned may be final and conclusive in relation to its *intra vires* facts and merit but not on matters of law. Because it is the High Court which is the final arbiter on matters of law and legality, there is always the possibility that the decision's legality can be challenged through one of the statutory or non-statutory remedies to be described in the next chapter. It is not unusual to find that Parliament has already addressed itself to the question of the status of the decision which emerges from an administrative remedy like an appeal. It has been seen in Chapter 5 that the decisions of some administrative tribunals are subject to a statutory appeal on a point of law to the High Court. A decision of the tribunal affected by an error of law can be taken to the High Court although one of the non-statutory remedies, *certiorari*, could be employed to quash the decision where the error was considered so fundamental as to render it *ultra vires*. In some instances and particularly in relation to decisions of the Secretary of State for the Environment in the area of town and country planning and compulsory purchase, it will be seen in the following chapter that an ouster clause often protects the decision while statutory provision is made for the limited terms on which the High Court can review its legality.

12.1.1 Varieties of administrative remedy

The administrative appeal is probably the best-known of the administrative remedies. There are two categories of appeal which are of considerable practical significance: appeals from decisions and other administrative action taken by local authorities and appeals from the decisions of government departments. Examples of these appeals are given in Chapter 4 on local government and in Chapter 5 on administrative tribunals. In the case of local authorities, one of the best-known appeals is that which is available to an applicant for planning permission where the local planning authority has refused planning permission or granted it subject to conditions. The appeal is to the Secretary of State for the Environment who is at liberty to look at the case afresh (perhaps with the help of a statutory inquiry) so that he could, for example, impose conditions which were even more stringent than those appealed against. The procedural requirements for these appeals are outlined in Chapter 9. Appeals from some local authority decisions go to administrative tribunals, as with disputes concerning Council Tax valuations, which go to the local valuation tribunals. Many appeals from decisions of government departments relate to welfare rights where the usual practice, as seen in Chapter 5, is to give an appeal against an adverse decision to an appropriate tribunal. Whatever the destination of an appeal, statutory rules of procedure will set out the detailed requirements for the process indicating the nature of any documentation required, time limits to be observed and so on. In some cases there are very distinct procedural requirements arising from an appeal, as in the case of appeals to the Social Security Appeal Tribunals where the initial decision is automatically reviewed when the appeal is notified.

In general, the administrative appeal stands out as the most common remedy for the person who is in some way affected by administrative action. There are, of course, other, more limited remedies for the individual such as the audit procedures dealt within Chapter 4 and the facilities for complaint to the appropriate minister in central government concerning the alleged failure of an administrative agency to undertake its statutory responsibilities. This latter facility will be dealt with later in the chapter. In addition, the individual can complain of maladministration which has caused him injustice at the hands of any one of a variety of different administrative agencies. Such a complaint of *intra vires* maladministration will go to one of the ombudsmen and this important remedy is described in Chapter 15. In any description of administrative remedies it should not be forgotten that such remedies may be available to agencies within a system of administration in order to permit some control of other agencies. Again, there are references to remedies such as directions and other default powers in Chapter 4 in the context of central government's control of local authorities as well as in Chapter 6.

12.2 Administrative Remedies and the Question of Legality

At the beginning of this chapter it was seen that where any challenge to a decision or other action is through an administrative remedy such as an appeal, there can be a complete re-examination of the decision. In other words, all the *intra vires* merits of the decision can be re-appraised and, if necessary, the appeal body can substitute its own decision for that made originally and which has now been brought to appeal. However, when the original decision is made by the administrative agency it may be suspected, on the basis of legal advice, that the legality of the decision is in doubt. It may be suspected, for example, that the decision is, in fact, *ultra vires*. For the individual who is affected by the decision there may be something of a dilemma. The decision may be made in respect of that activity from which he proposes to earn his livelihood. The licensing authority may have granted a licence by its decision but imposed perhaps onerous conditions. Should the individual pursue an administrative appeal in the hope that the onerous conditions might be lifted, or should he attempt to challenge the legality of the decision as a whole by applying to the High Court for one of the judicial remedies in administrative law? If the latter course is possible and the High Court found that the decision was *ultra vires*, that decision would probably be quashed or declared a nullity, so enabling the individual to start all over again with a fresh application to the licensing authority.

12.2.1 Administrative versus judicial remedies

For the individual faced with the dilemma described above there is the vital question of whether, in law, it is possible to go for the judicial remedy in the High Court where there is an administrative remedy already provided. The answer to this question emerges from the decision in *R v Hillingdon London Borough Council, ex p Royco Homes Ltd* (1974) where the administrative remedy was the appeal to the Secretary of State for the Environment against a conditional grant of planning permission by a local planning authority while the judicial remedy was an order of *certiorari* from the High Court to quash the decision by reference to *ultra vires* conditions. The crucial point was whether *certiorari* was available or whether the High Court would have to admit that the only remedy was the administrative remedy provided in this case by the Town and Country Planning Act. The Act provides that the applicant who is aggrieved by the decision of a local planning authority on an application for planning permission '... may by notice ... appeal to the Secretary of State'. On the face of it, the word 'may' seems to indicate that there is an option so that the aggrieved applicant does not necessarily have to take that route. It was decided by the High Court that the judicial remedy, ie in this case, the order of *certiorari*, would be available in a 'proper' case, where the only issue (as in this case) is the legality of a decision. Consequently, in any case where the only complaint about a decision is its legality, eg where there is an error of law on the face of the record, the administrative remedy can be ignored in favour of the judicial remedy from the High Court. The then Lord Chief Justice, Lord Widgery, giving judgment summarised the position by saying that:

> Whether the issue between [the parties] is a matter of law or fact, or policy or opinion, or a combination of some or all of those, one hearing before the Secretary of State has jurisdiction to deal with them all, whereas of course an application for *certiorari* is limited to cases where the issue is a matter of law ...

12.2.2 Administrative and judicial remedies serving the same purpose

It has been seen in the previous section that the two types of remedy available may not necessarily serve the same purpose although there would have been no objection to an appeal to the Secretary of State by Royco Homes under s 36. Indeed an administrative appeal is likely to be the cheaper option unless the parties become embroiled in an expensive public inquiry into the issues before the final decision is made. Had Royco Homes appealed against the conditions attached to its planning permission, a finding by the Secretary of State that they were *ultra vires* would not have necessitated a dismissal of the appeal in view of the fact that the Secretary of State can look at the application afresh and substitute his own decision (*Robert Hitchens (Builders) Ltd v Secretary of State for the Environment* (1979)). In another case from the background of town and country planning, *Pyx Granite Co Ltd v Minister of Housing and Local Government* (1959), the company sought a declaration (one of the judicial remedies to be described in the next chapter) that their quarrying operations could be carried out without planning permission because they were authorised by a 'private Act of Parliament' (the Malvern Hills Act 1924) for the purposes of a statutory order made under the Town and Country Planning Act. It was decided by the House of Lords that it could grant the declaration sought. One member observed that:

'It is surely proper that in a case like this involving ... difficult questions of construction of Acts of Parliament, a court of law should declare what are the rights of the subject who claims to have them determined' (Viscount Simonds). In this case, the court's declaration served the same purpose as the administrative remedy. This remedy, provided for in what is now s 64 of the Town and Country Planning Act 1990, provides than any person who wishes to ascertain whether proposed activities on land amount to 'development' requiring planning permission '... may ... apply to the local planning authority to determine that question'. In other cases where there is no overlap so that the respective remedies serve different purposes the court will require that the administrative or any other exclusive statutory remedy be followed, as in *Barraclough v Brown* (1897), which was distinguished by the House of Lords as a different case in *Pyx Granite*. In *Barraclough* the court was concerned with the statutory facilities which gave the plaintiff an entitlement to claim his expenses arising from the recovery of sunken vessels from the River Ouse. Such expenses were recoverable from a magistrates' court: this remedy, it was decided, was an exclusive remedy so that the plaintiff could not obtain a declaration from the High Court in respect of the validity of a claim, which was a matter entirely for the magistrates.

12.2.3 Exclusive administrative remedies

In the previous chapter reference was made to s 8 of the Education Act 1944 by which a local education authority is obliged '... to secure that there should be available for their area sufficient schools for providing full-time education' suitable to the requirements of pupils. The statutory definition of such broad duties is not uncommon: s 11 of the Water Act 1973 declared very broadly that: 'It shall be the duty of a water authority to supply water within their area.' This broad duty is now repeated in similar terms by the Water Industry Act 1991 in the case of the privatised water companies. However, any alleged failure of an administrative agency to undertake such a duty cannot be dealt with by means of a judicial remedy such as *mandamus*, which would direct that a statutory duty should be performed according to law. In many cases Parliament and the courts have foreseen that these very broad duties depend for their performance on all sorts of financial, economic and other variables. The Water Act 1989, for example, contained many duties which are enforceable by the Director General of Water Services and the Secretary of State through the service of provisional or final enforcement orders. As a consequence, the courts have decided that such duties (now consolidated in the Water Industry Act 1991) are not legally enforceable directly, a conclusion which is often fortified by statutory provisions which provide an alternative, exclusive remedy for those occasions when there is a failure to perform the duty or, to use a technical legal expression, a 'non-feasance'. Such a remedy is necessarily associated with default powers exercisable by various ministers in central government departments as illustrated in a section of Chapter 4 dealing with this type of central government control. One example mentioned in this section came from the Education Act 1944, s 99 of which states that:

> If [the Secretary of State] is satisfied, either upon complaint by any person interested or otherwise, that any local education authority ... have failed to discharge any duty imposed upon them by or for the purposes of this Act [the Secretary of State] may make an order declaring the authority ... to be in default in respect of that duty, and giving such directions for the purpose of enforcing the execution thereof as appear ... to be expedient; and any such directions shall be enforceable, on an application made on behalf of [the Secretary of State], by *mandamus*.

It will be seen from this provision that only at the end of the special procedure is there any possibility of enforcement by the law, but only through the Secretary of State's application for an order of *mandamus* where any directions have not been complied with.

13 Judicial Remedies

13.1 Judicial Remedies Generally

Despite the existence of a wide variety of administrative remedies such as the appeal, described in the previous chapter, the individual who wishes to defend, establish or assert his legal rights in the face of administrative action usually has an opportunity of so doing before a court of law. In this context the individual will look for the protection of the law through any one or more of the remedies which can be granted by a court of law, hence the reference to 'judicial remedies'. In most cases the remedy sought will attempt to deal with an *ultra vires* act or decision of an administrative agency in proceedings before the High Court, which has the inherent power to review the legality of the actions and decisions of administrative agencies and inferior courts. The judicial remedies for *ultra vires* actions and decisions are the declaration, injunction, *certiorari*, prohibition and *mandamus* which are described later in this chapter. It should not be forgotten that on a prosecution for non-compliance with an administrative order, notice, licence or some item of delegated legislation, it may be possible to raise what is, in effect, a defence of *ultra vires*. This form of remedy would apply equally to any civil enforcement where, again, the argument would be that there can be no breach of or non-compliance with something which does not exist in law, that is, something which is *ultra vires*. In some instances it is the case that statutory administrative schemes provide for general appeals to an inferior court where that court can look at the merits of any decision or other administrative action. In the case of such a general appeal the court has wide powers to look afresh at the decision or other action and to substitute its own decision, for example. Such general appeals are in contrast to the more restricted appeals on a point of law which go to the High Court. Both categories of appeal are dealt with in the present chapter which deals also with the limited remedy of damages in administrative law and the remedy of annulment before the European Court of Justice in respect of unlawful administrative action within the European Economic Community. It is proposed to deal first with the facilities for appeals, followed by the High Court's inherent powers of review by reference to the doctrine of *ultra vires*, the remedy of damages and the power of annulment in the European Court of Justice.

13.2   Appeals

An appeal can be made to a court of law only where it is expressly provided for by statute. As was stated in the opening section of this chapter, there are two varieties of appeal: the general appeal and the appeal on a point of law. Each variety is dealt with in turn.

13.2.1   The general appeal

A wide variety of statutory provisions contain facilities for appeals to inferior courts and for present purposes three examples are given covering the magistrates' courts, the county courts and the Crown Courts.

First, in the case of the magistrates' courts one function, seen in Chapter 8, may be to deal with appeals against licensing decisions of local authorities to which applications are made by persons wishing to set up sex establishments. The second example relates to the county courts' responsibility for appeals against repair notices served by local authorities in respect of houses which are unfit for human habitation and which may or may not be repairable at reasonable expense, as was explained in Chapter 5. Finally, the Crown Courts have dealt with appeals in connection with the validity of a local authority's rate as it affects a particular individual or hereditament. In each case the scope of the court's powers on appeal depends on the particular statutory provision. In the case of an appeal to a county court against a repairs notice, the county court judge is empowered to uphold, vary or quash a repairs notice. Similar powers exist under the Housing Act 1985 where the county courts also deal with appeals from improvement notices served by local authorities requiring the provision of standard amenities such as a bath and toilet in a house. Once again, a key factor is 'reasonable expense' and it is not uncommon to find that an appeal is being pursued on the ground that standard amenities cannot be provided at a reasonable expense so that the improvement notice should be quashed. In this case, the decision of the court whether to vary or quash the notice will depend on whether or not the cost of providing the standard amenities is more than any resulting increase in the value of the house on the market. Any such decision relates to the merits of the original decision of the local authority to serve the improvement notice, the crucial characteristic of an appeal which distinguishes it from review where the High Court is concerned only with the question whether a decision or other administrative action is outside the statutory powers, ie *ultra vires*.

13.2.2   The appeal on a point of law

Such appeals are clearly more restricted in that the court is concerned only with questions of law, its interpretation and application. As was seen in Chapter 5, the decisions of various tribunals included in Schedule 1 of the Tribunals and

Inquiries Act 1992 are subject to an appeal on a point of law to the High Court or, in more limited cases, the Court of Appeal.

Although the appeal on a point of law is primarily a feature of decision-making by administrative tribunals, there is one important instance where a minister's decision is subject to an appeal on a point of law. This is in relation to the decision of the Secretary of State for the Environment on an appeal against an enforcement notice served by a local planning authority under the Town and Country Planning Act 1990. Many such appeals are undertaken annually when the task of the High Court often centres on the question of whether, as a matter of law, the Secretary of State was right to confirm an enforcement notice alleging unlawful 'development' (as defined by the Act) without planning permission. Whether the decision subject to an appeal on a point of law is that of a tribunal or a minister, it is usual for there to be a requirement that if some error or mistake of law is found by the High Court the case is remitted back to the tribunal or minister for reconsideration and a fresh decision.

A person's legal standing or status (*locus standi*) to bring an appeal is closely controlled. In the case of tribunals, if the procedural rules say nothing about *locus standi* then the Tribunals and Inquiries Act requirement will apply, that is, that an appeal may be brought by '... any party to proceedings ... dissatisfied' with a decision. At the outset it was emphasised that the appeal is restricted to a point of law. This is clearly of fundamental importance and has been emphasised by the High Court in many cases, of which *Jolliffe v Secretary of State for the Environment* (1971) is typical. In that case the judge, Lyell J, referring to the appeal on a point of law from the decision of the Secretary of State on an enforcement notice appeal, stated that:

> The Court is not a court of appeal from the minister's decision. Its powers are closely circumscribed by statute, and it should not be tempted into substituting its own judgment for matters which fall to be decided by the minister.

13.3   Review

While an appeal can be pursued only where statute provides for an appeal, the High Court has an inherent power to review the legality of acts and decisions of administrative agencies and inferior courts. This supervisory jurisdiction of the High Court operates by reference to the rules of law described in Chapters 9 to 11. Although the High Court's inherent power of judicial review owes much of its development to the common law, statute has intervened quite frequently in recent times in order to amend or cut down the inherent powers of judicial review possessed by the High Court. Statute has intervened in two ways:

(1) to replace the inherent power of judicial review with a review process whose terms are found very largely in the legislation governing certain areas of decision-making and referred to in the present chapter as 'statutory review'; and

(2) to streamline the system of remedies in judicial review according to the High Court's inherent powers under a relatively new procedure known as the application for judicial review.

Despite the intervention of statute in this latter case in order to deal with the substantive changes in law relating to what are essentially, discretionary remedies, the procedures by which the remedies are sought continue to be governed by the Rules of the Supreme Court. In the next sections of this chapter it is proposed to describe the remedies which are available in the review process undertaken by the High Court, including a special section on statutory review, before going on to deal with the process referred to by the Rules of the Supreme Court as the application for judicial review which governs procedures for judicial review, with the exception of statutory review.

13.4   The Declaration

This discretionary remedy is one which confirms the legal status of a relationship and is now widely used in administrative law, even though it does not coerce or force a party to do or refrain from doing anything.

13.4.1   Uses of the declaration in administrative law

The declaration has its most obvious use on those occasions when it is declared that the act or decision of an administrative agency is *ultra vires*, as in the leading case of *Anisminic v Foreign Compensation Commission* (1969) seen in Chapter 11. The remedy can be used also where a relationship is affected by a breach of natural justice, as seen in Chapter 10 (*Ridge v Baldwin* (1963)), where it is desired to challenge the legality of delegated legislation, as seen in Chapter 8 (*Agricultural, Horticultural and Forestry Industry Training Board v Aylesbury Mushrooms Ltd* (1972)), and where it is desired to establish that an administrative agency is bound by an act or statement of its representative, as seen in Chapter 9 (*Lever (Finance) Ltd v Westminster (City) London Borough Council* (1970)). Most of these principal examples of the uses of the declaration indicate that in administrative law it is a remedy which, if granted, usually confirms that the act or decision of an administrative agency is *ultra vires*, that is, null and void. As such, the declaration is clearly unsuited to and will not be granted in respect of a merely voidable decision which is affected by an error of law on the face of the record which was explained in Chapter 11. In *Punton v Ministry of Pensions and National Insurance (No 2)* (1964) it was found that a decision of a National Insurance Commissioner was *intra vires* but voidable, being affected by an error of law on the face of the record. Unlike a remedy such as *certiorari*, which is dealt with later in this chapter, the declaration does not quash a decision, that is, it is not a 'coercive' remedy. Consequently, in this and similar cases, to grant a declaration would leave two decisions in force, the voidable decision of the Commissioner and the court's declaration. In these circumstances therefore, the remedy of *certiorari* is needed in order to quash the voidable decision so that from the date of quashing it has no force in law so that no one can rely on it for any purpose.

The scope of the declaration in administrative law has been further considered, on this occasion by the House of Lords, in *Equal Opportunities Commission v Secretary of State for Employment* (1994). The Commission sought declarations in judicial review proceedings that certain provisions of the Employment Protection (Consolidation) Act 1978 were not compatible with EU law regarding equal pay and equal treatment of workers. Thus the application amounted to a challenge to the legality of primary rather than delegated legislation. It was argued by the Commission that the provisions of the 1978 Act relating to the right to statutory redundancy pay and compensation for unfair dismissal amounted to indirect discrimination since the Act imposed thresholds, in terms of the number of hours worked in each week, which ensured that part-time male workers had more statutory rights than part-time female workers who formed the great majority of those who fell below the threshold of 16 hours per week. One of the central issues for the House of Lords to consider was whether a court had the jurisdiction to make a declaration that the domestic law of the UK was not in conformity with EU law. It was argued on behalf of the Secretary of State that declaratory relief would only be available in judicial review proceedings where one of the prerogative orders would be available under Order 53. However, the House of Lords refused to accept that the effect of Order 53 was that a declaration can only be made in lieu of a prerogative order. As Lord Browne-Wilkinson observed:

> I have sought to demonstrate that the history of declaratory relief, authority and the terms of Order 15, r 16 all point to the court having power to make a declaratory judgment in judicial review proceedings brought by a plaintiff who has *locus standi*, whether or not the court could also make a prerogative order.

The decision in the *Equal Opportunities Commission* case thus highlights the increasingly flexible and pragmatic approach taken by the courts in relation to the declaration. Evidently the procedural reforms that were made to the remedies in administrative law following the recommendations of the Law Commission, which are considered later in this chapter, have not been such as to prevent the granting of declaratory relief by itself. Prior to 1977, it was by no means uncommon for a plaintiff to seek to obtain a declaration of public rights in civil proceedings provided that it could be shown that there was sufficient *locus standi*. Indeed, it was this avenue that was pursued by the plaintiffs in both *Ridge v Baldwin* and *Anisminic v Foreign Compensation Commission*.

13.4.2   Exclusion of the declaration

It has been seen in the previous section that a declaration will not be granted in respect of a voidable decision. There are other circumstances in which (usually as a matter of discretion) the remedy will be excluded, where:

(1) there is some alternative statutory remedy;

(2) the issue before the court is purely hypothetical; and

(3) some alleged right or interest is not recognised by the law.

As to the first area of exclusion, there probably needs to be clear statutory words (*Barraclough v Brown* (1897)) as seen in the previous chapter on administrative remedies. The second area of exclusion is well illustrated by the decision in *Blackburn v Attorney General* (1971) where a challenge to the treaty-making powers of the Crown was unsuccessful. The challenge arose from a suggestion that accession to membership of the EEC by the UK as a result of signing the Treaty of Rome would lead to an irreversible loss of some of Parliament's sovereignty. Whether or not this would have been the case was regarded by the Court of Appeal as being purely hypothetical, for which reason the court declined to intervene by refusing the declaration sought. The third area of exclusion, where some alleged right or interest is not recognised by the law, arose in *Malone v Metropolitan Police Commissioner* (1979) where a declaration was sought, to the effect that telephone tapping was contrary to the European Convention on Human Rights. The declaration was refused and the case served to emphasise that telephone tapping was not unlawful, eg as an unlawful trespass on a person's property, and that the European Convention has no legally enforceable status in the UK. The Interception of Communications Act 1985 now defines an offence of intercepting communications transmitted by post or through a public telecommunication system. The Secretary of State is authorised to allow certain interceptions, subject to safeguards.

In addition to the foregoing categories of exclusion, it should be noted that there is one further category of exclusion – *locus standi*, ie where the applicant for a declaration does not have the requisite standing, status or interest in the issue before the court to qualify for an award of the remedy. Before the *locus standi* requirements for the declaration are examined, a section of the chapter will be devoted to *locus standi* requirements generally as they affect the remedies.

13.4.3   *Locus standi* generally

Where an individual is directly affected by the decision or other action of an administrative agency, eg as an applicant for a licence, he will have *locus standi* and so should be able to seek to obtain his remedy to deal with what he alleges to be an *ultra vires* decision. This assumes, of course, that the allegation can be established before the court and that other requirements for the remedy sought, such as an order of *certiorari* to quash, are present. Cases involving such a direct interest in the issue before the court do not usually raise any problems of *locus standi*, unlike those where a person has a less than direct interest. Typically, such a person will stand in a weaker position than the person with a direct interest. This being the case, the court has to decide whether Parliament could have intended that the applicant should have had any enforceable rights in relation to the administrative agency, its actions and decisions under the statutory provisions in question. It will be seen in a later section of this chapter devoted to the application for judicial review in the Queen's Bench Division of the High Court that most applicants for the administrative law remedies are now required to establish that they have a 'sufficient interest' in the matter before the court. The underlying test for sufficiency of interest is to be found in the House of Lords' decision in *Inland Revenue Commissioners v National Federation of Self-Employed and Small Businesses Ltd* (1981). In this case it was seen that, by virtue of a well-established practice in Fleet Street, casual workers on national newspapers received their wages without tax deductions. In order to avoid tax deductions, such workers did not give their true names on receipt of wage packets. Later an arrangement was made by which it was agreed between the employers, workers and the Commissioners that there would be a tax amnesty in respect of unpaid tax prior to 1977 in return for an agreement that the workers would register for the assessment of tax in the future. The Federation, claiming to represent a body of taxpayers, sought a declaration that the tax amnesty was unlawful and an order of *mandamus* directing the Commissioners to assess and collect tax from the workers as required by law. Among other things, it was decided by the House of Lords that the Federation did not have a 'sufficient interest' in the issues before the court so that the remedies were not available. The basis for this part of the decision is the nature of the Commissioners' statutory responsibilities. Lord Roskill, one member of the House of Lords, explained the position as follows:

> The Revenue are responsible for the overall management of the relevant part of the taxation system ... and for the assessment and collection of taxes from those who are, by law, liable to pay them. Such assessment and collection is a confidential matter between the Revenue and each individual tax-payer. Such confidence is allowed to be broken only in those exceptional circumstances for which the statute makes express provision ... It is clear that the Federation is seeking to intervene in the affairs of individual taxpayers ... [H]aving regard to the nature of the Revenue's statutory duty and the degree of confidentiality enjoined by statute which attaches to their performance ... in general it is not open to individual taxpayers or to a group of tax payers to seek to interfere between the Revenue and other taxpayers.

Another member of the same court in this case, Lord Fraser, summarised the present law of *locus standi* in a statement of principle now applicable whenever it is necessary to ascertain whether an applicant has a 'sufficient interest' for any of the remedies of declaration, injunction, *certiorari*, prohibition or *mandamus*. He stated that:

... a direct financial or legal interest is not now required, and ... the requirement of a legal specific interest is no longer applicable. There is also general agreement that a mere busybody does not have a sufficient interest. The difficulty is, in between those extremes, to distinguish between the desire of a busybody to interfere in other people's affairs and the interest of the person affected by or having a reasonable concern with the matter to which the application relates. In the present case that matter is an alleged failure by the Revenue to perform the duty imposed on them by statute. The correct approach in such a case is ... to look at the statute under which the duty arises, and to see whether it gives any express or implied right to persons in the position of the applicant to complain of the alleged unlawful act or omission.

In the recent case of *R v Inspectorate of Pollution, ex p Greenpeace (No 2)* (1994), the applicants, Greenpeace, sought judicial review of a decision taken by Her Majesty's Inspectorate of Pollution and the Minister of Agriculture, Fisheries and Food to grant applications by British Nuclear Fuels plc (BNFL) for variations of statutory authorisations which it had been granted to discharge radioactive waste from its thermal oxide reprocessing plant (THORP) at Sellafield in Cumbria. Although the substantive application failed, the case is of interest in the context of the *locus standi* question since Otton J considered that despite arguments advanced by counsel for BNFL, Greenpeace, which had some 2,500 supporters living in the immediate area, was more than a 'meddlesome' or 'mere' busybody; it did in fact have a sufficient interest in the matter to which the application related. In determining the *locus standi* issue at the hearing of a substantive application, it was felt that the court should take into account: the nature of the applicant; the extent of his interest in the issues raised by the application; the remedy which he sought to achieve; and, the nature of the relief sought. Thus the earlier decision in *R v Secretary of State for the Environment, ex p Rose Theatre Trust Co* (1990) was not followed where it had been held that an interest group which had been set up solely for the purpose of saving the Rose Theatre site did not have a sufficient interest in the matter.

In a further recent case the issue of *locus standi* was also of some importance. In *R v Secretary of State for Foreign Affairs, ex p World Development Movement Ltd* (1995), the applicants sought a declaration that the Foreign Secretary had acted unlawfully by deciding to grant aid for the construction of a dam and hydro-electric power station (the Pergau scheme) in Malaysia in the purported exercise of powers under the Overseas Development and Co-operation Act 1980. In granting the relief sought due to the fact that the project was economically unsound and therefore not within the criteria for the grant of aid under the 1980 Act, the Divisional Court held that the World Development Movement Ltd had a sufficient interest in the matter to which the application related. Their standing was based on a number of factors: the importance of vindicating the rule of law; the importance of the issue raised; the likely absence of any other responsible challenger; the nature of the breach of duty against which the relief was sought; the prominent role of the applicants in the tendering of advice, guidance and assistance with regard to aid; and, the applicants' national and international expertise and interest in the promotion and protection of aid granted to underdeveloped countries. In addition, Rose J pointed to the fact that 'the authorities referred to seem to me to indicate an increasingly liberal approach to standing on the part of the courts during the last 12 years'. In making such an observation, it would appear that his Lordship particularly had in mind the case of *R v Secretary of State for Foreign and Commonwealth Affairs, ex p Rees-Mogg* (1994) where the Divisional Court held that Lord Rees-Mogg had standing to challenge the UK's ratification of the Treaty on European Union (the Maastricht Treaty) 'because of his sincere concern for constitutional issues'. It may perhaps be argued that this is a somewhat tenuous reason for holding that the applicant had a sufficient interest in the matter, but before concluding that the Rees-Mogg case is evidence of a modern, increasingly liberal approach taken by the courts in relation to the issue of standing, it should be remembered that in 1971 the Court of Appeal was prepared to consider a challenge to the UK's accession to the Treaty of Rome by an individual even if ultimately the challenge failed because this exercise of the prerogative power was held not to be susceptible to review (*Blackburn v Attorney General*).

13.4.4   *Locus standi* for the declaration

It is by no means easy to generalise about the cases where *locus standi* has been in issue, very largely because each case depends on its own facts and individual judges' perceptions of the statutory background to administrative action and decisions for the purpose of deciding whether an applicant has a sufficient interest in relation to the remedy sought. In the *Equal Opportunities Commission* case, a majority of the House of Lords were of the opinion that the Commission did have *locus standi* to seek declarations that certain UK primary legislation was inconsistent with EU law. In a number of earlier cases such as *Equal Opportunities Commission v Birmingham City Council* (1989), it had never been suggested at any stage in the proceedings that the Commission lacked the necessary standing. Furthermore, the duties of the Commission under the Sex Discrimination Act 1975 included working towards the elimination of discrimination which was what the Commission were in effect trying to achieve in the present proceedings in the context of equal pay and equal treatment for male and female part-time employees.

A further two cases in this section come from the area of planning law. In *Steeples v Derbyshire County Council* (1981) the applicant for declarations was found to have *locus standi*. The County Council had by resolution granted itself planning permission to develop land as a leisure park, but the applicant persuaded the High Court that the decision had been taken in breach of certain statutory requirements under the Town and Country Planning Act. The strongest justification for the finding of *locus standi* lay in the fact that part of the proposed development involved the taking of a section of the applicant's land so that it could be said that his private rights were affected. This was not the case in *Gregory v Camden London Borough Council* (1966) where, again, the applicant sought a declaration that the decision of the local planning authority was *ultra vires*. The applicant was a neighbour of a convent for which the authority had decided to grant planning permission for the erection of school buildings. It was decided that the applicant did not have *locus standi* for a declaration since the Town and Country Planning Act did not give 'third parties' like Gregory any legally enforceable rights against the local planning authority. It will have been seen in the previous chapter that the applicant for planning permission does have *locus standi* to challenge the legality of a local planning authority's decision on an application (*R v Hillingdon London Borough Council, ex p Royco Homes Ltd* (1974)). In the case of Gregory involving a third-party neighbour, it appears that his remedies may be limited to objections made to his local councillor in advance of an application or complaints of maladministration causing injustice made to a local Commissioner for Administration. Two cases involving *certiorari – Covent Garden Community Association Ltd v Greater London Council* (1981) and *R v North Hertfordshire District Council, ex p Sullivan* (1981) – appear to put this view of the law in some doubt. These cases will be dealt with later under the section on *certiorari*. In many instances it is the task of the court to distinguish between an applicant's private rights and interests as they appear from statutory provisions, and purely public rights, which the individual cannot enforce in proceedings in his own name. The only exceptions to this latter proposition occur where the individual has suffered some special damage or loss peculiar to himself or where his own private rights are some way affected (*Boyce v Paddington Borough Council* (1903)). In *Gouriet v Union of Post Office Workers* (1977) it was decided by the House of Lords that only the Attorney General could sue on behalf of the public for an injunction to restrain a public wrong, more particularly a trade union threat to interrupt postal services to South Africa, contrary to provisions in the Post Office Act 1953. In the same way only the Attorney General could seek declarations as to the scope of public rights. Because Gouriet had no private rights at stake and had not suffered any loss or damage from the threatened interruption of postal services, he had no *locus standi*. Had Gouriet's mail been interrupted then his case would have been similar to that in *Dyson v Attorney General* (1911) where the plaintiff claimed that a notice served on him by the Inland Revenue Commissioners requiring certain returns within 30 days subject to a penalty, contained an unlawful requirement. Although other taxpayers could have made a similar claim, the court granted a declaration that the plaintiff was not obliged to comply with the notice since he was defending his own private rights and was not seeking to act on behalf of the public.

Finally, in *Barrs v Bethell* (1981) three ratepayers sought declarations against the local authority and some of the controlling councillors to the effect that there had been a breach of the duty owed to ratepayers in the way in which the authority's finances were managed. The case was brought in the Chancery Division of the High Court whereas most cases involving dispute about administrative action in public law now have to be brought before the Queen's Bench Division through the procedure known as the application for judicial review, which is explained later in the chapter. This latter procedure is in two stages, where the first stage requires the applicant to prove a 'sufficient interest' in the matter to which the application relates before he can go to the trial of the full case in the second stage. It was therefore decided in *Barrs* that, apart from this procedure and the audit procedure, which was covered in Chapter 4, a ratepayer was not able to sue the local authority except with the permission of the Attorney General, whose role and status will be dealt with in the next section on injunctions, unless the ratepayer could show some interference with a public right from which he has suffered damage peculiar to himself.

13.5   The Injunction

Unlike the declaration, the injunction is a coercive remedy which requires a party to proceedings before the court to discontinue or to undertake some specified act. In practice it is not uncommon to find that the court is asked for a declaration that some act of an administrative agency is *ultra vires*, and an injunction to prevent any reliance on or enforcement of the act. Indeed, there are some striking similarities between the declaration and the injunction, particularly in relation to questions of *locus standi*. In addition, there are circumstances in which the court may as a matter of discretion exclude the remedy, eg where the applicant is guilty of delay, as in *Bates v Lord Hailsham* (1972) where the application was made at 2pm for an injunction to restrain certain acts which may have taken place at 4.30pm on the same day where the proposals had been known for 10 weeks in general terms and for four weeks in specific terms. Other grounds for exclusion of the remedy include the availability of some alternative statutory remedy and any situation in which the applicant has suffered nothing more than a trivial loss or damage.

13.5.1   Varieties of injunction

There are three varieties of injunction:

(1) prohibitory;

(2) mandatory; and

(3) interlocutory.

13.5.2   The prohibitory injunction

This is perhaps the best-known of the injunctions in so far as it seeks to restrain any action which is found to be contrary to law. As such, it is employed in various areas of interest to administrative law. One of the more obvious areas concerns *ultra vires* acts of administrative agencies, as in *Sydney Municipal Council v Campbell* (1925), a case which was covered in Chapter 11. Breaches of statutory duty may be restrained by the prohibitory injunction, as in *Attorney General, ex rel McWhirter v Independent Broadcasting Authority* (1973) where a temporary injunction was at first granted against the Independent Broadcasting Authority to prevent the showing on television of an Andy Warhol film. The injunction was sought by reference to the Authority's duty in s 3(1)(a) of the Television Act 1954 '... to satisfy themselves that, so far as possible ... nothing is included in the programmes which offends against good taste or decency or is likely to be offensive to public feeling'. A third area where the prohibitory injunction is used is in relation to continuing breaches of the criminal law where the courts have had little difficulty in resisting the argument that breaches of the criminal law should be prosecuted in the usual way without resort to the injunction. One of many examples is *Attorney General v Sharp* (1931) where bus operators could only operate with a licence from the local authority. Failure to adhere to the licensing system was a criminal offence. Sharp operated buses without a licence and was accordingly fined on many occasions for continuing offences whereupon the Attorney General, acting at the request of the local authority, applied for and obtained an injunction to restrain the unlicensed bus services. Failure to comply with any such injunction is a contempt of court for which imprisonment is a penalty. On some occasions, the normal process of criminal prosecution may be ineffective in the face of some unlawful act which will bring lasting damage or loss unless it is restrained quickly by injunction. In *Attorney General v Melville Construction Co Ltd* (1968) an injunction was granted in order to restrain any further felling of trees protected by tree preservation orders, even though there had been no criminal prosecution. The leading statement of principle is now to be found in the House of Lords case of *Stoke on Trent City Council v B & Q (Retail) Ltd* (1984) where it was said that generally a local authority '... should try the effect of criminal proceedings before seeking the assistance of the civil courts [but can] take the view that the [defendants] would not be deterred by a maximum fine ...'

13.5.3 The mandatory injunction

This form of the injunction commands a person to act according to law where the applicant has a private right which arises out of a failure to perform some public duty. In *Attorney General v Bastow* (1957), the defendant had been fined on several occasions for failing to comply with an enforcement notice requiring the removal of caravans from a site which did not have the benefit of planning permission. Eventually, the Attorney General applied for and obtained an injunction on behalf of the local authority. The injunction was mandatory in directing that the offending caravans should be removed from the site. It may be difficult to obtain a mandatory injunction against an administrative agency where the effect of such an injunction would be to bind that body to undertake specified acts for the benefit of an individual where those acts would frustrate or compromise the performance of statutory responsibilities (*Dowty, Boulton Paul Ltd v Wolverhampton Corporation (No 1)* (1971)).

13.5.4   The interlocutory injunction

The interlocutory injunction is intended to preserve the *status quo* between the parties until the issue or issues between them can be tried fully. The court will grant an interlocutory injunction where:

(1) there is a serious question to be tried, and

(2) the court decides that on the balance of convenience the injunction should be granted (*American Cyanamid Co v Ethicon Ltd* (1975)).

Where the interlocutory injunction may be granted against an administrative agency there could be potential problems which were recognised by the Court of Appeal in *Smith v Inner London Education Authority* (1978). The Court of Appeal allowed an appeal against interlocutory injunctions on the ground that the Authority's action in introducing comprehensive education was lawful: those who had opposed the reorganisation of secondary education failed to show the court that there was a real prospect of success in any later action for permanent injunctions. It was emphasised that the interlocutory injunction applies to bodies exercising public duties in the same way as it applies to other individuals and organisations. However, Browne LJ added that:

> ... where the defendant is a public authority performing duties to the public one must look at the balance of convenience more widely, and take into account the interests of the public in general to whom those duties are owed.

One final point concerns the usual practice whereby an undertaking is expected from the applicant in proceedings for an interlocutory injunction to the effect that he will indemnify the defendant against any loss where it is found later that the injunction should not have been granted. However, where it is the Crown which acts as applicant for an interlocutory injunction, such an undertaking is not normally required. This was the case in *Hoffman-La Roche & Co AG v Secretary of State for Trade and Industry* (1974) where the Secretary of State sought an injunction in order to enforce an order which reduced drug prices, pending a later decision on its legality. The injunction was granted and the strong view of the House of Lords was that because it is the Crown's duty to see that the law is enforced, there should be no legal liability to any person or organisation alleged to be in breach of the order, which is presumed to be legally valid until it is set aside. In a recent case, *Kirklees Metropolitan Borough Council v Wickes Building Supplies Ltd* (1992), where a local authority sought an interlocutory injunction to restrain a do-it-yourself retailer from trading on Sundays contrary to the Shops Act 1950, the House of Lords held that the special privilege afforded to the Crown as law enforcer not to give a cross-undertaking in damages where such relief was sought also applied to other public authorities, including a local authority where it was exercising a law enforcement function in the public interest. Furthermore, the fact that the respondent might have a defence based upon a provision of the EEC Treaty did not require the court to extract an undertaking in damages from the local authority since such an undertaking would be superfluous in view of the fact that the UK government would itself be under an obligation to remedy any damage suffered by the respondent as a consequence of its own failure to ensure that its national law complied with EU law.

13.5.5   *Locus standi* for the injunction

The *locus standi* requirements for the injunction are very similar to those for the declaration. Much of the law in this area has been clarified in *Gouriet* which was described in the section on *locus standi* for the declaration. There are four categories of individuals and organisations with potential *locus standi* for the injunction:

(1) the Attorney General *ex officio*;

(2) the Attorney General *ex relatione*;

(3) the individual; and

(4) the local authority.

The first category is a recognition of the Attorney General's status as the defender of public rights and interests. Accordingly, the Attorney General may take the initiative in seeking an injunction to restrain unlawful expenditure by a local authority where (in the unlikely event) the auditor does not take action, for example. Applications *ex officio* are the exception. The second category is a reference to the 'relator action' which arises where an individual does not appear to have sufficient *locus standi*. In these circumstances, a request can be made to the Attorney General to use his name in the proceedings. Whether the Attorney General agrees to relator proceedings is entirely a matter for his discretion. In recent times, the Attorney General refused relator proceedings in *Gouriet* but agreed to them in *McWhirter*. Where relator proceedings are sanctioned, the relator (the individual) bears the cost of the action. Coming to the third category of the individual, whether he has *locus standi* for an injunction depends on the statement of principle in *Gouriet*, previously referred to in the section on declaration. In that House of Lords decision, mention was made of an important exception, the local authority, which is the final category. More particularly, this exception refers to the provision in s 222 of the Local Government Act 1972 which states that:

> ... where a local authority consider it expedient for the promotion or protection of the interests of the inhabitants of their area –
>
> (a) they may prosecute or defend or appear in any legal proceedings and, in the case of civil proceedings, may institute them in their own name ...

Prior to the appearance of this provision on the statute book, local authorities had to rely on relator proceedings in collaboration with the Attorney General. Section 222 now allows a local authority to apply for an injunction in its own name although specific powers to apply for injunctions still remain, eg under the Environmental Protection Act 1990 where criminal proceedings for statutory nuisances prove to be inadequate.

13.5.6 Injunctions and the Crown

In *M v Home Office* (1993) the House of Lords was required to consider issues of quite considerable constitutional importance concerning the relationship between the executive and the courts which arose out of a claim for political asylum by a citizen of Zaire. The claim was rejected by the Home Secretary and consequently, an application for judicial review of his decision was made to a judge in chambers. At this point a misunderstanding occurred between counsel for the Home Secretary and the judge who understood counsel to have given him an undertaking that the applicant would not, pending a further hearing, be returned to Zaire. However, that is exactly what did happen. Accordingly, the judge issued a mandatory injunction directing the Home Secretary to procure the return of the applicant. After having taken legal advice, the Home Secretary declined to comply with the order and thus he became the subject of proceedings for contempt of court. A unanimous House of Lords was of the opinion that if a minister acted in disregard of an injunction made against him in his official capacity, then a court was entitled to find him in contempt. Lord Templeman observed that:

> ... the argument that there is no power to enforce the law by injunction or contempt proceedings against a minister in his official capacity would, if upheld, establish the proposition that the executive obey the law as a matter of grace and not as a matter of necessity, a proposition which would reverse the result of the Civil War.

In view of the fact that ministers of the Crown or government departments are extremely unlikely to disobey decisions of the courts, the decision in *M v Home Office* is as much important in terms of principle as it is in terms of practice. Indeed, Lord Woolf, who gave the leading judgment in the case, drew attention to the fact that whilst the courts have jurisdiction to grant interim and final injunctions against government ministers, it was, despite this, a jurisdiction which would not be exercised 'except in the most limited circumstances'. Nevertheless, the decision not only serves to emphasise the comparative separation between the judicial and executive functions of government in the British constitution, but, it also reinforces the fundamental principle that the functions of government must be performed in accordance with the law. In addition and finally, the case casts considerable doubt upon the reasoning of Lord Bridge in *Factortame Ltd v Secretary of State for Transport* (1989) where his Lordship expressed the view that injunctive relief was not available against the Crown or its ministers in judicial review proceedings.

13.6 Certiorari

Certiorari, prohibition and mandamus (the latter two will be dealt with later in the chapter) are prerogative orders of great importance in the context of the remedies available in administrative law. These prerogative remedies were historically available only to the Crown and allowed the Crown an opportunity to monitor the activities of administrative agencies and inferior courts to ensure that they undertook their responsibilities according to law. Gradually these remedies were made available for individuals without any need to seek the consent of the Crown, and this explains the style of title for cases involving these remedies: R (Regina: the Crown) v Slagborough District Council (the name of the administrative agency against which the remedy is sought), ex parte (on behalf of) Jones (the applicant)). As to certiorari itself, the order removes proceedings from an administrative agency or inferior court with a view to any decision or similar action being quashed on any one or more of three grounds.

13.6.1 The grounds for certiorari

The three grounds for certiorari are:

(1) ultra vires;

(2) breach of natural justice; and

(3) error of law on the face of the record.

Examples of each of these three grounds in action can be drawn from previous chapters:

(1) ultra vires: R v Blackpool Rent Tribunal, ex p Ashton (1948) (Chapter 11);

(2) natural justice: R v Hendon Rural District Council, ex p Chorley (1933) (Chapter 10); and

(3) error of law on the face of the record: R v Crown Court at Knightsbridge, ex p International Sporting Club (London) Ltd (1981) (Chapter 11).

13.6.2 Bodies amenable to certiorari

Certiorari may be obtained against the following bodies:

(1) administrative tribunals;

(2) inferior courts;

(3) local authorities;

(4) ministers of the Crown;

(5) miscellaneous statutory and non-statutory bodies exercising public functions.

In relation to the first category of administrative tribunals, it was seen in Chapter 5 that a number of tribunals are within a special category where their decisions are subject to an appeal on a point of law to the High Court or, more rarely, the Court of Appeal. There are however, exceptions such as the Immigration Appeals Tribunal whose decisions are subject to review only, principally by *certiorari*. Inferior courts, such as the magistrates' courts, are subject to the High Court's supervisory powers by way of judicial review. The supervision of such courts by the High Court provides a reminder that the magistrates in particular undertook a great deal of local administration before the advent of local authorities as we now know them. That local authorities are amenable to *certiorari* means that, potentially, a great number of administrative powers are subject to the control of the law. The opportunities for control by *certiorari* of powers exercised by ministers of the Crown may not be as extensive as in the case of local authorities, very largely because any scheme of statutory powers is more likely to provide some exclusive system of statutory review, for example. As will be seen in the later section on statutory review, such a remedy will exclude the non-statutory remedies like the prerogative orders and substitute what may be a more restricted opportunity for the review of the minister's decisions under a particular statutory scheme. Finally, in the catalogue of bodies amenable to *certiorari* there is an ill-defined collection of miscellaneous statutory bodies exercising various public functions. In Chapter 10 reference was made to the disciplinary functions of prison boards of visitors in *R v Hull Prison Board of Visitors, ex p St Germain* (1979), though it was also pointed out that such functions have now been removed from the boards as a consequence of recommendations made in the Woolf Report. In *R v Police Complaints Board, ex p Madden* (1983) a decision of the Board was quashed by *certiorari* when it committed an error of law in refusing to consider a complaint which the Director of Public Prosecutions had decided did not justify the initiation of criminal proceedings. Although *certiorari* applies to bodies created by statute, there has been one notable exception on those occasions when decisions of the Criminal Injuries Board (which was created under the prerogative) have been quashed. In the first of these cases, *R v Criminal Injuries Board, ex p Lain* (1967), it appears that the High Court was concerned only with the fact that the Board performs public duties in conjunction with a duty to act judicially.

13.6.3   *Certiorari* and the duty to act judicially

As a general rule it can be said that *certiorari* applies to statutory bodies performing public duties with an obligation to act judicially. It was seen in Chapter 10 that the duty to act judicially arises where a body has legal authority to make decisions or take action which affects the rights of subjects (*R v Electricity Commissioners, ex p London Electricity Joint Committee Co (1920) Ltd* (1924) and *Ridge v Baldwin* (1963)). In practice, the definition of this requirement has been very flexible. On the one hand, it may not be difficult to identify a duty to act judicially in a case like *R v Crown Court at Knightsbridge, ex p International Sporting Club (London) Ltd* (1981) involving a decision of the Crown Court. On the other hand, it may be somewhat more difficult to conclude that a local authority has a duty to act judicially in deciding an application for planning permission as in a case like *R v Hillingdon London Borough Council, ex p Royco Homes Ltd* (1974). Bearing in mind that the Town and Country Planning Act 1947 took away an individual's virtually unfettered legal right to develop his land, it can be argued that wherever he applies for planning permission to develop the land, he does so as a person without any rights, that is, he is applying to regain his right to develop. In view of this argument, it is perhaps as well that the courts have usually adopted a much wider view of the duty to act judicially.

13.6.4 *Certiorari* and private bodies

Whereas *certiorari* applies to statutory bodies, including the prerogative Criminal Injuries Compensation Board, as previously described, it does not, of course, apply to purely private, domestic organisations. Accordingly, the remedy would not be available to challenge the legality of decisions of trade unions and professional organisations, for example, where the relationship between member and union or organisation is based on a privately concluded contract. By way of illustration, in *R v British Broadcasting Corporation, ex p Lavelle* (1982), Miss Lavelle, a tape examiner employed by the BBC, was dismissed from her employment as a result of what was described as a disciplinary interview and a decision of the managing director of BBC Radio upholding the formal letter of dismissal. The justification for dismissal was the unauthorised removal of tapes from the BBC. It was decided by the court that an order of *certiorari* was not available: although the BBC was a public corporation the matter in issue related to a private employment dispute and the decision of a domestic tribunal. It was pointed out that the scheme for obtaining *certiorari* and the other prerogative orders, through the application for judicial review prescribed by s 31 of the Supreme Court Act 1981 and Order 53 of the Rules of the Supreme Court, is concerned only with activities of a public nature. In the important Court of Appeal decision in *R v Panel on Takeovers and Mergers, ex p Datafin* (1987), it was decided that the Voluntary City Panel for Take-overs and Mergers (which enforces a voluntary code between companies in this field) is amenable to judicial review because it performs a public duty of a judicial nature that affects indirectly the rights of shareholders. The considerable powers that the panel enjoys in 'devising, promulgating, amending and interpreting the City Code on Take-overs and Mergers' did not owe their origin to statute or the prerogative, and neither were they founded on any sort of contractual relationship with those involved in the work of the financial market. Nevertheless, in the opinion of the Court of Appeal, the panel which is 'supported and sustained by a periphery of statutory powers and penalties' operated very much in the public domain and accordingly, it is a body which is susceptible to judicial review.

Dealing with the question of the jurisdiction of the courts in judicial review proceedings, Sir John Donaldson MR observed that:

> In all the reports it is possible to find enumeration of factors giving rise to the jurisdiction, but it is a fatal error to regard the presence of all those factors as essential or as being exclusive of other factors. Possibly the only essential elements are what can be described as a public element, which can take many different forms, and the exclusion from the jurisdiction of bodies whose sole source of power is a consensual submission to its jurisdiction.

In *Datafin*, it was argued that since the panel was exercising a decision-making power in which there was, as later described by Simon Brown J in *R v Chief Rabbi of the United Hebrew Congregation, ex p Wachmann* (1992), a 'governmental interest', it therefore followed that judicial review was available. This argument has been seized upon in later cases such as *R v Advertising Standards Authority Ltd, ex p Insurance Services plc* (1990) where it was held that the decisions of the Advertising Standards Authority were subject to judicial review and *R v Code of Practice Committee of the Association of the British Pharmaceutical Industry, ex p Professional Counselling Aids Ltd* (1990) where the court concluded that the committee is also a body subject to judicial review. The same applies to the functions of the Civil Service Appeal Board, dealing with employment disputes in the public service: *R v Civil Service Appeal Board, ex p Bruce* (1988). It is also clear from *Bank of Scotland, Petitioner* (1988) that the self-regulatory organisations in the financial markets, set up under the Financial Services Act 1986 perform sufficiently public, administrative tasks, to be amenable to judicial review.

The effect of *Datafin* has thus been to bring the decisions of a number of non-statutory bodies within the supervisory jurisdiction of the courts. However, in a string of cases concerned with applications for judicial review of the decisions of sports governing bodies such as *Law v National Greyhound Racing Club Ltd* (1983), *R v Football Association, ex p Football League* (1993), and, *R v Disciplinary Committee of the Jockey Club, ex p Aga Khan* (1993) where the Aga Khan sought among other things an order of *certiorari* to quash the decision of the Jockey Club to disqualify his horse for failing a dope test following its victory in the 1989 Oaks, the courts have steadfastly refused the invitation to extend their supervisory jurisdiction to such bodies. Despite the fact that these domestic tribunals enjoy powers which the courts have readily acknowledged as being virtually monopolistic, it is the view of the courts that the relationship between the body and the applicant in these cases is essentially contractual in nature. Accordingly, any disputes arising between these parties are to be settled via the private law rather than by way of an application for judicial review, the principles of which have been designed for the control of the abuse of power by government.

13.6.5 *Locus standi* for *certiorari*

Once again it can be said that *locus standi* is not a problem for the person directly affected by some administrative decision or other action, as in *R v Hillingdon London Borough Council, ex p Royco Homes Ltd* (1974). In other problem cases involving third parties, reference has to be made to the requirement of a 'sufficient interest' as explained in the *Inland Revenue Commissioners* case (the 'Fleet Street Casuals' case). The question, therefore, is whether the statutory background to the challenge gives the applicant any express or implied right to complain of the allegedly unlawful act or decision. In the case of *R v Hendon Rural District Council, ex p Chorley* (1933), the facts of which were seen in Chapter 10, Chorley was a third-party neighbour of land for which planning permission was obtained by a decision of the local planning authority which was quashed by *certiorari* for bias. Although the *locus standi* of Chorley was not discussed in the case, it may be explained by reference to the early Town and Country Planning Act under which the decision was taken. Where a grant of planning permission was made but later affected by a town planning scheme preventing the implementation of the permission, compensation was payable, the resources for which would come from the ratepayers, of whom Chorley was one. Such a case may be categorised as one where the statute gave Chorley an implied right to complain. In the later case of *R v Bradford-on-Avon Urban District Council, ex p Boulton* (1964) (where the applicant, who merely used a road through the area of the local planning authority each day, had no *locus standi* to challenge the legality of a planning decision by the authority), the court considered that Chorley had *locus standi* as an adjoining property owner. By contrast, in *Gregory*, the case where a declaration was refused, the court considered that Chorley had *locus standi* as a ratepayer, the argument which is set out towards the beginning of this section.

In two cases which were mentioned previously in the section on *locus standi* for the declaration, *Covent Garden Community Association Ltd v Greater London Council* and *R v North Hertfordshire District Council, ex p Sullivan*, it was decided that third parties did have *locus standi* for the orders of *certiorari* although the order was not granted in the first case because an *ultra vires* decision of the local planning authority could not be established. In the *Covent Garden* case the local residents' interests were represented by the specially formed company which attempted to challenge the legality of the council's resolution to grant itself planning permission. In *Sullivan* a neighbour succeeded in obtaining *certiorari* to quash a decision granting planning permission and listed building consent in respect of a development of land in relation to which she had been an objector and which would have interfered with her privacy. However, it was assumed without the point being argued that Sullivan had *locus standi* in this case, which may cast some doubt on the authority of the decision. The *Covent Garden* decision does, on the other hand, strengthen the position of third parties in the present context, but the question must be whether the present town and country planning legislation expressly or impliedly permits a third party to complain successfully to the High Court in respect of the legality of a decision of the local planning authority. The alternative approach to that in the *Covent Garden* case is that put forward in the declaration decision in *Gregory*, that the Act creates no legally enforceable rights for the third party. The basis of this approach is that the Act defines a very limited facility for objections and representations in respect of applications for planning permission, involving the democratic processes of the council (acting as guardian of the local planning process) and its members. If the courts prescribe that third parties have *locus standi* for *certiorari* in this context, the argument would be that there is no express or implied authorisation in the Act giving third parties such legally enforceable rights.

13.7 Prohibition

This remedy is very similar to the order of *certiorari* in seeking to prevent *ultra vires* action or action in breach of natural justice pending a final decision by a statutory agency exercising public functions with an obligation to act judicially. By way of illustration, an order of prohibition was granted in *R v Broadcasting Complaints Commission, ex p Thames Television Ltd* (1982) where the Commission was restrained from continuing to deal with a complaint about the Czech dissident movement pending the outcome of legal proceedings for libel which were associated with the complaint. In granting the order the court was enforcing a provision of the Broadcasting Act 1981 which placed certain restrictions on the Commission's powers to deal with complaints. A second illustration comes from *R v Kent Police Authority, ex p Godden* (1971), which was referred to in Chapter 10. The chief medical officer of a police authority certified that a chief inspector was suffering from a mental disorder. Thereupon, the policy authority, wishing to retire the inspector compulsorily, was obliged by statute to refer his medical condition to a doctor. The chief medical officer was selected for this purpose but an order of prohibition was granted in view of the likely impact of a decision on the inspector's future and the fact that the chief medical officer could have committed himself to a view in advance.

One final issue in relation to prohibition is the question of *locus standi* where the impression is that the law's attitude is perhaps more liberal than it can be in the case of the other remedies, almost certainly because the order is an interim remedy only. One of the most influential cases here is *R v Greater London Council, ex p Blackburn* (1976) where it was decided that a Mr and Mrs Blackburn had *locus standi* to prevent the local authority undertaking their film censorship functions by reference to a test which was found to be legally invalid. The applicants lived in the area of the local authority, Mrs Blackburn was a ratepayer and they had children who might be affected by pornographic films.

13.8 *Mandamus*

This prerogative order requires anybody obliged to perform a public duty by statute to perform that duty according to law. In most cases *mandamus* has been employed to compel the performance of a clear statutory duty on any occasion when the administrative agency has plainly and unlawfully refused to undertake the duty at the request of a person intended by Parliament to benefit from it. The need for a public duty means that *mandamus* would not be available to enforce a private duty arising by virtue of a contract, for example.

13.8.1 The legally enforceable duty

Mandamus can be used only in relation to a duty which, as a public duty, is also specifically enforceable. Such a duty, it was decided in *R v Kerrier District Council, ex p Guppys (Bridport) Ltd* (1976), occurs in s 189 of the Housing Act 1985 which states that:

> ... where a local authority ... are satisfied that any house is unfit for human habitation, they shall, unless they are satisfied that it is not capable at a reasonable expense of being rendered so fit, serve upon the person having control of the house, a notice requiring him ... to execute works specified in the notice ...

In this case it was decided that the local authority had refused unlawfully to serve a repairs notice so that an order of *mandamus* was available to enforce the specific public duty characterised by the use of the word 'shall' in the provision. In other words, once the requirements of the section were satisfied, the local authority had no choice but to serve the notice. By contrast, the duty formerly set out in s 14 of the Water Act 1973 was not specifically enforceable. The section declared that: 'It shall be the duty of every water authority to provide ... such public sewers as may be necessary for effectually draining their area'. As with any of the general duties covered in the previous chapter, the only remedy appears to be a complaint to the minister. Where, following any inquiry into such a complaint, the minister chose to issue directions, compelling compliance with some requirement arising from the duty, failure to comply with the directions was dealt with through the minister's statutory power to apply for *mandamus* in these circumstances.

In the same way that *mandamus* cannot be used to enforce a general duty, the order cannot be used to enforce the performance of a discretionary power. In *Re Fletcher's Application* (1970) *mandamus* was refused when it was sought in order to compel the Parliamentary Commissioner for Administration to investigate a complaint of maladministration made by the applicant. The court had no hesitation in finding that whether a complaint is investigated is entirely a matter for the Parliamentary Commissioner according to the words of the Parliamentary Commissioner Act 1967 which state that: 'In determining whether to initiate ... an investigation under this Act, the Commissioner shall ... act in accordance with his own discretion.' However, it is always possible that a discretionary power could be found to be linked with a duty and therefore enforceable by *mandamus*. This was the case in the important House of Lords decision in *Padfield v Minister of Agriculture* (1968), which has been encountered already in Chapters 9 and 11. Because the Agricultural Marketing Act gave rise to a well-defined object, the minister's discretion could be exercised only in conformity with that object. In other words, the minister could do nothing other than to refer a complaint to a committee without frustrating the object of the Act. The importance of this decision in *Padfield* lies in the fact that the potential scope of *mandamus* in judicial review has been extended considerably.

13.8.2 The scope of *mandamus*

In its application to the enforcement of public, specifically enforceable statutory duties, the order of *mandamus* extends to administrative and judicial functions. In this latter respect, therefore, it can be seen that the remedy had a wider cover-age than *certiorari* and prohibition and would apply equally to a statutory duty to undertake an investigation as well as to a duty to adjudicate a licensee's application for the renewal of a licence, for example. It was even suggested in *R v Commissioner for Metropolitan Police, ex p Blackburn* (1968) that *mandamus* might have been granted had the Commissioner not withdrawn a policy directive that aspects of the gaming laws should not be enforced by the police. One argument in this case was that *mandamus* should be refused because the applicant could resort to a suitable alternative remedy with private prosecutions against those who were allegedly acting in breach of the Gaming laws. Although the private prosecution was rejected as a suitable alternative remedy in this case, the court does have a discretion, as with the other remedies, to refuse an order of *mandamus* where a suitable alternative remedy is shown to exist, eg an administrative remedy such as an appeal to a tribunal or a minister. On some occasions the court may have to employ its discretion in potentially difficult circumstances as seen in *R v Bristol Corporation, ex p Hendy* (1974). In this case the court was concerned with the duty of a local authority to provide suitable alternative accommodation, where such accommodation is not otherwise available on reasonable terms, for any person displaced from accommodation for various reasons such as the demolition of a house by virtue of a demolition order served under the Housing Act 1985. Hendy had to vacate his flat when another Housing Act order, a closing order, required that it should not be occupied for the purposes of human habitation. Thereupon the local authority provided Hendy with temporary accommodation until more suitable, permanent accommodation was available. It was decided by the court that the local authority's statutory duty had been satisfied. In his judgment, Scarman LJ justified the court's decision by saying that:

> ... if, in a situation ... there is evidence that a local authority is doing all that it honestly and honourably can to meet [a] statutory obligation, and that its

failure, if there be failure, to meet that obligation arises out of circumstances over which it has no control, then I would think it would be improper for the court to make an order of *mandamus* compelling it to do that which either it cannot do or which it can only do at the expense of other persons not before the court who may have equal rights with the applicant and some of whom would certainly have equal moral claims.

13.8.3 *Locus standi* for *mandamus*

The order of *mandamus* was refused by the House of Lords in the 'Fleet Street Casuals' case, referred to earlier in the chapter. As to the broad legal principle in that case, it is difficult to speculate whether some of the older cases would have been decided in the same way had they occurred after the decision in the 'Fleet Street Casuals' case. *R v Commissioner for Metropolitan Police, ex p Blackburn* referred to previously is one of the more interesting cases. Blackburn sought an order of *mandamus* as a private citizen in order to compel the Commissioner to enforce the gaming laws. The Court of Appeal appeared to doubt whether Blackburn had *locus standi* although one member of the Court of Appeal thought that *mandamus* would be available to a householder where a chief constable directed that no housebreaker should be prosecuted in the district. In *R v Hereford Corporation, ex p Harrower* (1970) the Corporation placed a contract with the Electricity Board for the provision of central heating in council flats. Standing orders were broken because the Corporation did not seek tenders. The Corporation maintained a list of approved electrical contractors who now sought an order of *mandamus* requiring compliance with the standing orders. That order of *mandamus* was granted but only by reference to the applicants' status as ratepayers. The court also suspended the order to permit suspension of the standing orders in question. Whether there is *locus standi* in cases like these will continue to depend on the courts' conclusion as to whether the applicant has an implied right to complain of an unlawful decision or other action. While the first case of Blackburn would probably be decided in the same way, there may be a greater difficulty for the ratepayer if the *locus standi* requirements in *Barrs v Bethell*, albeit a declaration case, represent a trend in judicial policy.

13.9 The Application for Judicial Review

In 1976 the Law Commission published a report entitled *Remedies in Administrative Law* (Law Com No 73) which pointed to the deficiencies of the law then governing the remedies available to the individual intent on questioning the legality of administrative action in proceedings before the High Court. A section of the report headed 'The dilemma of the litigant seeking judicial review' observed that:

> The scope and procedural particularities of one remedy may suit one case except in one respect; but another remedy which is not deficient in this

respect may well be unsatisfactory from other points of view; and to add to his difficulties he may not be able to apply for both remedies in one proceeding.

The report proceeds to summarise the deficiencies, looking first at the declaration. It was noted that the declaration is available in respect of a wide range of acts, proposed acts or omissions of public authorities, including the Crown. Proceedings, it was said, can be initiated without leave, that is, the consent of the court, without any time limit constraint and with the advantage of full discovery, that is, the production by order of the court of documents and similar evidence connected with the claim. However, the declaration only states the legal position: it does not order or prohibit any action, it does not quash and there are doubts about *locus standi*. The report then observes that where the litigant looks to the prerogative orders to avoid the disadvantages of the declaration, he may lose some of the advantages of the declaration. *Certiorari*, for example, appeared to be more generous in relation to *locus standi* although leave to apply was necessary, discovery was not normally available, any application for the remedy had to be made within six months for the decision and claims for damages or an injunction could not be joined to the application for *certiorari*. A similar situation was seen to exist with *mandamus* and prohibition which, although they do not apply to the Crown, were subject to conditions similar to those for *certiorari* in relation to leave and discovery. Finally, it was suggested that the litigant, wishing to avoid the disadvantages of the declaration, might resort to the injunction. This remedy, it was said, gave the same advantages as the declaration in relation to the absence of leave, the full discovery of documents and the facility for joining a claim for damages or a declaration. Interim, interlocutory injunctions are available to preserve the *status quo* between the parties, but the injunction does not lie against the Crown.

13.9.1 Recommendation for reform: the application for judicial review

At the conclusion of the Law Commission's report there was a basic recommendation:

> ... that there should be a form of procedure to be entitled an 'application for judicial review'. Under cover of the application for judicial review a litigant should be able to obtain any of the prerogative orders, or, in appropriate circumstances, a declaration or injunction. The litigant would have to specify in his application ... which particular remedy or remedies he was seeking, but if he later desired to apply for a remedy for which he had not initially asked he would be able with the leave of the court to amend his application.

This recommendation was implemented with effect from 1 January 1978, when Order 53 of the Rules of the Supreme Court was amended accordingly. Some of the changes were confirmed by s 31 of the Supreme Court Act 1981. Nevertheless, references throughout will be to 'Order 53'.

13.9.2 Remedies available on an application for judicial review

Any application for *certiorari*, prohibition and *mandamus* is required always to be made under the Order 53 procedure known as the application for judicial review. The same is true of the declaration and injunction where either or both are sought in proceedings to challenge the legality of the actions or decisions of administrative agencies, that is, public authorities, arising from the exercise of their powers in public law. In other words, the Order 53 procedure will have to be used by a person seeking to establish that an administrative agency has acted *ultra vires* its statutory powers. On the other hand, such a person would be free to apply by writ to the Chancery Division of the High Court for a declaration where he is asserting that a local authority had no easement or right of way across his land, for example. In this latter case, the issue arises from the private law relationship between a landowner and another and does not involve the public, administrative law remedies prescribed by the Order 53 procedure. This important distinction is developed in a later section of the chapter.

13.9.3 Procedures and other requirements

Where the application for judicial review is made, any of the foregoing remedies may be claimed in the alternative or in addition to the remedy sought. Consequently, a declaration might be sought to the effect that the decision of an administrative agency is *ultra vires*, with an injunction to prevent any reliance on that decision by the agency.

The application for judicial review cannot be made unless the applicant has first obtained leave, that is, the permission of the Queen's Bench Division of the High Court. The application for leave is dealt with by a single member of that court and it is the task of the applicant by sworn evidence to establish that he has a 'sufficient interest' in the matter to which the application relates. Even where it is decided that the applicant has 'sufficient interest' and can proceed, it was decided by the House of Lords in the 'Fleet Street Casuals' case that this question of *locus standi* can be examined again and decided on when, at the second stage, the application comes to full trial. Suffice it to say at the moment, that the application for leave is designed as a filter to eliminate busybodies for the protection of the public, administrative agencies. Indeed, at this stage the administrative agency is not involved: the court is concerned only with the applicant's affidavits setting out his case. In granting leave, the court can impose conditions as to matters like costs. Any application has to be made promptly and in any event within three months from the date when grounds for the application first arose unless the court considers that there is good reason for extending that period. Where it is considered that there has been undue delay in making an application, the application for leave or for any of the remedies can be refused where otherwise there would be undue hardship or detriment to good administration. Good administration has to be understood from the point of view of the applicant and the person who may be subject to any remedy granted. The court will take account of the length of any delay and whether it is excusable, whether any action or inaction of an agent is attributable to the applicant, any further inexcusable delay following an application, a respondent's behaviour and any contribution to the delay, any adverse impact that may occur through a refusal of relief, any adverse affect on the respondent or third party through the grant of a remedy and the extent of any adverse impact on good administration: *R v Dairy Product Quotas Tribunal, ex p Caswell* (1988). In *R v Stratford-on-Avon District Council, ex p Jackson* (1985) an application for leave to apply outside the required period of three months was allowed because (through no fault of the applicant) there had been difficulty in obtaining a legal aid certificate.

Where leave is granted notice of the proceedings is served on those who are directly affected, together with all relevant supporting documents. At the hearing of the application the court is able to amend the statement of claim by specifying different or additional grounds or remedies. This facility means that where the initial application is for (say) a declaration that a decision is *ultra vires* that is, null and void and of no effect, the application can be amended so that the claim is for *certiorari* to quash where it becomes clear that the decision is merely voidable. This power to amend is a notable feature of Order 53. Whatever the content of an application the court can award damages if specified. The subject of damages is taken up in a later section of this chapter. Order 53 also provides for applications in respect of the discovery of documents (subject to some restrictions in the case of the Crown examined in Chapter 14), and, in particular, those held by an administrative agency concerned with the proceedings, together with applications for interrogatories and cross-examination. Proceedings in this context are normally conducted by reference to the parties' evidence contained in their affidavits, eg where one side will contend that there has been an *ultra vires* decision while the other will dispute the allegation. Consequently, the more traditional format of a trial involving questioning, cross-questioning and the discovery of documents is not commonly found in proceedings on an application in the present context. Indeed, there appears to be a well-founded fear that if this more traditional format does not become more common there would be a temptation for the court to substitute its own views of the facts and merits of a case thus likening the court to a court of appeal whereas its only concern here is with the legality of an administrative action or decision. There are two final points about procedure. First, where an application is made for *certiorari* and the court finds that there are grounds for quashing, the decision may be quashed and remitted to the administrative agency for reconsideration and a fresh decision in a manner similar to the procedure on an appeal on a point of law in the High Court. The administrative agency is perfectly at liberty to decide the matter in the same way as the decision which was quashed, provided that in so doing it acts *intra vires*. Secondly, where an application has been made for a declaration, an injunction or damages and the court considers that any such remedy should not be granted, eg because the main issue is the applicant's rights in private law, the court can order that the proceedings should continue as though they were begun by writ in another court.

13.9.4 The importance of the application for judicial review

This procedure is recognised as containing important safeguards, primarily for the benefit of the public, administrative agencies subject to the rules of public law. These safeguards, some of which have been seen already, are as follows:

(1) the need for leave to apply;

(2) the court's discretionary control of discovery, interrogatories and cross-examination;

(3) the ability of the court to expedite the proceedings;

(4) the avoidance of the courts involvement in the *intra vires* facts and merits of an application;

(5) the recognition of the consequences of delay in making an application;

(6) the channelling of applications through the Queen's Bench Division of the High Court with its judicial expertise in administrative law where the court has considerable control over the proceedings, so enabling the foregoing safeguards to be implemented.

13.9.5 The application for judicial review and the protection of rights in public law

It has been seen that the remedies available in the present context are concerned with the legality of action by public, administrative agencies arising from the exercise of their powers in public law. The applicant under Order 53 is therefore obliged to establish an infringement of his rights which are protected or mainly affected by public law. If that applicant attempts to avoid Order 53 and, for example, applies to the Chancery Division of the High Court for a declaration, the court would be obliged to strike out the action as an abuse of the court's process (*O'Reilly v Mackman* (1982)). Whether a case is one which must be pursued through the Order 53 procedure with its own special characteristics and safeguards rather than any other procedure is a matter of some difficulty. In *O'Reilly* it was decided by the House of Lords that a claim by a prisoner that a prison board of visitors should stay within their statutory jurisdiction and comply with the rules of natural justice should be dealt with under Order 53. In an earlier case from the same context, *Heywood v Hull Prison Board of Visitors* (1980), a prisoner who had been found guilty of certain disciplinary offences and punished by a board of visitors sought a declaration by writ in the Chancery Division that the decision was a nullity by virtue of breaches of natural justice. It was decided that although the remedies – the application by writ to the

Chancery Division for a declaration and the Order 53 procedure – were in the alternative, the characteristics of and safeguards contained in Order 53 meant that that procedure should be used. The decision shows the importance of the need for leave to apply in Order 53, a requirement that does not apply in the proceedings before the Chancery Division. The decision also suggest some of the practical difficulties in distinguishing between a procedure such as that by writ for a declaration before the Chancery Division, as opposed to the Order 53 procedure before the Queen's Bench Division. The process of discovering which is the correct procedure through additional litigation in the courts could prove very expensive and time-consuming for the individual. Some guidance emerges from two recent cases. In the first, *Cocks v Thanet District Council* (1982), it was decided by the House of Lords that a decision of a local authority under the Housing (Homeless Persons) Act 1977 (now part of the Housing Act 1985) to the effect that the applicant was intentionally homeless and not therefore entitled to permanent housing accommodation could be challenged only under Order 53. In such a case the individual applicant's rights would be affected by what was alleged to be an *ultra vires* decision. On the other hand, it was emphasised that once a decision of a local authority, for example, to grant permanent housing accommodation, had been given, this conferred private law rights. Consequently, in the unlikely event of a local authority refusing to provide such accommodation subsequently, the individual applicant would be able to look beyond Order 53 for the legal enforcement of his rights in private law, for example, through an action for damages for breach of statutory duty (*Thornton v Kirklees Metropolitan Borough Council* (1979)). In the second case, *Davy v Spelthorne Borough Council* (1983), it was decided that an injunction to restrain a local authority's implementation of an enforcement notice was a matter to be dealt with under Order 53 since the notice was made by a public administrative agency under public law powers with the intention that it should have effect against the applicant. In addition it was considered important by the court that the local authority should have the protection of the safeguards in Order 53. In addition a claim for damages was made in respect of allegedly negligent advice from the local authority as a result of which the applicant failed to appeal against the enforcement notice. In this case the claim arose from and affected the applicant's rights in private law so that although such a claim for damages could be pursued through Order 53, it would not be an abuse of the court's process if an alternative procedure was followed.

Both *Cocks* and *O'Reilly v Mackman* were distinguished by the House of Lords in *Wandsworth London Borough Council v Winder* (1985). Here the council sought possession of a house on the ground of non-payment of rent increases. The tenant sought to defend himself on the ground that the increases were *ultra vires*. The council unsuccessfully argued that such a defence should be processed through an application for judicial review in the High Court. The House of Lords disagreed: the tenant was complaining about infringement of his rights in private law, not public law; the tenant had not started the proceedings; the tenant was not wanting to gain some right or entitlement from a public authority, as in *Cocks*; there was a need for a speedy decision on the dispute in the interests of good administration; the tenant had not started the proceedings and merely sought to exercise his right to advance a defence against the claim. By contrast, in *Avon County Council v Buscott* (1988) a local authority decided to bring proceedings against trespassers. However, the Court of Appeal found that the court below was right to refuse an adjournment to allow argument of a case that eviction was unreasonable through the alleged failure of the Council to provide sites for gipsies. This matter had to be raised in Order 53 proceedings; no defence was raised on the merits of the case as in *Winder*.

The decision in *Cocks* has been followed in the recent case of *Ali v Tower Hamlets London Borough Council* (1992), where the issue before the court was whether the alleged failure of the council to discharge its statutory duty under ss 65 and 69 of the Housing Act 1985 to provide 'suitable accommodation' for homeless persons could only be challenged by way of judicial review proceedings as the council contended. In upholding the council's appeal, the Court of Appeal was of the opinion that whether or not accommodation was suitable was a matter of subjective judgment for the housing authority. The public law duties of the council were not discharged until the process of deciding on suitable accommodation had been completed. Therefore, since at this stage no private law rights had accrued in favour of the applicant, he had been wrong to bring an action for an injunction in the county court. Any challenge to the housing authority's decision could only be made by way of judicial review proceedings. On this basis, *Ali* can be distinguished from the decision in *Roy v Kensington and Chelsea and Westminster Family Practitioner Committee* (1992). In this case, Dr Roy commenced by writ an action against the Family Practitioner Committee in respect of among other things, payment of part of his basic practice allowance to which he believed he was entitled but which the Committee had withheld from him on account of the fact that in their view, he had failed to devote sufficient time to his National Health Service work. The Committee sought to have Dr Roy's action struck out as an abuse of the process since it was argued on their behalf that the issues raised by the case were public law issues and that therefore, Dr Roy's sole means of redress lay in judicial review proceedings. The House of Lords refused to accept this argument. Whilst Dr Roy may or may not have been in a contractual relationship with the Committee, he nevertheless had 'a bundle of rights which should be regarded as his individual private law rights against the Committee', and one of these private law rights was the right to be paid for the work that he had done. Accordingly, the effect of the rule in *O'Reilly v Mackman* is not such as to prevent a litigant possessed of a private law right from seeking to enforce that right by an ordinary action even when the proceedings necessarily involve a challenge to a public law decision.

13.9.6 Proposals for reforming judicial review

The Law Commission has recently returned to this area of administrative law in its report *Administrative Law: Judicial Review and Statutory Appeals* (Law Com No 226) in which it proposes a series of reforms which it considers ought to be made to the judicial review procedure as well as making certain recommendations with regard to the concept of public interest challenges. Dealing with the procedural proposals first, among the Law Commission's more important recommendations are that the term 'leave to apply for judicial review' ought to be removed and replaced by a 'preliminary consultation' stage which would, save in exceptional circumstances, be an exercise conducted on paper rather than by way of an oral hearing. Whether or not the case would proceed beyond this preliminary stage would depend on whether it was considered that there was a serious issue to be determined. With regard to the time limit for judicial review, the Law Commission is in favour of the retention of the three-month time limit together with the requirement that judicial review ought to be promptly sought within this three-month period. In addition, it is felt that an application ought not to proceed to a substantive hearing where an applicant has been unable to show that all alternative legal remedies have been exhausted. The Law Commission is evidently anxious to ensure that judicial review proceedings should only be pursued where the matter involved raises issues of a solely public law nature, thus emphasising the exclusive nature of the remedy. In the event that an applicant commences judicial review proceedings where a writ action would have been more appropriate, it is possible, as was stated in a previous section, for the court to convert the proceedings to a writ action. However, it has not been possible for an action begun by writ to be converted to judicial review proceedings. The Law Commission now proposes that machinery facilitating such a conversion ought to be put in place. Finally with regard to the Law Commission's recommendations for procedural reforms, it is suggested that the rather archaic terms for the remedies which are available ought to be changed on account of the fact that few people, including lawyers, can either pronounce them or know what they imply. Accordingly, an order for *certiorari* would subsequently be known as a quashing order, a prohibition would become a prohibiting order, and, *mandamus* would be replaced by mandatory orders.

Turning to the Law Commission's recommendations in relation to public interest challenges, principal among these is that an applicant's standing should no longer depend on whether they have a 'sufficient interest' in the matter to which the application relates. It is recommended that the new test for standing would be based upon either whether the court felt that the applicant had been or would be adversely affected by the matter to which the challenge was made, or, where the court considers that it is in the public interest for an application to be made. In addition, it is argued that pressure groups and other unincorporated associations should be allowed to make applications for judicial review in their own names. No doubt these recommendations will spark much debate among those actively involved in the judicial review process. However, whether these recommendations will ultimately receive statutory endorsement like their 1976 predecessors remains to be seen.

13.10   Statutory Review

In the case of some decision-making processes, Parliament has legislated to eliminate the process of judicial review as described in this chapter. In its place Parliament has legislated a special scheme of review, hence the expression 'statutory review' where statute dictates the substantive terms on which the legality of decisions may be challenged in the High Court. Applications for statutory review are a particular characteristic of the legislation governing town and country planning and compulsory purchase. In both cases, the Secretary of State for the Environment's decisions are subject to review by a single judge in the Queen's Bench Division of the High Court. For present purposes, the statutory review provisions of the Town and Country Planning Act 1990 will be used as an illustration.

13.10.1   The background to statutory review

Sections 284 and 288 of the Town and Country Planning Act contain the facilities for statutory review in respect of a full range of decisions by the Secretary of State under the Act. In practice, the most significant decision is that on an appeal from the decision of a local planning authority refusing planning permission or granting planning permission subject to conditions. Section 284 states that, the validity of any decision shall not be questioned in any legal proceedings whatsoever.

13.10.2   The scope of statutory review

Section 284 sets out a fairly common formula for statutory review. Where a person is aggrieved by a decision which is not within the powers of the Act or in respect of which relevant procedural requirements have not been complied with, he may apply to the High Court within six weeks of the decision. On such an application for statutory review, the High Court may quash the decision if it is found not to be within the powers of the Act, that is *ultra vires*. In the same way, the High Court may quash a decision where relevant procedural requirements are not complied with and the interests of the applicant are substantially prejudiced as a result.

13.10.3 The grounds for statutory review

The first ground, relating to substantive *ultra vires*, can be illustrated by referring back to Chapter 11 and, in particular, the case of *H Lavender & Son Ltd v
Minister of Housing and Local Government* (1970). The second ground relates to
the various rules of procedure which apply in the field of decision-making in
town and country planning, as described in Chapter 3. However, it will be
noticed that the court's discretion to quash applies only where the applicant's
interests have been substantially prejudiced. Consequently, the court would not
quash a decision affected by nothing more than a mere technical breach of the
rules in procedure.

13.10.4 The six-week limitation

The need to apply for statutory review within six weeks is the outstanding characteristic of this form of review. The time limit here is absolute: there is no possibility of proceedings beyond six weeks, an issue which was referred to
previously in the section on ouster clauses in Chapter 11 (*Smith v East Elloe Rural
District Council* (1956)). The prescription of a six-week time limit does mean that
there can be certainty as to the status of a decision granting planning permission, for example, after a relatively short period of time. Accordingly, the developer can go ahead with his development without fearing challenges to the
legality of his planning permission. The same comment can be made in respect
of the many confirmed compulsory purchase orders subject to the same pattern
of statutory review.

13.10.5 The person aggrieved

Once again it is necessary to look at the *locus standi* requirements for what is in
practice a very important remedy. The applicant for planning permission who
wishes to challenge an adverse appeal decision of the Secretary of State for the
Environment who confirms the local planning authority's refusal of planning
permission clearly has *locus standi* as a 'person aggrieved' (*Buxton v Minister of
Housing and Local Government* (1960)). The Town and Country Planning Act itself
specifies that the local planning authority has *locus standi* where the Secretary of
State reverses his decision on appeal. In *Buxton* the appeal against a local planning authority's decision resulted in a grant of planning permission to quarry
chalk adjacent to Buxton's farm. Because the application for planning permission had not fallen into a category where there was a statutory requirement for
publicity and a statutory obligation to take into account any objections arising
from the publicity, and because Buxton's common law rights had not been
infringed, eg by any nuisance, Buxton, it was decided, was not a person
aggrieved. However, it was decided that had Buxton been a statutory objector
within the above category, he would have been a 'person aggrieved' and able to
seek statutory review of the minister's decision. In *Turner v Secretary of State for*

the Environment (1974), the applicant for statutory review represented an amenity society which had objected to development at Richmond Hill. The society had been allowed by an inspector to appear at a public inquiry into the proposed development, which was a factor which weighed heavily in the decision that Turner was a person aggrieved. In practice most third parties have an opportunity of appearing at a public inquiry into a planning appeal so that the range of persons aggrieved is considerably widened by this decision in *Turner*. Desirable though this may be, it is probably contrary to the policy and objects of the Town and Country Planning Act which gives only limited statutory rights to the applicant for planning permission, the local planning authority and statutory objectors. Indeed, this limited background of statutory rights which must be presumed to be legally enforceable before the courts should be borne in mind when considering the question of *locus standi* for the declaration and *certiorari* in respect of decisions of the local planning authority.

13.11 Damages

English administrative law is concerned primarily with the quality of administrative action, that is, whether a decision is *ultra vires* and void or merely voidable. The law does not provide for damages in respect of unlawful administrative action so that the victim of *ultra vires* action by an administrative agency has no legal right to compensation for any loss, damage or injury which may have been sustained. An illustration of the way in which this gap in the law may occur in practice comes from the reference to estoppel in Chapter 9. Where an individual relies on an *ultra vires* statement from a representative of an administrative agency, it is not binding in law and can be denied. Any compensation which is paid will be *ex gratia* compensation, as will any compensation payable following a successful complaint to one of the ombudsmen (depending on the status of the administrative agency) described in Chapter 15. Earlier in the present chapter, it was seen that damages can be claimed under the Order 53 procedure in the High Court. Whether this or any other appropriate procedure is used, any damages claimed against a public administrative agency must fall within pre-existing categories of the law such as negligence, nuisance and breach of statutory duty which were outlined in Chapter 4. The difficulties in this area of administrative law are well summarised by Lord Wilberforce in *Hoffman-La Roche*, referred to earlier in the present chapter. He considered that, at the root of the various phrases describing the quality in law of an administrative action, lies:

> ... an unwillingness to accept that a subject should be indemnified for loss sustained by invalid administrative action. It is this which requires examination rather than some supposed visible quality of the order itself. In more developed legal systems this particular difficulty does not arise. Such systems give indemnity to persons injured by illegal acts of the administration. Consequently, where the prospective loss which may be caused by an order

is pecuniary, there is no need to suspend the impugned administrative act: it can take effect ... and at the end of the day the subject can, if necessary, be compensated.

13.12 Powers of Annulment in the European Court of Justice

The nature and sources of EU law have been dealt with previously in Part 2 where it was seen that the European Court of Justice has the task of overseeing the interpretation and application of the treaties governing the Union, the best-known of which is the Treaty of Rome. One facet of this task is the review of administrative action although there are other closely related tasks including the need to deal with preliminary references from courts in Member States requiring a conclusive interpretation of EU law, the adjudication of any alleged refusal to act by a Community institution, the adjudication of claims that regulations are illegal and the settlement of claims for damages against EU institutions. However, it is the power of review which occupies the place of importance for present purposes.

13.12.1 The power of review

The court's power of review is found in Article 173 of the Treaty of Rome as amended by Article G (53) of the Treaty on European Union (Maastricht). This states that:

> The Court of Justice shall review the legality of acts adopted jointly by the European Parliament and the Council, of acts of the Council, of the Commission and of the ECB [European Central Bank], other than recommendations and opinions, and acts of the European Parliament intended to produce legal effects *vis-à-vis* third parties. It shall for this purpose have jurisdiction in actions brought by a Member State, the Council or the Commission on grounds of lack of competence, infringement of an essential procedural requirement, infringement of this Treaty or of any rule of law relating to its application, or misuse of powers. The court shall have jurisdiction under the same conditions in actions brought by the European Parliament and by the ECB for the purpose of protecting their prerogatives. Any natural or legal person may, under the same conditions, institute proceedings against a decision addressed to that person or against a decision which, although in the form of a regulation or a decision addressed to another person, is of direct and individual concern to the former. The proceedings provided for in this Article shall be instituted within two months of the publication of the measure, or of its notification to the plaintiff, or, in the absence thereof, of the day on which it came to the knowledge of the latter, as the case may be.

13.12.2   The scope of review

The first crucial point to notice is that Article 173 applies to directives, regulations and decisions in the case of Member States, the Council and the Commission whereas review is more limited in the case of proceedings instituted by an individual or 'legal person', eg a company. Nevertheless, the court has attempted to widen its sphere of influence in relation to review by giving a generous interpretation of the concept of an EU 'act'. In approaching its task in the present context of review, the court assumes that the act complained of is legally valid until annulled, that is, in effect a voidable act.

13.12.3   The grounds for annulment

The four grounds for annulment listed above are closely related to each other and in some respects similar to the categories of the doctrine of *ultra vires* in English administrative law set out in Part 3.

The first ground, lack of competence, frequently arises from questions concerning delegation of functions by the Council to the Commission or any other EU institution. The leading case is *Meroni v Commission* (1958) where it was decided that there had been an unlawful delegation by the Commission of its functions to private organisations, as a result of which various legal safeguards could not operate as they would where the functions stayed within their authorised framework.

The second ground, the infringement of an essential procedural requirement, frequently appears in relation to the legal requirement for reasons to be given in respect of any 'binding' act (Article 190 of the Treaty of Rome) and in relation to the requirement for consultation arising from a number of provisions in the Treaty of Rome. It will be noticed that any procedural requirement for the purpose of Article 173 must be an 'essential' procedural requirement. Failure to give sufficient reasons has been justification for the annulment of a number of Union acts over the years. In the same way that the court has developed a body of law on the sufficiency of reasons, so it has developed a body of law on the requirement for consultation, bearing in mind the need to consult the European Parliament, for example, before certain legislative acts become legally effective.

The third ground involving the infringement of the Treaty or of a rule of law relating to its application probably covers most situations which occur where the court is invited to annul administrative action in the EU. Most action which is subject to annulment is likely to be an infringement of the Treaty in one way or another. Rules of law relating to the application of the Treaty include regulations, certain rules of international law at the foundation of the treaties and rules of law which crystallise particular fundamental rights from the legal systems of Member States and which provide guidance on the scope of EU law where it is silent on certain requirements.

Finally, there is the ground of misuse of powers which is particularly relevant on those occasions when it is alleged that administrative action in the EU is based on the unlawful abuse of discretionary powers.

13.12.4 Related functions of the European Court of Justice

Reference been made previously in this chapter and earlier in Part 2 to the function of the court in dealing with preliminary references on the interpretation of EU law made by national courts in Member States. This facility is particularly important on those occasions when the exercise of statutory powers for administrative purposes in a Member State may be subject to the constraints of EU law. In very general terms it may be said that any administrative activity which involves economic or associated regulation may come under the influence of constraints of EU law. Any doubts about the scope of that influence of those constraints can of course, be settled by a reference under Article 177. Another related function of the court occurs in Article 175 and deals with the alleged refusal of the Council or the Commission to act, in breach of the Treaty. Before the court can intervene, it is necessary to establish that a request was first made for the institution to act. In the face of a refusal to act, the institution has two months in which to define its position and any action that is then necessary may be brought within a further period of two months. As in Article 173, any individual or 'legal person' may take advantage of the facility in Article 175 where an institution has failed to address to that person any act other than a recommendation or opinion. A case of fundamental significance here is *European Parliament v Council of the European Communities* (1987). This case is the first action under Article 175 by one EU institution against another and the first admissible action under the Article brought before the European Court of Justice. The main issue was the Council's failure to create a Common Transport Policy. It was held that although the Council had a considerable discretion in this connection, thereby making a specific case of failure to act difficult, there were some aspects of the policy that could be defined with precision for the purpose of framing a case of failure to act.

Article 173 is reinforced by the provisions of Article 184 which relates to the regulations of the Union. Article 184 states that even though the two-month time limit in Article 173 has expired, any party may challenge the legality of a regulation on any of the four grounds in Article 173. Finally, Article 215 states that the EU shall make good any damage caused by its institutions or by its servants in the performance of their duties. However, provision is limited to non-contractual liability in conformity with the general principles common to the laws of the Member States. Potentially, therefore, this provision could open up very significant areas of legal liability whereby the individual could benefit from compensation for a wide variety of unlawful administrative action in the Union.

14 Crown Proceedings

14.1 The Background to Crown Proceedings

Going back through the course of legal history, a particularly harsh limitation prevented the Crown being sued in its own courts. This limitation resulted in considerable injustice. However, a process known as a 'petition of right' became available in some cases where legal proceedings could be brought against the Crown, but only with the consent of the Crown. This process did not unfortunately apply to torts, that is, civil wrongs, by virtue of the maxim that 'the Queen can do no wrong'. Nevertheless, there was an understanding that if damages were awarded against a servant or agent of the Crown for negligence, for example, those damages would be paid by the Crown. The legal liability of the Crown was altered quite considerably by the Crown Proceedings Act 1947.

14.1.1 The Crown Proceedings Act

The background to the passage of this piece of legislation is a useful illustration of the fact that moves for reform can sometimes take a long time to actually achieve their objective. It is not uncommon for the 1947 Act to be seen as the direct result of the decisions in *Adams v Naylor* (1946) and *Royster v Cavey* (1947) in which criticism was levelled at the Crown practice of nominating a Crown servant as a defendant in civil proceedings. However, such a view overlooks the complex departmental discussions that took place long before 1947 and which eventually resulted in a legislative initiative. In the House of Commons debates on the Crown Proceedings Bill, the Attorney General stated that the new legislation put '... the Crown, so far as may be, in matters of litigation in the same position as the subject, so that a subject who wants to bring an action against the Crown may proceed as though he were proceeding against another subject'. That the Crown's position in litigation is not the same as that of the subject will be seen in the following sections of this chapter. Indeed, it has been seen already in Chapter 2 that certain of the remedies described in the previous chapter do not apply to the Crown by virtue of the Crown Proceedings Act and that the Act confirmed that the rights and interests of the Crown shall not be prejudiced by statute unless that statute refers to the Crown.

14.2 Contracts and the Crown

Section 1 of the Crown Proceedings Act states that if a contract could have been enforced by the pre-1947 petition of right process or by virtue of any Act repealed by the Act of 1947, such a claim against the Crown can now be enforced in law without resort to the 'petition of right'. Although as a result of s 1 it now appears to be easier to sue the Crown in the law of contract, some of the restrictions previously existing still have to be taken into account. Those restrictions are of particular significance in three areas:

(1) employment contracts with the Crown;

(2) the funding of Crown contracts; and

(3) contracts which allegedly fetter future executive action by the Crown.

Before these three matters are examined, it should be pointed out that some statutory provisions repealed by the Act of 1947 permitted legal proceedings against a minister, without reference to the petition of right. Such statutory provisions in various Acts are referred to in the summary of s 1 at the beginning of this section. However, the Act of 1947 is not concerned with those Acts which incorporated various government departments and whose contracts are not made in the name of the Crown, as seen in Chapter 2.

14.2.1 Employment contracts

The legal position for the Crown servant is particularly weak and in the case of military servants there is virtually no legal protection at all. A member of the armed forces cannot resort to the law in order to enforce the provisions of any employment contract with the Crown. As far as the civil servant is concerned, his employer, the Crown, can dismiss him at will (*Dunn v R* (1896)). Although it has been suggested, even within the last 25 years, that a civil servant does not have an employment contract with the Crown but simply holds an appointment with the Crown, the position in law would not appear to be changing. In the previous chapter, for example, it was seen that decisions of the Civil Service Appeal Board are subject to judicial review. The Board has jurisdiction to hear appeals from civil servants in respect of dismissal notices, among other employment matters. Nevertheless, the court in *Bruce* confirmed that no contract exists between the Crown and its civil servant, simply because there is no intention to create legal relations on the evidence of the Civil Service Code of Pay and Conditions. However, there is deemed to be a contract of employment here by the Trade Union and Labour Relations (Consolidation) Act 1992 s 245. Without a deemed contract the civil service unions are not obliged to hold a strike ballot for the purposes of the 1992 Act and cannot be liable in tort for inducing breaches of contract. Although it remains the case that a civil servant cannot sue the Crown for 'wrongful' dismissal in breach of contract, there exists in the Civil Service a large number of voluntary employment agreements, many of which are negotiated and concluded with the trade unions. In addition, a good deal of legal protection has emerged from recent employment legislation. Perhaps the best example relates to the provisions of the Employment Protection (Consolidation) Act 1978 among which is the statutory right of an employee not to be dismissed unfairly. The Act of 1978 indicates that this part of the Act applies to the Crown, together with other parts such as those relating to maternity rights for women.

14.2.2 The funding of Crown contracts

Although it was at one time thought to be a prerequisite of a legally enforceable contract with the Crown that Parliament should have appropriated, expressly or impliedly, the funds for the contract, this seems not to be the present legal position. In an Australian case, *New South Wales v Bardolph* (1934), a government officer, on the authorisation of the state premier, purchased space in a newspaper for government advertising. A number of Acts of Parliament permitted 'government advertising' although this particular contract was not specifically authorised by Parliament. Following a change of government, there was a refusal by the new government to pay for the contracted advertising although the advertising continued. The newspaper sued the government for damages. In giving judgment for the newspaper, it was confirmed that the contract in question was a Crown contract and that while Parliament provided sufficient monies for its fulfilment it was binding on the Crown.

14.2.3 Contracts fettering future executive action by the Crown

This particular restriction is nothing more than a repetition of the broader legal principle governing other administrative agencies as seen previously in Chapter 11. One of the cases mentioned in this context in that earlier chapter was *Crown Lands Commissioners v Page* (1960). In that case it was decided that any implied covenant in a lease to which the Crown is a party and which relates to the quiet enjoyment of land would have to exclude executive acts undertaken in the national interest. Such acts might relate to national emergencies when the Crown, through the government, initiates measures under the prerogative. A further case of significance here is *Robertson v Minister of Pensions* (1949) where it was decided that the minister was bound by an assurance in circumstances where it was not considered necessary to invoke the Crown defence of 'executive necessity'. As was seen in Chapter 9 where *Robertson* was dealt with in some detail, it is clear that the correct decision was arrived at although there are technical legal objections to the decision. As to the defence of executive necessity, the case illustrates the fact that such a defence may often be irrelevant and its employment unjust against individuals whose dealings with the Crown have nothing to do with 'public security' or the 'national interest'.

14.3   Tortious Liability of the Crown

Section 2 of the Crown Proceedings Act provides that the Crown is subject to liability in tort in the same way that a private person of full age and capacity is so liable. The Act defines three main areas of liability:

(1) torts committed by a Crown servant or agent;

(2) torts arising from any breach of those common law duties owed by an employer to his servants and agents; and

(3) torts arising from any breach of those common law duties concerning the ownership, occupation, possession or control of property.

Three other areas of tortious liability dealt with by the Crown Proceedings Act should be mentioned:

(1) breaches of statutory duty;

(2) immunity from tortious liability in respect of acts or omissions by persons discharging responsibilities of a judicial nature; and

(3) immunity from tortious liability for certain acts of a member of the armed forces causing the death of or injury to another member of the armed forces.

Each of these six areas will be dealt with in turn.

14.3.1   Vicarious liability of the Crown

Although it has been possible to sue a Crown servant or agent personally for a tort which he has committed, the Act of 1947 adds to this remedy by stating that the Crown can be vicariously liable for a tort of its servant or agent, as long as that servant or agent would have been liable himself. One of the leading cases here is *Home Office v Dorset Yacht Co Ltd* (1970) where is was decided that there was liability in damages to the owner of a yacht which was damaged by borstal boys who, during an exercise outside the borstal, were not supervised with reasonable care by the officers in charge. A crucial finding in the case was that the damage to the yacht could have been foreseen by the officers on any lapse of their supervision so that this gave rise to a duty in favour of the yacht owner to take reasonable care. Clearly, therefore, the Crown can be liable in a situation of this sort since the servant or agent himself would be liable in negligence.

14.3.2   The employer's common law duties

Although the welfare of most employees is governed in so many ways by statute, eg by virtue of regulations made under the Health and Safety at Work Act 1974 governing various safety standards for the work place, there are some common law duties which fill any occasional gap in the statutory provision. One example for the area of the employer's common law duties is the duty to provide a safe place of work for the employee. Such a duty is owed by the Crown to any of its employees by s 2.

14.3.3 Common law duties relating to Crown property

It has been seen that the Crown is liable in tort for any breach of the common law duties relating to the ownership, occupation, possession or control of property. Consequently, where a person is injured while visiting Crown property it is likely that he will be able to sustain a successful action in tort where it can be established that there was a failure to maintain the premises in a safe condition. However, as in the case of the Crown's legal responsibilities as an employer, the Crown's tortious liability here is governed more often by statute. The Occupiers' Liability Acts 1957 and 1984, for example, bind the Crown and impose a statutory duty on any occupier to take reasonable care to ensure that premises are safe for those visitors who are invited or otherwise permitted to be on those premises. A third area of liability which could be related to this part of the Crown Proceedings Act was mentioned in Chapter 4. It was seen in that chapter that, even in the absence of negligence, there may be so-called 'strict' liability where a person, for his own purposes, brings on to his land and collects and keeps there anything likely to do mischief if it escapes (*Rylands v Fletcher* (1868)). Although there may be some doubt whether the Crown is acting for its own purposes in performing its usual public functions, there is at least potential liability against the Crown in this context.

14.3.4 Breach of statutory duty

Reference has been made to various statutory duties which are binding on the Crown. Where any such duty is binding on the Crown it is declared by s 2 of the Crown Proceedings Act that liability will attach in the normal way as if the defendant were a private person of full age and capacity. Of course, the Crown is not subject to the provisions of a statute unless referred to expressly or by implication so that liability for any alleged beach of statutory duty is subject to this crucial precondition.

14.3.5 The discharge of judicial responsibilities

Section 2 of the Crown Proceedings Act gives the Crown immunity from tortious liability in respect of any act or omission by a person who is discharging responsibilities of a judicial nature vested in him or any responsibilities in connection with the execution of judicial process. The crucial problem in assessing the scope of the Crown's legal immunity here lies in the definition of the term 'judicial'. The immunity clearly applies to the activities of judges in the Crown's courts although the fundamental need for an independent judiciary means that they cannot be regarded as Crown servants in the conventional sense. However, there are areas of uncertainty, eg in relation to the functions and responsibilities of administrative tribunals, although such uncertainty is reduced bearing in mind that the person allegedly responsible for the tort must be a Crown servant and that it is necessary to prove that he himself would have been liable. As to this latter point, a person with legal authority to undertake judicial function enjoys absolute privilege in relation to the words he uses. Such a defence could be used by the Crown in order to deny vicarious liability for the words used in these circumstances.

14.3.6 Immunity in respect of certain acts of members of the armed forces

The Crown Proceedings Act in s 10 prevented a member of the armed forces suing either the Crown or a fellow member of the armed forces in respect of personal injury sustained while on duty or on premises being used for the purposes of the armed forces where the alleged tort was committed by a member of the armed forces on duty. Where it was certified that the injury is attributable to pensionable service, the individual's claim for damages in tort was excluded by the Act. Section 10 was abolished by the Crown Proceedings (Amendment) Act 1987, with effect from 15 May 1987. However, the Secretary of State is empowered to revive s 10 if it is thought necessary or expedient in times of war or emergency, but not with retrospective effect. Such revival would be by statutory instrument.

14.4 Judicial Remedies and the Crown

Reference has been made at various points to the fact that some remedies are not available in legal proceedings against the Crown. In general terms, these remedies can be described as 'coercive' remedies and in law it is not considered appropriate that coercive measures should be exercised against the Crown in order to enforce these remedies. This is illustrated in s 25 of the Crown Proceedings Act, which prohibits any form of enforced payment by the Crown. As far as the prerogative orders are concerned, it is clear that since it is the Crown that acts as nominal applicant, the orders should not be available against the Crown. In reality, the only potential difficulty relates to the order of *mandamus*.

14.4.1 *Mandamus* and the Crown

Where an enforceable legal duty is conferred by statute on the Crown then the order of *mandamus* is not available. The same is true on those occasions when an enforceable duty is conferred on a servant or agent of the Crown, acting as such (*R v Lords Commissioners of the Treasury* (1872)). On the other hand, *mandamus* will be available on those occasions when the duty is conferred on a minister who is not required to exercise the duty on behalf of the Crown (*Padfield v Minister of Agriculture* (1968)). This state of affairs was left unaltered by the Crown Proceedings Act for the good reason that very few duties are conferred directly on the Crown. It has been seen already that most such duties are conferred on named ministers or other administrative agencies.

14.4.2 Injunctions and the Crown

The Crown Proceedings Act provides in s 21 that the injunction is not available against the Crown and that, in the same way, the injunction is not available against a Crown servant or agent where the effect would be to make the remedy available against the Crown indirectly. In lieu of the injunction here the Act does permit a declaration of the rights of the parties. Despite the limitation in s 21 it was argued that the injunction is available against the Crown or a minister of the Crown by virtue of the Supreme Court Act 1981 and the framework for judicial review. The Act of 1981 introduced a new framework whereas the Crown Proceedings Act made no provision for judicial review applications: *R v Licensing Authority, ex p Smith Kline and French Laboratories Ltd (No 2)* (1988). This view did not find favour with the House of Lords in *R v Secretary of State for Transport, ex p Factortame Ltd* (1989). The House of Lords took the view that no new jurisdiction to grant injunctions arose from the Act of 1981. However, in the light of the more recent decision of the House of Lords in *M v Home Office* (1993) discussed in Chapter 13, it is now beyond doubt that an injunction can be granted against a minister of the Crown. It was felt that the unqualified nature of the language of the 1981 Act was such that it did not warrant restricting its application in respect of ministers and other officers of the Crown.

14.5 Procedure

Where proceedings are brought against the Crown the litigation follows the usual procedures. In most cases the plaintiff will know the identity of the government department to be named as defendant but on those occasions when such a department cannot be identified the Attorney General will be the defendant. Whether the proceedings are dealt with by the High Court or a county court will depend on the amounts involved in any claim in contract, tort or for the recovery of property. During the course of the trial, discovery of documents is available against the Crown by virtue of s 28 of the Crown Proceedings Act. The Crown can also be required to answer any interrogatories. At the conclusion of the trial, any damages and costs will be payable by the department responsible although the normal measures of coercive enforcement of judgments are not available. In the same vein, the court may well make use of the declaration as a substitute for the coercive remedies, eg to declare the plaintiff's rights in property alleged to be in the unlawful possession of the Crown. Returning to the availability of discovery and interrogatories against the Crown under s 28, it should be noted that these facilities cannot affect any rule of law which:

(1) authorises the withholding of a document, or

(2) requires a refusal to answer a question, on the ground that any disclosure or revelation would be injurious to the public interest.

For a long time the Crown's ability to refuse to disclose certain documents or to answer particular questions in litigation was referred to as 'Crown privilege'. However, the law governing the sometimes difficult balance between the need to disclose and the need to retain information has wider implications so that this area of concern about disclosure is now more widely referred to as 'public interest immunity', which is the subject of the remaining sections of this chapter.

14.6 Public Interest Immunity

Before the Crown Proceedings Act came on to the statute book, a famous test-case came to the House of Lord for decision, a decision which was to influence the course of the law on disclosure of documents by the Crown for a long time. The case was *Duncan v Cammell, Laird & Co Ltd* (1942) and it arose from the loss of the submarine *HMS Thetis* in Liverpool Bay during trials after its launching. A claim for damages in negligence was made against the builders who were required by the Admiralty not to produce various design documents which had been demanded because their disclosure would be injurious to the national defence. This claim of Crown privilege for the documents was upheld by the House of Lords which decided that '... a court of law ought to uphold an objection, taken by a public department when called on to produce documents in a suit between private citizens that, on grounds of public policy, the documents should not be produced'. It will be remembered that the facilities for discovery of documents against the Crown given by s 28 of the Crown Proceedings Act are subject to any rule of law which authorised the withholding of a document. That rule of law seemed to be clearly defined as a result of the decision in *Duncan*. But notice that the claim of privilege for the documents was on the basis that their disclosure would be injurious to the national defence whereas the decision of the House of Lords apparently goes wider in referring to 'public policy' as the justification for a refusal to allow disclosure. This was just one crucial area of uncertainty left by the decision in *Duncan*. In addition, there was no certainty as to the circumstances in which a minister might oppose discovery in the public interest where two individuals are involved in private legal proceedings against each other, and no certainty whether a minister's claim for privilege would be conclusive in the eyes of the court.

The House of Lords in *Duncan* had appeared at first glance to endorse the approved practice which had been to treat a ministerial objection against disclosure as conclusive, provided that it was made in the proper form. Lord Simon stated with approval what has become known as the *Zamora* principle which holds that: 'Those who are responsible for the national security must be the sole judges of what the national security requires.' However, the seemingly unequivocal nature of this position became somewhat confused by Lord Simon's later observation that:

> Although an objection validly taken to production on the ground that this would be injurious to the public interest is conclusive, it is important to remember that the decision ruling out such documents is the decision of the judge.

14.6.1   The conclusiveness of claims opposing discovery

It was some years before there was any clarification of the uncertain position concerning the conclusiveness of a claim that documents should be protected from discovery. The important turning point came in another House of Lords' decision, *Conway v Rimmer* (1968). In this case, a probationer policeman had been prosecuted for the theft of a torch, acquitted and then dismissed from the force. In an action by the probationer against a superintendent for malicious prosecution (a tort), the probationer sought the discovery of certain reports which had been made about him by his superiors. Although both parties wanted this evidence produced, the Home Secretary resisted discovery on the ground that these documents belonged to a class whose production would be injurious to the public interest. In an important decision, the House of Lords ordered five of the documents to be produced for the court's inspection, indicating that it might not accept the Home Secretary's claim of privilege for at least four. The decision of the House of Lords shows that any claim of privilege which may be raised by a minister is not conclusive so that the court may balance any prejudice to the public interest if there is disclosure against any harm to the interests of justice if there is no disclosure. In balancing these factors to decide whether a claim of privilege should or should not be allowed, the court may examine the documents in private without disclosing them to the parties.

14.6.2   Public interest immunity recognised

In another decision of the House of Lords, *Rogers v Home Secretary* (1972), it was considered that the whole issue of discovery of documents should be seen against the broader background of the public interest. Lord Reid thought that the:

> ... real question is whether the public interest requires that [a document] shall not be produced and whether that public interest is so strong as to override the ordinary right and interest of a litigant that he shall be able to lay before a court of justice all relevant evidence. A minister of the Crown is

always an appropriate and often the most appropriate person to assert this public interest ... But, in my view, it must always be open to any person interested to raised the question and there may be cases where the trial judge should himself raise the question if no one else has done so.

In this case, a senior police officer wrote a report on an applicant to the Gaming Board for a gaming licence. The application for a licence was unsuccessful whereupon the applicant started legal proceedings against the officer alleging criminal libel arising from the letter sent to the Gaming Board. An attempt to obtain discovery of the letter was resisted by the Home Secretary and the Board. It was decided that the letter should remain confidential, primarily because any disclosure would make it that much more difficult for the Board to fulfil its function in relation to the issue of gaming licences where there was a need for candid assessment of applicants' characters. Consequently, the public interest in ensuring the suitability of applicants outweighed the possibility of injustice to a suitable applicant who might be concerned with possibly defamatory material in correspondence with the Board.

14.6.3   The application of public interest immunity

Public interest immunity is an issue which has arisen quite frequently in litigation. The final sections of the chapter contain an outline of some of the more significant cases where the immunity has been in issue. In *D v NSPCC* (1977) the court refused to allow the disclosure of the identity of informers in cases of alleged child abuse while in *Neilson v Laugharne* (1981) there was again a refusal to allow disclosure, this time of documents concerning police investigations of a complaint made by the plaintiff, for the purpose of an action in damages against the police. In refusing disclosure it was decided that the documents in question belonged to a class of documents whose disclosure would impede the proper functioning of the public service. It was in *Duncan* that the House of Lords decided that Crown privilege could be sought in two different ways, either on the ground that a document falls into a certain class, as seen in *Neilson*, or on the ground that the content of a document is such that its disclosure would be contrary to the public interest. The decision in *Neilson* emphasises the need for confidentiality in police investigations. As will be seen in some later cases, confidentiality is but one factor to be weighed in the balance when deciding whether there should be discovery. The 'class' basis for privilege was used in *Williams v Home Office* (1981) when it was claimed that documents about the formation of government policy on 'control units' in prisons should not be disclosed. In deciding that there should be disclosure to the judge, who eventually released some of the documents, the court considered it reasonably probable that they contained material which was relevant to the plaintiff's case that he had been detained unlawfully in a 'control unit'. The competing argument was that disclosure would attract criticism to the Home Office as the government department responsible for prisons. This objection to disclosure was not considered sufficiently serious to disallow disclosure if the parties concerned in the litigation undertook to use the documents only for the purpose of the litigation. Inspection of the documents took place in *Burmah Oil Co Ltd v Bank of England* (1980), but further disclosure was not permitted by the court following its inspection. The company had sued the Bank of England for the purpose of setting aside a sale of stock which formed part of its assets and sought discovery of certain documents which contained details of the government's intervention in the transaction. The decision not to allow disclosure provides a good example of the court's view that, on balance, the evidential value of documents to the individual may be outweighed by the fact that they belong to a class whose disclosure would impede the proper functioning of the public service in relation to the formation of important government policy. Since this case was decided, there has been a partial shift in government policy as to the type of documents that can be disclosed in the interests of open government so that 'documents are now being made available which in the past have been the subject of claims to immunity' (*per* Lord Woolf in *R v Chief Constable of West Midlands Police, ex p Wiley* (1994)). For example, it is now the case that the minutes of the meetings between the Chancellor of the Exchequer and the Governor of the Bank of England are disclosed some six weeks after the relevant meeting has taken place.

At a slightly less exalted level there are many day-to-day situations in which administrative agencies find themselves in possession of confidential information. The legal implications of any request for disclosure are dealt with in the following section of this chapter.

14.6.4 Administrative agencies and the disclosure of confidential information

It was seen previously in this chapter that on an application for discovery the factor of confidentiality is but one matter for the court's consideration. Two cases involving the Commissioners of Customs and Excise provide an illustration of the law in practice. In the first case, *Norwich Pharmacal Co v Customs and Excise Commissioners* (1973), the plaintiff company was the owner and licensee of a patent for a chemical compound. The company was aware that the compound was being imported into the country in breach of their legal rights. The names of the importers were in the possession of the Commissioners who refused to disclose them to the company. It was decided by the House of Lords that the company had a right to know the names of the importers since there were legally enforceable rights at stake so that, on this occasion, the interests of justice for the individual predominated. In the second case, *Alfred Crompton Amusement Machines Ltd v Customs and Excise Commissioners* (1973), the Commissioners had obtained information in connection with the fixing of purchase tax on the wholesale value of the plaintiff's amusement machines. The plaintiff company now sought disclosure of the information which had been obtained from their customers. The Commissioners' claim of privilege was upheld by the House of

Lords whose decision emphasised that even though information is given in confidence, this is not necessarily a reason for a refusal of discovery. It was decided that the arguments for and against disclosure were evenly balanced but it was decided finally that the information should be protected on the ground that its disclosure might be harmful to the efficient working of the legislation under which the Commissioners exercised their powers.

14.6.5   Public interest immunity and *Matrix Churchill*

The evidential doctrine of public interest immunity has recently been the subject of much academic and media debate as a direct consequence of the now infamous *Matrix Churchill* proceedings. The three defendants, all of whom were directors of a company, Matrix Churchill, which specialised in the manufacture and export of machine tools, were charged with deception in obtaining export licences. The prosecution's case was that between 1987 and 1989 Matrix Churchill had breached the government's export guidelines by exporting to Iraq machine tools which were capable of having military uses. In their defence, the directors argued that government ministers both knew about and indeed had authorised the company's trade with Iraq, and furthermore, it was contended that the secret intelligence service MI6 was also aware of the situation. What makes the proceedings of particular interest in the context of this Chapter is that a number of government ministers signed public interest immunity certificates, some of which were quashed by the trial judge, in an attempt to prevent the disclosure of certain information to the defence. Ultimately however the trial collapsed when it became apparent that the government had known all along that the intended use of the machine tools was for the manufacture of armaments. Clearly the episode has given rise to considerable cause for concern in many quarters since the use of public interest immunity certificates could perhaps have resulted in the unjust convictions of three innocent men. Accordingly, the so-called 'Arms to Iraq' Inquiry under the chairmanship of Lord Justice Scott was set up at the end of 1992 to:

> ... examine and report on decisions taken by the prosecuting authority and those signing public interest immunity certificates in *R v Henderson* and any other similar cases that he considers relevant to the inquiry; and to make recommendations.

The Scott Inquiry has yet to produce a final report but its recommendations are eagerly awaited. A number of issues need to be considered, such as the growing tendency, manifested in the *Matrix Churchill* proceedings as well as *Makanjuola v Commissioner of Police of the Metropolis* (1992), for the assertion of public interest immunity to be seen not in terms of the claim of a right, but rather, as the observing of a duty. It is to be hoped that the Inquiry will succeed in clarifying matters in what has become an increasingly opaque area of administrative law.

14.6.6 Public interest immunity certificates

Public interest immunity is commonly, but by no means always, claimed by way of a certificate signed by a government minister. There does not appear to be a prescribed format for such certificates and neither is there prescription with regard to the words to be used. However, the wording must clearly be such as to provide an unequivocal statement as to why the signatory believes that disclosure of the relevant documents should be withheld in the public interest. In *Conway v Rimmer* (1968), part of the affidavit sworn by the then Home Secretary was expressed in the following terms:

> ... 2. I personally examined and carefully considered all the said documents and I formed the view that those numbered 38; 39; 40 and 48 fell within a class of documents comprising confidential reports by police officers to chief officers of police relating to the conduct, efficiency and fitness for employment of individual police officers under their command and that the said document numbered 47 fell within a class of documents comprising reports by police officers to their superiors concerning investigations into the commission of crime. In my opinion the production of documents of each such class would be injurious to the public interest.

Thus public interest immunity may be claimed on a number of different grounds such as commercial confidentiality, national security, because secret intelligence matters are involved, in order to protect informer anonymity, or, as in the example above, so as to facilitate the proper functioning of the public service. Whether or not the certificate is accepted is of course a matter to be determined by the judge in the relevant proceedings, but it would seem likely that a strongly worded certificate raising the spectre of national security is as likely as anything to preclude the disclosure of the documents for which the immunity was sought.

Turning to the issue of who signs the certificate, dicta of Lord Simon in *Duncan v Cammell, Laird & Co Ltd* (1942) suggested that the decision to object to disclosure 'should be taken by the minister who is the political head of the department' once he has personally seen and considered the contents of the documents in question. The effect of these remarks has been such as to give rise to a challenge to a public interest immunity certificate in *Continental Reinsurance Corporation (UK) Ltd v Pine Top Insurance Ltd* (1986) on the basis that it was signed by a junior minister rather than the head of the department. However, the argument failed on account of the fact that Mr Justice Staughton did not believe that Lord Simon had ever intended to draw a distinction between a junior minister and his political superior, and moreover, even if he had so intended, it was:

> ... open to question whether the same doctrine should apply now when the activities of Governments are more widespread, the burden of senior ministers enormous and the occasions when Government Departments are both-

ered with requests for evidence or documents in disputes to which they are not a party more numerous.

This approach has found favour in cases such as *Gain v Gain* (1961) where both parties in matrimonial proceedings accepted a certificate signed by a departmental permanent under-secretary as though it had been signed by the political head of the department, and in the *Matrix Churchill* proceedings, no mention was made of the fact that one of the four signatories of the relevant certificates was a junior foreign minister rather than the Foreign Secretary himself. In many respects, there is little to cause alarm about such an arrangement, especially when it is borne in mind that the well known *Carltona* principle ensures that ultimately, it is the political head of the department who is accountable to Parliament for anything that his officials have done under his authority.

15 Remedies for Maladministration

15.1 The Ombudsman Remedy

It was seen in Chapter 1 that administrative law is concerned with the legal control of administrative action, that is, control by the courts. Chapters 9–11 and 13 have shown that such control is centred on the power of the High Court to review the legality of those mainly statutory functions exercised by the administrative agencies. However, to complete the picture of the controls available in respect of the administrative agencies and their functions it is necessary to appreciate that there are certain non-legal remedies which do not depend on the courts. Such non-legal remedies include the administrative remedies examined in Chapter 12 and the so-called ombudsman remedy which is to be examined in the present chapter. The various ombudsmen who have been established throughout the UK deal with and investigate complaints of injustice in consequence of maladministration. Any such complaint must relate to maladministration by an administrative agency where that agency is undertaking its administrative functions almost always within the scope of its statutory powers. The term 'ombudsman' is of Scandinavian origin and refers to a person who deals with grievances.

15.1.1 Ombudsmen in the UK

The first ombudsman to be established was the Parliamentary Commissioner for Administration whose office was created by the Parliamentary Commissioner Act 1967. The Parliamentary Commissioner Act (Northern Ireland) 1969 established the office in Northern Ireland to deal with complaints against the Northern Ireland government until it was suspended. The Commissioner for Complaints Act (Northern Ireland) Act 1969 established a Commissioner for Complaints who deals with complaints in the province against local bodies and certain other public bodies. In the remainder of the UK, the Local Government Act 1974 and the Local Government (Scotland) Act 1975 established Local Commissioners for Administration with responsibility for investigating maladministration in local government. Finally, in the National Health Service Reorganisation Act 1973 provision was made for Health Service Commissioners, with similar provision in Scotland under different legislation. Recent extensions to the law in this context are found in the Parliamentary and Health Service Commissioners Act 1987, the Local Government Act 1988 and the Health Service Commissioners Act 1993.

15.2 The Parliamentary Commissioner for Administration

The Parliamentary Commissioner is, as the name suggests, accountable to Parliament. In exercising his statutory function, the Parliamentary Commissioner reinforces the capacity of Parliament to deal with complaints against the executive. The Parliamentary Commissioner reports to Parliament through a series of annual reports, including reports of particular investigations and matters of concern, and his activities come under the scrutiny of the Select Committee on the Parliamentary Commissioner for Administration. Complaints to the Parliamentary Commissioner are required to be referred by a member of Parliament and it is likely therefore that a complainant will raise their concerns with their own constituency MP. This is particularly so in the light of the convention that MP's do not involve themselves in the business of other constituencies. The so-called 'MP filter' is a unique feature of the UK's ombudsman system. In some respects, it can be likened to the leave requirement in judicial review proceedings discussed in Chapter 13 since it represents an opportunity to identify at an early stage those grievances which do not fall within the remit of the Parliamentary Commissioner. In the event that an MP is unsure as to whether the subject matter of the complaint is an appropriate matter for the attention of the Parliamentary Commissioner, the complaint is likely to be referred so that the Parliamentary Commissioner will ultimately determine the jurisdiction issue. The need for a complaint to be referred by a member of Parliament serves to reinforce the MP's role as the elected representative dealing with complaints against the executive. This point was stressed by the government of the day in the White Paper (Cmnd 2767) which preceded the enactment of the 1967 Statute:

> In Britain Parliament is the place for ventilating the grievances of the citizen ... It is one of the functions of the elected member of Parliament to try to secure that his constituents do not suffer injustice at the hands of Government ... Members are continually taking up constituents complaints ... We do not want to create any new institution which would erode the function of members of Parliament in this respect... We shall give members of Parliament a better instrument which they can use to protect the citizen, namely, the services of a Parliamentary Commissioner for Administration.

15.2.1 Government departments and authorities subject to investigation

The Act of 1967 contains a schedule which includes all of those government departments and authorities whose administrative functions may be investigated on a complaint to the Parliamentary Commissioner. The list may be amended but may not include any body or authority whose functions are not exercised on behalf of the Crown. By way of an example, the Post Office was removed from the list when it was created a public corporation in 1969. The Parliamentary Commissioner is also empowered to investigate action taken by or on behalf of any of the bodies or authorities listed in the schedule. In general terms, the bodies included in the list are the government departments headed by their respective ministers, and certain other bodies which are related to those departments, such as the Inland Revenue Commissioners. References to particular departments include their respective ministers, whose own contribution to any maladministration can be investigated. One of the most famous investigations carried out by the Parliamentary Commissioner arose from many complaints from individuals who considered that the government had contributed to their loss when the holiday firm Court Line Ltd failed in 1974. The essence of the complaints was that holiday-makers who had booked with Court Line were given the impression by House of Commons statements from the Secretary of State for Industry two months before the failure that the firm was financially viable. In a special report, the Parliamentary Commissioner concluded that a misleading impression had been given by the Secretary of State. The conclusion was rejected by the government which refused to accept liability for any compensation for those who had suffered loss.

There have been recent extensions to the list of agencies subject to investigation. Following a report by the Select Committee and discussions with the government, a number of non-departmental public bodies were brought within the Parliamentary Commissioner's jurisdiction. The criteria for inclusion refer to executive or administrative functions directly affecting individuals or companies which would have been included if undertaken by a government department as well as subjection to some degree of ministerial accountability to Parliament and a dependency on government finance and policy. While the Monopolies and Mergers Commission is excluded as an advisory body, the Criminal Injuries Compensation Board is treated as being a tribunal and excluded also. Bodies that are added to the list include the Equal Opportunities Commission, the Commission for Racial Equality and the Horserace Betting Levy Board.

15.2.2   Matters excluded from investigation

The Act of 1967 expressly excludes certain matters from investigation by the Parliamentary Commissioner. The areas of exclusion are:

(1) foreign relations;

(2) action taken overseas;

(3) action affecting the administration of government in overseas territories such as colonies;

(4) action taken to extradite individuals by virtue of extradition treaties and to extradite fugitive offenders;

(5) investigation of crimes;

(6) proceedings before any court of law, international court or tribunal or disciplinary body in the armed forces;

(7) action taken in connection with the prerogative of mercy;

(8) the health service; see the Health Service Commissioners, whose functions are dealt with later in this chapter;

(9) commercial and contractual transactions;

(10) the grant of honours, awards, privileges and charters; and

(11) personnel matters in the civil service and armed services.

15.2.3 Complaints

The Act of 1967 prohibits any complaint by local authorities, public service bodies, nationalised corporations, bodies whose membership is appointed by the Crown, a minister or a department and bodies funded from monies provided by Parliament. Beyond these categories a complaint can be made by an individual or body which may or may not be incorporated. Consequently, a complaint may be made by a company or an unincorporated group of individuals such as a residents' association. In the more common case where the complaint is that an individual has suffered injustice in consequence of maladministration, that individual must complain personally as an 'aggrieved' person to the MP although there are exceptions to this requirement where, for example, an agent is used if a person is unable to act for himself, or where that person has died and the complaint is pursued through a personal representative. Any complainant is required to have been in residence in the UK or at least 'present' in the country when the action subject to the complaint occurred. The complaint to an MP must be made in writing not later than 12 months from the date when the complainant became aware or should have been aware of the issue which forms the basis of the complaint. In some exceptional cases, the Parliamentary Commissioner will allow a complaint to be considered beyond this time limit.

15.2.4 Alternative remedies

The Act of 1967 states that the Parliamentary Commissioner shall not undertake an investigation where the person aggrieved has or had a right of appeal, reference or review to or before a tribunal established by statute or under prerogative powers, or where the person aggrieved has or had a remedy by way of proceedings in any court of law. However, there is an exception in these circumstances, allowing the Parliamentary Commissioner to investigate where he is satisfied that it is not reasonable to expect the complainant to rely or to have relied on these remedies. This exception indicates that there is no clear division between the legal remedies and the non-legal ombudsman remedy. This lack of clarity is well illustrated in *Congreve v Home Office* (1976) referred to in Chapter 11, where the Court of Appeal decided that a threatened revocation of television licences prematurely renewed was *ultra vires* the Home Secretary's powers under the Wireless Telegraphy Act 1949. This decision followed a successful complaint to the Parliamentary Commissioner who was critical of the Home Office for a number of reasons, including the fact that there was a failure to advise the parties adequately of the department's attitude to premature renewal of licences. In many instances, the availability and suitability of the alternative remedy will be quite clear, eg where a decision of the Secretary of State for the Environment on a planning appeal can be challenged by way of statutory review within six weeks where the only issue is the legality of that decision. On the other hand, it may not be at all clear whether there is any matter of law or legality in issue so that the Parliamentary Commissioner might be more inclined to investigate the case. Despite the fact that the decision in *R v Commissioner for Local Administration, ex p Croydon London Borough Council* (1989) was concerned with the jurisdiction of the local commissioner, it nevertheless appears to be relevant to the present issue of alternative remedies and the Parliamentary Commissioner since there is a very close similarity between the relevant statutory provisions in the 1967 Act and the 1974 Local Government Act. Accordingly, in deciding whether his jurisdiction to investigate has been excluded by the 1967 Act, it would seem that the Parliamentary Commissioner is merely required to satisfy himself that the courts are the appropriate forum for the investigation of the complaint. He is not required to take a view as to the likelihood of success if legal proceedings were initiated. In addition, since the Parliamentary Commissioner is under a continuing duty to consider whether to carry on with an investigation, it may be that he will decide to discontinue an investigation where it becomes apparent in the course of that investigation that the issues raised are more suited to resolution by the courts.

15.2.5   The investigation of administrative functions

An important element in the Parliamentary Commissioner's powers is the limitation of investigations to administrative functions, as opposed to legislative (law-making) and judicial functions. While legislative functions such as the drafting and promotion of various types of statutory provision are outside the powers of the Parliamentary Commissioner because such functions are the concern of other Parliamentary processes, judicial functions are excluded because, as was seen in the previous section, there should be some remedy arising from those functions before a court or tribunal. In general, therefore, it can be said that if judicial functions are in issue, the individual's legal rights can be enforced in proceedings before a court and any appropriate tribunal. This is well illustrated in a complaint by an ambulance driver against the Department of Health and Social Security in respect of his classification for natural insurance purposes (*Case No C96/T*: First Report of the Parliamentary Commissioner, 1973–74). The ambulance driver had been paying national insurance contributions as a self-employed person but he considered that he should be classified as an employed person, in which case the contributions are payable by the employer. When he applied to the Secretary of State for a decision, an inquiry was convened and the complainant was represented by a trade union official. Subsequently, it was decided that the complainant had been a self employed person for national insurance purposes. The complainant and his representative then complained to the Department about alleged procedural irregularities at the inquiry and requested a new inquiry. At about the same time, the complainant's MP wrote to the Secretary of State about the matter and, not being satisfied with the response, referred the case to the Parliamentary Commissioner. It was recognised at the outset that the decision of the Secretary of State on a question of classification is final, subject only to an appeal on a point of law to the Court of Session in Scotland or, in England, the High Court. It was also recognised that the Secretary of State may review the decision if new facts are brought to his notice, or if he is satisfied that the decision was given in ignorance of, or was based on a mistake as to, some material fact. Although the existence of the appeal on a point of law was noted, it appears that the investigation proceeded because it was not considered reasonable that the complainant should have to rely on that remedy, possibly because the complaint appeared at the stage to raise questions relating to the Secretary of State's power to review a decision. Following the investigation it was found that there had been criticism of the conduct of the inquiry but that the complainant and his representative recognised that the decision had been taken on the correct facts. In conclusion, it was stated by the Parliamentary Commissioner:

... that the complaint is fundamentally a disagreement with the Secretary of State's judicial decision, which is not a matter I am entitled to question; alternatively it may constitute a contention that the Secretary of State did not correctly apply the law to the facts, in which case the proper course open to the complainant was to exercise his right of appeal to the Court of Session.

15.2.6 Procedures for investigations

Whether a complaint should be investigated is entirely a matter of discretion for the Parliamentary Commissioner (*Re Fletcher's Application* (1970)). If a complaint is to be investigated, the Parliamentary Commissioner proceeds in private and gives the head of any department or official concerned an opportunity to make comments. Relevant files are examined and officials interviewed. In some cases the complainant will be interviewed, which is what happened in the investigation described in the previous section where the Parliamentary Commissioner was particularly concerned to ensure that, despite procedural irregularities at the inquiry, the correct facts had been reported to the Secretary of State for the purpose of his decision. The Parliamentary Commissioner has wide powers through which he can obtain his information. However, no person can be compelled to provide information which relates in any way to cabinet proceedings and a certificate from the Secretary to the Cabinet for this purpose is regarded as conclusive in relation to such information. Otherwise, the Parliamentary Commissioner cannot be met by any claim from the Crown that any documents or other information are privileged from disclosure. Where the Parliamentary Commissioner considers that he has been obstructed or in any way prevented from carrying out an investigation he can apply to the High Court which can deal with any such difficulty as a contempt of court. In the course of an investigation the Parliamentary Commissioner may permit a person concerned in that investigation to be legally represented while, in addition, an investigation may sometimes comprise a more formal hearing. Whatever the form of investigation adopted, the Parliamentary Commissioner has a power to require that evidence is given on oath. At the conclusion of an investigation, a report is sent to the MP who referred the complaint in the first place. The Parliamentary Commissioner may be prohibited from including information in a report on the ground that its disclosure would be contrary to the public interest as certified by a minister. In addition, the Parliamentary Commissioner is subject to the Official Secrets Acts.

15.2.7   Injustice in consequence of maladministration

The Act of 1967 allows the Parliamentary Commissioner to investigate complaints from those who allege that they have suffered injustice in consequence of maladministration where they consent to a reference of that complaint by the MP to the Parliamentary Commissioner. This central feature of the Act of 1967 is also a prime characteristic of the powers conferred on the other ombudsmen in the UK. The Act fails to define the meaning to these important terms, but the statute's silence in this respect has in fact been welcomed by one former Parliamentary Commissioner on the basis that 'to define maladministration would be difficult and unprofitable'. In practice, 'injustice' receives a wide interpretation which goes beyond some tangible loss or damage which may be suffered when there is an unjustified delay in adjusting a person's liability for income tax, for example. Inconvenience, frustration and annoyance are all facets of injustice even though they may not be capable of being quantified. When the Act of 1967 was being debated in Parliament it was considered that 'maladministration' would include 'bias, neglect, inattention, delay, incompetence, ineptitude, arbitrariness and so on'. In the early years of his office, the Parliamentary Commissioner tended to concentrate on what may be described as 'procedural' maladministration comprising things like delay, loss of documents or a failure to follow internal procedures in decision-making. With the encouragement of the Select Committee on the Parliamentary Commissioner, there has been a greater willingness to investigate complaints of 'substantive' maladministration where the decision itself is 'bad' in quality as where a successful objector to an administrative scheme is refused the costs he had incurred in that context. Sir Cecil Clothier, the former Parliamentary Commissioner, has suggested that the approach he encouraged whilst in office was to treat 'any departure from what the average reasonable man would regard as fair, courteous, efficient and prompt administration as maladministration'. However, it must be remembered that the Parliamentary Commissioner is in no sense an appeal body so that he is not able to substitute his own decision for that of the administrative agency subject to investigation. In this respect, his role is rather like that of the Queen's Bench Division of the High Court when it is exercising its supervisory jurisdiction in relation to judicial review proceedings as seen in Chapter 13. Nevertheless, he is able to point out the areas where the decision-making exercise has departed from the standards of good administration. That the Parliamentary Commissioner is in no way an appeal body is emphasised by the Act of 1967 which states that the merits of a discretionary decision taken without maladministration cannot be questioned.

15.2.8 Maladministration and injustice in practice

To illustrate the operation of the Parliamentary Commissioner's powers of investigation, one particular case has been chosen: *Case No 213/T* from the First Report of the Parliamentary Commissioner, 1973–74. The complaint was made against the Property Services Agency of the Department of the Environment which was acting for the Post Office (not subject to investigation by the Parliamentary Commissioner in his powers under the Act of 1967) in the sale of a strip of land. The land in question was at the rear of the complainant's garden and the gardens of her neighbours on either side. Despite instructions from the Post Office, the surveyor employed by the Agency failed to approach the complainant and accepted the view of one of the neighbours that the complainant's husband would not want to buy the strip of land at the rear of his garden. As a result, the Post Office undertook to convey the strip of land passing at the rear of all three properties to the neighbour. When the complainant indicated that she and her husband would be interested in buying the strip of land at the rear of their garden, they were told by the Agency that there had been an exchange of contracts for the sale of the complete strip to the neighbour and that they had had many years in which to secure a purchase of the land in question. Subsequently, the ground behind the complainant's garden had been levelled, trees and bushes removed and old building timber deposited on the land. The complainant and her husband had incurred expense in erecting a new fence, planting new trees and bushes and seeking legal advice. On investigation it was found that the failure to give an opportunity to make an offer for the land, compounded by wrong information about an exchange of contracts together with a lack of sympathy and understanding in dealing with the complaints made amounted to maladministration. It was also found that injustice through distress and expense had been caused as a result of the maladministration. The status quo could not be restored and the injustice removed but the Department agreed to made an *ex gratia* payment of £100 to cover the distress suffered and the expenses incurred.

15.2.9 Judicial review of reports and decisions

It has recently been established in *R v Parliamentary Commissioner for Administration, ex p Dyer* (1994) that both the decisions and reports made by the Parliamentary Commissioner relating to an investigation into an alleged case of maladministration are susceptible to judicial review. This case was the first occasion on which a substantive application for judicial review of the Parliamentary Commissioner had come before the courts. An earlier application for leave had been refused in *R v Parliamentary Commissioner for Administration, ex p Lithgow* (1990) on the basis that there had been a lengthy delay in making the application which greatly exceed the three month time limit stipulated in Order 53. In *Ex p Dyer*, the applicant's original complaint centred upon the mishandling by the Department of Social Security of various claims made by her relating to invalidity benefit, supplementary benefit and income support. Following the Parliamentary Commissioner's investigation which found that her complaints were justified, the department made an *ex gratia* payment of £500 to the applicant to cover the costs incurred in pursuing her claim as well as issuing her with an apology for its shortcomings. The applicant was not satisfied with either the outcome or the fact that the Parliamentary Commissioner had chosen to investigate only certain of her complaints and hence she applied for judicial review of his decision not to reopen the investigation. Despite the fact that the application was ultimately dismissed, the Divisional Court in *Ex p Dyer* were not prepared to accept the argument that the Parliamentary Commissioner is beyond the supervisory control of the courts simply because he is answerable to Parliament. There was, the court felt, nothing in the Parliamentary Commissioner's role or for that matter the statutory framework within which he operates to take him wholly outside the reaches of judicial review. Moreover, the court did not accept the argument that there was a parallel between the decisions of the Parliamentary Commissioner regarding matters appropriate for investigation and the conduct of the investigation on the one hand, and the decisions made regarding national economic policy on the other hand. This was because the latter were decisions that clearly involved an exercise of political judgment (see *Hammersmith and Fulham London Borough Council v Secretary of State for the Environment* (1990)), whereas the former were not.

Interestingly, the court did not think that two earlier cases relating to the judicial review jurisdiction over local commissioners' reports, *R v Commissioner for Local Administration, ex p Eastleigh Borough Council* (1988) and *R v Commissioner for Local Administration, ex p Croydon London Borough Council* (1989) were of any great assistance in the present case. This was because the issue before the courts in each of those cases was not the review of the local commissioners' discretionary powers, but rather, it related to an allegation that he had contravened the requirements of the Local Government Act 1974. Finally with regard to the issue of whether the Parliamentary Commissioner is entitled to reopen an investigation, the court agreed with his view that he was precluded from doing so since once his report had been sent to both the MP who referred the complaint and the department concerned, the Parliamentary Commissioner was *functus officio*. Therefore, an investigation could not be reopened without a further referral of a complaint under the relevant provision of the 1967 Act.

It may be that the decision in *Ex p Dyer* will prove to be more important in terms of principle than practice. This view is based on the fact that the 1967 Act confers a wide discretion on the Parliamentary Commissioner when he is considering whether to initiate, continue or discontinue an investigation. The subjective nature of these judgments is such that, as was accepted by the court in *Ex p Dyer*, it is likely to prove difficult to show that the Parliamentary Commissioner has exercised his discretionary power unreasonably in a public law sense. Indeed in the present case, the Divisional Court felt that in the exercise of his discretion, the Parliamentary Commissioner had been perfectly entitled to select which of the applicants' complaints he would address in his investigation.

15.3   Health Service Commissioners

Since the National Health Service Reorganisation Act 1973 and similar statutory provisions in Scotland, the ombudsman remedy has been established with Health Service Commissioners for England, Wales and Scotland. The Parliamentary Commissioner for Administration also acts as Health Service Commissioner in each of these areas of the country. Many aspects of the ombudsman remedy in the Health Service are very similar to those previously described in relation to the functions of the Parliamentary Commissioner. One of the outstanding differences lies in the fact that the Health Service Commissioners are empowered to investigate injustice or hardship. A complaint must be pursued within 12 months of the date when the complainant had notice of the issue.

15.3.1   Matters excluded from investigation

As with the Parliamentary Commissioner, a complaint may not be investigated where the complainant has some alternative remedy in a court of law, for example. The Health Service Commissioners are excluded from investigations into:

(1) clinical decisions;

(2) the functions of any Family Practitioner Committee where it operates as an administrative tribunal;

(3) personnel issues;

(4) contracts and commercial matters except in so far as they relate to the provision of services for patients; and

(5) matters subject to a statutory inquiry by the Secretary of State.

In addition, various individuals and organisations are excluded from investigation. Of particular interest here are the community health councils and general practitioners who provide the basic medical, dental and other services.

15.3.2 Complaints

Any complaint is made directly to a Commissioner, even by a health authority which may be anxious to have an investigation of a matter for which it is responsible. The person directly affected and aggrieved by a failure to provide a service, or a failure of a service or any other action taken by or on behalf of a health authority or other body subject to investigation may also complain through a representative where he is unable to undertake a complaint himself. A personal representative may also complain on behalf of a person who is deceased. Complaints range across a wide field and include the treatment of patients by hospital staff, the management of hospital waiting lists and the transfer of patients between different hospitals. In all of these complaints, it is the task of the Commissioner to investigate injustice or hardship in consequence of a failure to provide a service or a failure of that service, or injustice or hardship in consequence of maladministration in relation to any other action. Following an investigation, a report is sent to the complainant and the Secretary of State for Health or the health authority. Annual and special reports are made to the Secretary of State and laid by him before Parliament.

15.4 Local Commissioners for Administration

The Local Government Act 1974 created two Commissions for Local Administration, one for England and one for Wales. The English Commission comprises a number of Commissioners with responsibility for different areas of the country while one Commissioner deals with complaints about maladministration among local authorities in Wales. Parish councils and their equivalent community councils in Wales cannot be investigated by the Commissioners. Otherwise, the Commissioners have been empowered to investigate all local authorities including the regional water authorities and police authorities, except for the Metropolitan Police Authority, which is the responsibility of the Home Secretary. The Commissioners are responsible for investigating complaints of injustice in consequence of maladministration in these authorities. As in the case of the Parliamentary Commissioner, there is an exclusion of cases where the complainant can reasonably resort to a suitable alternative remedy although another alternative applies under the Act of 1974, namely where the complainant can pursue an appeal to a minister. Because third party objectors to a grant of planning permission do not have an appeal to the Secretary of State for the Environment against a grant of planning permission, many complaints have been entertained by the Commissioners in this area.

15.4.1 Matters excluded from investigation

Apart from the complaint which may be pursued through a suitable alternative procedure, there are five areas of exclusion from Commissioners' investigations:

(1) decisions in relation to legal proceedings;

(2) the investigation or prevention of crime;

(3) personnel matters;

(4) the internal organisation and operation of schools and other educational establishments; and

(5) contracts and commercial matters.

It is notable in Northern Ireland that the Commissioner for Complaints is not excluded from the investigation of complaints about commercial and personnel matters. On the same parallel, the Northern Ireland Parliamentary Commissioner is empowered to investigate personnel matters. As in the cases of Parliamentary Commissioner for Administration and the Health Service Commissioners, the Local Commissioners have a general discretion in deciding whether to investigate a complaint.

15.4.2 Complaints

As in the case of the Parliamentary Commissioner and the Health Service Commissioners, there are few limitations on the categories of complainant who need not be ratepayers, residents or electors. Complaints must be made in writing to a member of the local authority within 12 months but, exceptionally, when a complaint cannot be so referred, it may be made directly to a Local Commissioner. Local Commissioners now enjoy a greater discretion to accept complaints made out of time. Whatever the method of referral, the Local Commissioner can refuse to undertake an investigation where the complaint appears to affect all or most of the inhabitants in the local authority's area. Where a complaint is accepted for investigation, the Commissioner responsible is obliged to give the local authority concerned a reasonable opportunity to investigate and comment on the complaint. At the conclusion of an investigation a report is sent to the complainant, the member who referred the complaint and the local authority responsible for the action which forms the basis of the complaint. The authority is obliged to make copies of the report available for public perusal and to advertise the fact of its availability. If the report concludes that there has been injustice in consequence of maladministration, the local authority is obliged to consider the report and to advise the Local Commissioner of the action to be taken to deal with its findings. Where the local authority fails to advise the Local Commissioner in this respect a special report can be prepared by that Commissioner, highlighting the problem. Local authorities are now specifically empowered to make payments or provide other benefits for the purpose of redressing any reported injustice. Each Commissioner reports to the Commission on an annual basis while the Commissions report to a representative body, one for England and one for Wales, comprising persons from those local authorities subject to investigation by the Local Commissioners. Each Commission publishes a triennial report. The Parliamentary Commissioner is a member of the Local Commissions as well as being an *ex officio* member of the Council on Tribunals, so emphasising the importance of a close relationship between bodies which operate in areas where complaints of administrative injustice can be closely related.

15.4.3 Maladministration and injustice in practice

Some of the more frequent complaints to the Local Commissioners arise from the functions of local authorities in relation to town and country planning and housing. By comparison, the Parliamentary Commissioner, operating by reference to the same formula of injustice in consequence of maladministration, also finds most of his complaints in the area of town and country planning, in addition to income tax disputes. Both ombudsmen suffer from the fact that there is no facility for the legal enforcement of any suggested remedy for a finding of injustice in consequence of maladministration. By contrast, any such finding by the Northern Ireland Commissioner for Complaints permits the person aggrieved to apply to a county court for damages or an injunction. The Attorney General also has the opportunity to make application to the High Court where any maladministration is likely to continue, despite the efforts of the Commissioner for Complaints.

15.5 The European Ombudsman

In addition to the prospect of lodging a complaint with a domestic ombudsman, it is now possible for citizens of the UK, together with the other citizens of the European Union, to make a complaint to the EU Ombudsman. The post was established by virtue of Article 138e of the Treaty of Rome which was inserted by Article G(41) of the Treaty on European Union (the Maastricht Treaty). In some respects, the European Ombudsman closely resembles his UK counterpart. For example, he is appointed by the European Parliament to investigate complaints concerning instances of maladministration in the activities of the institutions or bodies of the Union, with the exception of the European Court of Justice and the court of First Instance where they are performing a judicial function. As with the UK position, there is no authoritative definition of what is meant by the term 'maladministration' despite the central nature of the concept in terms of the jurisdiction of the ombudsman. With regard to the actual conduct of an investigation, the EU Ombudsman is required to inform the institution or body concerned as soon as a complaint is referred to him, and in return, the institution or body is obliged to supply him with any information that he has requested as well as affording him access to the relevant files. However, they may refuse to supply the information required but only on the basis of 'duly substantial grounds of secrecy'.

Two notable distinctions that can be made between the UK Ombudsman and the EU Ombudsman relate to the issues of access and initiative. Whilst the UK Ombudsman cannot be approached directly by a complainant as was indicated in a previous section, the EU Ombudsman can be approached either directly or through a member of the European Parliament. Furthermore, in terms of the impetus for his investigation, the EU Ombudsman may act upon his own initiative in addition to responding to a complaint, whereas his UK counterpart must of course wait for a complaint to be referred to him. In the event that the EU Ombudsman finds that there has been maladministration, he is required to inform the institution or body concerned, and where appropriate, he may make draft recommendations as to how to put matters right. For their part, the relevant institution or body is under an obligation to send the ombudsman a detailed opinion within three months of the date of the notification. The investigative process is brought to a conclusion by the ombudsman sending a report to both the European Parliament and the institution or body concerned. It is a requirement that the complainant shall be informed by the ombudsman of the outcome of his inquiries, of the opinion expressed by the institution or body, and of any recommendations that he has made. Thus as with the UK Ombudsman, the EU Ombudsman does not possess any powers of enforcement in relation to the recommendations which he may make since there is no express provision made for a sanction in the event of a failure to comply with his findings. Consequently it would seem that as is the case in the UK, there will be an expectation that a finding of maladministration will be all that is required for the relevant institution or body to undertake the necessary remedial action. However, it is worth noting that in a rare and interesting recent development in the UK, the Transport Secretary has to date refused to compensate people whose houses fell in value where they were situated close to the Channel Tunnel rail link despite a recommendation made by the Parliamentary Commissioner to this effect.

Self-assessment Questions

Chapter 1

1 Why is the judicial review of administrative action such an important characteristic of administrative law?

2 What is the essential task of the High Court in relation to the doctrine of *ultra vires*?

3 In what circumstances could it be said that statutory powers conferred on an administrative agency are contrary to the Rule of Law?

4 Why is it true to say that accession to membership of the EU has radically altered the sovereignty and supremacy of the United Kingdom Parliament?

5 Identify any matters of interest to administrative law arising from any separation of powers that occurs in the United Kingdom.

6 What are the main differences between prerogative and statutory powers?

Chapter 2

1 In what circumstances and to what extent will the courts now review and question the exercise of prerogative powers?

2 Why might it be so important to ascertain whether it is the Crown, or a Crown servant or agent which is responsible for the discharge of administrative functions?

3 In the absence of any express definition of an administrative agency's Crown status, what factors may nevertheless suggest that that status is implied?

4 What broad guidelines are there for the allocation of functions to administrative agencies involving (1) the adjudication of disputes and (2) the initiation of administrative action?

5 Why is the element of policy in any decision-making process an important factor in deciding the type of administrative agency to which that process should be allocated?

Chapter 3

1 What is the status of the statutory inquiry in relation to decision-making in many central government departments?

2 To what extent can it be said that the statutory inquiry is a facility which is provided in order to satisfy the public that there is a proper reconciliation of competing interests in certain areas of decision-making?

3 What legal safeguards are provided to ensure a proper functioning of the inquiry-based decision-making process?

4 In the case of planning inquiries, what are the essential differences between a decision to be taken by the Secretary of State and a decision to be taken by an inspector?

5 What reasons may justify any exclusion, restriction or modification of the system of statutory, public inquiries?

6 What are the disadvantages of the conventional system of planning inquiries as a means of dealing with proposals for large-scale energy developments?

7 What are the arguments for and against public inquiries examining the merits of government policy?

Chapter 4

1 What is the essential legal relationship between the council of a local authority and its members?

2 Why is it necessary for there to be a realistic application of the doctrine of *ultra vires* to the functions and activities of local authorities?

3 Define the possible legal effects of an *ultra vires* contract which is approved by a local authority.

4 How does statute affect the considerations to be ignored by local authorities in their making of contracts?

5 What means are available to control unlawful expenditure by a local authority?

6 Do local authorities enjoy any autonomy in relation to the management of their finances?

7 What part does the law play in the audit of local authorities' accounts?

8 To what extent can it be said that the relationship between central and local government is based on 'collaborative partnership'?

9 Does the law provide the local authority with any significant immunities from legal liability in the exercise of its functions?

Chapter 5

1 How do administrative tribunals differ from courts of law?

2 What is the distinction between administrative tribunals and statutory inquiries?

3 Why may the standards of 'openness, fairness and impartiality' be in doubt in the case of some administrative tribunals?

4 Identify the main factors which determine the allocation of functions to administrative tribunals.

5 To what extent does the Tribunals and Inquiries Act govern the operation of administrative tribunals?

6 What part is played by the High Court and the Court of Appeal in the supervision of administrative tribunals?

Chapter 6

1 What factors will tend to indicate that an administrative function should be conferred on a public corporation?

2 To what extent are public corporations subject to central government control?

3 Are there circumstances in which total privatisation may be deemed impossible? If so how can government continue to exercise effective control over a company's activities?

4 What are the possible legal consequences where a public corporation has the status of a Crown servant or agent?

5 Can it be said that a public corporation is more amenable to judicial control if it is not one of the so-called nationalised industries?

Chapter 7

1 To what extent can the common law be described as a source of administrative powers?

2 What are the legally defined objectives of the European Union?

3 Define the extent to which EU law is superior to the law of the United Kingdom.

4 Why is EU law of interest to the administrative lawyer?

5 What is the essential difference between the discretionary and non-discretionary statutory power? Indicate which administrative agencies are more likely to have discretionary powers with which to perform their functions.

6 Are there any special factors which will tend to determine the characteristics of administrative powers, eg to the extent that a system of licensing may be preferred to contractual regulation?

Chapter 8

1 What are the disadvantages of legislation as a means of providing the statutory framework for an administrative system?

2 In what circumstances is it likely that the promotion of a Private or Local Bill will fail?

3 What factors would be relevant in deciding whether a proposed major development should seek approval through the planning system (involving a public inquiry) or by means of a Private Act?

4 Define the importance of the statutory instrument.

5 What functions are normally undertaken by regulations, rules and orders?

6 What is the purpose of bylaws?

7 Explain the background to each of the grounds on which a bylaw may be found to be unlawful.

8 Summarise the basic sources of EU law and define their different characteristics.

9 How might a Belgian worker, required by order of the Home Secretary under the Immigration Act to leave the United Kingdom, enforce his legal rights under Article 48 of the Treaty of Rome?

Chapter 9

1 What is the legal consequence of a breach of a mandatory and a directory procedural requirement?

2 Indicate the broad legal requirements for consultation.

3 Is it always true to say that administrative functions can be delegated, but not judicial functions?

4 What is the likely effect of s 101 of the Local Government Act on the delegation of functions by a local authority?

5 Define the requirements for common law estoppel and indicate how the courts may be able to avoid the application of estoppel.

6 Why should the law presume that the time limit for the communication of a decision is directory while the time limit for notification of an appeal is mandatory?

7 To what extent can the law ensure that there is an effective, universal obligation to give adequate, intelligible reasons for all administrative decisions?

Chapter 10

1 In what circumstances will the law exclude the rules of natural justice?

2 Outline the circumstances in which the law is likely to require that all the rules of natural justice will apply or that some of the rules will apply or that the rules will not apply.

3 What is meant by the duty to act 'fairly'?

4 How important is the requirement of a 'judicial' function in relation to natural justice?

5 What are the legal requirements for the rule against bias?

6 What are the basic requirements for the *audi alteram partem* rule?

7 Do the rules of natural justice insist that a person should be able to put his case with the aid of an oral hearing and legal representation?

8 If there is a denial of natural justice at the first stage of a two-stage disciplinary process within a domestic organisation, can this omission be remedied at the second, appeal stage?

Chapter 11

1 Where it is claimed that a decision of an administrative agency is *ultra vires*, but not in relation to matters of procedure, what will the court look for to confirm that claim?

2 Are the rules of substantive *ultra vires* more or less stringent in the case of decisions taken by inferior courts?

3 What is the difference between a decision which is *ultra vires* as opposed to a decision which is affected by an error of law on the face of the record?

4 How can the court identify those matters which relate to the merits of a decision within the powers of an administrative agency and beyond judicial review?

5 In what circumstances will an ouster clause exclude judicial review of a decision?

6 What are the difficulties confronting the judicial review of decisions taken by reference to discretionary powers? How are they overcome?

7 Why are some policies regarded as unlawful, 'preclusive' policies?

Chapter 12

1   Where it appears that there is an administrative and judicial remedy available to challenge a decision of an administrative agency, what are the requirements which will indicate whether the remedies can be sought in the alternative?

Chapter 13

1   What is the difference between review and appeal?

2   What is the task of the High Court in dealing with an appeal on a point of law?

3   Comment on the role of the declaration in administrative law and outline the circumstances in which the court is likely to refuse to grant this remedy.

4   In what circumstances is the injunction available to the administrative agency and the individual in order to restrain unlawful action?

5   Are there any significant restrictions on the availability of *certiorari* to control the unlawful actions of any organisation?

6   Is *mandamus* available to enforce the performance of any public, statutory duty?

7   What purposes are served by the application for judicial review?

8   Outline the criteria by which the law insists that certain claims against public, administrative agencies are pursued through the application for judicial review.

9   In what circumstances will a court permit a person to question the legality of action where the court is now deciding his criminal responsibility for failing to comply with that action?

10 Identify the significant distinctions between the requirements for statutory review and those for judicial review in general.

11 Indicate the general legal criteria for locus standi in relation to judicial review.

Chapter 14

1   What are the main effects of the Crown Proceedings Act in relation to the legal position of the Crown?

2   In what circumstances will any injunction be available against the Crown?

3   Explain the scope of any legally enforceable employment rights available to the civil servant.

4 In the course of legal proceedings against the Crown what approach is the court likely to adopt where the Crown claims privilege for certain information?

Chapter 15

1 Describe the various limits beyond which the Parliamentary Commissioner for Administration cannot pursue an investigation of maladministration.

2 In the case of the Parliamentary Commissioner for Administration's investigations, explain the significance of the complainant's alternative remedies and the fact that the merits of a discretionary decision cannot be questioned.

3 What are the main differences between the functions of the Parliamentary Commissioner for Administration, the Health Service Commissioners and the Local Commissioners for Administration?

Selected Bibliography

B Abel-Smith and R Stevens, *In Search of Justice*, Allen Lane.

J Beatson and M H Matthews, *Administrative Law: Cases and Materials*, Oxford.

P Birkinshaw, *Grievances, Remedies and the State*, Sweet & Maxwell.

A W Bradley and K D Ewing, *Constitutional and Administrative Law*, Longman.

A Charlesworth and H Cullen, *European Community Law*, Pitman.

L Collins, *European Community Law in the United Kingdom*, Butterworths.

Council for Science and Society, JUSTICE, Outer Circle Policy Unit, *The Big Public Inquiry*.

Council on Tribunals, *Annual Reports*, Her Majesty's Stationery Office.

P P Craig, *Administrative Law*, Sweet & Maxwell.

C A Cross, *Principles of Local Government Law*, Sweet & Maxwell.

K Davies, *Local Government Law*, Butterworths.

Lord Denning, *The Discipline of Law*, Butterworths.

B Denyer-Green, *Development and Planning Law*, Estates Gazette.

A Doig, *Corruption and Misconduct*, Pelican.

C T Emery and B Smyth, *Judicial Review*, Sweet & Maxwell.

J M Evans, *de Smith on Judicial Review of Administrative Action*, Sweet & Maxwell.

J A Farmer, *Tribunals and Government*, Weidenfeld & Nicolson.

D Foulkes, *Administrative Law*, Butterworths.

G Ganz, *Administrative Procedures*, Sweet & Maxwell.

G Ganz, 'Allocation of Decision-making', [1972] *Public Law* at 215 and 299.

G Ganz, *Quasi-Legislation*, Sweet & Maxwell.

L Grant and I Martin, *Immigration, Law and Practice*, The Cobden Trust.

J A G Griffith, *The Politics of the Judiciary*, Fontana.

I Harden and N Lewis, *The Noble Lie*, Hutchinson.

C Harlow and H F Rawlings, *Law and Administration*, Weidenfeld and Nicolson.

T C Hartley, *The Foundations of European Community Law*, Oxford University Press.

T C Hartley and J A G Griffith, *Government and Law*, Weidenfeld & Nicolson.

House of Commons Select Committee on the Parliamentary Commissioner, *Reports*, Her Majesty's Stationery Office.

D Hughes, *Environmental Law*, Butterworths.

D Hughes, *Public Sector Housing Law*, Butterworths.

P Jackson, *Natural Justice*, Sweet & Maxwell.

B L Jones, *Garner on Administrative Law*, Butterworths.

P Leyland, T Woods and J Harden, *Textbook on Administrative Law*, Blackstone Press.

M Loughlin, *Local Government in the Modern State*, Sweet & Maxwell.

G Marshall, 'Maladministration', [1973] *Public Law* 32.

P McAuslan and J F McEldowney, *Law, Legitimacy and the Constitution*, Sweet and Maxwell.

J F McEldowney, *Public Law*, Sweet and Maxwell.

P Morgan and S Nott, *Development Control*, Butterworths.

Parliamentary Commissioner for Administration, *Annual and Other Reports*, Her Majesty's Stationery Office.

D Pearl and K Gray, *Social Welfare Law*, Croom Helm.

H F Rawlings, *Law and the Electoral Process*, Sweet & Maxwell.

H Street and R Brazier (eds), *de Smith on Constitutional and Administrative Law*, Penguin Education.

A E Telling, *Planning Law and Procedure*, Butterworths.

H W R Wade and C F Forsyth, *Administrative Law*, Oxford University Press.

R J Walker and R W Ward, *The English Legal System*, Butterworths.

D W Williams, *Maladministration Remedies for Injustice*, Oyez.

Index

U

Ultra Vires, doctrine of: see Delegated
legislation, Discretionary powers,
Natural Justice, No evidence,
Procedural
ultra vires, Substantive *ultra vires*

V

W